Research Papers

A Complete Guide

Ninth Edition

005

James D. Lester
Austin Peay State University

 LONGMAN

An imprint of Addison Wesley Longman, Inc.

New York • Reading, Massachusetts • Menlo Park, California • Harlow, England
Don Mills, Ontario • Sydney • Mexico City • Madrid • Amsterdam

Editor-in-Chief: Patricia Rossi
Associate Editor: Lynn M. Huddon
Development Editor: Thomas Maeglin
Marketing Manager: Ann Stypuloski
Supplements Editor: Donna Campion
Project Coordination and Text Design: Electronic Publishing Services Inc., NYC
Cover Designer/Manager: Nancy Danahy
Cover Illustration: ©Garry Nichols (s)/SIS
Full Service Production Manager: Valerie L. Zaborski
Publishing Services Manager: Al Dorsey
Electronic Page Makeup: Electronic Publishing Services Inc., NYC

Cover Printer: The Lehigh Press, Inc.

Library of Congress Cataloging-in-Publication Data
Lester, James D., 1935–
      Writing research papers : a complete guide / James D. Lester. —
9th ed.
          p.   cm
      Includes bibliographical references (p.) and index.
      ISBN 0-321-04980-2 (pbk.)—ISBN 0-321-04978-0 (spiral)
      1. Report writing. 2. Research. I. Title.
LB2369.L4   1998   98–12163
808'.02—dc21   CIP

Please visit our website at http://longman.awl.com

ISBN 0-321-04980-2 (paper)

ISBN 0-321-04978-0 (spiral)

12345678910—VH—01009998

Contents

Preface

W*riting Research Papers*, always a good guide to the entire research and writing process, is now a great guide with the most up-to-date information on finding, evaluating, and citing Internet sources. This book offers students time-tested advice and step-by-step instruction for discovering a topic, conducting research, taking notes, and writing and formatting the completed paper in a particular documentation style. Several factors have influenced the development of the ninth edition of *Writing Research Papers: A Complete Guide*, as explained below.

New MLA Style

In 1998 The Modern Language Association published *The MLA Style Manual and Guide to Scholarly Publishing*, which is the professional companion to *MLA Handbook for Writers of Research Papers*, Fourth Edition. We have chosen to update this text to its specifications.

For Internet sources we have followed the guidelines of the MLA. While this text is as up-to-date as possible, we recommend that you keep current by consulting one of my Web sites at http://www.apsu.edu/~lesterj/lester.htm or http://longman.awl.com/englishpages/. At either site you will find free access to *Citing Cyberspace*, an up-to-date guide to Internet sites for about 20 disciplines and the documentation format for Internet sources in MLA style, APA style, Chicago footnote style, and CBE number style.

New Standards for the APA Style

The *Publication Manual of the American Psychological Association*, fourth edition, continues in print; however, the APA Web site gives new instructions about form and style for citing Internet sources and the format of student research papers. (See http://www.apa.org/journals/webref.html or http://www.apa.org/journals/faq.html.) This edition of *Writing Research Papers* provides APA citations in the new, correct style.

Emphasis on Researching and Writing with Computers

Throughout this edition, you will see a special emphasis on the student's use of electronic sources and the computer to write the research paper. Today most students will use the computer to discover a topic; find sources on the computerized public access catalog, InfoTrac, Silverplatter, or on the Internet with search engines; discuss their topics within chatgroups; and then keyboard on a computer their bibliography list, their notes, and the various drafts of the paper. While *Writing Research Papers* does not abandon the traditional methods, this edition emphasizes first the electronic methods and tools for researching and writing, addressing such topics as bookmarks and evaluation of Internet sources. Also, new Appendix B identifies 35 important and credible Internet sources for research in 19 disciplines.

Emphasis on Writing Across the Curriculum

The elements of writing across the curriculum also receive special emphasis in *Writing Research Papers*. Chapter 10 explains APA documentation style and gives methods for writing in the social sciences. Chapter 11 explains the documentation styles for several disciplines across the curriculum with samples demonstrating the "number" style and the "footnote" style. In addition, the annotated Appendix A lists the best reference guides, bibliographies, databases, and journals for each major discipline.

Plagiarism

A full section on plagiarism explains the role of a researcher, who must cite sources honestly and accurately. Rather than merely warning against plagiarism, the text encourages critical thinking so that students learn to document ideas in their notes and to incorporate them clearly and smoothly in the manuscript. The section explains the rules and methods for achieving correct citations clarifying the often misunderstood concept of "common knowledge," and it condemns blatant disregard for scholarly conventions.

Sample Papers

The text includes many sample papers, new or updated in this edition, so that students can see how to write and format their own manuscripts.

- Research proposals
- An annotated bibliography
- A review of the literature on the topic
- Abstracts in MLA and APA style
- A short essay with documentation of a few sources in MLA style
- A new lengthy research paper in MLA style
- A research paper in APA style

- A research paper in the number style
- A portion of a paper in footnote style

Additional sample papers appear in the text's supplements, discussed below.

Collecting Data Outside the Library

Many instructors now require students to search for material beyond the library, so the text features comprehensive sections on observation, interviews, collaborative reports, letters and questionnaires, visits to government archives, television programs, and original experiments. The text also shows how to cite and document each type of source.

Supplements

Guides to Literature, Argument, and Writing Across the Curriculum

Three supplemental student guides are available to adopters of *Writing Research Papers*. *Literature and Research* introduces the nuances of literary research, showing students how to identify a problem, investigate the literature, and interpret and analyze the work employing various methods of inquiry. It also shows how to maintain a proper focus in the introduction, body, and conclusion and includes a sample paper in MLA style.

Argument and Research introduces students to the complexities of developing a persuasive essay. The text explains methods for discovering a valid argument and investigating the evidence; methods of inquiry and systems of reasoning, such as the rhetorical triangle and the Toulmin system; and the design of the introduction, the body, and the conclusion. A sample paper in MLA style is included.

Writing Across the Curriculum and Research introduces students to the conventions and requirements of research in different disciplines. This guide explains methods for identifying and investigating a problem and methods of inquiry. It explains what constitutes acceptable evidence and how to report it in science and technology, the social sciences, and the humanities. Guidelines for design and format of a paper in CBE, APA, and Chicago styles are explained and illustrated with sample papers.

Instructor's Manual

A chapter-by-chapter manual offers classroom activities and questions, worksheet duplication masters, and unit tests as well as MLA, APA, CBE, and *Chicago* style sample research papers.

Model Research Papers

Model Research Papers from Across the Disciplines examines eight student papers on topics from a variety of disciplines. Introductions and annotations examine each paper's features in detail. Models illustrate use of MLA in-text reference and footnote, APA, and CBE documentation styles. Models include one sample World Wide Web hypertextual paper/group project.

World Wide Web Site

A new companion Web site at ⟨http://longman.awl.com/lester⟩ with additional information and examples expands the scope of the text into the ever-changing and growing World Wide Web. Features include chapter summaries and learning objectives, online activities, a collection of links for each chapter, a searchable glossary of Internet and Web terms, an electronic style guide, a Web tutorial, and *Citing Cyberspace*.

Acknowledgments

Many of the students and instructors who have used this text in its previous eight editions have made contributions to the quality of the book. For that I am grateful.

Special thanks goes to Anne May Berwind, Head of Library Information Services at Austin Peay State University. She revised the list of references in the Appendix and added a few annotations for selected works on the list.

Professional reviewers for the ninth edition offered many helpful ideas; they were Louise Ackley, Boise State University; Bege Bowers, Youngstown State University; Peggy Brent, Hinds Community College; P. J. Colbert, Marshalltown Community College; Janice Erwin, Kilgore College; Diane Gould, Shoreline Community College; Angie Green, Lee College; Jaime Herrera, Mesa Community College; Michael Howley, Alabama State University; David Karrfalt, Edinboro University of Pennsylvania; Elizabeth Kirchoff, St. Cloud State University; Colleen Lloyd, Cuyahoga Community College; Kim Brian Lovejoy, Indiana University at Indianapolis; Anne Maxham-Kastrinos, Washington State University; Tim McGee, College of New Jersey; Nancy J. Moore, Edmunds Community College; John Orr, Fullerton College; Sid Parham, St. Cloud State University; Randall Popken, Tarleton State University; Diane Price, Wayne Community College; Debbie Reinders, Mesa Community College; Arthur G. Ritas, Macomb Community College; Kurt Spellmeyer, Rutgers University; James Stokes, University of Wisconsin, Stevens Point; Joanne Tardoni, Western Wyoming Community College; Judith B. Williamson, Sauk Valley Community College.

The following instructors kindly reviewed *Citing Cyberspace*, and their observations have contributed to *Writing Research Papers* as well: James L. Brown, Kansas City Kansas Community College; Brion Champie, St. Edward's University; Marica Lavely, The University of Tennessee, Martin; Janeen Myers, Oklahoma State University.

I appreciate also the support of my family, and so I thank Martha, Jim, Mark, Debbie, Caleb, and Sarah for their unending enthusiasm and encouragement.

James D. Lester

Introduction

Your creation of a long, scholarly paper will seldom develop in a neat, logical progression. You will probably take a few steps forward and then find yourself retracing your steps. Nevertheless, one way to succeed will be to follow the orderly nature of this text—choose a topic, gather data, plan and write a draft, revise and polish the manuscript, and develop a final bibliography. Word processing makes each of these tasks easier, and this manual explains computer technology as appropriate to the task. However, it does not presume to be a computer manual; that task is best left to others. The goal of this book is to help you write well.

This writing manual provides a step-by-step explanation of the research-writing process. It encourages you to take one step at a time—from selecting a significant topic to producing a polished manuscript. You will become adept at several skills.

1. Narrowing your focus to a manageable topic
2. Locating source materials and taking notes
3. Analyzing, evaluating, and interpreting materials
4. Arranging and classifying materials
5. Writing the paper with a sense of purpose as well as with clarity and accuracy
6. Handling problems of quoting and properly documenting your sources

In time, you will come to understand that knowledge is not always something conveyed by experts in books and articles for you to copy onto the pages of your research papers. You will learn to generate new ideas about the issues and defend your position with the weight of your argument backed up by valid evidence. You will use the evidence to support *your* ideas.

Chapter 1 shows how to search both the library and Internet sources for a worthy topic that confronts a scholarly issue, asks a research question, or poses an argument. It asks you to:

Examine your own experience.
Reconsider your cultural background.
Evaluate issues within your favorite academic disciplines.

Chapter 2, "Gathering Data," offers you three distinct methods for gathering ideas—(1) the electronic library and Internet sources, (2) the printed resources, and (3) information found outside the library, such as interviews, letters, lectures, or questionnaires. Thus, a portion of Chapter 2 serves as an introduction to researching by computer.

Chapters 3, 4, and 5 will help you organize a plan, practice critical reading, and write your notes. Included in Chapter 5 is a discussion of *plagiarism,* an error of scholarship that afflicts many students who think proper scholarly credit is unnecessary or who become confused about proper placement of references.

Chapters 6 and 7 provide details about writing the paper—from title and outline to introduction, body, and conclusion. In particular, Chapter 6 will help you frame the argument in the introduction, develop it in the body, and discuss it in the conclusion. You will also be reminded of three vital phases—revising, editing, and proofreading. Chapter 7 explains the value of in-text citations to help you distinguish your own comments from paraphrases and quotations borrowed from the source materials.

Chapters 8 and 9 explain matters of formatting and mechanics. They show you how to design the paper, from the title page to the works cited page. Sample papers serve as guides to the MLA (Modern Language Association) style.

Chapter 10 explains the APA (American Psychological Association) style and correlates its features with MLA style. You will need to use the APA style for papers in several disciplines, such as psychology, education, political science, and sociology.

Chapter 11 explains the documentation style for disciplines other than English and psychology. It explains and gives examples of the name and year system for papers in the social sciences, business, and the physical or biological sciences; the CBE number system for use with papers in the applied sciences and medical sciences; and the footnote and endnote systems of *The Chicago Manual of Style* for use with some papers in the liberal arts.

Finally, Appendix A offers a list of reference works and journals shown alphabetically by many fields of study. For every discipline listed, you will find a list of study guides, database sites, the appropriate printed bibliographies, and the most useful indexes to literature in the journals. Appendix B shows important Internet sites by discipline.

1 Finding a Topic

Choosing a topic for the research paper can be easy (any topic will serve) yet very complicated (an informed choice is crucial). Select a person, a person's work, or a specific issue to study—President Bill Clinton, John Steinbeck's *Of Mice and Men,* or learned dexterity with Nintendo games. Select a subject from these general areas:

Current events (effects of maternal smoking)
Education (standardized testing in public schools)
Social issues (parents who lie to their children)
Science (genetic engineering and cloning)

Try to select a topic that will meet three demands.

1. It must examine a significant issue.
2. It must address a knowledgeable reader and carry that reader to another plateau of knowledge.
3. It must have a serious purpose, one that demands analysis of the issues, argues from a position, and explains complex details.

Choose a topic with a built-in issue or argument so that you can interpret the issue and cite the opinions of outside sources. You need not abandon a favorite topic, such as "Fishing at Lake Cumberland." Just be certain to give it a serious, scholarly perspective: "The effects of toxic chemicals on the fish of Lake Cumberland."

For example, the topic "Internet Addiction" raises two questions about a serious issue: How do some people get addicted to the Internet? With what results? When your topic addresses a problem or raises an issue, you have a reason to:

Examine specific sources in the library.
Share your point of view with the reader.
Write a meaningful conclusion.

Start with personal reflection about your interests (see Section 1a). If that doesn't produce a good topic, use a computer search (see Section 1b). If computers are unavailable, use the library's printed sources to search out a topic (see Section 1c).

1a   Generating Ideas for a Research Paper Project

Begin with four activities before you enter the library.

1. Reflect on your personal experiences.
2. Talk with other people.
3. Speculate about the subject by listing issues, asking questions, engaging in free writing, and utilizing other techniques.
4. Keep abreast of current events via Internet, newspapers, radio, and television.

By beginning with these four activities, you will begin (1) to find a primary topic, (2) to discover issues, terms, and questions, and (3) to write notes.

Using Personal Experience for Topic Discovery

Most people have special interests as demonstrated by their television viewing, their choice of magazines, their clubs, and their activities. One of three techniques can spark your interest and, perhaps, help you discover a writing topic.

1. Combine a personal topic with some aspect of your academic studies:
   a. Skiing and Sports Medicine: A personal interest in skiing combined with an academic study of sports medicine might yield this topic: "Therapy for Strained Muscles."
   b. Video Games and Mathematics: Your love for video games might prompt you to study the mathematical formulas for developing the games.
2. Consider economic or scientific subjects. For example:
   a. Child Care and Economics: Your concern about the cost of child care might prompt you to make a cost-benefit analysis of different child-care options.
   b. The Family Farm and Chemistry: The contaminated well water on your family's farm combined with a study of chemical toxins might yield: "The Poisoning of Underground Water Tables."
3. Let your cultural background prompt you toward detailed research into your roots, your culture, and the mythology and his-

tory of your ethnic background. Five students developed these topics:

a. The Indian Wars from the Native American's point of view
b. Chinese theories on the roles of women
c. Bicultural experiences of Hispanic students
d. Pride as motivation for the behavior of young black Americans
e. The Irish migration to America

Talking with Others to Find a Subject

Like some researchers, you may need to start your research sitting on a park bench with a friend or across the coffee table from a colleague or relative. Listen to people in your school and community as they express their concerns. Something said might trigger an idea for your paper.

1. Consult with your instructor.
2. Consult with three or four students about your topic.
3. Listen to the concerns of others.
4. Take careful notes.
5. Adjust your research accordingly.

For example, one writer discovered a topic by chatting about television with a few friends. One friend said, "The talk shows are just entertainment, like soap operas; they're not news and not reality." The writer seized upon the idea and produced a paper called, "Television Reality Check: The Fine Line between Fact and Fiction on Talk Shows." (See also Section 2j for methods of conducting an interview.)

Speculating About Your Subject to Discover Ideas

At some point you may need to sit back, relax, and use your imagination to contemplate the issues and generate ideas. Out of meditation may come topics and subtopics worthy of investigation. Ideas can be generated in these ways.

Keeping a Research Journal

Unlike a diary of personal thoughts about your daily activities or a journal of creative ideas (poems, stories, or scenarios), the research journal records ideas on specific issues. You can maintain the journal on your computer or in a notebook to list issues, questions, notes, and bits of free writing (following in this section). In effect, you can keep all your initial ideas and materials in one source book or computer file. A notebook that has pockets on the inside jacket will give you a place for photocopied materials and other miscellaneous items. If you keep the journal on a computer file, you can download materials from the Internet and use a scanner for other items.

Free Writing

To free write, merely focus on a topic and write whatever comes to mind. Continue writing with your mind on the topic. Do not worry about grammar, style, or penmanship. The result? You have started writing. Your brain is engaged, and ideas flow forth. The exercise requires nonstop writing for a page or so to develop valuable phrases, comparisons, personal anecdotes, and specific thoughts that help focus issues of concern. Note this brief example that establishes the writer's concerns about the subject:

> Tabloid television seems to me a good name for what's been happening with the talk shows on tv. The shows just sensationalize the personal, private misery of lots of people. How many times have I wondered, "Is this really true?" It seems like people will say or do just about anything to get on tv. What's worse, the tv producers encourage extreme behavior by kooks and weirdos.

This free writing has set the path for this writer's investigation into the somewhat bizarre world of television talk shows.

Listing Key Words

During your search for a subject, be alert for fundamental terms and concepts that might focus the direction of your research. One student, while considering a topic for his Native American Studies course, listed several terms and phrases about oral traditions of the Blackfoot tribe:

boasting	invoking spirits	singing
making medicine	story telling	reciting history
war chants	jokes and humor	

Key words set the stage for writing the rough outline, as explained below.

Arranging Key Words into a Rough Outline

As you develop ideas and begin listing key terms and subtopics, you should recognize the hierarchy of major and minor issues.

Native American Oral Traditions

Chanting	Narrating	Singing
for war	history	hymns
for good health	stories	folk songs
for religion	jokes	
	boasts	

This initial ranking of ideas will mature during the research process.

Clustering

Another method for discovering the hierarchy of your primary topics and subtopics is to cluster ideas around a central subject. The cluster of related topics can generate a multitude of ideas, which are all joined and interconnected, as shown in the illustration.

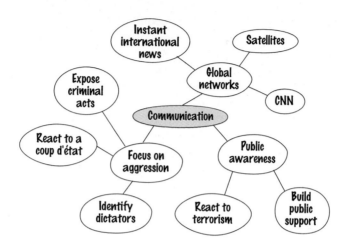

Asking Questions

Stretch your imagination with questions. Ask questions that focus your attention on primary issues and that help you frame a workable topic. Having read Henry Thoreau's essay "Civil Disobedience," one writer asked:

> What is "civil disobedience"?
> Is dissent legal? Is it moral? Is it patriotic?
> Is dissent a liberal activity? Conservative?
> Should the government encourage or stifle dissent?
> Is passive resistance effective?

Answering the questions can lead the writer to a central issue and even produce a thesis statement: "Civil disobedience has helped to shape our nation."

Another student framed questions by using the rhetorical modes of composition, as illustrated:

COMPARISON	How does a state lottery compare with horse racing?
DEFINITION	What is a lottery in legal terms? In religious terms?
CAUSE/EFFECT	What are the consequences of a state lottery on funding for education, highways, prisons, and social programs?
PROCESS	How are winnings distributed?
CLASSIFICATION	What types of lotteries exist and which are available in this state?
EVALUATION	What is the value of a lottery to the average citizen? What are the disadvantages?

Any one question above can identify a key issue worthy of research.

A third student framed questions for a study across the curriculum on the subject of sports gambling:

ECONOMICS	Does sports gambling benefit a college's athletic budget? The national economy?
PSYCHOLOGY	What is the effect of gambling on the mental attitude of the college athlete who knows huge sums hang in the balance on his/her performance?
HISTORY	Does gambling on sporting events have an identifiable tradition?
SOCIOLOGY	What compulsion in human nature prompts people to gamble on athletic prowess?

Such questions help to identify a working topic.

1b Using a Computer Search to Discover a Topic

The Internet, CD-ROMs, and even your library's public access catalog can quickly show you what research has been done on a topic and even lead you to think about your subject in new ways.

Surfing the Internet for a Topic

The Internet is a worldwide computer network consisting of millions of computers and computer files that form a huge library of source materials. Most researchers now use the **World Wide Web** (for more on the Web, see pages 28–37).

Use a subject directory if you have no subject but need one. Subject directories categorize websites, moving you methodically from the general to more narrow topics. Looking at the available subjects, you might start with *history,* move to *military history,* move to *Civil War History,* move to *Civil War Battles,* and arrive finally at *The Battle at Gettysburg.*

Many of these same sites allow **key-word searches.** These searches reveal addresses and descriptions of web sites that use your key words. The results of a key-word search can tell you if a topic has been researched by others. For example, entering

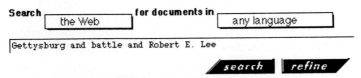

will direct you to such sites as:

http://gettysburg.welcome.com/battle.html

or

http://www.gettybg.com/battle.html

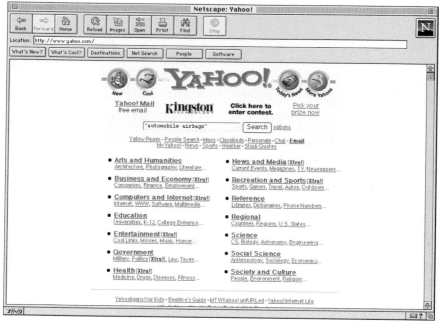

Figure 1
Example of a subject directory with "hot" text.

Figure 1 shows a subject directory on the Internet with highlighted "hot" text, which will move you, with a click of the mouse, to an Internet site. Read the information at these sites to see what others are saying on the subject.

> "The Electronic Library: Using a Computer Search" in Chapter 2, pages 28–37, discusses the matter of Internet searches in great detail, so you may need to look there for specific advice.

Using CD-ROM to Find a Topic

CD-ROM comes in two forms—individual disks and databases. For general information as you begin your research, consult encyclopedias on individual disks, such as *Grolier's Encyclopedia, Encarta,* or *Electronic Classical Library.* Also, the individual cassettes give you access to research tools, such as the *Oxford English Dictionary, IBM Dictionary of Computing,* or *McGraw-Hill Encyclopedia of World Economies.* Other examples are *The History of American Literature, America's Civil War: A Nation Divided,* and *Leading Black Americans.* Your library may not house the individual disk relevant to your search, so look for additional disks at department offices and at the offices of individual professors.

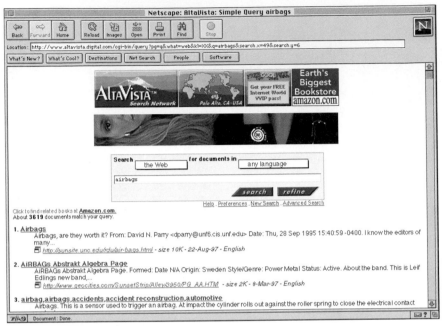

Figure 2
Example of hypertext with "hot" links. Reproduced with the permission of Digital Equipment Corporation. Alta Vista, the Alta Vista logo, and the Digital logo are trademarks of Digital Equipment Corporation.

Figure 2 shows highlighted "hot" text, which will take you to specific articles on the Web.

Most college libraries now have CD-ROM databases, such as *InfoTrac, Silverplatter,* or *UMI-Proquest.* These database files refer you to thousands of magazine and journal articles. The search engine of the database will help you work from a general subject to a narrowed topic and, finally, to descriptions of specific articles. In many cases you can read an abstract of the article, and sometimes get a computer printout of an entire article. Libraries will vary in their CD-ROM holdings, so it is important for you to develop a working relationship with the reference librarians. Follow these steps:

1. **Select a database.** The computers in the reference room will feature a variety of databases. *InfoTrac* is general; PSYCINFO (psychological sources) and ERIC (educational sources) are specific.

2. **List a general subject.** Use a key word search to launch the investigation.

    women

3. **Scan the subtopics.** Read the list of subtopics provided on the screen and narrow your search to one.

    women in business
    women in popular culture

women in politics
women in public life

4. **Select one topic.** Enter a choice, such as *women in politics,* to get a printout of articles. Scan these titles to see what others are writing about and look carefully for a topic that interests you.

> Gender differences in support for women candidates: is there a glass ceiling in American politics? Kathleen Dolan Women & Politics, Spring 1997 v17 n2 p27 (15). —full text available—
> Tough mothering. (women in politics) (Editorial) Jeffrey Klein. Mother Jones, Jan–Feb 1997 v22 nl p3 (1). —abstract available—
> Might women have the edge? Open-seat house primaries. Robert A. Bernstein. Women & Politics, Spring 1997 v17 n2 p1 (26). —abstract available—

At this point, since you are still searching for a topic, you need not examine too closely the abstracts or articles nor print the list of sources; however, see Section 2c for information on reading the abstracts and printing documents of interest.

5. **Search several topics at once.** You can speed up the keyword search by using two or three words at the start joined by "and" or "or":

> women and politics
> politics or diplomacy or congress and women
> "gender politics"
> "White House reporters"
> (Women and politics and congress) not Hillary Clinton

"Using CD-ROM" in Chapter 2, pages 37–38, discusses these requests in greater detail. Also, read the instructions at the terminal, press the HELP key, or confer with a reference librarian.

Using the Public Access Catalog (PAC) to Find a Topic

Most college libraries now have a *Public Access Catalog* (PAC), which is a computer version of the card catalog files. It indexes books, film strips, video tapes, and similar items, but usually not articles in magazines and journals. Like the CD-ROM databases, it will help you find a topic by guiding you quickly from general subjects to subtopics and finally to specific books. Follow five steps in your search for a good subject.

1. **General subject.** Type in a general subject at the keyboard of the PAC.

> women

2. **Subtopics.** Examine the various subtopics for an interesting topic:

> 1—women
> 2—women in art
> 3—women in business
> 4—women in industry
> 5—women in medicine
> 6—women in politics

3. **List of references.** As you search deeper in the subject, you will find a specific list of book titles, and one might trigger your interest:
   a. Electoral systems in comparative perspective: Their impact on women and minorities (1994)
   b. Women in power: the secrets of leadership (1997)
   c. Women, politics, and a changing environment (1997)
   d. The warrior queens (1989)
   e. Toward a feminist theory of the state (1989)
4. **Printout.** If the subject matter of one book looks interesting, you can investigate it. Just enter the proper codes, get a complete description of the book on the screen, and print it:

> ***Bibliographic Record—***
> Rule, Wilma, and Zimmerman, Joseph F., eds. Electoral systems in comparative perspective: Their impact on women and minorities / 1st ed. / Westport, Conn.: Greenwood Press, 1994. xi, 259 p.: ill.; 25cm. Bibliography: page 247-250. LOCATION; Political science stacks. CALL NUMBER: JF/1057/E43/1994 12/7/94. Not charged to a user.

Examining the book can suggest additional topics. Keep cruising the library sources until you find something that excites your interest. (See Section 1c for ways to examine a book.)

> Use a computer search to control the size of the project. If the computer lists 50 or 60 books and 200 or more articles, the topic is too broad, and you should narrow it. If it provides one book and only two or three articles, you probably need to broaden the topic.

5. **Gateways.** Use gateways or hypertext links to other library collections. At your library's public access catalog you may discover headings that will link you with other libraries or to networked

information, even the Internet at some libraries (see pages 28–29 for more on hypertext links). The gateway enables you to examine the holdings in a nearby library that you might visit personally or to examine the holdings at distant libraries that offer interlibrary loans (that is, the distant library will ship material to your library for your use).

1c Using Printed Sources to Formulate a Topic

If you have not yet discovered a workable topic for your research, go into the library for exploratory reading in reference books, biographies, or periodicals.

Scanning Periodicals and Books

As with Internet sources, look to see how your topic is discussed in the literature. Carefully read the **titles** of books and articles and make a record of key terminology, as shown here:

"The Lessons of the French Revolution"
"Napoleon's Ambition and the Quest for Domination"
"Perspectives: Napoleon's Relations with the Catholic Church"

These titles provide several key words and possible subjects for a research paper: *Napoleon's ambition, Napoleon and the church, the French Revolution.* Investigation of these will lead to other possible topics.

Inspect a book's **table of contents** to find a subject that interests you. A typical history book might display these headings in the table of contents:

The French Revolution
The Era of Napoleon
Reaction to Napoleon and More Revolutions
The Second Empire of France

If any of these headings look interesting, go to the book's **index** for additional headings, such as this sample:

Napoleon
    becomes Emperor, 174–176
    becomes First Consul, 173
    becomes Life Consul, 174
    and the Catholic Church, 176–178
    character of, 168–176
    and codes of law, 178–179
    defeated by enemies, 192–197
    defeats Austrians, 170

encounters opposition, 190–191
extends empire in Europe, 180–189
seizes power for "One Hundred Days"
sent to Elba, 197
sent to St. Helena, 199

If you see something that looks interesting, the logical follow-up involves reading the designated pages to consider issues and to find a general subject for your research. For example, the list above might suggest a student's investigation of Napoleon's return from Elba for a few additional days of glory before the darkness of confinement at St. Helena.

Scanning an Encyclopedia Article

An encyclopedia contains not only an alphabetical list of topics but also in-depth discussions that can trigger your own ideas. Keep in mind that encyclopedias vary in complexity. The most accessible is *The World Book Encyclopedia,* then *Collier's Encyclopedia* and *Encyclopedia Americana.* Then the level of complexity increases with *Encyclopedia Britannica,* followed by subject-specific encyclopedias, such as *Encyclopedia of World Literature in the 20th Century.* Many encyclopedias are also available on CD-ROM or online. Note this brief encyclopedia passage and the method of evaluating it for possible topics:

> History would have given Napoleon Bonaparte a high place even if he had followed only one career. His military campaigns inspired many commanders, who sought the secret of his success. Napoleon's genius at making war lay in the ability to exploit an enemy's weakness.
> Napoleon's achievements in government influenced both dictators and liberators of the 1800's and 1900's. His contributions to French law, embodied in the Code Napoléon, survive today. He also made major developments in education and banking.—Vernon J. Puryear, *The World Book Encyclopedia.* 1976.

Several topics emerge from this passage: Napoleon's military campaigns, his effect on French law, the elements of the Code Napoléon, his effect on French education, and the changes he made in the banking system. All are worthy of additional research. *Caution:* Encyclopedias serve only your preliminary search; they are seldom cited in a final manuscript.

Searching the Headings in the Printed Indexes

Any major index collection in the reference room, such as the *Readers' Guide to Periodical Literature, Bibliographic Index,* or *Humanities Index,* categorizes and subdivides topics in alphabetical order. Searching under a key word or phrase will usually locate a list of critical articles on the subject. The following entry under the heading "Single Mothers" from *Social Sciences Index,* 1997, produces several titles.

Single Mothers
  Constructing the objects of our discourse: the welfare wars, the orphanage, and the silenced welfare mom. R. Asen. Bibl *Polit Commun* v13 p393–307 Jl/S '96
  Sex roles and soap operas: what adolescents learn about single motherhood. M. S. Larson. bibl *Sex Roles* v35 p97–110 Jl '96

Economic Conditions
  Child support in black and white: racial differentials in the award and receipt of child support during the 1980s. J. S. Graham and A. H. Beller. Bibl *Soc Sci Q* v77 p528–42 S '96
  Single mothers in various living arrangements: differences in economic and time resources. K. F. Folk. bibl *Am J Econ Sociol* v55 p277–92 Jl '96
  Welfare stigma among low-income, African American single mothers. R. L. Jarrett. bibl *Fam Relat* v45 p368–74 O '96

Studying the titles of these articles might suggest a good topic.

> **Note:** Topic selection goes beyond choosing a general category (e.g., "single mothers"); it includes finding a research-provoking issue or question, such as "Has the foster parent program effectively replaced the orphanage system?" That is, you need to take a stand and adopt a belief.

1d   Drafting a Research Proposal

A research proposal helps clarify and focus the project. It comes in two forms: (1) a short paragraph to identify the project for yourself and your instructor, or (2) several pages to give background information, your rationale for conducting the study, a review of the literature, your methods, and conclusions you hope to prove.

The Short Proposal

A short proposal will quickly identify four essential ingredients of your work:

  a. The purpose of the paper (explain, analyze, argue)
  b. The intended audience (general or specialized)
  c. Your position as the writer (informer or advocate)
  d. The preliminary thesis sentence or opening hypothesis

One writer, sitting at the computer, developed this research proposal:

> This paper will examine objectivity on television talk shows, which promote their news value but seem more concerned about titillating the audience to build their ratings and advertising dollars. Objectivity is an ideal, and viewers should understand that television gives us symbolic reality like a novel or a staged drama. The talk show host, the guests, the studio audience, and even the viewer at home are all participants in a staged show that has little to do with reality.

This writer has identified the basic nature of the project and can now go in search of evidence that will defend the argument.

The Long Proposal

The long proposal will be necessary for instructors in some courses, and it will certainly be necessary if you are asking an agency to approve and fund a proposed project. (*Note:* Submissions to an agency will usually require you to follow a set of furnished guidelines.) The long proposal may include some or all of the following elements:

1. *Cover page* with title of the project, your name, and the person or agency to whom you are submitting the proposal:

   The Dangers of Internet Addiction
   Submitted to
   The University Committee on Computers
   By Tiffany Bledsoe

2. An *abstract* that provides a summary of your project in 50 to 100 words (see page 176 for an example).
3. A *purpose statement* with your *rationale* for the project. In essence this is your thesis sentence, your identification of the audience that your work will address, and the role you will play as investigator and advocate (see the short proposal above for an example).
4. A *statement of qualification* that explains your experience and the special qualities you bring to the project: "I bring first-hand experience to this study, for I watched my mother become addicted to the Internet to the point that she abandoned our family and divorced my father just so she could sit at the computer day and night. I want to examine the psychological allure of this new medium." *Note:* Such an intense experience is not required, and this section can even be omitted.
5. A *review of the literature* that surveys the articles and books that you have examined in your preliminary work (see pages 99–103 for an explanation with an example).

6. A description of your *research methods,* which is the design of your study, the *materials* you will need, your *timetable,* and, where applicable, your *budget.*

Explaining Your Purpose in the Research Proposal

Research papers accomplish different tasks:

1. They explain and define the topic.
2. They analyze the specific issues.
3. They persuade the reader with the weight of your evidence.

Usually, one of these purposes will dominate the paper, but you will probably employ all the purposes in one way or another. For example, the writer on page 16 must *persuade* his readers that talk shows are not objective, he must *explain* the structure of the shows, and he must *analyze* the role of the various participants.

1. Use *explanation* to review and itemize factual data. For example, one writer defined cocaine and explained how it comes from the coca shrub of South America. Another writer explained how advertisers have gained entrance into classrooms by providing free educational materials.
2. Use *analysis* to classify various parts of the subject and to investigate each one in depth. For example, one writer examined the effects of cocaine on the brain, the eyes, the lungs, the heart, and so on. Another writer classified and examined the methods used by advertisers to reach school children with their messages.
3. Use *persuasion* to reject the general attitudes about a problem and affirm new theories, advance a solution, recommend a course of action, or—at the least—invite the reader into an intellectual dialogue. For example, one writer condemned the use of cocaine and warned of its dangers. Another writer argued that advertisers have enticed children into bad habits: eating improperly, smoking cigarettes, drinking alcohol, or behaving violently.

Identifying Your Audience in the Research Proposal

You will want to design your research paper for an audience of interested readers who expect a depth of understanding on your part and evidence of your background reading on this special topic. Readers of a paper on social issues (working mothers, latchkey children, overcrowded prisons) expect analysis that points toward a social theory or answer. Readers of an academic interpretation of a novel expect to read literary theories on the novel's symbolism, narrative structure, or characterization. Readers of a business report on outdoor advertising expect statistical evidence that will defend a general proposition, especially as it reflects the demographics of the targeted consumers and the cost of reaching them.

Checklist on Addressing the Reader

1. Identify your audience and respond accordingly. How will your audience affect your topic, your development, your voice and style, and even your choice of words?

2. Meet the needs of your readers. Are you telling them everything they need to know without insulting their intelligence? Are you saying something worthwhile? Something new? Do not bore them or insult their intelligence by retelling known facts from an encyclopedia. (This latter danger is the reason many instructors discourage your use of an encyclopedia as a source.)

3. Invite your readers into the discussion by approaching the topic from an interesting and different point of view; that is, address literature students with an economic interpretation of a novel; address marketing students with a biological study of human behavior in the marketplace; address history students with a geographical study of a nation's destiny.

Identifying Your Role as a Researcher in the Proposal

Your voice should reflect the investigative nature of your work, so try to display your knowledge. In short, make it *your* discourse, not a collection of quotations from experts in the books and journals. Your role is to investigate, explain, defend, and argue the issue at hand with proper citations. Do not hide authorities that you have consulted but refer to them and offer quotations. After all, the ideas of others are of paramount interest to you and to your readers. Provide charts or graphs that you have created or copied from the sources. (Your instructors will give you credit for using the sources in your paper.) Just be certain that you give in-text citations to the sources to reflect your academic honesty.

Expressing Your Thesis Sentence in the Research Proposal

A thesis sentence expands your topic into a scholarly proposal, one that you will try to prove and defend in your paper. It does not state the obvious, such as: "Too much television is harmful to children." That sentence will not provoke an academic discussion because your readers know that excess in anything is harmful. The writer must narrow and isolate one issue by finding a critical focus, such as:

> Violence in children's programming echoes an adolescent's fascination with brutality.

This sentence advances an idea that the writer can develop fully and defend with the evidence. The writer has made a connection between the subject *television violence* and the focusing agent, *adolescent behavior.* Look at two more examples:

THESIS   Television cartoons can affect a child's personality because they are so violent.

THESIS   Objectivity can never be perfectly presented by any television broadcast nor perceived by any viewer.

In the first, the writer combines television viewing with psychological development. In the second, the writer advances his comparison of reality and the creative arts of television.

Accordingly, a writer's critical approach to the subject affects the thesis. One writer's social concern for battered wives will generate a different thesis than another person's biological approach:

SOCIAL APPROACH   Public support of "safe" houses for battered wives seems to be a public endorsement of divorce.

BIOLOGICAL APPROACH   Battered wives may be the victims of their own biological conditioning.

PSYCHOLOGICAL APPROACH   The masochism of some women traps them in a marriage of painful love.

Each thesis statement shown above will provoke a response from the reader, who will demand a carefully structured defense of any unstated assumptions.

Your thesis is not your conclusion or your answer to a problem. Rather, the thesis anticipates your conclusion by setting in motion the examination of facts and pointing the reader toward the special idea of your paper, which you will save for the conclusion. Note below how three writers developed different thesis sentences even though they had the same topic, "Santiago in Hemingway's *The Old Man and the Sea.*"

Note: This novel narrates the toils of an old Cuban fisherman named Santiago, who desperately needs the money to be gained by returning with a good catch of fish. On this day he catches a marlin. After a long struggle, Santiago ties the huge marlin to the side of his small boat. However, during the return in the darkness, sharks attack the marlin so that he arrives home with only a skeleton of the fish. He removes his mast and carries it, like a cross, up the hill to his home.

THESIS   Poverty forced Santiago to venture too far and struggle beyond reason in his attempt to land the marlin.

This writer will examine the economic conditions of Santiago's trade.

THESIS   The giant marlin is a symbol for all of life's obstacles and hurdles, and Santiago is a symbol for all suffering humans.

This writer will examine the religious and social symbolism of the novel.

THESIS   Hemingway's portrayal of Santiago demonstrates the author's deep respect for Cuba and its stoic heroes.

This writer takes a social approach in order to examine the Cuban culture and its influence on Hemingway.

Make the preliminary thesis sentence a part of your research proposal:

> This paper will interpret a novel, <u>The Old Man and the Sea</u>, by Ernest Hemingway. My purpose is to explain to fellow literature students the novel's setting and the social conditions of the old Cuban. I suspect that poverty forced Santiago to venture too far and struggle beyond reason in his attempt to land the marlin.
> —Ramon Lopez

This writer and his instructor now have an understanding of the paper's purpose, its audience, the role of the student as a literary interpreter, and the paper's narrow focus on Santiago's economic status.

Using an Enthymeme

Some of your instructors might want the research paper to develop an argument as stated in an enthymeme, which is a claim supported with a reason as stated in a *because* clause. Let's look at some examples:

ENTHYMEME   Some battered women accept their fate of bad marriages because of their own masochism.

The claim that some women accept the batterings is supported by the stated reason that their masochism gives them a passive, compliant nature. This writer will perhaps need to address any unstated assumptions, for example, that a battered woman is in a "bad" marriage.

ENTHYMEME   Violence in children's television programming should be controlled because the violence triggers an adolescent's fascination with brutality.

The claim that violence on television should be controlled is supported by the stated reason that violence affects a child's interest in brutality. Again, this writer will need to address any unstated assumptions, for example, that fascination with brutality will make a child brutal or violent.

ENTHYMEME   Television talk shows seldom provide objective viewpoints because both the producers and the

television viewers have their own subjective agendas
about the sensational social issues raised.

The claim that objectivity seldom occurs on talk shows is supported by the
stated reason that a producer as well as a viewer usually has ready-made re-
actions to an issue. Again, this writer will need to address any unstated assumptions, for example, that producers and viewers really do have subjective attitudes.

1e   Narrowing the General Subject to a Specific Topic

Research requires accurate facts and evidence in support of a specific proposition. Drafting a research proposal (1d) will narrow the topic, but use the
following techniques if needed.

Narrowing the Topic by a Comparison

Comparison will limit a discussion to specific differences. Historians compare
Robert E. Lee and Ulysses S. Grant. Political scientists compare conservatives
and liberals. Literary scholars compare the merits of free verse with patterned
verse. Any two works, any two persons, any two groups may serve as the
basis for a comparative study. However, the study should focus on issues.
Note how a rough outline sets up the differences between Alexander Hamilton and Thomas Jefferson on fiscal issues:

National Bank	Currency	Tariffs
Jefferson	Jefferson	Jefferson
Hamilton	Hamilton	Hamilton

Rather than talk about Jefferson's policies and then Hamilton's, this writer
will focus on the issues—the national bank, the currency, and tariffs. The
plan limits the discussion to specific differences between the two statesmen.

Restricting and Narrowing with Disciplinary Interests

Every discipline, whether sociology, geology, or literature, will limit a discussion to analytical categories that require detailed study, such as the *demographics* of a target audience (marketing) or the *function* of loops and ar-
rays (computer science). Those who write about literature-related topics
must learn to write about *symbols, images,* or *themes.* In contrast, a researcher in psychology must proceed with an *observation* of subjects, may
conduct *tests* on rats, or might take a *cognitive approach* to the data. Avoid
overusing the language of the discipline; yet do use the terms of the field to
help narrow your subject.

Narrowing the Topic to Match Source Materials

Library sources often limit the scope of your research. Your preliminary work should include a brief search for available sources. Will you have enough books and articles on the topic? Are they up-to-date? What have other writers focused on? For example, one writer started with the general subject, the Internet, but it was too broad. Thousands of sources were listed on the Alta Vista search engine. She responded to personal experience (her mother had become addicted to the Internet to the point that it affected the family). She searched "Internet Addiction" with the search engine and found 400 sources. On InfoTrac she found several journal and magazine articles. At the Online Public Access Catalog she found several books that addressed *addiction*. She was then ready to turn her attention to gathering the data she would need for her paper, as discussed in detail in the next chapter.

2 Gathering Data

For most writing projects you must research a specific subject, perhaps politically correct language, world banking networks, or DNA fingerprinting. Today, the search for source materials has become easier, thanks to modern technology—book catalogs on computers, the Internet, and compact disks within computers that can search thousands of journal articles for you and print out a bibliography list. For that reason, researchers need to learn how to use the new electronic library as well as know how to use the printed sources.

This chapter is therefore divided into five distinct parts:

The layout of the library
Format for bibliography entries
Electronic sources
Printed bibliographies, indexes, and catalogs
Sources outside the library

The search for sources is a serious task. Some leads will turn out to be dead ends; other leads will provide only trivial information. Some research will be duplicated, and a recursive pattern will develop; that is, you will go back and forth from reading, to searching indexes, and back again to reading. One idea modifies another, you discover connections, and a fresh perspective emerges. First-hand data, found in various ways, can also be the principal support for the research paper. That is, go beyond information found by computer or in the library. See pages 61–67 for details about conducting interviews, using questionnaires, writing letters, and other methods that work well outside the library.

Your research strategy should include these steps, with adjustments for individual needs:

Search the available sources: Access electronic sources as well as the printed indexes, abstracts, bibliographies, and reference books. This preliminary work serves several purposes:

1. It gives you an overview of the subject.

2. It provides a beginning set of references.
3. It defines and restricts the subject.
4. It suggests the availability of sufficient source materials with diverse opinions and disagreements.

Refine the topic and evaluate the sources: Narrow your topic to something that you believe will be manageable, then spend time browsing, reading abstracts, skimming articles, and examining pertinent sections of books. Look to see if you will have enough source material from scholarly sources. That is, have a mix of journal articles and books to accompany your Internet articles and magazine features.

Read and take notes: Examine books, articles, essays, reviews, computer printouts, government documents.

Use computer searches: If available, you can save time by accessing the public access catalog (PAC), the Internet, the CD-ROM services, and other electronic sources. Without leaving the work station, you can develop a working bibliography, you can scan abstracts and some entire articles, and make substantive advances before you enter the library.

Use the Appendixes of this book: They highlight the best Internet sources as well as the best printed indexes. They advise you about the best sources in psychology, art, African-American literature, chemical engineering, myth and folklore, and many other disciplines. For example, it tells writers in the field of education to search ERIC, *Current Index to Journals in Education* and Edweb, but it sends computer science students to INSPEC, to *Computer Literature Index,* and to the Internet's Virtual Computer Library.

2a   Learning the Organization of Your Library

Because of the sheer number of books and magazines and because of the vast array of retrieval systems, it will be to your advantage to tour the library and learn its arrangement—from the circulation desk, to the reference room, and on to the stacks.

Circulation Desk

The circulation desk is usually located at the front of the library where personnel can point you in the right direction and later check out your books for withdrawal. Whenever you cannot find a book on your own, check with the circulation desk or at the computer terminals to determine whether it is checked out, on reserve, or lost. If the book is checked out, you may be able to place a hold order so the librarians will contact you when the book is returned. The circulation desk also handles most general business, such as renewals, collection of fines, and handling keys and change for video and photocopying machines.

Reference Room

Here you will find general and specialized encyclopedias, biographical dictionaries, and other general works to help refine your topic. Reference librarians know the best resources for most topics, so take advantage of their expertise. After your subject is set, the reference room provides the bibliographies and indexes for your search of the sources (see 2d, "Using the Printed Bibliographies," pages 38–44, and 2e, "Searching the Printed Indexes," pages 44–55). In the reference room you should develop a working bibliography on individual cards or in a computer file. It should provide call numbers and information for your search of books and articles.

Public Access Catalog (PAC)

Most libraries have converted their card catalog files to the computer. The PAC will locate all books, listing them by author, title, and subject—all interfiled in one alphabetical catalog. For examples, see Section 1b, pages 8–13. If your library still uses the card catalog system, see 2i.

CD-ROM Database Facilities

A new type of library has emerged, one with access to sources by local computer and also by national networks that dispatch information on almost any topic—bibliographies, abstracts, and even the full text of some articles. (See Section 2c, "The Electronic Library: Using a Computer Search," pages 28–38.)

Reserve Desk

Instructors often place books and articles on reserve with short loan periods—two hours or one day—so that large numbers of students will have access to them. This system prevents one student from keeping an important, even crucial, book for two weeks while others suffer its absence. Your library may also place on reserve other valuable items that might otherwise be subject to theft, such as recordings, videotapes, statistical information, or unbound pamphlets and papers.

Stacks

The numerous shelves (stacks) of the library hold books organized by call numbers. Here you can locate specific books and browse for others that interest you. However, libraries with closed stacks will not permit you into the stacks at all. Rather, you provide the call numbers of the books you want, and an attendant will retrieve the book for you.

Interlibrary Loans

One library may borrow from another. The interlibrary loan service thereby supplements a library's resources by making additional materials available from other libraries. However, receiving a book or article by interlibrary loan may take seven to ten days. Ask your librarian about interlibrary loans available at your library. *Note:* Some libraries are networking with others by fax machine. You may also use a document delivery service, but the cost is high.

Photocopiers

Photocopying services provide a real convenience, enabling you to carry home articles from journals and reserve books that cannot be withdrawn from the library. However, copyright laws protect authors and place certain restrictions on the library. You may use the copying machines and duplicating services for your own individual purposes only, but be sure that you give proper credit to the sources (see "Understanding Plagiarism," pages 118–22, and also "Copyright Law," page 194).

Nonprint Materials

Libraries serve as a storehouse for recordings, videotapes, film, microfilm, and many other items. These nonprint materials are usually listed in the general catalog or in a special catalog. By searching these overlooked holdings, you may uncover a valuable lecture on cassette tape or a significant microfiche collection of manuscripts. Ask your librarian about vertical files, which are articles clipped from magazines and newspapers and kept in alphabetical order by topic, not by title.

Archives and Special Collections

You might select a topic that will use a special collection at your library. Many libraries are government depository libraries and house special collections and archives. Others, through donations and purchases, house collections of special import—the Robert Browning collection at Baylor University, the James Joyce holdings at Tulsa University, and so forth.

> **Library Etiquette**
>
> Some behavior is rudimentary, such as silence, respect for others, and no food or drinks in the library. Here are a few guidelines:
>
> 1. Do not reshelve books and periodicals; leave them at the reshelving bins so that librarians can return them to the correct place.
> 2. Rewind microfilm and leave it in the reshelving bin.
> 3. Do not hide material so that only you can find it, thereby depriving other researchers of the material.
> 4. Do not rip out pages of books or periodicals; if desperate, ask librarians for free copying privileges.
> 5. Be aware that others might need to use the computer station that you have camped at for too long.
> 6. At the computer station, analyze sources and then print; do not randomly print everything.

2b Developing a Working Bibliography

A working bibliography is a list of the sources that you plan to read before drafting your paper. Too few sources will indicate that your topic is too narrow or obscure. Too many sources will indicate that you need a tighter focus. Producing a set of bibliography entries has three purposes:

1. It locates articles and books for note-taking purposes.
2. It provides information for the in-text citations, as in this example in MLA style: "The numerous instances of child abuse among step fathers has been noted by Stephens (31–32) and McCormick (419)."
3. It provides information for the final reference page (see Chapters 9, 10, and 11). Therefore, you should preserve all computer printouts and handwritten notes.

Whether you keyboard your sources or make handwritten notes, each working bibliography entry should contain the following information, with variations, of course, for books, periodicals, and government documents:

1. Author's name
2. Title of the work
3. Publication information
4. Library call number
5. (Optional) A personal note about the contents of the source

Bibliography Entry for a Book (MLA Style):

> E477.6/T78/1994
> Trudeau, Noah Andre. <u>Out of the Storm: The End of the Civil</u>
>   <u>War, April–June 1865</u>. Boston: Little, 1994. Bibliography on
>   437–57.

Use the same format in your working bibliography that you will need for your finished manuscript—MLA, APA, and so forth, as explained in Chapters 9, 10, and 11.

Bibliograpy Entry for a Journal Article (MLA Style):

> Bloomfield, Josephine. "Chaucer and The Polis: Piety Desire in the
>   <u>Troilus and Criseyde</u>." <u>Modern Philology</u> 94 (1997): 291–304.

Bibliography Entry for a Magazine (MLA Style):

> Greer, Germaine. "Making Art, Making Revolution." <u>Ms.</u> May/June
>   1997: 72–77.

For other sources (e.g., anthology, lecture, map), consult the Index, which will direct you to appropriate pages in Chapters 9, 10, and 11 for samples of almost every imaginable type of bibliographic entry.

2c The Electronic Library: Using a Computer Search

The Internet, a worldwide computer network, offers instant access to hundreds, even thousands of computer files relating to almost any subject, including articles, illustrations, sound and video clips, and raw data. For access to this network, most researchers now use the World Wide Web, which is a set of specially linked computer files (articles, images, or programs). You access the Web by means of special software called a browser. The most common browsers are *Netscape Navigator* and *Microsoft Internet Explorer.*

The connections between web sites appear as hypertext links. Links are "hot" text or icons that, when clicked, instruct the computer to perform certain functions, such as to go to another file within this vast network (web). You will know that text is hot when it is underlined and colored blue, green, red, or some color other than black. Normally you will not see (or need to know about) the sets of underlying computer instructions called HTTP (hypertext transfer protocol) and HTML (hypertext markup language) that make hypertext work.

Web browsers are able to find files because each file on the Web is given a unique address that follows a specific format. An address in this format is called a Uniform Resource Locator (URL). Thus, by clicking the computer mouse on various URL addresses or icons, you can find specific articles within this vast network (web). Let's look at one URL. It follows this pattern: protocol/server.domain/directory/file.

http://www.georgetown.edu/labyrinth/library/library_catalogues.html

The *protocol* is a technological process for transmitting data. The protocol gives instructions that tells the computer how to handle incoming data. Without the protocol and without an address, your files cannot move on the Intenet. Other Internet protocols that you will see are FTP, gopher, telnet, and others, which are explained below.

The *server,* in this case *www* (World Wide Web), is the global Internet service that connects a multitude of computers and their files.

The *domain* names the organization that is feeding information into the server with a *suffix* to label the type of organization—*.com* commercial, *.edu* educational, *.gov* government, *.mil* military, *.net* network organization, and *.org* nonprofit organization. Often, knowing just the protocol and the server.domain name will get you to a home site from which you can search deeper for files. The site *www.georgetown.edu* will take you to Georgetown University's home page, where you can ask for a specific directory, such as *labyrinth,* which offers the researcher a wide assortment of files. In this case, the file *library* contains a subfile called *library_catalogues,* which is a catalogue of libraries and ways to access them.

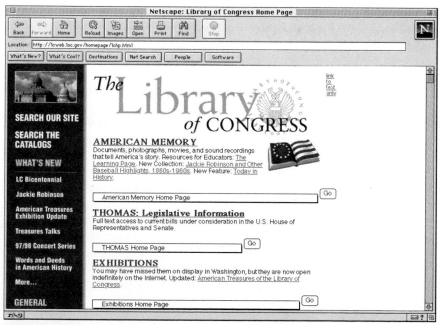

Figure 3
Example of a site's home page.

The closing code, *html,* signals to readers that *hypertext markup language* was used to write the files.

> ***Note:*** The technology of the Internet is advancing so rapidly that the instructions in this text may be dated. However, the author of this book is committed to keeping it current, so consult the following Web site for up-to-date advice and examples:
>
> > http://longman.awl.com/englishpages/
>
> Here you will find Lester's *Citing Cyberspace.*

Using a Search Engine

Search engines are Internet sites that look for and index other sites. Many search engines provide both subject directories and key-word searches. General, commercial sites provide access to subject menus and key-word searches. The commercial sites will entice you with advertisements for various products, but they do an excellent job of directing you to a wide variety of sources. These are a few of the most popular:

AltaVista	http://altavista.digital.com/
Excite	http://www.excite.com
Hotbot	http://www.hotbot.com
Infoseek	http://guide.infoseek.com
Lycos	http://www.lycos.com
Open Text Index	http://www.opentext.com/omw/f-omw.html
Search	http://www.search.com
Webcrawler	http://webcrawler.com
Yahoo!	http://www.yahoo.com

Other search engines appear almost monthly, and they often specialize in one area, such as *WWWomen* (women's studies), *TribalVoice* (Native American Studies), *Bizweb* (business studies). In addition, large web sites sometimes have search engines just for themselves.

Educational search engines provide subject indexes to the various disciplines (Humanities or Sciences) and to subtopics under those headings (History, Literature, Biochemistry, etc.). These four will help you get started:

Clearinghouse	http://www.clearinghouse.net
Internet Public Library	http://ipl.sils.umich.edu/
Planet Earth Virtual Library	http://www.nosc.mil/planet_earth/info.html
SavvySearch	http://www.cs.colostate.edu/~dreiling/ smartform.html

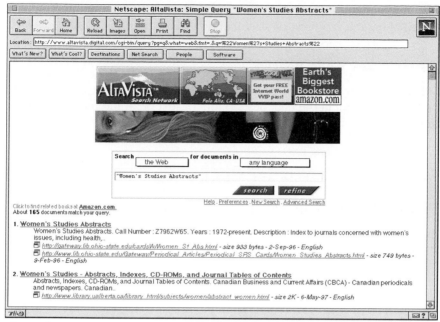

Figure 4
Example of a Web search on Alta Vista. Reproduced with the permission of Digital Equipment Corporation. Alta Vista, the Alta Vista logo, and the Digital logo are trademarks of Digital Equipment Corporation.

Bookmarks

Most web programs, such as *Netscape,* include a tool for configuring a bookmark icon that enables you to revisit addresses with just a click of the mouse. When you find a search engine or a file that you need to access on a regular basis, make a bookmark. For example, in *Netscape* simply click on *Bookmarks,* then click on *Add Bookmark.* This will automatically add the URL to the list of bookmarks. In *Microsoft Internet Explorer* use the button bar marked *Favorites* to make your bookmarks. *Note:* if you are working at a university computer laboratory, do not add bookmarks to the hard drive. Instead, save the bookmarks to your disk by using *save as* in the *file* menu of Netscape.

Using a Subject Directory

A **subject directory** indexes a sequence of hierarchical subjects. That is, it moves you methodically to narrower topics. You might start with *history,* move to *military history,* move to *Civil War History,* move to *Civil War Battles,* and arrive finally at *The Battle at Gettysburg.* In effect, the subject directory will have carried you from the general to the specific. The sites found along the way may be useful and pertinent to your work.

Using a Key-Word Search

When you know your topic, perform a key-word search using the words you would like to find in the title, description, or text of an Internet site. For example, to find information on Robert E. Lee's role at the Battle of Gettysburg, you would enter the words:

Gettysburg and battle and Robert E. Lee

The engine will direct you to a list of sites, such as:

http://gettysburg.welcome.com/battle.html

or

http://www.gettybg.com/battle.html

You can then read the articles to determine their relevance to your research efforts. *Note:* Designers of the sites usually put the most relevant sites first, so the first 5–10 will be likely sources, not the 45th of 50 sites.

Tips for Searching

1. If you write a single word, such as *gettysburg,* you will get a mammoth list of every document that contains this term, most having little relevance to your thesis. Use lower case words, if you like, because they will also find capitalized words (e.g., "gettysburg" will find *gettysburg, Gettysburg, GETTYSBURG*).

> ***Note:*** Not all search engines use words and symbols interchangeably, so you may need to read the HELP menu of each one for details.

2. If you provide two or more words with *and* or the "+" sign between each one, the search engine will find sources that feature these words.

   gettysburg *and* Lee
   gettysburg + Lee

3. Attach a *not* or a minus (–) sign in front of words that *must not* be a part of the search:

   gettysburg + Lee – Lincoln
   gettysburg *and* Lee *not* Lincoln

This request will give you documents that mention gettysburg and Robert E. Lee but will eliminate any documents that include Lincoln's name.

4. Use a *t:* to restrict the search to titles of sites:

> *t:* "*gettysburg address*"

5. Use quotation marks around two words to make them one unit (although proper names do not need quotation marks).

> "stone henge" + Thomas Hardy

This request will give you documents that combine both stone henge and Thomas Hardy. The use of phrases is perhaps the best way to limit the number of hits by the search engine. Compare:

> *gettysburg and lincoln and address* (40,000 documents found) and
> "*Lincoln's Gettysburg Address*" (200 documents found)

Therefore, make your request with phrases whenever possible; that is, ask for "migraine headaches" (2,000 hits), not "migraine and headaches" (10,000 hits). *Netscape Navigator Gold 3,* for example, gives you a search option for *phrase* as well as by *any* word or *all* words.

What should you do, however, when the search engine only produces one or two sources or useless sources? First, you can try another search engine because not all search engines work in the same way, so they give different results. Second, you can change the key-word selection.

Accessing Online Magazines and Journals

Search out articles on your topic by accessing online journals, magazines, and newspapers.

Journals

Begin by looking for scholarly journals that might be online. First, try making a key-word query if you know the title, such as *Psycholoquy,* a social science journal.

Second, if you want a comprehensive list of periodicals on a subject, access a search engine where you might find them in a subject directory. In *Yahoo!* for example, this writer selected "Social Science" from the key directory, clicked on "Journals," then on "Social Work," and accessed links to five online journals.

Third, access a search engine and use a key-word search using the words *journals* or *periodicals* and the name of your discipline. For example, this writer accessed *Alta Vista* and used a key-word search for "journals + social work." From the list provided, one of the sites, *Social Work and the*

Internet-Journals, produced links to 23 online journals devoted to social work. In another search, a request for "women's studies + journals" produced a list of journals, such as *Feminist Collections, Resources for Feminist Research,* and *Differences.* By accessing one of these links, you can examine abstracts and articles.

Many of the online periodicals offer an index to articles and some even provide key-word searches. Of more importance, these journal sites will often provide full-text articles from hard-to-find periodicals that may not be housed in your library. (Caution: some journals will require a fee or require you to join the association before permitting access.)

Magazines

Several directories exist for searching out magazine articles:

Ecola's 24-Hour Newstand	http://www.ecola.com/new/
Electric Library	http://www3.elibrary.com/
Pathfinder	http://pathfinder.com/
Monster Magazine List	http://enews.com/monster/index.html
Ziff-Davis Magazines	http://www.zdnet.com/hom/filters/mags.html

The *Electric Library,* for example, offers key-word searches as well as a directory. This writer used *child abuse* for a key-word search, and the engine found thirty articles on this topic in such periodicals as *Futurist, Mother Jones,* and *Research on Social Work Practice.*

Using Online Versions Rather than Print Versions

There are certain advantages to the use of the online versions of these works. First, you can find them almost instantly on the moniter screen rather than having to search microfilm or microfiche. Second, you can use the online indexes or search engines to find an appropriate article on your topic. Third, you can save or print out an abstract or article without the hassle of using the photocopying machine. Fourth, you can download material to your disk and, where appropriate, insert it into your research paper. However, disadvantages also exist. You may have to subscribe at a modest cost. The texts may not be the same as printed versions; some may be digest versions of the original. Abstracts may not accurately represent the full article. Therefore, act with caution.

Newspapers

Most major magazines maintain commercial sites. Here are a few:

The Chronicle of Higher Education	http://www.chronicle.com
The New York Times	http://www.nytimes.com

USA Today	http://www.usatoday.com
U.S. News Online	http://www.usnews.com
Wall Street Journal	http://www.wsj.com

Using Gopher, FTP, Telnet, and Other Protocols

Although HTTP sources now dominate the Web, valuable material still exists on other protocols, such as **Gopher, FTP,** and **telnet.** These sources will look different because they have no hypertext format (they are not linked to other sources) and most do not have graphics and color.

Gopher is an Internet browser that burrows deeper and deeper into layers of information, unlike the web, which allows you to move from site to site regardless of level of specificity.

Gopher requires you to select items from a general menu, then from a more specific menu, and so on, until you arrive at a specific site. Its name comes from the Golden Gophers at the University of Minnesota where the software was developed. Unlike *http* sites, *gopher* will not transfer you quickly from site to site. If you see a plain text file with no hot keys, it is probably a gopher site. They look like this gopher menu from the University of Virginia library:

psyc.95.6.01.group-selection.1.caporael
psyc.95.6.02.language-network.11miikkulainen
psyc.95.6.03.language-network.12.miikkulainen
psyc.95.6.04.language-network.13.miikkulainnen
psyc.95.6.05.sex-brain.1.fitch
pscy.95.6.06.memory-brain.1.klimesch

Fortunately, most *gopher* files have been redesigned as files for the World Wide Web. *Note:* The process for accessing *gopher* files varies from place to place, so you will need specific instructions at your school. Two key-word search engines for *gopher* are:

gopher://veronica.psi.net:2347/7-tl
gopher://empire.nysernet.org:2347/7

File Transfer Protocol (ftp) is a step-by-step process by which you copy computer files—text, graphics, video, sound, and so forth—from the Internet into your computer file. Thus, you can access files then use *ftp* to copy what you need. As with *gopher,* you will need specific instructions for the system at your school. In some cases you will need a user account.

Telnet, which will give you access to various computer databases, will require the use of directories and menus to find items. Unlike *ftp,* it is not a protocol for file transfer but a remote operations protocol. Telnet is a protocol that lets you access a computer somewhere on the net and use it as though it were your own terminal. To do this, you will need a username or password that will permit you to login and begin working. In *Netscape* you can access a known program by selecting *Options* → *General Preferences* → *Apps*. At the window you can install the *telnet* client that will work within *Netscape*. Again, you will need to get help for your specific system from a librarian, instructor, or an expert at the computer center.

Listserv provides ongoing E-mail discussion on technical and educational topics. To participate, you must have an E-mail address and, in some cases, subscribe to the list. To access *Listserv,* write to a server, such as ⟨listserv@list-serv.net⟩ for a list of discussion groups on your topic. For example, student Wes Cochran made a request for groups on "health." The return e-mail message gave Wes a list of discussion groups from which to choose. The student sent this message:

To	listserv@listserv.net
Name	cochranw@apsu01.edu
Subject	subscribe
Message	subscribe SHS SHS@UTKVM1 (Student Health Services)

He soon received word that his subscription had been activated, along with instructions for participating and the means of canceling the subscription once his research had ended.

Another way to find discussion groups is through a key-word search for "List of LISTSERV lists" at one of the search engines (see page 30).

A few additional aspects of *listserv* are FAQ, lurking, and moderated and unmoderated lists. FAQ (frequently asked questions) provides answers to questions by new members. Lurking is to watch the messages on the list without participation. A moderated list has an editor who screens messages that go out. Unmoderated lists have an automatic process that distributes any message that comes through.

Usenet provides access to newsgroups (discussion groups) via the web. One list of newsgroup lists can be found at this site:

http://www.dejanews.com

Some Internet search engines, such as *Alta Vista,* give you the choice of searching *Usenet* rather than the Web. Also, some versions of browers, such as *Netscape,* can be set to read newsgroups and perform key-word searches of them.

This text does not pretend to be a manual on all possible sites and protocols, and the sites change almost weekly. However, you should realize that many search engines exist for your particular needs. Seek authoritative advice on using the wide variety of documents.

Examining Library Holdings Via Internet Access

Consult libraries through the Internet. Many libraries now offer an OPAC (Online Public Access Catalog), which will allow you to search on the Web their collections for books, videos, dissertations, audiotapes, special collections, and other items. You may sometimes order books through interlibrary loan online. Additionally, some of the libraries now post full-text documents, downloadable bibliographies, databases, and links to other sites. Also, if you need identification of all books on a topic, as copyrighted and housed in Washington, DC, consult:

> Library of Congress http://www.loc.gov

This site allows you to search by word, phrase, name, title, series, and number. It also provides special features, such as an American Memory Home Page, full-text legislative information, and exhibitions. You can view, for example, the various drafts of Lincoln's *Gettysburg Address*.

For an Internet overview of online libraries, their holdings, and addresses, consult:

> LIBCAT → http://www.metronet.lib.mn.us/lc/lc1.html
> LIBWEB → http://sunsite.berkeley.edu/libweb

LIBCAT gives you easy access to almost 3000 online library catalogs. LIBWEB takes you to home pages of academic, public, and state libraries. For many library connections, the library's computer will prompt you with a public-access login name, so follow the directions for entering and exiting the programs.

Another kind of online library is Carl UnCover:

> http://www.carl.org.uncover/

This site offers you a keyword search of 17,000 journals by author, title, or subject. Copies of the articles will be faxed, usually within the hour, for a small fee.

Using CD-ROM

CD-ROMS are good for (1) obtaining information, (2) searching large bodies of text, such as Shakespeare's tragedies, (3) copying and pasting text into your manuscript, and (4) accessing reference tools.

You will find CD-ROM in two forms. One version is a single disk that you can load into your computer. Many games come in this form, but scholarly material is also available. The other is a disk or set of disks preloaded as a database into the computer(s) at your library. For general information as you begin your research, consult encyclopedias on the individual disks, such as *Grolier's Encyclopedia, Encarta,* or *Electronic Classical Library.* Like the Internet, a CD-ROM offers multimedia products as opposed to text-based references. With disks loaded onto your CD-ROM drive, such as *The History of American Literature* or *America's Civil War: A Nation Divided,* you can examine the biographical and critical articles and, again, download material to your paper (while giving scholarly credit, of course). Finally, many large and hefty research tools, such as the *Oxford English Dictionary* or the

McGraw-Hill Encyclopedia of World Economies have been published in convenient CD-ROM form. Libraries may not hold all CD-ROMs relevant to your research. Look for additional disks in other locations at your school: department offices, department libraries, and individual professor's offices.

UMI-ProQuest, Silverplatter, InfoTrac, and *Eric* are CD-ROM databases loaded into your library's computer. Like the search engines on the Internet, these databases direct you to articles on your listed subject. For additional discussion, see Chapter 1, pages 9–11.

2d   Using the Printed Bibliographies

Generally speaking, Internet sources and CD-ROM databases only give access to sources written in the last five years. That is why it is important in many cases to augment your search with printed sources. Thus, you may need to supplement your computer printouts with the old-fashioned searching of various printed sources, especially the bibliographies and indexes.

In the reference section of your library you will find many types of printed bibliographies. Each is appropriate for different stages of the research process. If you have a clearly defined topic, skip to page 40, "Using a Shortcut: Searching the Specialized Bibliographies." However, if you are still trying to formulate a clear focus, begin with general guides, as discussed next.

Starting the Search with General Bibliographies

One important work, annually updated, provides page numbers to many different books and journals that contain bibliographies on numerous subjects.

> *Bibliographic Index: A Cumulative Bibliography of Bibliographies.*
> New York: Wilson, 1938–date.

Although *Bibliographic Index* originally covered only the years 1937-42, it is kept current by supplements. Figure 5 gives an example.

If it fits your research, you would probably want to write a bibliography entry for this source and go in search of it.

> Sarnoff, Susan Kiss. <u>Paying for Crime: The Policies and Possibilities</u>
> <u>of Crime Victim Reimbursement.</u> New York: Praeger, 1996.
>   Bibl on 105–12

Other bibliographies that direct you to sources on a wide range of subjects are:

> Besterman, Theodore. *A World Bibliography of Bibliographies.* 4th ed.
> 5 vols. Lausanne: Societas Bibliographica, 1965.
> Hillard, James. *Where to Find What: A Handbook to Reference Service.*
> 3rd ed. Metuchen, NJ: Scarecrow, 1991.

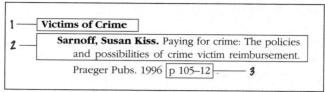

Figure 5
Example of Bibliographic Index, *1997, shows (1) Subject
heading (2) Entry of a book that contains a bibliography on
crime victims (3) Specific pages on which bibliography is located.*

McCormick, Mona. *The New York Times Guide to Reference Materials.*
   Rev. ed. New York: Times Books, 1986.
Sheehy, Eugene P., ed. *Guide to Reference Books.* 10th ed. Chicago:
   ALA, 1986.

Using the Trade Bibliographies

Trade bibliographies, intended primarily for use by booksellers and librarians, can help you in three ways: (1) to discover sources not listed in other bibliographies or in the card catalog; (2) to locate facts of publication, such as place and date; and (3) to learn if a book is in print. Start with a search for your topic in this work:

   Subject Guide to Books in Print (New York: Bowker, 1957–date).

Use this work for its subject classifications, any one of which will provide a ready-made bibliography to books on your subject. Figure 6 shows a sample from the 1997 issue.

Figure 6
From Subject Guide to Books in Print, *1997 (1) Subject (2)
Author (3) Title (4) Library of Congress number (5) Number of
pages (6) Date of publication (7) Price (8) International
Standard Book Number (used when ordering) (9) Paperback
book (10) Publisher.*

Make a note for any promising source:

> Aefsky, Fern. <u>Inclusion Confusion: A Guide to Educating Students with Exceptional Needs</u>. New York: Corwin, 1995.

You may also find valuable sources in the following trade bibliographies:

Books in Print. New York: Bowker, 1948–date.
> This work provides an author-title index to the *Publisher's Trade List Annual* (New York: Bowker, 1874–date), which lists all books currently in print.

Publishers' Weekly. New York: Bowker, 1872–date.
> This journal offers the most current publication data on new books and new editions.

Paperbound Books in Print. New York: Bowker, 1955–date.
> Use this work to locate paperback books on one topic, especially books available at local bookstores rather than the library.

Cumulative Book Index. New York: H. W. Wilson, 1900–date.
> Use this work to find complete publication data on one book or to locate all material in English on a particular subject.

The National Union Catalog: A Cumulative Author List. Ann Arbor: Edwards, 1953–date.
> Basically, this work is the card catalog in book form, but use it to find titles reported by other libraries.

Library of Congress Catalog: Books, Subjects. Washington, DC: Library of Congress, 1950–date.
> Use this work for its subject classification which provides a ready-made bibliography to books on hundreds of subjects. Separate volumes are available for the years 1950–54, 1955–59, 1960–64, and annually thereafter.

Union List of Serials in Libraries of the United States and Canada. 3rd ed. New York: H. W. Wilson, 1965. Supplements, *New Serial Titles,* Washington, DC: Library of Congress, 1953–date.
> Consult this work to determine if a nearby library has a magazine or journal that is unavailable in your library.

Ulrich's International Periodicals Directory. Ed. Merle Rohinsky. 15th ed. New York: Bowker, 1973.
> Use this work to locate current periodicals, both domestic and foreign, and to order photocopied reprints of articles.

Using a Shortcut: Searching the Specialized Bibliographies

If you have narrowed your subject, you can go directly to reference guides, bibliographies, and indexes for your special discipline. You can do this in one of three ways.

1. Go to Appendix A of this book, pages 333–66. For example, one student narrowed his subject to "The role of female talk show hosts on network television." He looked under the heading *Women's Studies* on pages 365–66 of Appendix A and found twenty sources, such as these four:

    Women in Popular Culture: A Reference Guide
    Womanhood Media: Current Resources about Women
    Women in America: A Guide to Information Sources
    Women's Studies Abstracts

2. At a search engine on the Internet, such as *Alta Vista,* enter a descriptive phrase, such as "Child Abuse Bibliographies." You will get a list of bibliographies, and you can click the mouse on one of them, such as:

    Child Abuse
    Child Abuse. Child Abuse Articles. Child Abuse Reports
       http://www.childwelfare.com/kinds/pr01.htm

    Clicking with the mouse on the hypertext address will carry you to a list:

    Child Abuse Articles
    Child Abuse Reports
    Child Sexual Abuse
    Substance Abuse

    Clicking on the first item will produce a set of hypertext links to articles that you might find helpful, such as this one:

    Suffer the Children: How government fails its most vulnerable citizens—abused and neglected kids by David Stoesz and Howard Jacob Karger (*The Washington Monthly,* 1996)

3. At the Public Access Catalog, type in the word *bibliographies* and your general subject. For instance, one student in a study of Robert Frost's poetry, typed in *bibliographies* and *literature* at the PAC. It directed him to *Magill's Bibliography of Literary Criticism,* an index to literary interpretations (see Figure 7, page 42).

    If one of the citations looks promising to your research, you would need to make a bibliography entry, as shown below in MLA style:

    Brower, Reuben A. <u>The Poetry of Robert Frost:</u>
       <u>Constellations of Intention.</u> New York: Oxford UP,
       1963.
    See esp. 23–27

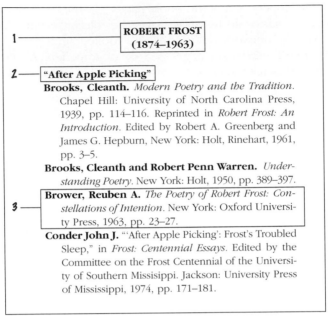

Figure 7
From Magill's Bibliography of Literary Criticism (1) Author and dates (2) Title of work (3) Citation of a critical work on the poem.

Works similar to Magill's bibliography are *Poetry Explication* and *Twentieth Century Short Story Explicator.* Language and literature students should also examine the *MLA International Bibliography,* which indexes literary interpretations annually, as demonstrated in Figure 8. *Note:* The MLA bibliography is also available at many libraries on a CD-ROM database. Check for it because it will usually be more up-to-date than the printed version.

Another shortcut is searching out encyclopedias for your field at the Public Access Catalog (PAC). Locate such works as *Encyclopedia of Social Work, Encyclopedia of Psychology, or Encyclopedia of Geographic Information.* Look especially for bibliographies at the end of encyclopedia articles, such as the one shown in Figure 9 from *Encyclopedia of Psychology.*

When you get into the stacks, look for bibliographies at the end of the books. An example of one is shown in Figure 10.

Bibliographies also appear in most scholarly journals at the end of the articles. For example, students of history depend upon the bibliographies within various issues of *English Historical Review* and students of literature find bibliographies in *Studies in Short Fiction.* In addition, the journals themselves provide subject indexes to their own contents. For example, if your subject is

1— **FROST, ROBERT (1874–1963)**

[8762] Iwayama, Tajiro. "Robert Frost." 439–475 in Ogata. Toshihiko, ed. American *Bungaku no Jikotenkai: 20-seiki no America Bungaku II.* Kyoto: Yamaguchi; 1982. ii, 638 pp.

[8763] Monteiro, George. "'A Way *Out* of Something': Robert Frost's Emily Dickinson." *CentR.* 1983 Summer; 27(3): 192–203. [†Relationship to Dickinson, Emily: includes comment on Bogan, Louise: MacLeish, Archibald; Wilbur, Richard.]

Poetry

[8764] Daniel, Charles L. "Tonal Contrasts in the Imagery of Robert Frost." *WGCR.* 1982 May; 14:12–15 [†Light imagery; dark imagery.]

[8765] Gage, John T. "Humour en Garde: Comic Saying in Robert Frost's Poetic." *Thalia.* 1981 Spring-Summer; 4(1):54–61. [†Role of humor.]

[8766] Gonzàlez Martín, Jerónimo P. "Approximación a la poesía de Robert Frost." *CHA.* 1983 Apr.; 394: 101–153. [†Includes biographical information.]

[8767] Greenjut, D. S. "Colder Pastoral: Keats, Frost, and the Transformation of Lyric." *MHLS.* 1983; 6: 49–55. [†Lyric poetry. Use of pastoral. Treatment of landscape compared to Keats, John.]

2— [8768] Marks, Herbert. "The Counter-Intelligence of Robert Frost." *YR.* 1982 Summer; 72(4):554–578. [†Treatment of revelation, concealment. Sources in Bible; Milton, John: *Paradise Lost.*]

[8769] Slights, William W. E. "The Sense of Frost's Humor." *CP.* 1983 Spring; 16(1):29–42. [†Humor; comedy; relationship to reader.]

[8770] Sutton, William A. "Some of Robert Frost 'Fooling'." *MTJ.* 1983 Spring; 21(3): 61–62. [†Relationship to Clemens, Samuel.]

[8771] Trinkha, Manoramma B. *Robert Frost: Poetry of Clarifications.* Atlantic Highlands, NJ: Humanities; 1983. 259 pp. [†Use of metaphor; symbolism. Sources in Emerson, Ralph Waldo; James, William.]

Poetry/"Away"

3— [8772] Kau, Joseph. "Frost's 'Away!': Illusions and Allusions." *NMAL.* 1983 Winter; 7(3): Item 17.

Poetry/"Beech"

[8773] Will, Normal P. "Robert Frost's 'Beech': Faith Regained." *NMAL.* 1982 Spring-Summer; 6(1): Item 2.

Poetry/A Boy's Will (1913)

[8774] Wordell, Charles B. "Robert Frost from *A Boy's Will to North of Boston.*" *SALit.* 1983 June; 19:1–13. [†*North of Boston.*]

Figure 8

From MLA International Bibliography *(1) Author and dates (2) General articles about Frost's poetry (3) An article about a specific poem.*

FURTHER REFERENCES

Clarke, E., & Dewhurst, K. *An illustrated history of brain function*. Clarke, E., & O'Malley, C. D. *The human brain and spinal cord*. Ferrier, D. *The functions of the brain*.

Finger, S., & Stein, D. G. *Brain damage and recovery: Research and clinical perspectives*.

McHenry, L. C., Jr. *Garrison's history of neurology*.

Figure 9
Sample bibliography from the end of an article in Encyclopedia of Psychology, *2nd ed., Vol. 1, p. 287, edited by Raymond J. Corsini. Copyright © 1994 John Wiley & Sons, Inc. Reprinted by permission of John Wiley & Sons, Inc.*

SECONDARY SOURCES

Abbott, Edith. "The Civil War and the Crime Wave of 1865–70." *Social Service Review,* 1977.

Amis, Mosews N. *Historical Raleigh,* 1913.

Andrews, Marietta M. *Scraps of Paper.* 1929.

Badeau, Adam. *Military History of U. S. Grant.* 1885

Bailey, Mrs. Hugh. "Mobile's Tragedy: The Great Magazine Explosion of 1865." *Alabama Review,* 1968.

Bakeless, John. "The Mystery of Appomattox." *Civil War Times Illustrated,* 1970.

Figure 10
A portion of a bibliography list at the end of N. A. Trudeau's book, Out of the Storm.

"Adoption," you will discover that a majority of your sources are located in a few key journals. In that instance, going straight to the index of one of these journals will be a shortcut.

2e Searching the Printed Indexes

An index furnishes the exact page number(s) to specific sections of books and to individual articles in magazines, journals, and newspapers. In general, a bibliography is a list of complete works without any mention of page numbers. Note that *Bibliographic Index* features both words: it indexes the page numbers of bibliographies to be found in various sources.

Fundamentally, there are five types of indexes: (1) indexes to literature in periodicals, (2) indexes to materials in books and collections, (3) indexes to materials in newspapers, (4) indexes to pamphlets, and (5) indexes to abstracts, which are short descriptions of books and articles (see pages 116–17 for an example).

When you have a well-developed idea of your topic, go to the specialized indexes of your discipline, as found in Appendix A of this book, such as *Music Index* or *Philosopher's Index* (see pages 40–44). Or at the PAC request "Music Indexes." Or at a search engine of the Internet request "Music Indexes," which will produce such entries as:

> Music Indexes
> Music Library Music Indexes
> http://www.nsceee.edu/unlv/Libraries/music/musref/indexes.html

Clicking on this site will take you to a list of sources, such as:

> Blom, Eric. A General Index to Modern Musical Literature in the English Language.

Searching the Printed Indexes to Periodicals

Use a CD-ROM database (such as *InfoTrac* or *Silverplatter*) for quick access to current articles (see pages 9–11). Otherwise, consult the printed indexes, as described below.

> *Readers' Guide to Periodical Literature.* New York: H. W. Wilson, 1900–date.

Although it indexes many nonscholarly publications, such as *Teen, Needle and Craft,* and *Southern Living,* the *Readers' Guide* also indexes important reading for the early stages of research in magazines such as:

Aging	*Foreign Affairs*	*Psychology Today*
American Scholar	*Foreign Policy*	*Scientific Review*
Astronomy	*Health*	*Science Digest*
Bioscience	*Negro History*	*Science*
Business Week	*Oceans*	*SciQuest*
Earth Science	*Physics Today*	*Technology Review*

Figure 11 shows an entry from *Readers' Guide to Periodical Literature.* Make a bibliography entry to sources that look promising, as shown below in APA style:

> Pierce, C. (1994, April). Is everything okay? Gentleman's Quarterly, 64, 196–203.

If your study involves a social science, consult the following index.

> *Social Sciences Index.* Vols. 1–. New York: H. W. Wilson, 1974–date.

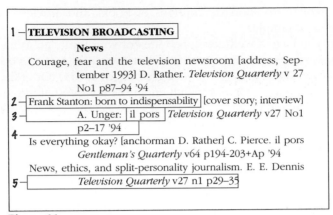

Figure 11
From Readers' Guide to Periodical Literature *(1) Subject (2) Title of article (3) Author (4) Illustrated with portraits (5) Name of periodical and publication data.*

Social Sciences Index searches for journal articles in 263 periodicals in these fields:

anthropology	geography	political science
economics	law and criminology	psychology
environmental science	medical science	sociology

Researchers in the humanities should consult:

Humanities Index. New York: H. W. Wilson, 1974–date.

This work catalogs 260 publications in several fields:

archaelogy	folklore	performing arts
classical studies	history	philosophy
language and literature	literary	religion
area studies	political criticism	theology

For sources prior to 1974, consult two works that preceded *Humanities Index* and *Social Sciences Index:*

International Index. Vols. 1–18. New York: H.W. Wilson, 1907–65.
Social Sciences and Humanities Index. Vols 19–61. New York: H. W. Wilson, 1965–1974.

Also consult the following indexes for articles in these specific disciplines:

Chemistry, engineering, computer science, electronics, geology, mathematics, photography, physics, and other related fields:

Applied Science and Technology Index. New York: Wilson, 1958–date.

Biology, zoology, botany, agriculture, and related fields:

> *Biological and Agricultural Index.* New York: Wilson, 1947–date.

Education, physical education, and related fields:

> *Education Index.* New York: Wilson, 1929–date.

Business, marketing, accounting, advertising, and related fields:

> *Business Periodicals Index.* New York: Wilson, 1958–date.

History and related fields:

> *Recently Published Articles.* American Historical Association, 1976–date.

In addition to these major indexes, you should examine the indexes for your discipline as listed in Appendix A of this book, pages 333–66.

Searching an Index to Abstracts

An index to abstracts can accelerate your work by allowing you to decide whether a source is useful before you read the entire work.

Appendix A of this book (pages 333–66) lists by discipline the important indexes to abstracts, or you may find them at the PAC by entering the word *abstracts* or something more specific, such as *sociology abstracts.* You will find such works as:

> *Abstracts of English Studies* *Psychological Abstracts*
> *Biological Abstracts* *Sociological Abstracts*

For example, a student with the topic *child abuse* found and searched an issue of *Psychological Abstracts* as shown in Figure 12. *Note:* Many libraries have this same information on a CD-ROM Database, *PsycLIT,* so check the computer stations for its availability.

If a source appears useful, the writer should make an appropriate working bibliography entry, and then read and perhaps quote from the original work, *Journal of Family Violence.* If the journal is not available, the researcher may quote from the abstract but must note that fact in the bibliography entry (see pages 262–63 [MLA style] and 289 [APA style]). That is, let your readers know that you are citing from an abstract, not from the entire article.

You may wish to read the abstracts to the dissertations of graduate students, as listed in this reference source:

> *Dissertation Abstracts International* (Ann Arbor: Univ. Microfilms, 1970–date.

Look for issue No. 12, Part II, of each volume, for it contains the cumulated subject and author indexes for Issues 1–12 of the volume's two sections—

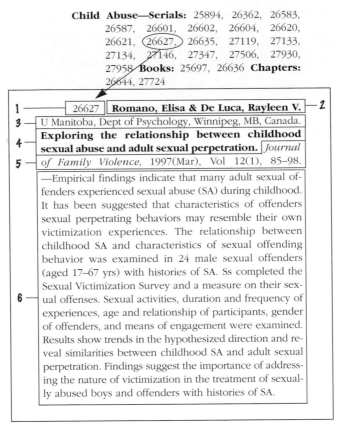

Child Abuse—Serials: 25894, 26362, 26583, 26587, 26601, 26602, 26604, 26620, 26621, 26627, 26635, 27119, 27133, 27134, 27146, 27347, 27506, 27930, 27958 **Books:** 25697, 26636 **Chapters:** 26644, 27724

1 — 26627 **Romano, Elisa & De Luca, Rayleen V.** — *2*

3 — U Manitoba, Dept of Psychology, Winnipeg, MB, Canada.

4 — **Exploring the relationship between childhood sexual abuse and adult sexual perpetration.** *Journal*

5 — *of Family Violence,* 1997(Mar), Vol 12(1), 85–98.

6 — —Empirical findings indicate that many adult sexual offenders experienced sexual abuse (SA) during childhood. It has been suggested that characteristics of offenders sexual perpetrating behaviors may resemble their own victimization experiences. The relationship between childhood SA and characteristics of sexual offending behavior was examined in 24 male sexual offenders (aged 17–67 yrs) with histories of SA. Ss completed the Sexual Victimization Survey and a measure on their sexual offenses. Sexual activities, duration and frequency of experiences, age and relationship of participants, gender of offenders, and means of engagement were examined. Results show trends in the hypothesized direction and reveal similarities between childhood SA and adult sexual perpetration. Findings suggest the importance of addressing the nature of victimization in the treatment of sexually abused boys and offenders with histories of SA.

Figure 12
From Psychological Abstracts, *August, 1997 Vol. 84.8 (1) Abstract number (2) Authors (3) Affiliation (4) Title of the article (5) Citation that tells you where to find the full article (6) Abstract of the article.*

A: Humanities and Social Sciences and *B: Sciences and Engineering.* For example, the index of *Dissertation Abstracts International* of July 1997 shown in Figure 13 lists the following entries under the heading "Artificial Intelligence."

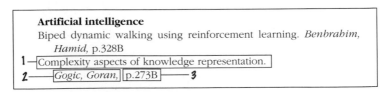

Artificial intelligence
Biped dynamic walking using reinforcement learning. *Benbrahim, Hamid,* p.328B

1 — Complexity aspects of knowledge representation.

2 — *Gogic, Goran,* p.273B — *3*

Figure 13
From the Index to Vol. 58.1, Dissertation Abstracts International, *1997 (1) Title of Dissertation (2) Author (3) Page number where abstract can be found.*

The abstract of Goran Gogic's dissertation is shown in Figure 14.

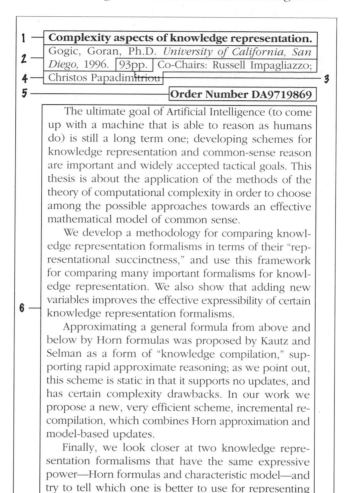

1 — **Complexity aspects of knowledge representation.**

2 — Gogic, Goran, Ph.D. *University of California, San Diego,* 1996. 93pp. Co-Chairs: Russell Impagliazzo;

4 — Christos Papadimitriou ——— **3**

5 ———————————————— Order Number DA9719869

6 —
The ultimate goal of Artificial Intelligence (to come up with a machine that is able to reason as humans do) is still a long term one; developing schemes for knowledge representation and common-sense reason are important and widely accepted tactical goals. This thesis is about the application of the methods of the theory of computational complexity in order to choose among the possible approaches towards an effective mathematical model of common sense.

We develop a methodology for comparing knowledge representation formalisms in terms of their "representational succinctness," and use this framework for comparing many important formalisms for knowledge representation. We also show that adding new variables improves the effective expressibility of certain knowledge representation formalisms.

Approximating a general formula from above and below by Horn formulas was proposed by Kautz and Selman as a form of "knowledge compilation," supporting rapid approximate reasoning; as we point out, this scheme is static in that it supports no updates, and has certain complexity drawbacks. In our work we propose a new, very efficient scheme, incremental recompilation, which combines Horn approximation and model-based updates.

Finally, we look closer at two knowledge representation formalisms that have the same expressive power—Horn formulas and characteristic model—and try to tell which one is better to use for representing knowledge in various contexts.

Figure 14
Dissertation Abstracts International, *1997 (1) Title of dissertation (2) Author, degree earned, school, and date (3) Total number of pages of the dissertation (4) Faculty chairmen of the dissertation committee (5) Order number if you desire to order a copy of the complete work (6) The abstract.*

An abstract, of course, only briefly summarizes the entire work. Again, you may cite the abstract in your paper if you include the words "dissertation abstract" in the text and in your works cited entry (see page 266). If you need the full dissertation and have time, order a copy of the complete work from University Microfilms, Inc., Ann Arbor, MI 48106.

Searching the Biographical Indexes for Authors and Personalities

When writing about a specific person, the reference section will provide multiple sources, some specific to a field, such as *American Men and Women of Science: The Physical and Biological Sciences* or *Who's Who in Hard Money Economics.* Appendix A of this book, pages 333–66, will list biographical studies by discipline. Several general indexes have value.

> *Biography Index: A Quarterly Index to Biographical Material in Books and Magazines.* New York: H. W. Wilson, 1946/47–date.

Biography Index is a starting point for studies of famous persons. It gives clues to biographical information for people of all lands. Note the short excerpt from *Biography Index* in Figure 15.

Other valuable biographical indexes are:

> *Current Biography Yearbook.* New York: Wilson, annually.
>> This annual work provides a biographical sketch of important people. Most articles are three to four pages and they include references to other sources at the end. It is current, thorough, and has international scope.
>
> *Contemporary Authors.* Detroit: Gale, annually.
>> Use this annual biographical guide for current writers in fiction, nonfiction, poetry, journalism, drama, motion pictures, television, and a few other fields. It provides a thorough overview of most contemporary writers, giving a list of writings, biographical facts (including a current address and agent), a list of writings, sidelights, and in many cases an interview by the editors of *CA* with the author. Most entries include a bibliography of additional sources to the writer. It has good coverage of major writers and stays current with second and third articles.
>
> *Dictionary of Literary Biography.* Detroit: Gale, 1978–date.
>> In more than 100 volumes, this work provides a profile of thousands of writers, both national and international, under such titles as these:
>>
>>> *American Humorists, 1800–1950*
>>> *Victorian Novelists after 1885*
>>> *American Newspaper Journalists, 1926–1950*
>>
>> This work has a comprehensive index that will help you locate the article on your author. Use *Dictionary of Literary Biography* not only for the profile of the author but for the reference to other sources

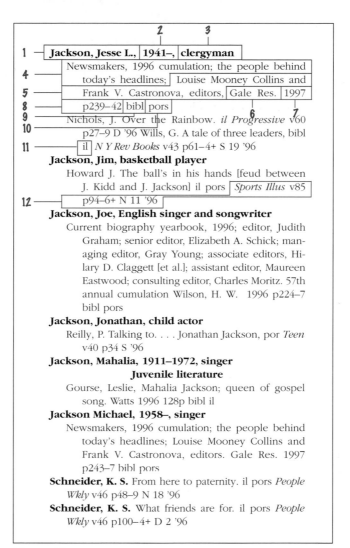

Figure 15
From Biography Index, *1997 (1) Subject (2) Dates of subject's
birth and death (3) Subject's profession (4) Title of the biography
(5) Author of the biography (6) Publisher (7) Date of publication
(8) Number of pages (9) Contains a bibliography (10) Contains
portraits (11) Illustrated (12) Publication data for a periodical.*

that ends each essay. Figure 16 shows a portion of the bibliography
on poet Anne Sexton.

You would need to make bibliography cards for any sources that show
promise for your research.

WORKS OF ANNE SEXTON

POEMS

To Bedlam and Part Way Back. Boston: Houghton Mifflin, 1960.

Ally My Pretty Ones. Boston Houghton Mifflin, 1962.

Selected Poems. London: Oxford University Press, 1864.

Live or Die. Boston: Houghton Mifflin, 1966; London: Oxford University Press, 1967.

Poems. London: Oxford University Press, 1968. With Thomas Kinsella and Douglas Livingstone.

Love Poems. Boston: Houghton Mifflin, 1969; London; Oxford University Press, 1969.

Transformations. Boston: Houghton Mifflin, 1971; London; Oxford University Press, 1972.

The Book of Folly. Boston: Houghton Mifflin, 1972. London: Chatto and Windus, 1974.

The Death Notebooks. Boston: Houghton Mifflin, 1974; London: Chatto and Windus, 1975.

The Awful Rowing Toward God. Boston: Houghton Mifflin, 1975; London: Chatto and Windus, 1977.

45 Mercy Street, edited by Linda Gray Sexton. Boston: Houghton Mifflin, 1976. Martin and

BIBLIOGRAPHY

Northouse, Cameron, and Thomas P. Walsh. *Sylvia Plath and Anne Sexton: A Reference Guide.* Boston: G. K. Hall and Co., 1974.

CRITICISM AND REVIEWS

Alvarez, A. *Beyond This Fiddle: Essays, 1955–57.* New York: Random House, 1969.

Boyers, Robert. *"Live or Die:* The Achievement of Anne Sexton." *Salmagundi,* 2, no. 1:41–71 (Sprint 1967). Reprinted in *Anne Sexton, The Artist and Her Critics,* edited by J. D. McClatchy. Bloomington and London: Indiana University Press, 1978 (hereafter referred to as McClatchy).

Dickey, James. "Five First Books." *Poetry,* 97, no. 5:318–19 (February 1961). Reprinted in his *Babel to Byzantium.* New York: Farrar, Straus and Giroux, 1968. Also in McClatchy.

Fields, Beverly. "The Poetry of Anne Sexton." In *Poets in Progress,* edited by Edward Hungerford. Evanston Ill.: Northwestern University Press, 1967. Pp. 251–85

Gullans, Charles. "Poerty and Subject M from Hart Cr Turner he So 7.

Figure 16
Sample excerpt from Dictionary of Literary Biography.

Searching the Newspaper Indexes

Newspapers provide contemporary information. Each of these indexes is helpful:

> *Bell and Howell's Index to the Christian Science Monitor.* Christian Science Publishing Society, annually.
> *The New York Times Index* (New York: New York Times, 1913–date).

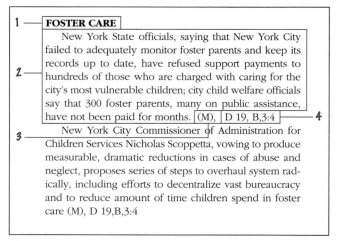

Figure 17
From The New York Times Index, *1996 (1) Subject (2) Description of the article (3) Length of the article (S) short, (M) medium length, (L) long (4) Date, section number, page number, and column (April 18, section B, page 5, column 1).*

Official Index [to *The London Times*] (London: *Times,* 1907–date).
Wall Street Journal Index. New York: Dow Jones, annually.

Many libraries have *The New York Times* and *The Wall Street Journal* on microfilm (see "Using the Microforms," page 57). The index can send you to the correct microform. One student, writing about foster parents, found the list of sources shown in Figure 17.

> *Note:* The year is not given in the entries, so get it from the front of the volume you use, in this case 1994. The title is not listed; you must record it when you read the article. For a sample bibliography entry, see page 255.

Searching the Pamphlet Files and Pamphlet Indexes

Librarians collect bulletins, pamphlets, folders, and miscellaneous materials that they file alphabetically by subject in loose-leaf folders. You should make the pamphlet file a regular stop during preliminary investigation. Sometimes called the *vertical file,* it will have brochures on many topics, such as: "Asbestos in the Home," "Carpel Tunnel Syndrome," "Everything Doesn't Cause Cancer," and "Medicare and Coordinated Care Plans." For a preview of what these pamphlet files can contain, find one of these principal indexes to published pamphlets:

Vertical File Index: A Subject and Title Index to Selected Pamphlet Material. New York: H. W. Wilson, 1932/35–date. This work gives a description of each entry, the price, and the information for ordering the pamphlet.

Social Issues Resources Series (SIRS). This work collects articles on special topics and reprints them as one unit on a special subject— *abortion, AIDS, prayer in schools, pollution*. With *SIRS* you will have 10 or 12 articles readily available.

The CQ Researcher. With this work, like *SIRS,* you will have one pamphlet devoted to one topic, such as "School Choice Debate: Are Tuition Vouchers the Answer to Bad Schools." It will examine central issues on the topic, give background information, show a chronology of important events or processes, express an outlook, and provide an annotated bibliography. In one place you have quotable and paraphrasable material as well as a list of additional sources, as shown in Figure 18.

Books

Lieberman, Myron, *Privatization and Educational Choice,* St. Martin's Press, 1989.

Lieberman, an education policy consultant, covers the entire sweep of the school choice debate, from the effect of competition to the constitutionality of vouchers. He also examines the political landscape, describing the groups and interests lined up on both sides of the issue.

McGroarty, Daniel, *Breaking These Chains: The Battle for School Choice,* Prima Publishing, 1996.

McGroarty, a fellow at the Institute for Contemporary Studies, chronicles the efforts of parents and community leaders in inner-city Milwaukee to establish and sustain a voucher program. McGroarty argues that for many of these mostly black residents, the fight for school choice is akin to the civil rights battles of the 1960s.

Moe, Terry M., and John E. Chubb, *Politics, Markets and America's Schools,* The Brookings Institution, 1990.

Moe and Chubb look at the recent history of education and education reform in the United States and the problems that have plagued America's schools in the last three decades. The authors come to the conclusion that the institutions governing the nation's schools hamstring them and prevent real reform from taking hold. Moe and Chubb argue that vouchers are a way to break this institutional vise grip.

Figure 18
A portion of a bibliographical list from The CQ Researcher *7.27 (1997).*

Remember, too, that the federal government publishes many pamphlets and booklets on a vast array of topics, as discussed next.

2f Searching the Indexes to Government Documents

All branches of the government publish massive amounts of material. Many documents have great value for researchers, so look especially for the following:

> United States. Superintendent of Documents. *Monthly Catalog of United States Government Publications.* Washington: GPO, 1895–present. Monthly.

This work indexes all the documents published by the Government Printing Office. An index will provide a catalog number, and the catalog number will send you to a bibliographic description, as shown in Figure 19.

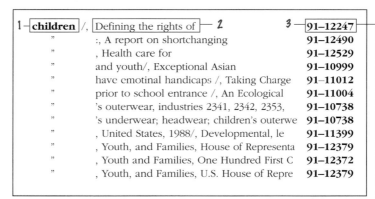

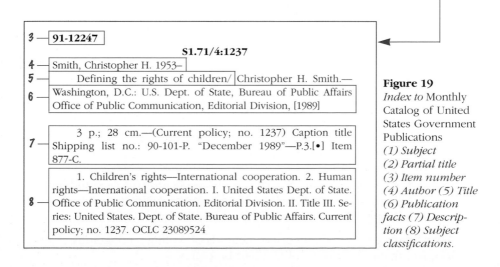

Figure 19
Index to Monthly Catalog of United States Government Publications
(1) Subject
(2) Partial title
(3) Item number
(4) Author (5) Title
(6) Publication facts (7) Description (8) Subject classifications.

Note: Most federal publications are published by the Government Printing Office (GPO) in Washington, DC, regardless of the branch of government that issues them. Thus, a working bibliography entry to the source in Figure 19 should look like this:

> S1.71/4:1237
> Smith, Christopher H. <u>Defining the Rights of Children</u>.
>   Washington: GPO, 1989.

If your library does not house a government document that you need for your research, write a request to:

> Superintendent of Documents
> Government Printing Office
> Washington, DC 20402

Most documents are free and will be shipped immediately.

Search out other indexes in the government documents section of your local library and learn their resources. In many libraries a separate catalog lists governmental holdings. The Government Printing Office, like other publishers, is converting to CD-ROM, so look for government documents on a computer database if one is available. Look also for the following:

Public Affairs Information Service Bulletin (PAIS)
> This work indexes articles and documents published by miscellaneous organizations. It's a good place to start because of its excellent index.

Congressional Record
> This daily publication provides Senate and House bills, documents, and committee reports. *Congressional Record* should be available at your library. If not, write either the Senate Documents Room or the House Documents Room for free copies of specific legislation.

> Senate Documents Room   House Documents Room
> SH-B04 Capitol Building   B-18 Ford Building
> Washington, DC 20510   Washington, DC 20515

Public Papers of the Presidents of the United States
> This work is the publication of the executive branch, including not only the president but also all members of the president's cabinet and various agencies.

The U.S. Code
> The Supreme Court regularly publishes decisions, codes, and other rulings, as do appellate and district courts. State courts also publish rulings and court results on a regular basis.

Note: See pages 257–58 for correct methods of writing bibliography citations to government documents of all three branches.

2g Searching for Essays within Books

Some essays get lost within collections and anthologies. You can find such essays, listed by subject, in the following reference work:

> *Essay and General Literature Index, 1900–1933.* New York: H. W. Wilson, 1934. Supplements, 1934–date.

This reference work helps you find essays hidden within anthologies. It indexes material of both a biographical and a critical nature. The essay listed in the example below might easily have been overlooked by any researcher.

> **King, Martin Luther, 1929–1968**
> About
> > Raboteau, A. J. Martin Luther King and the tradition of black religious protest. (*In* Religion and the life of the nation; ed. By R. A. Sherrill, p. 46–65).

The Public Access Catalog will give you the call number to Sherrill's book.

2h Using the Microforms

When ordering periodicals, libraries can either buy expensive printed volumes or purchase inexpensive microform versions of the same material. Most libraries have a combination of the two. Your library will specify in the cardex files (the list of periodicals) how journals and magazines are housed.

In particular, most libraries now store national newspapers, weekly magazines, and dissertation abstracts on microfilm. Use a microfilm reader, usually located near the microfilm files, to browse the articles. Should you need a printed copy of a microfilmed article, the library will supply coin-operated machines or the clerks will copy it for you.

Your library may also house guides to special microform holdings, which carry such titles as *American Culture 1493–1806: A Guide to the Microfilm Collection* or perhaps *American Periodicals 1800-1850: A Guide to the Microfilm Collection.*

Every library has its own peculiar holdings of microfilm and microfiche materials; the librarian can help you.

2i Using the Printed Catalog Cards

Your library's card catalog may exist as a traditional card bank in file cabinets, rather than as a PAC computer file. In theory, it will include every book in the library filed by subject, author, and title. In truth, it is not always kept current with the lastest holdings, so check with a librarian if you need a recently published work.

Begin your research at the catalog by searching a subject. Theoretically, books will be filed under one or more common headings, which will be printed at the top of the card. Searching under a common heading, such as "TELEVISION AND CHILDREN," would produce a number of books, as shown in Figure 20.

TELEVISION AND CHILDREN.

HQ
784   Durkin, Kevin
T4   Television, sex roles, and
D88   children: a developmental social
1985   psychological account / Kevin Durkin-
        Milton Keynes: Philadelphia:
        Open University Press. c1985

TELEVISION AND CHILDREN.

HQ
784   Cullingford, Cedric.
T4   Children and television / Cedric
C84   Cullingford.—New York: St. Martin's
1984   Press, 1984.
            x. 239 p.; 23 cm.
            Includes index.
            ISBN 0-312-13235-2

TELEVISION AND CHILDREN.

HQ
784   Buckingham, David. 1954–
T4   Children talking television:
B83   the making of television literacy /
1993   by David Buckingham.–London;
        Washington, D.C.: Falmer Press, 1933.
        xiv, 321 p.; 25 cm.–(Critical perspectives
        on literary [i.e. literacy] and education)
            Includes bibliographical references
        (p. 298–314) and index.

Figure 20
Subject cards.

The next procedure is to record call numbers onto appropriate working bibliography entries on cards or in your computer file.

HQ/784/T4/B83/1993
    Buckingham, David. <u>Children Talking Television: The Making
        of Television Literacy</u>. London: Falmer Press, 1993.
        bibliography on 298–314

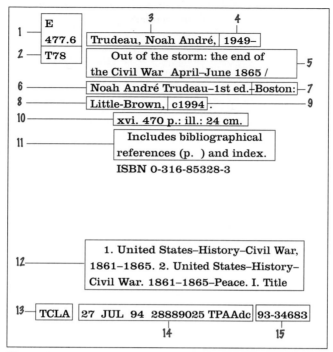

Figure 21
*Main Entry Card (Author Card) (1) Classification number
(2) Author number (3) Author (4) Life span of author (5) Title
(6) Author and edition number (7) Place of publication
(8) Publisher (9) Date of publication (10) Technical description
(11) Note on contents of the book (12) Separate card filed under
United States–History (13) Publisher of this card (14) Library of
Congress number (15) Order number.*

Note: Writing the correct form now will save you time when you are rush-
ing to complete the manuscript.

You can also search the catalog by an author's name (the author card)
or by the book's title (the title card). The author card is shown in Figure 21.

Distinguishing the Dewey Decimal System from the Library of Congress System

Your library will classify its books by one of two call number systems, the
Dewey Decimal System or the Library of Congress (LC) system. Understanding the system your library uses is necessary if you want to use it fully as a resource. The Dewey system, for example, lists Noah Trudeau's *Out
of the Storm* (Figure 21) with the number 973.7 T78o, yet the LC system uses
the number E477.6/T78/ 1994.

Dewey Decimal System

The Dewey system has 100 divisions as shown in Figure 22.

Second Summary*
The Hundred Divisions

000	**Generalities**	**500**	**Natural Sciences & mathematics**
010	Bibliography	510	Mathematics
020	Library & information sciences	520	Astronomy & allied sciences
030	General encyclopedic works	530	Physics
040		540	Chemistry & allied sciences
050	General serials & their indexes	550	Earth sciences
060	General organizations & museology	560	Paleontology Paleozoology
070	News media, journalism, publishing	570	Life sciences
080	General collections	580	Botanical sciences
090	Manuscripts & rare books	590	Zoological sciences
100	**Philosophy & psychology**	**600**	**Technology (Applied sciences)**
110	Metaphysics	610	Medical sciences Medicine
120	Epistemology, causation, humankind	620	Engineering & allied operations
130	Paranormal phenomena	630	Agriculture
140	Specific philosophical schools	640	Home economics & family living
150	Psychology	650	Management & auxiliary services
160	Logic	660	Chemical engineering
170	Ethics (Moral philosophy)	670	Manufacturing
180	Ancient, medieval, Oriental philosophy	680	Manufacture for specific uses
190	Modern Western philosophy	690	Buildings
200	**Religion**	**700**	**The arts**
210	Natural theology	710	Civic & landscape art
220	Bible	720	Architecture
230	Christian theology	730	Plastic arts Sculpture
240	Christian moral & devotional theology	740	Drawing & decorative arts
250	Christian orders & local church	750	Painting & paintings
260	Christian social theology	760	Graphic arts Printmaking & prints
270	Christian church history	770	Photography & photographs
280	Christian denominations & sects	780	Music
290	Other & comparative religions	790	Recreational & performing arts
300	**Social sciences**	**800**	**Literature & rhetoric**
310	General statistics	810	American literature in English
320	Political science	820	English & Old English literatures
330	Economics	830	Literatures of Germanic languages
340	Law	840	Literatures of Romance languages
350	Public administration	850	Italian, Rumanian, Rhaeto-Romanic
360	Social services: association	860	Spanish & Portuguese literatures
370	Education	870	Italic literatures Latin
380	Commerce, communications, transport	880	Hellenic literatures Classical Greek
390	Customs, etiquette, folklore	890	Literatures of other languages
400	**Language**	**900**	**Geography & history**
410	Linguistics	910	Geography & travel
420	English & Old English	920	Biography, genealogy, insignia
430	Germanic languages German	930	History of ancient world
440	Romance languages French	940	General history of Europe
450	Italian, Rumanian, Rhaeto-Romanic	950	General history of Asia Far East
460	Spanish & Portuguese languages	960	General history of Africa
470	Italic languages Latin	970	General history of North America
480	Hellenic languages Classical Greek	980	General history of South America
490	Other languages	990	General history of other areas

*Consult schedules for complete and exact headings

Figure 22
From the Dewey Decimal Classification and Relative Index.

The Trudeau book (Figure 21) belongs to the 970 category, "General history of North America," so it is designated **973.7**. Immediately below the Dewey classification numbers are letters and numbers based on the Cutter Three-Figure Author Table. For example, **T78o** is the author number for Trudeau's *Out of the Storm*. The letter **T** is the initial of the author's last name. Next the Cutter table subclassifies with the Arabic numerals **78**, and the lowercase **o** designates the first important letter in the title to distinguish this entry from similar books by Trudeau. Thus, the complete call number for Trudeau's book is **973.7 / T78o**. You must use the entire set to locate the book.

Library of Congress Classification System

The LC system also uses a combination of letters and numerals for its divisions, as shown in Figure 23. Note that *E–F* designates "History: America (Western Hemisphere)." Accordingly, Trudeau's book is assigned **E** with the subentries **477.6**. Then, like the Cutter system, LC uses the first letter of the author's name and a number, **T78**.

Here, for example, are the LC and Dewey Decimal system call numbers for the same text, *Understanding and Controlling Air Pollution* by Howard E. Hesketh.

Library of Congress:		**Dewey Decimal:**	
TD	[Environmental Technology]	628.53	[Engineering & Allied operations]
833 .H461u	[Air Pollution] [Author Number]	.H48	[Author Number]

2j Collecting Data Outside the Library

Without doubt, the library contains invaluable sources, but some information can only be found in other places. Therefore, conduct primary research in the laboratory and in the field whenever your topic permits it. Converse with other people in person, by letter, or E-mail, and if time permits conduct in-depth interviews or use a questionnaire. Watch for television specials, visit the courthouse archives, and perhaps do some empirical research under the guidance of an instructor (see pages 66–67).

Firsthand data, found in these various ways, can be the principal support for a research paper. That is, go beyond information found by the computer or the library.

Interviewing Knowledgeable People

Talk to persons who have experience about your subject. Personal interviews with knowledgeable people can elicit valuable in-depth information that few others will have. Look to organizations for experienced persons (for

**LIBRARY OF CONGRESS
CLASSIFICATION SCHEDULES**

For sale by the Cataloging Distribution
Service, Library of Congress, Building 159,
Navy Yard Annex, Washington, D.C. 20541,
to which inquiries on current availability
and price should be addressed.

A	General Works
B–BJ	Philosophy, Psychology
BL–BX	Religion
C	Auxiliary Sciences of History
D	History: General and Old World (Eastern Hemisphere)
E–F	History: American (Western Hemisphere)
G	Geography. Maps. Anthropology. Recreation.
H	Social Science
J	Political Science
K	Law (General)
KD	Law of the United Kingdom and Ireland
KE	Law of Canada
KF	Law of the United States
L	Education
M	Music
N	Fine Arts
P–PA	General Philology and Linguistics Classical Languages and Literatures
PA Supplement	Byzantine and Modern Greek Literature Medieval and Modern Latin Literature
PB–PH	Modern European Languages
PG	Russian Literature
PJ–PM	Languages and Literatures of Asia, Africa, Oceania, American Indian Languages, Artificial Languages
P–PM Supplement	Index to Languages and Dialects
PN, PR, PS, PZ	General Literature, English and American Literature, Fiction in English Juvenile Belles Lettres
PQ Part 1	French Literature
PQ Part 2	Italian, Spanish, and Portuguese Literatures
PT Part 1	German Literature
PT Part 2	Dutch and Scandinavian Literatures
Q	Science
R	Medicine
S	Agriculture
T	Technology
U	Military Science
V	Naval Science
Z	Bibliography, Library Science

Figure 23
From the Library of Congress System.

example, the writer on folklore might contact the county historian, a senior citizens's organization, or a local historical society). Another way to accomplish this task is to request information on a *Listserv* list, which will bring you commentary from a group of experts interested in a particular field (see page 36 for more details).

Keep in mind these guidelines when preparing for the interview:

Consult with experienced persons.

Consult with several people, if possible, and weigh their different opinions.

Be courteous and on time for interviews.

Conduct telephone interviews as necessary.

Be prepared in advance with a set of focused, pertinent questions for initiating and conducting the interview.

For accuracy, record the interview with a tape recorder (with permission of the person interviewed, of course).

When you are finished with the interview, make a bibliography entry just as you would for a book:

Thornbright, Mattie Sue. Personal interview. 15 Jan. 1997.

Writing Letters

Correspondence provides a written record for research. Ask pointed questions so that correspondents will respond directly to your central issues.

Dear Mrs. Beach:
I am a college student conducting research into folklore of Montgomery County. In particular, I need specifics on tales of ghosts. Do any ghosts haunt homes in this region? Which homes? Do the ghosts have names?

As a courtesy, provide a self-addressed stamped envelope. If you receive information that you can use in the paper, write a thank you note and make a bibliography entry.

Beach, Mary W. Letter to the author. 5 Apr. 1994.

Examining Audiovisual Materials, Television, and Radio

Important data can be found in audiovisual materials: films, filmstrips, music, phonograph recordings, slides, audio cassettes, and video cassettes. You will find these sources both on and off campus. Consult such guides as *Educators Guide* (film, filmstrips, and tapes), *Media Review Digest* (nonprint materials), *Video Source Book* (video catalog), *The Film File,* or *International Index to Recorded Poetry*. Again, write bibliography entries for any materials that contribute to your paper.

"Nutrition and AIDS." Narr. Carolyn O'Neil. CNN. 12 Jan. 1997.

Numerous programs of quality are available if you watch the schedules carefully. In particular, check the programming of the Public Broadcast System. In addition, national and local talk shows often discuss important issues. Remember to keep accurate notes on names, statements, and program titles.

Attending Lectures and Public Addresses

Watch bulletin boards and the newspaper for a featured speaker who might visit your campus. Take careful notes and, if necessary, request a copy of the lecture or speech. Remember too that many lectures, reproduced on video, will be available in the library or in departmental files. Always make a bibliography entry for any words or ideas you use from a lecture.

> Petty-Rathbone, Virginia. "Edgar Allan Poe and the Image of Ulalume." Lecture. Perry Hall, U of Kentucky, 1997.

Investigating Local Government Documents

Documents are available at three levels of government—local, state, and federal. As a constituent, you are entitled to examine many kinds of records on file at various agencies. If your topic demands it, you may contact the mayor's office, attend and take notes at a city council assembly, or search out printed documents.

Local Government

Visit the courthouse or county clerk's office where you can find facts on each election, census, marriage, birth, and death. These archives will include wills, tax rolls, military assignments, deeds to property, and much more. Therefore, a trip to the local courthouse can be rewarding, helping you trace the history of the land and its people or examine contemporary records, such as zoning plans on traffic projections or flood control.

State Government

Contact by phone a state office that relates to your research, such as Consumer Affairs (general information), Public Service Commission (which regulates public utilities such as the telephone company), or the Department of Human Services (which administers social and welfare services). The agencies may vary by name in your state. Remember, too, that the state will have an archival storehouse which will make its records available for public review.

Federal Government

A U.S. senator or representative can send you booklets printed by the Government Printing Office. A list of these materials, many of which are free, appears in a monthly catalog issued by the Superintendent of Documents, *Monthly Catalog of United States Government Publications,* Washington, DC 20402. Most college libraries will have this catalog. Use the Web to search such sites as *Fedworld, Library of Congress, Thomas,* and *White House Web* (see pages 8–13). In addition, you can gain access to the National Archives Building in Washington, D.C., or to one of the regional branches in Atlanta, Boston, Chicago, Denver, Fort Worth, Kansas City, Los Angeles, New York, Philadelphia, or Seattle. Their archives contain court records and government documents which you can review in two books: *Guide to the National Archives of the United States* and *Select List of Publications of the National Archives and Record Service.* You can borrow some documents on microfilm if you consult *Catalog of National Archives Microfilm Publications.* One researcher, for example, found the table shown in Figure 24 while looking for information on shifts in population. The researcher also made a bibliography entry to record the source of this table.

REF/HA/202/A37

"Population Change, 1980–1990." <u>1993 County and City</u>
<u>Extra:Annual Metro, City and County Data Book.</u> Ed. Courtney
M. Slater and George E. Hall. Lanham, MD: Bernan Press,
1993.

Population change, 1980-1990
Cities with the most rapid population growth

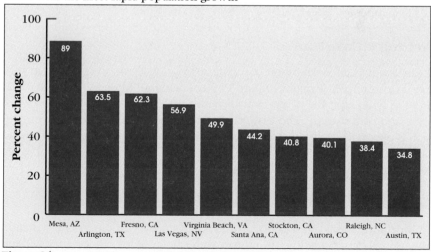

Figure 24
Table on population from Courtenay M. Slater and George E. Hall, eds., 1993 County and City Extra. *Reproduced by permission of Slater–Hall Information Products, from Bernan Press, Lanham, MD, 1993 (copyright).*

Reading Personal Papers

Search out letters, diaries, manuscripts, family histories, and other personal materials that might contribute to your study. In particular, the college library will house private collections, and the city librarian may help you contact the county historian and other private citizens who collect local documents. Again, make a bibliography entry for such materials:

> Joplin, Lester. "Notes on Robert Penn Warren." Unpublished paper. Nashville, 1997.

Conducting a Survey with a Questionnaire

Questionnaires can produce firsthand data that you can tabulate and analyze. The information will be current and localized. Of course, to achieve meaningful results, you must survey a random sample, one that is representative of the whole population in terms of age, sex, race, education, income, residence, and other factors. Various degrees of bias can creep into the questionnaire unless you remain objective. Be advised that most schools have a Human Subjects Committee that sets guidelines, draws up consent forms, and requires anonymity of participants for information gathering that might be intrusive. Thus, use the formal survey as an information-obtaining device only when you are experienced with tests and measurements as well as with statistical analysis or when you have an instructor who will help you with the instrument. Label your work in the bibliography entry:

> Mason, Valerie, and Sarah Mossman. "Child Care Arrangements of Parents Who Attend College." Questionnaire. Knoxville: U of Tennessee, 1997.

Writing a Case Study

A case study is a formal report based upon your observation of a human subject. For example, it might require you to examine patterns of behavior in order to build a profile of a person as based on biographical data, interviews, tests, and observation. The case study then becomes evidence for your research paper. Each discipline has its own ways and means of conducting the case study, and you should not begin examining any subject without guidance of your instructor or supervisor.

Conducting Experiments, Tests, and Measurements

Empirical research, often performed in a laboratory, can determine why and how things exist, function, or interact with one another. Your paper will explain your methods and findings in pursuit of a hypothesis (your thesis). An experiment thereby becomes primary evidence for your paper. For example, your experiments with a species of reptiles at a local lake area would require you to write a report with four distinct parts:

Introduction to explain the design of your experiment:
    Present the point of the study
    State the hypothesis and how it relates to the problem
    Provide the theoretical implications of the study
    Explain the manner in which this study relates to previously published work

Method to describe what you did and how you conducted the study:
    Describe the subjects who participated, whether human or animal
    Describe the apparatus to explain your equipment and how you used it
    Summarize the procedure in execution of each stage of your work

Results to report your findings:
    Summarize the data that you collected
    Provide the necessary statistical treatment of the findings with tables, graphs, and charts
    Include findings that conflict with your hypothesis

Discussion that explains the implications of your work:
    Evaluate the data and its relevance to the hypothesis
    Interpret the findings as necessary
    Discuss the implications of the findings
    Qualify the results and limit them to your specific study
    Make inferences from the results

Your experiment and the writing of the report will require the attention of your instructor. Seek his or her advice often.

3 Organizing Ideas and Setting Goals

After the initial search for sources, you need to organize your ideas so that reading and note taking will relate directly to your specific needs. Your needs become clear when you draw plans, such as a research proposal, a list of ideas or questions that will establish your key terminology, or a rough outline. In addition, the design of your study might match an appropriate organizational model, called a *paradigm* (see Section 3b, pages 73–77). You may also be required to create a final outline to accompany your final manuscript. Having said all that, we must also recognize that developing a paper is usually haphazard, with bits of information scattered everywhere and in different forms—notes, photocopied material, printouts from the Internet, and so forth. You will find your own way through the maze. The organizational ideas that follow may serve your needs in small or large measure.

3a Charting a Direction and Setting Goals

Do not plunge too quickly into note taking. You need to know *what* to look for and *why* you need it; therefore, frame your key ideas in a chart or outline. These tools can also help you label your notes with terms that you will use in your writing.

Using Your Research Proposal to Direct Your Note Taking

Your research proposal (see pages 15–21) is a way of talking to yourself about the project. It introduces issues you will want to explore in your research. For example, the last sentence of this research proposal names four topics worthy of research.

> I want to address young people who think they need a tan in order to be beautiful. Preliminary investigation indicates that ultraviolet radiation causes severe skin damage that is cumulative; that is, it builds adverse effects with each exposure. My role is to investigate the facts and explore options for those

who desire a good tan. I need information on skin types, sun
exposure, tanning beds, and types of skin damage.

Another writer sketched the following research proposal, which lists a cou-
ple of key terms (objectivity, symbolic reality) and names four classes of people that need investigation—host, guest, studio audience, and the viewer at
home. This writer will know what to search for in articles and books.

This paper will examine objectivity on television talk shows,
which promote their news value but seem more concerned about
titillating the audience to build their ratings and advertising
dollars. Objectivity is an ideal, and viewers should understand
that television gives us symbolic reality like a novel or a staged
drama. The talk show host, the guests, the studio audience, and
even the viewer at home are all participants in a staged show that
has little to do with reality.

Listing Key Words and Phrases to Set Directions for Note Taking

A list focuses your research using the terms most important to your central
issue.

One researcher started with this set of key words:

natural sun	tanning beds
sunscreens	time in the sun or under the screen
skin damage	ultraviolet radiation

The writer could begin note taking with this list and write one of the words
at the top of each note.

Writing a Rough Outline

As early as possible, present the topics into a brief outline, which will
arrange the words and phrases in an ordered sequence, as shown in this example.

The tanning process
    Natural sun
    Artificial light at tanning salons
    Time in the sun or under the screen
Effects of radiation on the skin
    Immediate skin damage
    Long-term skin damage
Protection
    Oils

      Sunscreens
      Time control

This outline, although sketchy, provides the terminology for scanning sources, checking alphabetical indexes, and conducting interviews or questionnaires (see Section 2j).

Using Questions to Identify Issues

Questions will invite you to develop answers in your notes. (See also Section 1a, "Asking Questions," pages 7–8.)

      Is there such a thing as a healthy tan?
      How does a tan differ from sunburn?
      What causes skin damage?
      How prevalent is skin damage?
      What are short-term consequences of a sunburn?
      What are long-term consequences of a sunburn?

You should try to answer every question with at least one written note. One question might lead to others, and your answer to a question might produce a topic sentence for a paragraph:

Skin damage   Rennick 63

      One source argues that no tan is healthy. "Anything that damages the skin--and burning certainly does that--cannot be considered safe" (Rennick 63).

Setting Goals by Using the Modes of Development

Try to anticipate the kinds of development you will need and write notes based upon the modes of development (*definition, comparison and contrast, process, illustration, cause and effect, classification, analysis,* and *description*) to build effective paragraphs and to explore your topic fully. One writer developed this list:

      Define sunburn
      Contrast natural tanning with a tanning-bed tan
      Illustrate sunburn with several examples
      Use statistics and scientific data
      Search out causes with a focus on the sun and its ultraviolet rays
      Determine the consequences of burning
      Read and use a case study
      Explore the step-by-step stages of the process
      Classify the types and analyze the problem
      Give narrative examples

With this list in hand, a writer can search for material to develop as *contrast, process, definition,* and so forth. One student keyboarded this note that contrasts several items:

> Tanning at its best is a light burning of the skin that darkens the pigment. At its worst it blisters the skin and damages the tissue. In either case, the burned skin is now susceptible to Squamous Cell Carcinoma, a surface tumor, or Basal Cell Carcinoma, an ulcer that burrows deep into the skin tissue, or Malignant Melanoma, a rapidly growing neoplasm that can kill if left untreated.

Using Approaches Across the Curriculum to Chart Your Major Ideas

Each scholarly field gives a special insight into any given topic. Suppose, for example, that you wish to examine an event from U. S. history, such as the Battle of Little Big Horn. Academic disciplines will force you to approach the topic in different ways.

POLITICAL SCIENCE	Was Custer too hasty in his quest for political glory?
ECONOMICS	Did the government want to open the western lands for development that would enrich the nation?
MILITARY SCIENCE	Was Custer's military strategy flawed?
PSYCHOLOGY	Did General Custer's ego precipitate the massacre?
GEOGRAPHY	Why did Custer stage a battle at this site?

These approaches will produce valuable paragraphs, such as this:

> The year 1876 stands as a monument to the western policies of Congress and the President, but Sitting Bull and Custer seized their share of glory. Custer's egotism and political ambitions overpowered his military savvy (Lemming 6). Also, Sitting Bull's military tactics (he told his braves to kill rather than show off their bravery) proved devastating for Custer and his troops who no longer had easy shots at "prancing, dancing Indians" (Potter 65).

Using Your Thesis to Chart the Direction of Your Research

Once you have developed a tentative thesis sentence, you should list concepts that will expand upon it, as shown next:

THESIS   Objectivity can never be perfectly presented by any television broadcast nor perceived by any viewer.

1. Objectivity requires real sensory data.
2. Television provides a symbolic reality.
3. Viewers develop their own subjective reality.

The outline above, though brief, gives this writer three categories that require detailed research in support of this thesis. Notice that the next writer's very different thesis on the same topic points the way to four different areas worthy of investigation.

THESIS Television can have positive effects on a child's language development.

1. Television introduces new words.
2. Television reinforces word usage and proper syntax.
3. Literary classics come alive verbally on television.
4. Television provides the subtle rhythms and musical effects of accomplished speakers.

Revising Your Goals During Research

Your preliminary plans are not a binding contract, so revise your plans periodically to reflect changes in your thinking and alterations in your response to the source material. Allow the paper to develop and grow: add new topics and discard others, rearrange the order, identify and develop new code words, and subordinate minor elements.

Writing a research paper is a recursive process, which means that you must reexamine your goals several times, rechart your direction, and move forward again. The parts of your general plan will expand or shrink in importance as you gather data and write the drafts. Therefore, use these questions to evaluate your overall plan:

Revision Checklist

1. What is my role as researcher? Am I reviewing, discovering, interpreting, or theorizing?
2. What is my thesis? Will my notes and records defend and illustrate my proposition? Is the evidence convincing?
3. How specialized is my audience? Do I need to write in a nontechnical language, or may I assume that the audience is knowledgeable in this field and expects in-depth discussion of substantive issues?

Your answers will determine, in part, the research notes you will need. (See also Section 3c, "Writing a Formal Outline.")

3b Using Academic Models (Paradigms) to Stimulate Your Note Taking

A paradigm is a universal outline, one that governs most papers of a given type. It is not content specific; rather, it provides a general organizational model, a broad scaffold, and a basic academic pattern of reasoning for all papers of a certain purpose. In contrast, a traditional outline, with its specific detail on various levels of subdivision, is useful for only one paper. To phrase it another way, the paradigm is an ideal pattern for many different papers, and the outline is a content-oriented plan for one paper only. Start with a paradigm and finish with an outline.

A General All-Purpose Model

If you have any hesitation about the design of your paper, start with this bare-bones model and expand it with your material. Readers, including your instructor, are accustomed to this sequence for research papers. It offers plenty of leeway.

> Identify the subject
> > Explain the problem
> > Provide background information
> > Frame a thesis statement
> Analyze the subject
> > Examine the first major issue
> > Examine the second major issue
> > Examine the third major issue
> Discuss your findings
> > Restate your thesis and point beyond it
> > Interpret the findings
> > Provide answers, solutions, a final opinion

To the introduction you can add a quotation, an anecdote, a definition, comments from your source materials, and other items discussed more specifically in Section 6e (see pages 133–37). Within the body you can compare, analyze, give evidence, trace historical events, and handle many other matters as explained in Section 6f (see pages 137–42). In the conclusion you can challenge an assumption, take exception to a prevailing point of view, and reaffirm your thesis, as explained in Section 6g (see pages 142–45). Flesh out each section, adding subheadings as necessary, and you will create an outline.

Paradigm for Advancing Your Ideas and Theories

If you want to advance a theory in your paper, adjust this next design to eliminate some items and add new elements as necessary.

> Introduction
> > Establish the problem or question
> > Discuss its significance
> > Provide the necessary background information
> > Introduce experts who have addressed the problem
> > Provide a thesis sentence that addresses the problem from a perspective not yet advanced by others

Body
  Trace issues involved in the problem
  Develop a past to present examination
  Compare and analyze the details and minor issues
  Cite experts who have addressed the same problem
Conclusion
  Advance and defend your theory as it grows out of evidence in the
    body
  Offer directives or a plan of action
  Suggest additional work and research that is needed

Paradigm for the Analysis of Creative Works

If you plan a literary analysis of poetry, fiction, or drama or if you must study
music, art, or other artistic works, use this next paradigm and adjust it to your
subject and purposes.

Introduction
  Identify the work
  Give a brief summary in one sentence
  Provide background information that relates to the thesis
  Offer biographical facts about the author that relate to the specific
    issues
  Use quotations and paraphrases of authorities that establish the
    scholarly traditions
  Write a thesis sentence that establishes your particular views of the
    literary work or other art form
Body
  Provide an analysis divided according to such elements as imagery,
    theme, character development, structure, symbolism, narration,
    language, and so forth
Conclusion
  Keep a fundamental focus on the author of the work, not just the
    elements of analysis as explained in the body
  Offer a conclusion that explores the contributions of the writer in
    concord with your thesis sentence

Paradigm for Argument and Persuasion Papers

If you must write persuasively or argue from a set position, your paper
should conform in general to this next paradigm. Select the elements that fit
your design.

Introduction
  In one statement establish the problem or controversial issue that
    your paper will examine
  Summarize the issues
  Define key terminology

Make concessions on some points of the argument

Use quotations and paraphrases of sources to build the controversial nature of the subject

Provide background to establish a past/present relationship

Write a thesis to establish your position

Body

Argue in defense of one side

Analyze the issues, both pro and con

Give evidence from the sources, including quotations as appropriate

Conclusion

Expand your thesis into a conclusion that makes clear your position, which should be one that grows logically from your analysis and discussion of the issues

Paradigm for Analysis of History

If you are writing a historical or political science paper that analyzes events and their causes and consequences, your paper should conform in general to the following plan.

Introduction

Identify the event

Provide the background leading up to the event

Offer quotations and paraphrases from experts

Give the thesis sentence

Body

Provide a thorough analysis of the background leading up to the event

Trace events from one historic episode to another

Offer a chronological sequence that explains how one event relates directly to the next

Cite authorities who have also investigated this event in history

Conclusion

Reaffirm your thesis

Discuss the consequences of this event on the course of history; that is, explain how the course of history was altered by this one event

Paradigm for a Comparative Study

A comparative study requires that you examine two schools of thought, two issues, two works, or the positions taken by two persons. The paper examines the similarities and differences of the two subjects, as outlined in the following general plan. It shows three arrangements for the body of the paper.

Introduction
    Establish A
    Establish B
    Briefly compare the two
    Introduce the central issues
    Cite source materials on the subjects
    Present your thesis

Body (choose one)

Examine A	Compare A and B	Issue 1
		Discuss A and B
Examine B	Contrast A and B	Issue 2
		Discuss A and B
Compare and contrast A and B	Discuss the central issues	Issue 3
		Discuss A and B

Conclusion
    Discuss the significant issues
    Write a conclusion that ranks one over the other
      or
    Write a conclusion that rates the respective wisdom of each side

Remember that the models provided above are general guidelines, not iron-clad rules. Use them in that spirit and adjust each as necessary to meet your special needs. (See page 292 for the paradigm to a scientific report.)

3c Writing a Formal Outline

A formal outline classifies the issues of your study into clear, logical categories with main headings and one or more levels of subheadings. Not all papers require the formal outline, nor do all researchers need one. A short research paper can be created from key words, a list of issues, a rough outline, and a first draft.

Many writers, however, benefit by developing a formal outline that classifies the investigation into clear, logical divisions. It should be started fairly early, during the drafting stages and modified as the writing progresses. The outline will thereby change miscellaneous notes, computer drafts, and photocopied materials into an ordered progression of ideas. *Note:* A formal outline is not rigid and inflexible; you may, and should, modify it while writing and revising. In every case, treat an outline or organizational chart as a tool. Like an architect's blueprint, it should contribute to, not inhibit, the construction of a finished product.

You may wish to experiment with the Outline feature of your word processor. If you use this feature when composing the original document, it will allow you to view the paper at various levels of detail and to highlight and "drop" the essay into a different organization.

Using Standard Outline Symbols

List your major categories and subtopics in this form:

I. _____ First major heading
  A. _____ Subheading of first degree
    1. _____ Subheadings of second degree
    2. _____
      a. _____ Subheadings of third degree
      b. _____
        (1) _____ Subheadings of fourth degree
        (2) _____
          (a)_____ Subheadings of fifth degree
          (b)_____
  B. _____ Subheading of first degree

The degree to which you continue the subheads will depend, in part, upon the complexity of the subject. Subjects in a research paper seldom carry beyond subheadings of the third degree, the first series of small letters.

    An alternative form, especially for papers in business and the sciences, is the *decimal outline,* which divides material by numerical divisions, as follows:

1. ____
  1.1. ____
      1.1.1. ____
      1.1.2. ____
      1.1.3. ____
  1.2. ____
      1.2.1. ____
      1.2.2. ____
2. ____

Writing a Formal Topic Outline

If your purpose is to arrange quickly the topics of your paper without detailing your data, build a topic outline of balanced phrases. The topic outline may use noun phrases:

III. The senses
    A. Receptors to detect light
      1. Rods of the retina
      2. Cones of the retina

It may also use gerund phrases:

  III.   Sensing the environment
      A. Detecting light
         1. Sensing dim light with retina rods
         2. Sensing bright light with retina cones

And it may also use infinitive phrases:

  III.   To use the senses
      A. To detect light
         1. To sense dim light
         2. To sense bright light

No matter which grammatical format you choose, you should follow it consistently throughout the outline. A portion of one writer's topic outline follows.

    I.   Distorting the truth with television news and talk shows
       A. Skewing and distorting objectivity
          1. Recognizing television as a presentation, like a drama
          2. Contriving an illusion
          3. Falsifying the line between fact and fiction
       B. Perceiving objectivity in television broadcasts
   II.   Finding the scholarly issues in the way we construct reality
       A. Identifying three categories
          1. Recognizing the objective social reality
          2. Accepting a symbolic social reality
          3. Building our own subjective social reality
       B. The producers: Dressing television as "real" or "objective"
          1. Presenting both sides of a controversy
          2. Squeezing out reality to conform to a format
          3. Rehearsing and editing to compromise objectivity

Writing a Formal Sentence Outline

The sentence outline requires full sentences for each heading and subheading. It has two advantages over the topic outline:

1. Many entries in a sentence outline can serve as topic sentences for paragraphs, thereby accelerating the writing process.
2. The subject/verb pattern establishes the logical direction of your thinking. (For example, the phrase "Vocabulary development" becomes "Television viewing can improve a child's vocabulary.")

Consequently, the sentence outline brings into the open any possible organizational problems rather than hiding them as a topic outline might do. The time devoted to writing a complete sentence outline, like writing complete, polished notes (see pages 105–08), will serve you well when you write the rough draft and revise it.

A portion of one writer's outline follows.

I. All couples make plans for the type of baby they expect.
    A. Most accept the reality of natural birth.
       1. Childbirth carries its gambles and risks.
       2. Parents expect the child to carry on the family traits--the best features as well as the quirks and even the disorders.
    B. Some might use genetic engineering to design the child.
       1. Genetic engineering involves taking a section of DNA and reattaching it to another section.
       2. It has a variety of uses--control of various diseases; better production of grains, poultry, and cattle; a decrease in the use of pesticides; and even the gift of a problem-free baby.
    C. However, one of the greatest arguments against genetic engineering of human beings is the matter of natural law; it is simply wrong to tamper with and to change natural childbirth.

As shown above, you should write the thesis sentence into the outline where it will appear in the paper, usually at the end of the introduction, as shown in item "C" above. The thesis is the main idea of the entire paper, so do not label it as Item I in the outline. Otherwise, you may search fruitlessly for parallel ideas to put in II, III, and IV. (See also page 133 on using the thesis in the opening.)

Using Your Notes, Photocopies, Internet Printouts, and Research Journal to Enrich an Outline

If you have kept a research journal, you have probably developed a number of paragraphs on the topic. Therefore, review the journal and assign each paragraph to a section of your outline. Do this by making a note, such as "put in the conclusion," or by assigning an outline number, "use in II.A.1." Do the same thing with your source materials. Then assign them to a spot in your outline, as shown in this brief example from an outline:

    A. Television viewing can improve the vocabulary of children.
        1. Negative views
            Cite Powell; cite Winkeljohann
        2. Positive views
            Cite Rice and Woodsall; cite Singer; cite Postman

Using Basic, Dynamic Order to Chart the Course of Your Work

Finally, the finished paper should trace the issues, defend and support a thesis, and provide dynamic progression of issues and concepts that point forward to the conclusion. Each section of the paper should provide these elements:

Identification of the problem or issue
Analysis of the issues
Presentation of evidence
Interpretation and discussion of the findings

In every case you must generate the dynamics of the paper by (1) building anticipation in the introduction, (2) investigating the issues in the body, and (3) providing a final judgment. In this way, you will satisfy the demands of the academic reader who will expect you to:

- examine a problem,
- review what is known about it,
- offer your ideas and interpretation of it.

All three are necessary in almost every instance. Consequently, your early organization may determine, in part, the success of your research paper.

4 Finding and Reading the Best Sources

The research paper tests your ability to find and cite appropriate and relevant sources. So your task is twofold: (1) you must read and personally evaluate the sources for your own benefit as a writer, and (2) you must present them to your reader in your text as validated and authentic sources.

This chapter offers tips about selecting and using the sources. It cuts to the heart of the matter: How do I find the best sources? Should I read all or just part of a source? How do I respond to it? The chapter also demonstrates how to write both an annotated bibliography and a review of the literature on a limited topic.

Some student researchers photocopy entire journal articles and carry armloads of books from the library. Such diligence is misplaced. The quality of your citations far outweighs the quantity of your source materials.

4a Finding the Best Source Materials

Be skeptical about accepting every printed word as being the truth. Constantly review and verify to your own satisfaction the words of your sources. Use some of the following techniques for finding the most reliable sources.

Consulting with Your Instructor and the Librarians

Do not hesitate in asking your instructor or the librarians for help in finding sources. Instructors know the field, know the best writers, and can provide a brief list to get you started. Sometimes instructors will pull books from their office shelves to give you a starting point.

Librarians know the resources of the library. Their job is to serve your needs. If you ask for help, they will often walk into the stacks with you to find the appropriate reference books or relevant journal articles.

Using Recent Sources

A book may look valuable, but if its copyright date is 1938 the content has probably been replaced by recent research and current developments. Scientific and technical topics always require up-to-date research. Learn to consult monthly and quarterly journals as well as books.

Evaluating Internet Sources

The Internet supplies mammoth amounts of material, some of it excellent and some not so good. You must make judgments about the validity of these materials. In addition to your common sense judgment, here are a few guidelines:

1. Use the "edu" and "org" sites. These will be home pages developed by an educational instutition, such as Ohio State University, or by a professional organization, such as the American Psychological Association. The "gov" (government) and "mil" (military) sites usually have reliable materials. The "com" (commercial) sites become suspect.
2. Look for the *professional* affiliation of the writer, which you will find in the opening credits or in an E-mail address.
3. A bibliography that accompanies the article will usually indicate the scholarly nature of this writer's work.
4. Be wary of usenet discussion groups. Some of these people are just airing complaints without sound and fundamental evidence to support their opinions.
5. Treat E-mail messages as "mail," not scholarly articles.
6. Access the hypertext links to other professional sites. However, in your search of new sites remember that many commercial sites want to sell you something.

Using Journals Rather than Magazines

Beware of biased reporting. In general, scholarly journals offer more reliable evidence than popular magazines. The authors of journals write for academic honor, and they document all sources. In addition, journal writers publish through university presses and academic organizations that require every article to pass the scrutiny of a jury of critics before its publication. A journal article about child abuse found in *Child Development* or in *Journal of Marriage and the Family* should be reliable. A magazine article about child abuse in a Sunday newspaper supplement or in a popular magazine may be less reliable in its facts and opinions.

Usually, but not in every case, you can identify a journal in these ways:

1. The journal does not have a colorful cover; in fact, the table of contents is often displayed on the cover.

2. There are no colorful graphics and photography to introduce each article, just a title and name of the author.
3. The word *journal* often appears in the title (e.g., *The Journal of Sociology*).
4. The yearly issues of a journal are bound into a book.
5. Usually, the pages of a journal are numbered continuously through all issues for a year (unlike magazines which are always paged anew with each issue).
6. You can find a journal article with just the volume number and the page numbers. You can best find a magazine article with day/month/year and the page numbers.

Using Scholarly Books Rather than Trade Books and Encyclopedias

Like journal articles, scholarly books are subjected to careful review before publication. They are published because they give the very best treatment on a subject. They are not published to make money; in fact, many scholarly books lose money for the publishers. Scholarly books, including textbooks, treat academic topics with in-depth discussions and careful documentation of the evidence. A college library is a repository for scholarly books—technical and scientific works, doctoral dissertations, publications of the university presses, and many textbooks.

Trade books are published to make money for the authors and the publishers. They seldom treat with depth any scholarly subject. *How to Launch a Small Business* or *Landscaping with Rocks* are typical titles of nonfiction trade books to be found in book stores, not in a college library (although public libraries often have vast holdings in trade books).

Encyclopedias, by design, contain brief surveys of every well-known person, event, place, and accomplishment. They will serve you well during preliminary investigation, but most instructors prefer that you go beyond encyclopedias in order to cite from scholarly books and journal articles.

Using Biographies to Evaluate an Author

You may need to search out information about an author for several reasons:

1. To verify the standing and reputation of somebody that you want to paraphrase or quote in your paper.
2. To provide biographical details in your introduction. For example, the primary topic may be Carl Jung's psychological theories of the unconscious, but some information about Jung's career might be appropriate in the paper.
3. To discuss a creative writer's life in relation to his or her work. That is, Joyce Carol Oates's personal life may shed some light on your reading of her stories or novels.

You can learn about a writer and his or her work on the Internet or in a printed biography. At a search engine, such as *Alta Vista,* just type in the name of an author and see what develops. The best writers will usually have several sites devoted to them with articles by and about them.

The librarian can help you find appropriate printed biographies, such as these:

> *Contemporary Authors,* a set of biographies on contemporary writers
> *Dictionary of American Negro Biography,* a review of writers and important figures in African-American history
> *Who's Who in Philosophy,* a list and discussion of the best writers and thinkers in the field

You can find reference works similar to these three books for almost every field. Appendix A, pages 333–66, lists many of them.

Conducting a Citation Search

Citation searching discovers authors who have been cited repeatedly in the literature. For example, one writer located the same name, *Kagan, J.,* in the bibliographies of three articles (see Figure 25). That information signals Kagan's importance to research in this area. The student researcher would be wise to read Kagan's material.

You should search several bibliographies and mark your bibliography cards with stars or circles each time a source is cited. Two or more stars will suggest *must* reading. The sources themselves have suggested a few important books and articles. Three citation indexes will do some of this work for you:

> *Arts and Humanities Citation Index (AHCI)* 1977–date.
> *Science Citation Index (SCI)* 1961–date.
> *Social Sciences Citation Index (SSCI)* 1966–date.

Examining the Book Reviews

Whenever one book serves as the cornerstone for your research, you can test its critical reputation by reading a review or two. Two works provide summaries and critical points of view:

> *Book Review Digest.* New York: H. W. Wilson, 1905–date.
> > Arranged alphabetically by author, this work provides an evaluation of several thousand books each year. It features summaries and brief quotations from the reviews to uncover the critical reception of the work.
> *The Booklist.* Chicago: American Library Assn., 1905–date.
> > A monthly magazine that reviews new books for librarians. This work includes brief summaries and recommendations.

Graham, S., & Folkes, V. S. (1990). *Attribution theory: Applications to achievement, mental health, and interpersonal conflict.* Hillsdale, NJ: Erlbaum.

Kagan, J., Kearsley, R. B., & Zelazo, P. R. (1978). *Infancy: Its place in human development.* Cambridge, MA; Harvard University Press.

Levy, D. M. (1937). Studies in sibling rivalry. Research Monographs, *American Orthopsychiatric Association*

Kagan, J. (1984). *The nature of the child.* New York: Basic.

Kagan, J. (1992). Yesterday's premises, tomorrow's promises. *Developmental Psychology, 28,* 990–997.

Kagan J. (1994). *Galen's prophecy: Temperament in human nature.* New York: Basic.

Kagan, J., Rossman, B. L., Day, D., Albert, J., & Phillips, W. (1964). Information processing in the child: Significance of analytic and reflective attitudes. *Psychological Monographs, 78* (Whole No. 578).

Goldsmith, H. H., & Rothbart, M. K., (1992). *Laboratory Temperament Assessment Battery (LABTAB).* Pre- and Locomotor Versions. University of Oregon.

Kagan, J. (1984). *The nature of the child.* New York: Basic Books.

Kochanska, G. (1993). Toward a synthesis of parental socialization and child temperament in early development of conscience. *Child Development, 64,* 325–347.

Figure 25
From Child Development, *1997, author who appears in three different bibliographies.*

Other reviews are hidden here and there in magazines and journals. To find them, use one of the following indexes:

Book Review Index. Detroit: Gale, bimonthly.
    This work indexes reviews in 225 magazines and journals.
Index to Book Reviews in the Humanities. Williamston, Michigan: Phillip Thompson Publ., annually.
    This index to reviews in humanities periodicals has entries listed by author, title, and then reviewer.
Index to Book Reviews in the Social Sciences. Williamston, Michigan: Phillip Thompson Publ., annually.
    This index to reviews in social science periodicals has entries listed by author, title, and then reviewer.
Current Book Review Citations. New York: H. W. Wilson, annually.
    This work gives an author-title index to book reviews published in more than 1,000 periodicals.

The sample page of *Book Review Digest* shown in Figure 26 shows you the type of information available in a review of books. After bibliographic details, it summarizes the book and then provides the reviews, one from *Booklist* and another from *The Library Journal*. Both reviewers give a positive response to the book, so a researcher could feel good about using it as a source.

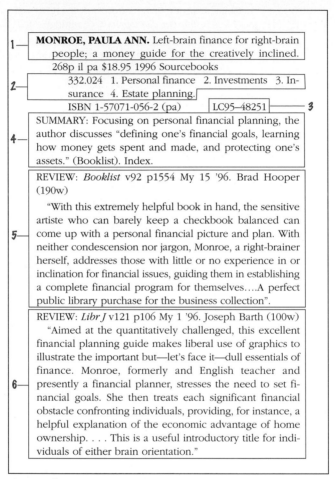

1 — **MONROE, PAULA ANN.** Left-brain finance for right-brain people; a money guide for the creatively inclined.
268p il pa $18.95 1996 Sourcebooks

2 — 332.024 1. Personal finance 2. Investments 3. Insurance 4. Estate planning.

ISBN 1-57071-056-2 (pa)   LC95–48251 — 3

4 — SUMMARY: Focusing on personal financial planning, the author discusses "defining one's financial goals, learning how money gets spent and made, and protecting one's assets." (Booklist). Index.

REVIEW: *Booklist* v92 p1554 My 15 '96. Brad Hooper (190w)

5 — "With this extremely helpful book in hand, the sensitive artiste who can barely keep a checkbook balanced can come up with a personal financial picture and plan. With neither condescension nor jargon, Monroe, a right-brainer herself, addresses those with little or no experience in or inclination for financial issues, guiding them in establishing a complete financial program for themselves....A perfect public library purchase for the business collection".

REVIEW: *Libr J* v121 p106 My 1 '96. Joseph Barth (100w)

6 — "Aimed at the quantitatively challenged, this excellent financial planning guide makes liberal use of graphics to illustrate the important but—let's face it—dull essentials of finance. Monroe, formerly and English teacher and presently a financial planner, stresses the need to set financial goals. She then treats each significant financial obstacle confronting individuals, providing, for instance, a helpful explanation of the economic advantage of home ownership. . . . This is a useful introductory title for individuals of either brain orientation."

Figure 26
From Book Review Digest, *1997 (1) Author and title, (2) Dewey call number and subject entries for card catalog (3) Library of Congress call number (4) First entry is a description of the work (5)* Booklist's *evaluation of the book (6)* Library Journal's *evaluation of the book.*

4b   Reading All or Part of a Source

Confronted by several books and articles, many writers have trouble determining the value of material and the contribution it will make to the research paper. To save time, you must be selective in your reading. To serve your reader, you must cite carefully selected material that is pertinent to the argument. Avoid dumping huge blocks of quotation into the paper because you will lose your voice as the writer.

Evaluating an Article

1. The *title*. Look for key words that have relevance to your topic before you start reading the article. For example, *Children and Parents* may look ideal for child abuse research until you read the subtitle: *Children and Parents: Growing up in New Guinea.*
2. An *abstract*. If an abstract is available on CD-ROM or on an abstracting service (e.g., *Psychological Abstracts*), read it before going in search of the printed article. If a printed article is preceded by an abstract, read it first. Reading an abstract is the best way to ascertain if an essay or a book will serve your specific needs.
3. The *opening paragraphs*. If the opening of an article shows no relevance to your study, abandon it.
4. Each *topic sentence* of paragraphs of the body. These first sentences of each paragraph will give you a digest of the author's main points. See Figure 27 for an article highlighted in vital places.
5. The *closing paragraphs*. If the opening of an article seems promising, skim the closing for relevance. Read the entire article only if this survey encourages you.
6. *Author credits*. Learn something about the credientials of the author. Magazine articles often provide brief biographical profiles of authors. The backs of book jackets often do the same. Even journal articles will include the author's academic affiliation and some credits. Internet home pages provide the same sort of information.

Evaluating a Book

A book requires you to check several additional items:

1. The *table of contents*. A book's table of contents may reveal chapters that pertain to your topic. Often, only one chapter is useful. For example, Richard Ellmann's book *Oscar Wilde* has one chapter, "The Age of Dorian," devoted to Wilde's book *The Picture of Dorian Gray*. If your research focuses on this novel, then the chapter, not the entire book, will demand your attention.
2. The *book jacket,* if one is available. For example, the jacket to Richard Ellmann's *Oscar Wilde* says:

   Ellmann's *Oscar Wilde* has been almost twenty years in work, and it will stand, like his universally admired *James Joyce,* as the

Second thoughts about integration

Black ambivalence about busing has less to do with ideology than with results

By Jerelyn Eddings

Since court-ordered school busing began in 1971, it has been the subject of rancorous debate. Many white opponents have decried busing as too disruptive to neighborhoods, while black communities and civil rights activists hailed it as the only solution to separate and unequal school systems. Now there's a new twist: A number of black leaders are pushing to jettison busing and get out of the desegregation business. Frustrated with the slow pace of progress in their schools, prominent blacks in places as varied as Prince George's County, Md., Yonkers, N.Y., and Seattle are challenging the old line on busing: Better to spend scant resources on improving their schools, they argue, than on chasing the rainbow of integration.

Even the National Association for the Advancement of Colored People, whose name is synonymous with the fight for desegregation, appears torn on the issue. Chairman Myrlie Evers-Williams had promised a major debate on the subject at the organization's annual convention in Pittsburgh last week, but then backed off. She used her keynote address instead to make a firm statement in support of integration—and against the "rats" trying to divide the organization.

The tensions that had been simmering below the surface since the NAACP fired two local presidents for arguing against busing were in full view at the convention. In a letter distributed to convention delegates, Robert H. Robinson, one of the ousted presidents, argued: "The NAACP establishment is using the same arguments for desegregation that it made in the 1950s."

Demographic changes. Although it is taking place within the context of a larger debate about integration vs. separatism, the new busing controversy is less about political philosophy than about practical concerns like the quality of schools and the best use of scant educational resources.

Twenty-five years ago, Prince George's County was a mostly white, largely rural jurisdiction with a racial past so bitter that blacks referred to it as "little Georgia." In 1972, the NAACP won a school desegregation case against the county, and the school system has been operating un-

Figure 27
Article with highlighting on the opening, the topic sentences, and the closing.
(Source: *U.S. News & World Report*, July 28, 1997)

definitive life. The book's emotional resonance, its riches of authentic color and conversation, and the subtlety of its critical illuminations give dazzling life to this portrait of the complex man, the charmer, the great playwright, the daring champion of the primacy of art.

Such information can stimulate your reading and note taking from this important book.

der court orders to bus students ever since.

But busing in Prince George's may no longer make sense, as the area has undergone a dramatic demographic shift. The county now boasts one of the largest middle-class, African-American populations in the country, and the school system is 73 percent black. As a result, busing programs that once carried black students to white neighborhoods now often simply move them from one black neighborhood to another. "Busing was useful in the early years, but now the black population is too large," says school board Chairman Kenneth Johnson.

While demographic changes have undermined busing's popularity in Prince George's and other "white flight" communities, the main reason for the growing ambivalence toward busing is that it often hasn't raised educational achievement. In Yonkers, N.Y., for example, blacks still score nearly two grade levels below whites on standardized tests a decade after a federal court ordered busing; as a result, an effort is underway in Yonkers to do away with busing. Similarly, in Seattle, the new school superintendent—John Standord, an African-American retired Army general—has maintained that busing is doing nothing to improve test scores.

Better education. In places such as these, the focus is shifting away from trying to avoid "separate" schools and toward efforts to achieve "equal" ones instead. "The issue with the NAACP is that some of the membership is saying we can't just keep emphasizing integration. We have to put some emphasis on improving schools and the economic life of the black community, and I think frankly that most of the people within the NAACP realize that," says Alvin Poussaint, a Harvard University professor and expert on racial attitudes.

Prince George's is trying to win court approval to replace busing with a new plan that concentrates on building and improving neighborhood schools. "We need to look at what busing was intended to do," says the school board's Johnson. "It was never about black kids sitting next to white kids; it was about an inequitable distribution of resources."

"We need to redefine what desegregation is," sals Alvin Thornton, who devised the neighborhood-schools plan. "It's about making the black child whole—even if that means educating them in schools that happen to be all black."

*With Jeannye Thornton
and Barbra Murray*

3. The *foreword, preface,* or *introduction.* Often an author's *preface* or *introduction* serves as a critical overview of the entire book, pinpointing the primary subject of the text and the particular approach of this author. Read an author's preface to find a statement of purpose or an author's perspective on the subject. For example, Ellmann opens his books *Oscar Wilde* by saying:

> Oscar Wilde: we have only to hear the great name to anticipate that what will be quoted as his will surprise and delight us. Among

the writers identified with the 1890s, Wilde is the only one whom everyone still reads. The various labels that have been applied to the age—Aestheticism, Decadence, the Beardsley period—ought not to conceal that fact that our first association with it is Wilde, refulgent, majestic, ready to fall.

Such an introduction describes the nature of the book: Ellmann will portray Wilde as the dominating literary figure of the 1890s. A *foreword* is often written by somebody other than the author. It is often insightful and worthy of quotation.

4. The *index*. A book's *index* will list names and terminology with page numbers for all items mentioned within the text. For example, the index to *Oscar Wilde* lists about eighty items for *The Picture of Dorian Gray,* among them:

> writing of, 310–14; possible sources for, 311; W's Preface to, 311, 315, 322, 335; homosexuality and, 312, 318; magazine publication of, 312, 319, 320; W's self-image in, 312, 319; literature and painting in, 312–131; underlying legend of, 314–15

The index, by virtue of its detailed listing, has determined the relevance of the book to your research.

4c   Responding to the Sources

After you find source material relevant to your subject, you must respond in several ways:

1. Read the material.
2. As you read, write notes that record key ideas.
3. Write notations on the margins of photocopied materials.
4. Outline the key ideas of an article.
5. Write a précis (see definition on page 94) to summarize the whole.
6. Identify the source information and relevant page numbers.

Selecting Key Ideas for Your Notes

In many instances you may borrow only one idea from a source that you can rephrase into your own words. One student borrowed from a portion of a bulletin on air bag safety.

**New Rules Proposed by NHTSA
to Reduce Dangers of Air Bags**

The National Highway Traffic Safety Administration (NHTSA) is considering new rules to minimize the dangers of air bags to children and small adults, while preserving the lifesaving benefit of the devices.

Calling for a phase-in of smart air bag technology, the proposal also contains more immediate measures such as enhanced warning labels and a reduction in the deployment force of bags.

Smart Technology

"Smart" air bag technology will allow the deployment force of the bag to be determined by factors such as the weight or position of the occupant. Development of the technology has been underway for some time, and Mercedes has already introduced a Seiman system which can detect the presence of a child safety seat in the front passenger position and disable the air bag.

— Use this idea!

Depowering

NHTSA will propose a reduction of between 20-35 percent of the deployment force of air bags until smart technology is in place. The agency believes this action will reduce the incidence of injury and improve the performance of air bags for belted occupants including children, individuals with acute medical conditions and small-stature adults, while still providing significant protection for unbelted occupants.

Options for Owners

NHTSA will also propose allowing dealers to deactivate the air bags of any vehicle owner who requests it, such as families who need to have children in the front seat for medical monitoring purposes, car pools with front-seated children, short-stature individuals and others who have reasonable concerns about a potential danger....

Rather than copy the entire piece or copy the one paragraph, the researcher read first, related the reading to her thesis and her own outline, and wrote this summary:

From "New Rules," page 1

Technology is now being developed for the automatic disabling of an air bag when it detects a child or small adult in the seat.

The writer has selected only a small portion of the text for her notes, that which relates to technological advances.

Outlining the Key Ideas of a Source

Most books have a table of contents which outlines the basic ingredients of the book. Consult it for issues that deserve your critical reading. In the case of an essay, you can frame your own outline to capture an author's primary themes; that is, list the main ideas and subtopics to show the hierarchy of issues, to identify parallel parts, and to locate supporting ideas. The goal is to discover the author's primary and secondary ideas. The outline of the "New Rules" article might look like this:

New Rules for Air Bags
    Smart technology
        Detects position
        Detects weight
        Detects child safety seat
    Depowering the bags
        Reduce deployment power
        Make a 20–35 percent reduction
    Give options to owners
    Allow them to deactivate
        For children
        For medical monitoring
        For short-statured individuals

Such an outline gives the researcher a clear overview of the issues.

Making Notations on Photocopied Materials

Avoid making marks on library books and magazines, but *do* make marginal notes in your own books and magazines or on photocopied materials. Underline sentences, circle key ideas, ask questions, and react with your own comments.

Writing a Summary or a Précis

A *summary* condenses into a brief note the general nature of a source. In some cases you might use the summary in your paper, but more than anything else it serves to remind you later on about the source's relevance to your study. Note this example of a *summary* and compare it with the *précis* below:

From "New Rules," page 1

NHTSA wants smart technology to detect little people in the seats, to put less power in the air bag, and to give more options for auto owners to deactivate air bags.

For further details about writing a summary, see Section 5e, page 114.

A *précis* is a highly polished summary, one that you can transfer to your paper or use in an annotated bibliography. It often uses direct quotation from the original source. Use the précis to review a piece of writing or to write a plot summary.

From "New Rules," page 1

NHTSA asks for "smart" air bags that will "allow the deployment force of the bag to be determined by factors such as the weight or position of the occupant" (1). It suggests reducing the deployment force of air bags by 20–35 percent. It also recommends that dealers be permitted to "deactivate the air bags of any vehicle owner who requests it" (1).

For further details and examples, see Section 5f, pages 115–17.

4d Selecting a Mix of Both Primary and Secondary Sources

Primary sources are the original words of a writer. The primary sources include novels, speeches, eyewitness accounts, letters, autobiographies, interviews, or the results of original research. Feel free to quote often from a primary source because it has direct relevance to your discussion. If you examine a poem by Dylan Thomas, you must quote the poem. If you examine Bill Clinton's domestic policies on health care, you must quote from White House documents.

The best evidence you can offer, when writing about a poem, story, novel, or drama, will be the words of the author. Therefore, quote often from these works in order to defend the thesis of a literary paper. The same is true with a history paper, in which you should cite the words of the key figure, whether it be Thomas Jefferson, Marie Antoinette, or Karl Marx.

In the social sciences your best evidence will be found in the wording of original case studies and reports of social workers and psychiatrists. In a similar fashion, education will offer test data, interviews, pilot studies, and other forms of primary information. Thus, every discipline will offer you plenty of primary source material, as shown on page 96.

Secondary sources are writings about the primary sources, about an author, or about somebody's accomplishments. Examples of secondary sources are a report on a presidential speech, a review of new scientific findings, or an analysis of a poem. A biography provides a second-hand view of the life of a notable person. A history book interprets events. These evaluations, analyses, or interpretations provide ways of looking at original, primary sources.

Do not quote too liberally from secondary sources. Be selective. Use a well-worded sentence, not the entire paragraph. Incorporate a key phrase into your text, not eight or nine lines. (See "Selecting Key Ideas," 92–93.)

The subject area of a research paper determines in part the nature of the source materials. Use the chart on page 96 as a guide:

Citing from Primary and Secondary Sources

	Primary Sources	*Secondary Sources*
Literature	Novels, poems, plays, short stories, letters, diaries, manuscripts, auto biographies, films, videos of live performances	Journal articles, reviews, biographies, critical books about writers and their works
Government Political Science History	Speeches, writings by presidents and others, the *Congressional Record,* and reports of agencies and departments, documents written by historic figures	Newspaper reports, news magazines, political journals and newsletters, journal articles, history books
Social Sciences	Case studies, findings from surveys and question-naires; reports of social workers, psychiatrists, and lab technicians	Commentary and evalua-tions in reports, docu-ments, journal articles, and books
Sciences	Tools and methods, exper-iments, findings from tests and experiments, observa-tions, discoveries, and test patterns	Interpretations and discussions of test data as found in journals and books (scientific books, which are quickly dated, are less valuable than up-to-date journals)
Fine Arts	Films, paintings, music, sculptures as well as re-productions and synopses of these for research pur-poses	Evaluations in journal articles, critical reviews, biographies, and critical books about the authors and their works
Business	Market research and test-ing, technical studies and investigations, drawings, designs, models, memo-randums and letters, com-puter data	Discussion of the busi-ness world in news-papers, business mag-azines, journals, government documents, and books
Education	Pilot studies, term pro-jects, sampling results, tests and test data, sur-veys, interviews, observa-tions, statistics, and com-puter data	Analysis and evaluation of educational experi-mentation in journals, pamphlets, books, and reports

4e Preparing an Annotated Bibliography

An *annotation* is a summary of the contents of a book or article. A *bibliography* is a list of sources on a selected topic. Thus, an annotated bibliography does two important things: (1) it gives a bibliographic entry to all your sources, and (2) it summarizes the contents of each book or article. The annotated bibliography will evaluate the strength of your sources.

- For instructions on writing an annotation, see 5f, "Using the Précis to Write an Annotated Bibliography," page 116.
- For instructions on writing the citation to a source in MLA style see Chapter 9 (for other styles, consult Chapters 10–11).

Note: This writer chose the Arial font for developing the paper and used italic lettering rather than underscoring. You may also prepare your paper in this fashion; that is, you are not required to use the Courier font for all of your papers.

Annotated Bibliography

Clark, Charles S. "Pursuing the Paranormal." *The CQ Researcher* 6.12 (29 Mar. 1996): 265–288. Clark explores the new interest in paranormal activity and unexplained phenomena ranging from UFO sightings to alien abduction testimonials to psychic abilities. This new interest in the paranormal is attributed by Clark to the high level of mistrust in government, which is due in part to the decade-old rumors about the coverup of the Roswell Incident. A brief chronology of paranormal activity from the 1940 to 1996 is given, as well as annotated bibliographical information on sources pertaining to paranormal activity.

Headquarters United States Air Force. *The Roswell Report: Fact Versus Fiction in the New Mexico Desert.* D301.82/7:R73. Washington: GPO, 1995. In an attempt to end rumors of government conspiracy, this is the first official report on the "Roswell Incident" issued by the Department of the Air Force regarding the alleged UFO crash in Roswell, New Mexico. The report contains Colonel Richard L. Weaver's report of Air Force research and a synopsis of balloon research findings. A number of interviews with and statements of airmen stationed at Roswell in 1947 are also disclosed.

Hesemann, Michael and Philip Mantle. *Beyond Roswell: The Alien Autopsy Film, Area 51, & the U.S. Government Coverup of UFOs.* New York: Marlowe, 1997. This book by a cultural anthropologist, Hesemann, and the Director of Investigations for the British UFO Research Association, Mantle, delves into the specifics of the Roswell UFO crash and the alien autopsy that followed. A number of eyewitness accounts and affidavits are included to provide support for the argument that such an event actually occurred and to prove the contradictions present in the official Air Force report on the subject.

"Interview with Carl Sagan, Author, Astronomer." *NOVA Online*. 1996. 31 July 1997 ⟨http://www.pbs.org/wgbh/pages/nova/aliens/ carlsagan.html⟩. In this interview, the fact that Sagan believes in extraterrestrial life is evident; however, he is skeptical of "alien abductions." Sagan fails to see psychological evidence as being proof that such events have occurred and rather sees the lack of physical evidence as proof that they did not occur. He says of two believers in alien abductions, John Mack and Budd Hopkins, that they "want the validation of science" without the "standards of evidence."

"Interview with John Mack, Psychiatrist, Harvard University." *NOVA Online*. 1996. 31 July 1997 ⟨http://www.pbs.org/wgbh/pages/nova/ aliens/johnmack.html⟩. Not only does Mack believe in extraterrestrial life, but he also believes that aliens have visited earth and abducted human beings. The basis of his belief lies in the numerous interviews with abductees in which common experiences are described and common injuries are evident. In the interview, Mack gives the details of the commonalities of abductees that provide the foundation for his belief in such occurrences.

Naeye, Robert. "OK, where are they?" *Astronomy 24.7* (July 1996): 36+. *InfoTrac: Expanded Academic Index*. CD-ROM. Information Access. July 1997.Naeye writes that there is little scientific evidence to support the hypothesis that intelligent forms of life exist on other planets in the universe. Having only life on earth to study, scientists consider the fundamental characteristics of life on this planet to be universal. When these fundamental characteristics are combined with the theories of the evolution of life, there is little scientific basis for the belief that intelligent life actually exists elsewhere in the universe.

"Poll: Most in U.S. Believe in Space Life." *Yahoo! News*. 28 July 1997. 31 July 1997 ⟨http://www.yahoo.com/headlines/970828/news/stories/ space_1.html⟩.This news story gives the statistical findings of a Harris poll released Monday, July 28, 1997. The poll of 1,002 adults was taken between July 9 and 14; it revealed that the belief in intelligent life in space has increased from fifty-three to fifty-nine percent since last year. Other specific statistical information is also included where space exploration is concerned.

"Poll: U.S. Hiding Knowledge of Aliens." *CNN Interactive*. 15 June 1997. 31 July 1997 ⟨http://www.cnn.com/US/9706/15/ufo.poll/index.html⟩. The statistic that eighty percent of Americans think that the government is hiding knowledge of extraterrestrial life forms is included in this report of a CNN/Time poll released July 15th. Other statistical data includes the belief of sixty-four percent that aliens have contacted humans and the belief of fifty percent that aliens have abducted humans. Statistical data on the Roswell incident and personal knowledge of alien encounters is also included.

Rayl, A.J.S. "Inside the Military UFO Underground." *Omni* 16.7 (Apr. 1994): 48+. *InfoTrac: Expanded Academic Index.* CD-ROM. Information Access. July 1997. In 1969, the U.S. Government abandoned unidentified flying object research; however, three insiders give testimony in this article to the contrary. Robert O. Dean, retired Command Sergeant Major; Bob Lazar, independent contract scientist and businessman; and Charles I. Halt, retired United States Air Force Colonel, report that underground investigations are still being conducted by the U.S. Government. In this article, the claims, backgrounds, and stories of these three men are reported, as well as critical and official responses to their claims.

"Roswell Report: Case Closed." *Air Force Web Information Service.* 24 June 1997. 31 July 1997 ⟨http://www.af.mil/lib/roswell/⟩. In this executive summary, the release of a second report on the "Roswell Incident" is discussed. This report, "The Roswell Report: Case Closed," discloses the Air Force activities and experiments conducted on the base at Roswell, New Mexico, in an attempt to disprove claims of a governmental cover-up of UFO activity and "alien bodies." The web page summarizes the conclusions drawn from documented research.

Stacy, Dennis. "Cosmic Conspiracy: Six Decades of Government UFO Cover-Ups." *Omni* 16.7 (Apr. 1994): 34+. *SIRS Researcher on the Web.* 31 July 1997 ⟨http://researcher.sirs.com/cgi-bin/res-article-display?4PR030A⟩. In this article, Stacy follows the reported incident of a UFO crash in Roswell, New Mexico, and the recovery of the debris by the Army Air Corps. In addition, he examines the information on Project Blue Book released by the U.S. Government. Interviews with many believers in the conspiracy to coverup knowledge of alien encounters are also included in the article.

4f Preparing a Review of the Literature on a Topic

The review of literature presents a set of summaries in essay form for two purposes.

1. It helps you investigate the topic because it forces you to examine and then to show how each source addresses the problem. *Note:* Do not simply list summaries of the sources without relating each source to your thesis.

2. It organizes and classifies the sources in some reasonable manner for the benefit of the reader.

The essay below introduces the issue of alien life forms, discusses the debate, sets science against psychiatry, and offers a summary.

To write summaries of your key sources, see Section 5e, page 114.
To blend source material into your survey, see Section 7a, pages 156–57.
To write the bibliography entries, see Chapter 9, pages 233–72.

Bonds 1

Leigh Bonds
English 101
24 October 1997

Selected Review of Literature:
Is the Earth Being Visited by Intelligent Alien Life Forms?

According to a CNN poll taken on June 15, 1997, eighty percent of Americans feel that the government is hiding knowledge of the existence of extraterrestrial life forms and sixty-four percent believe that aliens have contacted humans. According to Gallup polls, over twenty-three million people in the United States believe they have seen UFOs and about two percent of the population believe themselves to be abductees. With the numbers of believers in the existence of intelligent extraterrestrial life increasing from fifty-three to fifty-nine percent from 1996 to 1997, the question must ultimately surface: Is the earth being visited by intelligent life forms?

The purpose of this survey is to examine two of the numerous debates over alien encounters. The first involves the reports on the "Roswell incident" and UFO research issued by the U.S. Government, which has spawned a debate between those who stand by these reports and those who feel that these reports are merely coverups withholding of the actual truth. The second places the theories of science against the findings of psychiatry in a debate over the substantiality of alien encounter allegations.

The Debate Over Roswell

In 1995, the Headquarters of the United States Air Force released *The Roswell Report: Fact Versus Fiction in the New Mexico Desert*. This report, compiled by Colonel Richard L. Weaver and First Lieutenant James McAndrew, addressed the request made by Representative Steven H. Schiff for information on the alleged UFO crash in Roswell in 1947. The report concluded that there was no evidence that a UFO had crashed at Roswell, and rather, it was a classified, experimental weather balloon, Project MOGUL, designed for atmospheric monitoring.

According to the "Roswell Report: Case Closed" web site, the Headquarters of the United States Air Force released a second report on the Roswell incident on June 24, 1997, that shares the name of the web site. The report supports the claims of the first report that the Air Force was engaged in high-altitude balloon experimentation. However, this report adds that the "aliens" observed at Roswell were, in fact, anthropomorphic test dummies, and that the military units previously thought to arrive at the base to retrieve the UFO wreckage were in fact engaged in the anthropomorphic dummy recovery operations.

In the April 1994 issue of OMNI, an article appeared entitled "Inside the Military UFO Underground." Having claimed to abandon UFO research in 1969, the United States government continued to conduct underground investigations on the matter according to three informants interviewed in this article. With one informant being a propulsion system engineer and the other two being highly ranked military personnel, credibility is lent to their stories. An official response, which is essentially no response, follows each story along with a critical statement by personnel from the Center for UFO Studies.

In the same issue of *OMNI,* another article entitled "Cosmic Conspiracy: Six Decades of Government UFO Cover-Ups" analyzes the story issued by the Air Force involving the Roswell incident. The article builds upon the statement made by Colonel William Blanchard to the *Roswell Daily Record* for July 8, 1947 that the intelligence office of the 509th Bomb Group "was fortunate enough to gain possession of a disc through the cooperation of local ranchers and the Sheriff's office of Chaves County." Opinions of both skeptics and supporters of the government's report on Project Blue Book are included in the article.

In the March 29, 1996, *CQ Researcher,* skepticism is voiced by Richard Hall, chairman of the Washington, D.C.-area Fund for UFO Research, where the Air Force's report on Roswell is concerned. He refers to the article as a "terrible example of overkill" designed by its size to discourage the public from analyzing its argument. He says that the balloons were actually launched long after 1947, and that the eyewitness accounts can hardly be discounted.

The book *Beyond Roswell* examines all of the information known about the Roswell incident from that released by the U.S. Government to a number of written affidavits and eyewitness accounts of what occurred after the bright lights were spotted in the sky on July 4. Believing that the alien autopsy film, the Santilli film, that aired on the FOX network two years ago was real, Hesemann and Mantle interview numerous individuals who corroborate the story that alien bodies were extracted from the UFO wreckage sight and that autopsies were performed on these lifeless forms.

Science v. Psychiatry

On the side of science is the prominent astronomer Carl Sagan. In an interview for the PBS television show, *NOVA,* Sagan's belief in extraterrestrial life is evident; however, he is skeptical of the increasing numbers of allegations of "alien abductions." Sagan sees the lack of physical evidence that such events occur as being the proof to refute them and fails to see psychological evidence as being proof that such events have occurred. He says of two believers in alien abductions, John Mack and Budd Hopkins, they "want the validation of science" without the "standards of evidence."

In an article entitled "OK, where are they?," Robert Naeye searches for scientific evidence to support the hypothesis that extraterrestrial life exists. Naeye comes to the conclusion that there is actually very little scientific evidence to support the hypothesis that intelligent forms of life exist on other planets in the universe. Scientists consider the fundamental characteristics of life on this planet to be universal; therefore, the absence of many of these fundamentals on other planets makes life, as science knows it, to be improbable. When these fundamental characteristics are combined with the theories of the evolution of life, there is little scientific basis for the belief that intelligent life actually exists elsewhere in the universe.

On the other side of the debate is Harvard psychiatrist, John Mack. In an interview on the PBS program NOVA, Mack talks about his findings from interviews with over a hundred alien encounter "experiencers." Not only does Mack believe in extraterrestrial life, but he also believes that aliens have visited earth and abducted human beings. The basis of his belief lies in the common experiences described by "experiencers" and the common injuries that are evident on their bodies following the abductions. The details of the commonalities among the testimonies of abductees are given by Mack to NOVA in this interview.

Conclusion

Though the literature selected for this review hardly represents the vast amount of literature on the "Roswell Incident" and the alleged "government cover-up," nor the numerous press releases issued by the Air Force on the subject, it does reflect the issues of the debate. Where the debate between science and psychiatry is concerned, there are also numerous articles written to support the findings of each. The common ground between the two debates is that there is no concrete evidence to support any of the positions, although each position feels that it has such evidence.

Bonds 4

Until a concrete piece of physical evidence is found that can shed more light on the subject, the government will continue to stand by the two released reports and the skeptics will continue to believe that something is being withheld from them; scientists will continue to demand physical evidence and psychiatrists will firmly stand by their findings in the testimonies of "experiencers." It has been said that Americans have been distrustful of their government since the country was established; however, where information of alien encounters are concerned, many Americans feel that they have every reason to be.

Works Cited

Clark, Charles S. "Pursuing the Paranormal." *The CQ Researcher* 6.12 (29 Mar. 1996): 265–288.

Edergreen, Katarina. "Alien Abductions—Dream or Reality?" *Alien Abductions.* 31 July 1997 ⟨http://www.jmk.su.se/mark/global/ edergreen/alien.html⟩.

Headquarters United States Air Force. *The Roswell Report: Fact Versus Fiction in the New Mexico Desert.* D301.82/7:R73. Washington: GPO, 1995.

Hesemann, Michael and Philip Mantle. *Beyond Roswell: The Alien Autopsy Film, Area 51, & the U.S. Government Coverup of UFOs.* New York: Marlowe, 1997.

"Interview with Carl Sagan, Author, Astronomer." *NOVA Online.* 1996. 31 July 1997 ⟨http://www.pbs.org/wgbh/pages/nova/aliens/ carlsagan.html⟩.

"Interview with John Mack, Psychiatrist, Harvard University." *NOVA Online.* 1996. 31 July 1997 ⟨http://www.pbs.org/wgbh/pages/nova/ aliens/johnmack.html⟩.

Naeye, Robert. "OK, where are they"? *Astronomy* 24.7 (July 1996): 36+. *InfoTrac: Expanded Academic Index.* CD-ROM. Information Access. July 1997.

"Poll: Most in U.S. Believe in Space Life." *Yahoo! News.* 28 Jul. 1997. 31 July 1997 ⟨http://www.yahoo.com/headlines/970828/news/stories/ space_1.htm⟩.

"Poll: U.S. Hiding Knowledge of Aliens." *CNN Interactive.* 15 Jun. 1997. 31 July 1997 ⟨http://www.cnn.com/US/9706/15/ufo.poll/index.html⟩.

Rayl, A.J.S. "Inside the Military UFO Underground." *Omni* 16.7 (April 1994): 48+. *InfoTrac: Expanded Academic Index.* CD-ROM. Information Access. July 1997.

"Roswell Report: Case Closed." *Air Force Web Information Service.* 24 June 1997. 31 July 1997 ⟨http://www.af.mil/lib/roswell/⟩.

Stacy, Dennis. "Cosmic Conspiracy: Six Decades of Government UFO Cover-Ups." *Omni* 16.7 (April 1994): 34+. *SIRS Researcher on the Web.* 31 July 1997 ⟨http://researcher.sirs.com/cgi-bin/ res-article-display?4PR030A⟩.

5 Writing Notes

The inventor Thomas Edison depended upon documented research by others. He built upon their beginnings. How fortunate he was that his predecessors recorded their experiments. They kept good notes. Scholarship is the sharing of information. The primary reason for any research paper is to announce and publicize new findings. A botanist explains the discovery of a new strain of ferns in Kentucky's Land Between the Lakes. A medical scientist reports the results of cancer research. A sociologist announces the results of a two-year pilot study of Native Americans in the Appalachian region.

Similarly, you must explain your findings from a geology field trip, disclose research on illegal dumping of medical waste, or discuss the results of an investigation into overcrowding of school classrooms. You will often support your position by citing the experts in the field, so accuracy in your quotations and paraphrases is essential.

Accordingly, you will need to write notes of high quality so that they fit appropriate places in your outline, as discussed in Chapter 3. In addition, you will need to write different types of notes that reflect your evaluation of the sources—quotations for well-phrased passages by authorities but paraphrased or summarized notes for less notable materials. This chapter explains the following types of notes:

Personal notes (5b) expressing your own ideas as opposed to borrowed viewpoints or a string of quotations.

Quotation notes (5c) preserving the wisdom and distinguished syntax of an authority.

Paraphrase notes (5d) interpreting and restating what the authority has said.

Summary notes (5e) distilling factual data that has marginal value; you can return to the source later if necessary.

Précis notes (5f) capturing the essence of one writer's ideas in capsule form.

Field notes (5g) recording interviews, questionnnaire tabulations, lab experiments, and various types of field research.

> ***Note:*** The Internet now offers many articles that you can print or download to a file. Treat these as you would a printed source; that is, develop notes from them that you can transfer into your draft. If you download an article to your files, you can mark passages and transfer them quickly into your notes or draft. See pages 158–60.

5a Creating Effective Notes

Whether you write your notes with word processing or by hand, you should keep in mind some basic rules:

1. *Write one item per note.* One item of information for each note facilitates shuffling and rearranging the data during all stages of organization. On a computer make single files for each note or one file with notes labeled and recorded for easy retrieval.
2. *List the source.* Abbreviate the exact source (for example, "Thornton 431" or "Smith, 1998, p. 62") to serve as a quick reference to the full address. Make it a practice to list name, year, and page number on your notes; then you will be ready to make in-text citations for MLA, APA, or other academic styles.
3. *Label each note.* Arrange your notes by describing each one (for example, "objectivity on television") or by putting one of your outline headings on it (for example, "Television as a presentation").
4. *Write a full note.* When you have a source in your hands, write full, well-developed sentences to speed the writing of your first draft. They may require editing, later, to fit the context of your draft. Avoid photocopying everything because the writing will remain to be done at a later time.
5. *Keep everything.* Try to save every card, sheet, scrap, and note in order to authenticate dates, page numbers, or full names.
6. *Label your personal notes.* To distinguish your thoughts with those from authorities, label personal ideas with "PER" (personal note), "my idea," "mine," or "personal note."
7. *Conform to conventions of research style.* This suggestion is somewhat premature, but if you know it, write your notes to conform to your discipline—MLA, APA, CBE, Chicago—as shown briefly below and explained later in this book.

> **MLA:** Lawrence Smith states, "The suicidal teen causes severe damage to the psychological condition of peers" (34).
>
> **APA:** Smith (1997) has commented, "The suicidal teen causes severe damage to the psychological condition of peers" (p. 34).

Chicago footnote: Lawrence Smith states, "The suicidal teen causes severe damage to the psychological condition of peers." [3]

CBE Number: Smith (4) has commented, "The suicidal teen causes severe damage to the psychological condition of peers."

The *default* style shown in this chapter is MLA. Figure 28 provides another sample of MLA style with sidebars to direct you to detailed instructions.

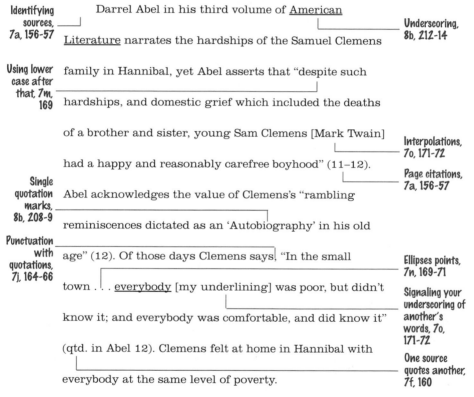

Figure 28
Conventions of style for writing notes.

Using a Computer for Note Taking

The computer affects note taking strategies in several ways:

1. You can enter your notes into the word processor using one of two methods:
   a. Write each note as a separate temporary file under a common directory so that each can be moved later into the appropriate section of your TEXT file by a COPY, READ, or INSERT

command. In other words, you should first create a directory, perhaps with the title *FAULKNER*. Second, build a set of files, each with its distinctive title, perhaps the name of a critic, *WATSON,* the name of a character, *SNOPES,* or the name of an issue, *GREED*. Periodically, you ought to print a hard copy of these notes, which should include the name of the file. You can then edit them on the printed sheets as well as on the computer monitor. *Note:* your instructor may also request a copy of these notes. Or:

b. Write all notes into a single file, labeled with a short title, such as "NOTES." With this method, your notes will be gathered in *one* file, not numerous ones. It is advisable to give each new note a code word or phrase. When you begin the actual writing of the paper, you merely open this same file of notes and begin writing at the top of the file, which will push the notes down as you write. When you need one of your notes, you can use FIND or SEARCH with the code word(s) or you can scan down through the file to find the appropriate note. Again, printing a hard copy of the notes before beginning the actual writing will provide reference points for your work. You can also move your notes easily within the one document by CUT and PASTE moves or BLOCK and COPY moves that will transfer them quickly into your text. With luck, you will finish the paper at the same time you exhaust your notes.

2. Computer notes, once keyboarded, will not need retyping. You need only move the note into your rough draft and then revise it to fit the context (see Chapter 7, "Blending Reference Material into Your Writing").

3. You can record the bibliography information for each source you encounter by listing it in a BIBLIO file so that you build the necessary list of references in one alphabetical file. Chapters 9, 10, and 11 give you the correct forms.

Developing Handwritten Notes

Handwritten notes should conform to these additional conventions:

1. *Use ink.* Write notes legibly in ink because penciled notes become blurred after repeated shuffling of the cards.

2. If you are writing by hand, use *index cards*. In fact, you might want to use two sizes of cards, one for notes and one for bibliography entries. This practice keeps the two separate.

3. *Write on one side of a card.* Material on the back of a card may be overlooked. Use the back side, if at all, for personal notes and observations, but mark the front with "OVER." Staple together two or more cards.

5b Writing Personal Notes

During your research, record *your* thoughts on the issues by writing plenty of personal notes in your research journal. Personal notes are essential because they allow you to express your discoveries, to reflect on the findings, to make connections, to explore another point of view, and to identify prevailing views and patterns of thought.

Remember, the content of a research paper is not a collection of ideas transmitted by experts in books and articles; it is an expression of your own ideas as supported by the scholarly evidence. Readers are primarily interested in *your* thesis sentence, *your* topic sentences, and *your* personal view of the issues.

Personal notes should conform to these standards:

1. The idea on the note is exclusively yours.
2. The note is labeled with "my idea," "mine," "personal thought" so that later you can be certain that it has not been borrowed.
3. The note can be a rough summary, an abstract sketch of ideas, or a complete sentence or two. Most personal notes will need to be revised later when you draft the paper.
4. The note lists other authorities who address this same issue.
5. The jottings in your research journal are original and not copied from the sources.

A sample of a personal note follows:

> My note
> ___
>
> Geraldo, Morton Downey, Jr., Oprah, and all the others will sometimes uncover a bit of truth out of the weird people interviewed, but any sense of objectivity goes out the window.

5c Writing Direct Quotation Note Cards

Copying the words of another person is the easiest type of note to write. However, you must obey the conventional rules.

1. Select quoted material that is worthy of quotation and well written, not something trivial or something that is common knowledge. NOT "John F. Kennedy was a democrat from Massachusetts" (Rupert 233) BUT "John F. Kennedy's Peace Corp left a legacy of lasting compassion for the downtrodden" (Rupert 233).
2. Use quotation marks correctly. Do not copy the words of a source into your paper in such a way that readers will think *you* wrote the material.

3. Use the author's exact words and punctuation.
4. Provide an in-text citation to author and page number, like this (Henson 34–35), or give the author's name at the beginning of the quotation and put the page number after the quotation, like this:

> Cohen, Adoni, and Bantz label the construction a <u>social</u> process "in which human beings act both as the creators and products of the social world" (34).

5. The in-text citation goes *outside* the final quotation mark but *inside* the period.
6. Write notes from both primary sources (original words by a writer or speaker) and secondary sources (comments after the fact about original works). See Section 4d, "Selecting a Mix of Both Primary and Secondary Sources," pages 95–96.
7. Try to quote key sentences and short passages, not entire paragraphs. Find the essential statement and feature it; do not force your reader to fumble through a long quoted passage in search of the relevant statement. Make the quotation a part of your work, in this way:

> Tabloid television is not merely the news as much as it is entertainment. For example, one source notes that "the networks live by the dictum 'keep it short and to the point'" so they make the news "lively" (Kuklinsky and Sigelman 821).

Quoting the Primary Sources

Frequent quotation of *primary sources* is necessary because you should cite poetry, fiction, drama, letters, and interviews. In other cases, you may want to quote liberally from a presidential speech, quote a businessman, or reproduce computer data. As shown in the next example, quote exactly, retain spacing and margins, and spell words as in the original.

> Images of frustation in Eliot's "Prufrock," 5
> -----------
> "For I have known them all already,
>   known them all:--
> Have known the evenings, mornings,
>   afternoons,
> I have measured out my life with
>   coffee spoons;
> I know the voices dying with a
>   dying fall
> Beneath the music of a farther room.
>   So how should I presume?"

The student has copied an entire unit of the poem even though she may use only a line or two. Having in her notes an entire verse (or entire paragraph of prose) assures accuracy in handling the quotation within the body of the research paper. With a computer note, you should double-space all material so that you can transfer it, without alteration, into your text.

Quoting the Secondary Sources

Quote from secondary sources for three specific reasons:

1. To display excellence in ideas *and* expression by the source.
2. To explain complex material.
3. To set up a statement of your own, especially if it spins off, adds to, or takes exception to the source as quoted.

The overuse of direct quotation from secondary sources indicates either (1) that you did not have a clear focus and copied verbatim just about everything related to the subject, or (2) that you had inadequate evidence and used numerous quotations as padding. Therefore, limit quotations from secondary sources by using only a phrase or a sentence.

Incorporate a quoted phrase into your note by making it a grammatical part of your sentence, as shown in this note:

> The geographical changes in Russia require "intensive political analysis" (German 611).

If you quote an entire sentence, make the quotation a direct object. It tells *what* the authority says. Headings on your notes will help you arrange them.

> Geographic changes in Russia
> --------------
>
> In response to the changes in Russia, one critic notes, "The American government must exercise caution and conduct intensive political analysis" (German 611).

The next writer develops two separate notes and then blends the two quotation notes to build a paragraph.

Note 1:

> TV as Reality   Keller 202
> --------------
>
> "For shows that are often referred to as 'reality' shows, there's a lot of theatre going on. 'Current Affair' and 'America's Most Wanted' are the most extreme, but others indulge in their share of re-creations. The problem is that the line between news/entertainment, fact/fiction, accuracy/effect is more than blurred--it's intentionally trampled."

Note 2:

> TV & Objectivity   Schiller 2
> --------------
> "News reports repeatedly claim that, ideally at least, they recount
> events without the intrusion of value judgments or symbols. News
> is a map, a verifiable representation, a report on reality, and hence
> not really a story at all, but merely the facts--this is the claim.
> But news--akin to any literary or cultural form--must rely upon
> conventions. Formally created and substantially embodied
> conventions alone can be used to contrive the illusion of objectivity.
> How else could we recognize news as a form of knowledge?"

Draft (Incorporates the Two Notes):

> Don Schiller says that we accept television news as reality because
> "news--akin to any literary or cultural form--must rely upon
> conventions. . . . to contrive the illusion of objectivity" (2), while
> Teresa Keller proclaims that "the problem is that the line between
> news/entertainment, fact/fiction, accuracy/effect is more than
> blurred--it's intentionally trampled" (202).

Additional examples of handling quoted materials can be found in Chapter 7.

5d Writing Paraphrased Notes

A paraphrase is the most difficult note to write. It requires you to restate in
your own words the thought, meaning, and attitude of someone else. The
paraphrase maintains the sound of your voice, sustains your style, and
avoids an endless string of direct quotations. It both interprets and rewrites.
With *interpretation* you act as a bridge between the source and the reader
as you capture the wisdom of the source in approximately the same number of words. Your *rewriting,* developed by careful reading and evaluation
of the sources, requires you to (1) name the source, (2) indicate the source's
attitude (i.e., positive, negative, ironic), and (3) rewrite the material as shown
here: "Morris Smith condemns a defendant's claim that he or she is a victim"
(21).

Keep in mind these five rules for paraphrasing a source:

1. Rewrite the original in about the same number of words.
2. Provide an in-text citation to the source (the author and page
   number in MLA style).
3. Retain exceptional words and phrases from the original by enclosing them within quotation marks.
4. Preserve the tone of the original by suggesting moods of satire,
   anger, humor, doubt, and so on. Show the author's attitude with

appropriate verbs: "Edward Zigler condemns . . . defends . . . argues . . . explains . . . observes . . . defines."

5. Put the original aside while paraphrasing to avoid copying word for word. Return to the original for comparison of the finished paraphrase with the original source to be certain that the paraphrase truly rewrites the original and that it uses quotation marks with any phrasing or key words retained from the original.

Note: When instructors see an in-text citation but no quotation marks, they will assume that you are paraphrasing, not quoting. Be sure that their assumption is true.

Here are examples that show the differences between a quotation note and a paraphrased one.

Quotation:

> Heredity   Hein 294
> --------------
>
> Fred Hein explains, "Except for identical twins, each person's heredity is unique" (294).

Paraphrased Note:

> Heredity   Hein 294
> --------------
>
> Fred Hein explains that heredity is special and distinct for each of us, unless a person is one of identical twins (294).

Quotation Note (More Than Four Lines):

> Heredity   Hein 294
> --------------
>
>   Fred Hein clarifies the phenomenon:
>   Since only half of each parent's chromosomes are
>   transmitted to a child and since this half represents a
>   chance selection of those the child could inherit, only
>   twins that develop from a single fertilized egg that
>   splits in two have identical chromosomes. (294)

(*Note:* In MLA style, long quotations require a 10-space indention.)

Paraphrased Note:

> Heredity   Hein
> --------------
>
> Hein specifies that twins have identical chromosomes because they grow from one egg that divides after it has been fertilized. He affirms that most brothers and sisters differ because of the "chance selection" of chromosomes transmitted by each parent (294).

Remember that paraphrasing keeps the length of the note about the same as the original but converts the original into your own language and style. Place any key wording of the source within quotation marks.

5e   Writing Summary Notes

You may write two types of summary notes: one, a quick sketch of material, as discussed here and, two, the more carefully drawn *précis,* as explained next in Section 5f.

The *summary note* describes and rewrites the source material without great concern for style or expression. Your purpose at the moment will be quick, concise writing without careful wording. If its information is needed, you can rewrite it later in a clear, appropriate prose style and, if necessary, return to the source for revision. Use summary notes for several types of information:

1. Source material that appears to have marginal value
2. Facts that do not fit a code word or an outline heading
3. Statistics that have questionable value for your study
4. The interesting position of a source speaking on a closely related subject but not on your specific topic
5. A reference to several works that address the same issue, as shown in this example:

   > This problem of waste disposal has been examined in books by West and Loveless and in articles by Jones et al., Coffee and Street, and Abernathy.

Like other notes, a summary needs documentation of the author and page number. However, a page number is unnecessary when the note summarizes the entire article, not a specific passage.

> TV & Reality   Epstein's Book
> --------------
> Now dated but cited by various sources, the 1973 book by Epstein seems to lay the groundwork for criticism of distorted news broadcasts.

Eventually, this summary note was incorporated into the final draft of one student's research paper, as shown here:

> Television viewers, engulfed in the world of communication, participate in the construction of symbolic reality by their perception of and belief in the presentation. Edward Jay Epstein laid the groundwork for such investigation in 1973 by showing in case after case how the networks distorted the news and did not, perhaps could not, represent reality.

5f Writing Précis Notes

A *précis* note differs from the quick summary note. It serves a specific purpose, so it deserves a polished style for transfer into the paper. It requires you to capture in just a few words the ideas of an entire paragraph, section, or chapter. Use the précis for these reasons:

- To review an article or book
- To annotate a bibliography entry
- To provide a plot summary
- To create an abstract

Success with the précis requires the following:

1. Condense the original with precision and directness. Reduce a long paragraph into a sentence, tighten an article into a brief paragraph, and summarize a book into a page.
2. Preserve the tone of the original. If the original is serious, suggest that tone in the précis. In the same way, retain moods of doubt, skepticism, optimism, and so forth.
3. Write the précis in your own language. However, retain exceptional phrases from the original, enclosing them in quotation marks. Guard against taking material out of context.
4. Provide documentation to the source and page.

Use the Précis to Review Briefly an Article or Book

The review of literature, see pages 99–103, will require you to briefly describe the contents of various articles and books. Note this example of the short review:

> On the "Fairness Doctrine" CQR 370
> --------------
>
> The CQ Researcher indicates that Congress has begun efforts to implement again the "fairness doctrine," which the Federal Communications Commission repealed in 1987. The law would require stations to air equal sides of an argument. Talk show hosts, as might be expected, are fighting the legislation.

With three sentences, the writer has made a précis of the entire article. The next précis note reviews two entire articles in only a few words.

> On Proliferation of Talk Shows McClellan
> --------------
>
> Steven McClellan has two closely related articles on this subject, but both are about the proliferation of talk shows. He opens both with "Talk, Talk, Talk."

Use the Précis to Write an Annotated Bibliography

An annotation is a sentence or paragraph that offers explanatory or critical commentary on an article or book. The précis can serve you in this case because it explains the contents of a source, as shown here:

> Steele, Janet. "TV's Talking Headaches." <u>Columbia Journalism Review</u> 31.2 (1992): 49–52. This writer examines the networks' use of experts to comment on national and international events. She finds, however, that persons with real expertise in the history of a country, its language, and its customs are bypassed for experts who have contacts, can telephone the right people, and explain what's happening, whether it is true or not.

This annotation briefly clarifies the nature of the work. It seldom extends beyond two or three sentences. The difficulty of this task is to capture the main idea of the source. (See also 4e, "Preparing an Annotated Bibliography," pages 97–99.)

Use the Précis in a Plot Summary Note

In just a few sentences a précis summarizes a novel, short story, drama, or similar literary work, as shown by this next note:

> <u>Great Expectations</u> by Dickens describes young Pip, who inherits money and can live the life of a gentleman. But he discovers that his "great expectations" have come from a criminal. With that knowledge his attitude changes from one of vanity to one of compassion.

Furnish a plot summary in your paper as a courtesy to your readers to cue them about the contents of a work. *Caution:* Make the plot summary a précis to avoid a full-blown retelling of the whole plot.

Use the Précis as the Form for an Abstract

An abstract is a brief description that appears at the beginning of an article to summarize the contents. It is, in truth, a précis. Usually, it is written by the article's author, and it helps readers make decisions about reading or skipping the article. You can find entire volumes devoted to abstracts, such as *Psychological Abstracts* or *Abstracts of English Studies.* An abstract is required for most papers in the social and natural sciences. Here's a sample from one student's paper.

> This study examines the problems of child abuse, especially the fact that families receive attention after abuse occurs, not before. With statistics on the rise, efforts devoted to prevention rather than coping should focus on parents in order to discover those

adults most likely to commit abuse because of heredity, their own childhood experiences, the economy, and mental depression. Viewing the parent as a victim, not just a criminal, will enable social agencies to institute preventive programs that may control abuse and hold together family units.

(See also pages 291–92 for the use of the abstract in a paper that uses the APA style.)

5g Writing Notes from Field Research

You will be expected to conduct field research in some instances. This work will require different kinds of notes kept on charts, cards, note pads, laboratory notebooks, a research journal, or the computer.

If you *interview* knowledgeable people, make careful notes during the interview and transcribe those notes to your draft in a polished form. A tape recorder can serve as a backup to your notetaking; however, *do* get permission. In some states it is a criminal offense to tape a conversation without expressed consent.

If you conduct a survey using a *questionnaire,* the results will become valuable data for developing notes and graphs and charts for your research paper.

If you conduct *experiments, tests,* and *measurements,* the findings serve as your notes for the "results" section of the report and will give you the basis for the "discussion" section. (See page 67.)

5h Avoiding Plagiarism

Plagiarism is purposely using another's person's writing as your own. It is a serious breach of ethics. Knowledgeable, ethical behavior is necessary whenever you handle sources and cite the words of other people.

Documenting Your Sources for a Purpose

Blending the sources into your text is a major part of the assignment as explained in Chapter 7. You will get credit if you:

- Cite borrowed ideas
- Quote a well-worded phrase (with appropriate credit to the speaker)
- Summarize the best ideas on a topic as expressed by several of the best minds (provided again that you name them).

Research writing is an exercise in critical thinking that tests your ability to collect ideas and then to share them in clear, logical progression. Therefore, one of your roles as researcher is to share with the reader the fundamental scholarship on a narrow topic. You will explain not only the subject matter, *the dangers of air bags,* but also the *literature* of the topic, the articles from the Internet and current periodicals. Rather than secretly stuffing your paper with plagiarized materials, announce boldly the name of your sources to let readers know the scope of your reading on the subject, as in this student's note:

> Christianity and Political Activists
>
> --------------
>
> Commenting on the political activities of the Christian coalition within the Republican party, Steven V. Roberts makes this observation in <u>U. S. News and World Report</u>: "These incidents have triggered a backlash among establishment Republicans who fear that religious conservatives are pulling their party too far to the right and undermining their ability to win national elections" (43).

This sentence serves the reader, who can identify the political spokesman of a national news magazine. It gives clear evidence of the writer's investigation into the subject. It is intellectually honest.

Critical Thinking Tip

To avoid plagiarism, develop personal notes full of your own ideas on a topic. Discover how you feel about the issue. Then, rather than copy sources onto your pages of text, try to synthesize the ideas of the authorities with your own thoughts by using the précis and the paraphrase. Rethink and reconsider ideas gathered by your reading, make meaningful connections, and when you refer to a specific source—as you inevitably will—give it credit.

Understanding Plagiarism So You Can Avoid It

Fundamentally, the plagiarist offers the words or ideas of another person as his/her own. A major violation is the use of another student's work or the purchase of a "canned" research paper. Also flagrantly dishonest are writers who knowingly use sources without documentation (see student version A, page 120). These two instances of plagiarism are cause enough for failure in the course.

A gray area in plagiarism is a student's carelessness that results in an error. For example, the writer fails to enclose quoted material within quotation marks, yet he or she provides an in-text citation (perhaps because the note card was mislabeled or carelessly written); or the writer's paraphrase never quite becomes paraphrase—too much of the original is left intact (see student version B, page 121). Although these cases are not flagrant instances of plagiarism, these students face the scrutiny of instructors who demand precision in citations.

Admittedly, a double standard exists. Magazine writers and newspaper reporters quote people constantly without documentation. But as an academic writer, you must document original ideas borrowed from source materials. The reason goes back to this chapter's opening discussion. Like Thomas Edison's, your research in any area borrows from others and advances your findings and theory. Somebody else, perhaps, will continue your research and carry it to another level. Without proper documentation on your part, the research will grind to a halt.

Rules for Avoiding Plagiarism

1. Let the reader know when you begin borrowing from a source by introducing the quotation or paraphrase with the name of the authority.
2. Enclose within quotation marks all quoted materials.
3. Make certain that paraphrased material has been rewritten into your own style and language. The simple rearrangement of sentence patterns is unacceptable.
4. Provide specific in-text documentation for each borrowed item, but keep in mind that styles differ for MLA, APA, the number system, and the footnote system (see Chapters 9–11).
5. Provide a bibliography entry in the "Works Cited" for every source cited in the paper.

Quotation marks are an absolute *must* when using someone else's exact words. Citing a page number to the source is good, but you must also put quotation marks around a key word, a phrase, or a clause if the words are not your own.

These are the rules, but facts available as common knowledge are exceptions. Even though you might read it in a source, you need not cite the fact that Illinois is known as the "Land of Lincoln," that Chicago is its largest city, or that Springfield is the capital city. Information of this sort requires *no* in-text citation, as shown in the following example.

> The flat rolling hills of Illinois form part of the great midwestern Corn Belt. It stretches from its border with Wisconsin in the north to the Kentucky border in the south. Its political center is Springfield in the center of the state, but its industrial/commercial center is Chicago, that great boisterous city camped on the shores of Lake Michigan.

However, if you borrow specific ideas or exact wording from a source, you must provide an in-text citation to the source.

> Early Indian tribes on the plains called themselves Illiniwek (which meant strong men), and French settlers pronounced the name Illinois (Angle 44).

Here are two more examples: the first needs no documentation, but the second does because the opinion belongs to the source.

> President George Bush launched the Desert Storm attack against Iraq with the support of allies and their troops from several nations.

> Bush demonstrated great mastery in his diplomatic unification of a politically diverse group of allies (Wolford 46).

Checklist for Common Knowledge Exceptions

Would an intelligent person know this information?
Did you know it before you discovered it in the source?
Is it encyclopedia-type information?
Has this information become general knowledge by being reported repeatedly in many different sources?

The next four examples in MLA style will demonstrate the differences between genuine research writing and plagiarism. First is the original reference material; it is followed by four student versions, two of which constitute plagiarism and two of which do not.

Original Material

> Despite the growth of these new technologies and the importance of the mass media in our lives, our schools have failed to do anything in the way of developing a systematic curriculum aimed at helping students to understand the form, content, ownership, and organization of the mass media.—David M. Considine, "Visual Literacy and the Curriculum: More to It Than Meets the Eye," *Language Arts* 64 (1987): 635.

> While schools continue to operate as though print were the main means of communication in our culture, an increasingly high-tech society requires a new definition of literacy that encompasses visual, computer, and media literacy.—Considine 639.

Student Version A (Unacceptable)

> Despite new technology that makes the mass media important in our lives, the schools have failed to develop a systematic curriculum aimed at helping students to understand television. In fact, schools operate as though print were the main means of communication in our culture. But young people have a high-tech, visual sense of communication.

This piece of writing is a clear example of plagiarism. Material stolen without documentation is obvious. The writer has simply borrowed abundantly from the original source, even to the point of retaining the essential wording. The writer has provided no documentation whatsoever, nor has the writer named the authority. In truth, the writer implies to the reader that these sentences are an original creation when, actually, nothing belongs to the writer.

The next version is better, but it still demonstrates blatant disregard for scholarly conventions.

Student Version B (Unacceptable)

Modern communication technology is here to stay and cannot be ignored. We live in the information age, bombarded by television and radio in our homes and automobiles, annoyed by ringing telephones, and infatuated by computers and their modems for networking across the nation. Despite this new technology that makes the mass media important in our lives, the schools have failed to develop a systematic curriculum aimed at helping students to understand television. In fact, schools operate as though print were the main means of communication in our culture. But young people have a high-tech, visual sense of communication (Considine 635–39).

Although this version provides original opening sentences by the student and a citation to the authority David Considine, it contains two serious errors. First, readers cannot know that the citation "(Considine 635–39)" refers to most of the paragraph; readers can only assume that the citation refers to the final sentence. Second, the borrowing from Considine is not paraphrased properly; it contains far too much of Considine's language—words that should be enclosed within quotation marks.

The next version is correct and proper.

Student Version C (Acceptable)

Modern communication technology is here to stay and cannot be ignored. We live in the information age, bombarded by television and radio in our homes and automobiles, annoyed by ringing telephones, and infatuated by computers and their modems for networking across the nation. David Considine sees the conflict as chalk boards and talking by teachers versus an environment of electronic marvels (635). He argues, "While schools continue to operate as though print were the main means of communication in our culture, an increasingly high-tech society requires a new definition of literacy that encompasses visual, computer, and media literacy" (639).

This version represents a satisfactory handling of the source material. The authority is acknowledged at the outset of the borrowing, a key section has been paraphrased in the student's own words with a correct page citation to Considine's article, and another part has been quoted directly with page citation at the end.

Let's suppose, however, that the writer does not wish to quote directly at all. The following example shows a paraphrased version:

Student Version D (Acceptable)

Modern communication technology is here to stay and cannot be ignored. We live in the information age, bombarded by television and radio in our homes and automobiles, annoyed by ringing telephones, and infatuated by computers and their modems for networking across the nation. David Considine sees the conflict as chalk boards and talking by teachers versus an environment of electronic marvels (635). He argues that our public schools function with print media almost exclusively, while the children possess a complex feel and understanding of modern electronics in their use of computers, television, and other media forms (639).

This version also represents a satisfactory handling of the source material. In this case, no direct quotation is employed, and the authority is acknowledged and credited, yet the entire paragraph is paraphrased in the student's own language.

Required Instances for Citing a Source

1. An original idea derived from a source, whether quoted or paraphrased.

   Genetic engineering, by which a child's body shape and intellectual ability is predetermined, raises memories of Nazi attempts in eugenics (Riddell 19).

2. Your summary of original ideas by a source.

   Genetic engineering has been described as the rearrangement of the genetic structure in animals or in plants, which is a technique that takes a section of DNA and reattaches it to another section (Rosenthal 19–20).

3. Factual information that is not common knowledge.

   Genetic engineering has its risks: a nonpathogenic organism might be converted into a pathogenic one or an undesirable trait might develop as a result of a mistake (Madigan 51).

4. Any exact wording copied from a source.

   Kenneth Woodward asserts that genetic engineering is "a high stakes moral rumble that involves billions of dollars and affects the future" (68).

6 Writing the Paper

Meals, class sessions, social functions, daydreaming—these activities and others interfere with drafting a long paper. Because of many starts and stops, do not expect a polished product at first. Treat the initial draft as exploratory, one that examines both your knowledge and the strength of your evidence. At this point, supporting evidence may be weak, and you may need to abandon the manuscript at times to retrace previous steps—reading, researching, and note taking.

If you get writer's block and find yourself staring at the wall, relax and learn to enjoy the break rather than get frustrated. Lean back in your chair and change depression into prime time for reflecting. Nature has a way of reminding us that we need to pause now and then, catch our breath, and rethink our problems. Even if the manuscript is only a page or two, read back over your writing. Rereading might restart your thought processes.

Three rules for drafting may serve your needs:

Be practical. Write what you know and feel, not what you think somebody wants to hear. Write portions of the paper when you are ready, not only when you arrive there by outline sequence. If necessary, leave blank spots on the page to remind you that more evidence will be required.

Be uninhibited. Initial drafts must be attempts to get words on the page rather than to create a polished document. Write without fear or delay.

Be judicious. Treat the sources with respect—citing names, enclosing quotations, and providing page numbers to the sources.

Write without procrastination or fear, reminding yourself that a first draft is a time for discovery. Later, during the revision period, you can strengthen skimpy paragraphs, refine your prose, and rearrange material to maintain the momentum of your argument.

Begin with these tasks:

1. Refine your thesis sentence (6a).
2. Write a title that identifies your key terms (6b).

3. Understand your purpose and your role as a writer (6c).
4. Begin writing from your notes and outline (6d).

6a Writing a Final Thesis Sentence

A thesis sentences expresses a theory that you hope to support with your evidence and arguments. It is a proposition that you want to maintain, analyze, and prove. Thus, it functions as the principal component of any theoretical presentation. A final thesis sentence will:

1. Set the argument to control and focus the entire paper.
2. Give order to details of the essay by providing unity and a sense of direction.
3. Specify to the reader the point of the research.

For example, one student started with the topic "television talk shows." The student narrowed it to "truth and reality on television talk shows." Ultimately, this thesis emerged:

> Television objectivity is nothing more than an ideal which can never be perfectly presented by any broadcast nor perceived by any viewer.

This statement focuses the argument on the objective/subjective nature of television broadcasting. Without such focus, the student might have drifted into other areas and confused his readers.

Using Questions to Focus the Argument

If you have trouble focusing on a thesis sentence, ask yourself a few questions. One of the answers might serve as the thesis.

What is the point of my research?

THESIS   Recent research demonstrates that self-guilt often prompts a teenager to commit suicide.

What do I want this paper to do?

THESIS   The public needs to understand that advertisers who use blatant sexual images have little regard for moral scruples and ordinary decency.

Can I tell the reader anything new or different?

THESIS   The evidence indicates clearly that most well water in the county is unsafe for drinking.

Do I have a solution to the problem?

THESIS   Public support for "safe" houses will provide a haven for children who are abused by their parents.

Do I have a new slant and new approach to the issue?

THESIS   Personal economics is a force to be reckoned with, so poverty, not greed, forces many youngsters into a life of crime.

Should I take the minority view of this matter?

THESIS   Give credit where it is due: Custer may have lost the battle at Little Bighorn, but Crazy Horse and his men, with inspiration from Sitting Bull, *won* the battle.

What exactly is my theory about this subject?

THESIS   Trustworthy employees, not mechanical safeguards on computers and software, will prevent theft of software, sabotage of mainframes, and destruction of crucial files.

These sample thesis sentences all use a declarative sentence that focuses the argument toward an investigative issue that will be resolved in the paper's general discussion and conclusion. The thesis may also be expressed as an enthymeme (see Chapter 1, pages 20–21).

Using Key Words to Focus Your Argument

Use the important words from your notes and rough outline to refine your thesis sentence. For example, during your reading of several novels or short stories by Ernest Hemingway, you might have jotted down certain repetitions of image or theme or character. The key words might be "death," "loss of masculinity," "the code of the hero," or other issues that Hemingway explored time and again. These concrete ideas might point you toward a general thesis, such as one of these:

The tragic endings of Hemingway's stories force his various heroes into stoic resignation to fate.

Hemingway's code of the hero includes a crippling degree of pessimism that clouds the overstated bravado.

Final Thesis Checklist
The thesis will fall short of expectations if it fails to answer "yes" to each question that follows:

1. Does it express your position in a full, declarative sentence, which is not a question, not a statement of purpose, and not merely a topic?
2. Does it limit the subject to a narrow focus that grows out of research?
3. Does it establish an investigative, inventive edge to the discovery, interpretation, or theoretical presentation?

Adjust Your Thesis During Research If Necessary

Abandon your preliminary thesis if research leads you to new, different issues. For example, one writer began research on child abuse with this preliminary thesis: "A need for a cure to child abuse faces society each day." Investigation, however, narrowed her focus: "Parents who abuse their children should be treated as victims, not criminals." The writer moved, in effect, to a specific position from which to argue that social organizations should serve abusing parents in addition to their help to abused children.

6b   Writing a Title

Develop early a clearly expressed title which, like a good thesis sentence, will control your writing and keep you on course. However, the title may not be feasible until the paper is written. In either case, the title should provide specific words of identification. For example, one writer began with this title: "Television Reality Check." To make it more specific, the writer added another phrase: "Television Reality Check: The Fine Line between Fact and Fiction on Talk Shows." Readers thereby have a clear concept about the contents of the research paper. Note that long titles are standard in scholarly writing. Consider the following strategies for writing your title.

1. Name a general subject, followed by a colon and a phrase that renames the subject.

   Computer Control: Software Safeguards and Computer Theft

2. Name a general subject and narrow it with a prepositional phrase.

   Gothic Madness in Three Southern Writers

3. Name a general subject and cite a specific work that will illuminate the topic.

   Religious Imagery in Faulkner's <u>The Sound and the Fury</u>

4. Name a general subject, followed by a colon, and followed by a phrase that describes the type of study.

   Black Dialect in Maya Angelou's Poetry: A Language Study

5. Name a general subject, followed by a colon, and followed by a question.

   AIDS: Where Did It Come From?

6. Establish a specific comparison.

   Religious Imagery in Momaday's <u>The Names</u> and Storm's <u>Seven Arrows</u>

Be sure to avoid fancy literary titles that may fail to label issues under discussion.

POOR	"Let There Be Hope."
BETTER	"Let There Be Hope: A View of Child Abuse."
BEST	"Child Abuse: A View of the Victims."

For placement of the title, see "Title Page or Opening Page," pages 173–75.

6c Understanding Your Purpose and Your Role as a Writer

Your writing style in a research paper needs to be factual, but it should also display human emotion. Build your research paper around the facts of the study and your feelings about the topic. As an objective writer, you will need to offer evidence and analysis and keep a distance from the subject. You must examine a problem, make your claim (your thesis sentence), and produce your supporting evidence. As a subjective writer, you should argue with flashes of human passion about the subject. Complete objectivity, then, is unlikely for any research paper, which displays in fact and form an intellectual argument. Of course, you must avoid the extremes of subjective writing—demanding, insisting, quibbling. Moderation of your voice, even during argument, suggests control of the situation—both emotionally and intellectually.

You will win the audience to your point of view in two ways.

1. **Ethical appeal.** The reader will recognize your deep interest in the subject and your carefully crafted argument if you project the image of one who knows and cares about the topic.
2. **Logical appeal.** The reader may believe in your position if you provide sufficient evidence in the form of statistics, paraphrases, and direct quotations from authorities on the subject.

For example, in an examination of *automobile airbags,* a writer might remain objective in presenting the evidence and statistics; yet the ethical problem remains close to the surface: children need protection from the explosive power of the airbags.

6d Drafting the Paper from Your Notes and Outline

At some point you must write a draft of the whole paper. You may work systematically through the outline, or you may start anywhere in order to write what you know at the time, keeping the pieces of manuscript controlled by your thesis and overall plan. Your notes will usually keep you focused on the subject.

In the initial draft, leave plenty of space as you write—wide margins, double-spacing, and blank spaces between some paragraphs. The open areas will invite your revisions and additions later on. If you write on a word processor, the process is simplified because the paper is keyboarded one time and revisions can take place on the computer screen.

Use your notes and research journal to:

Transfer personal notes, with modification, into the draft.
Transcribe précis notes and paraphrased materials directly into the text.
Quote primary sources.
Quote secondary sources from notes.

Write with caution when working from photocopied pages of articles or books. You will be tempted to borrow too much. Quote or paraphrase key phrases and sentences; do not quote an entire paragraph unless it is crucial to your discussion and you cannot easily reduce it to a précis.

Citing More Than One Source in a Paragraph

Readers want to discover your thoughts and ideas. For this reason, a paragraph should seldom contain source material only; it needs at least a topic sentence to establish a point for the research evidence. Every paragraph should explain, analyze, and support a thesis, not merely string together research information. The following passage cites effectively two different sources.

> Tabloid television is not so much news as entertainment. One source notes that "the networks live by the dictum 'keep it short and to the point,'" so they make the news "lively" (Kuklinsky and Sigelman 821). Many programs, "Hard Copy" and "A Current Affair" come to mind, go for "show over substance with an ongoing commentary to let listeners know how they should be reacting and to keep emotional involvement high" (Keller 201). The re-creations of some newscasts are designed, according to Keller, for the same scintillating purpose, "show over substance," an enhancement or abbreviation of the facts, a breach of objectivity (201).

This passage illustrates four points. A writer must:

- Weave the sources effectively into a whole.
- Cite each source separately, one at a time.
- Provide different in-text citations.
- Use the sources as a natural extension of the discussion.

Note: Drafting a paragraph or two by using different methods of development is one way to build the body of your paper, but only if each part fits the purpose and design of your work. Write a comparison paragraph, classify and analyze one or two issues, show cause and effect, and ask a question and answer it. Sooner than you think, you will draft the body of the paper. See 6g for detailed discussion of these methods of development.

Writing from Your Outline and Notes

If you have not used a word processor to store your notes, you should now gather all materials and begin typing. Follow the outline in a general way so that the notes expand the outline. Let the writing find its own way, guided but not controlled by your preliminary plans. Consult also the paradigm (see 3b) that best fits your design. Weave source material into the paper as support of *your* ideas, not as filler. Your handwritten notes will let the essay grow, blossom, and reach up to new levels of knowledge.

If you have developed your outline and notes on a word processor, you can draft the paper from your outline and notes. You can do this in several ways, and you may even have a method beyond the four mentioned here.

Method one requires the complete outline on file so that you can enter information onto the screen underneath any of the outline headings as you develop ideas (see Chapter 3 for details on outlining). You can import your notes to a specific location of the outline. This technique allows you to work anywhere within the paper to match your interest of the moment with a section of your outline. In effect, you expand your outline into the first draft of your research paper.

Method two requires separate note files within a specially named directory, as explained in 5a. All your note files will be located here, so during the drafting stage, you can use the INSERT, COPY, or READ command to transfer your notes into your text.

Method three assumes that you have placed all your notes within one file. Begin writing your paper in a new file. As you need a note, minimize this text file and maximize your file of notes. Find the note you wish to transfer, highlight it, and then CUT or COPY it. Go back to your text file and PASTE the note into your text.

Method four assumes that you have placed all your notes within one file and that you have labeled each with a code word or title. Begin drafting your paper at the top of this file, which will push the notes below as you write. When you need a note, use FIND or SEARCH with the code word or title. The computer will place you at the note, which you can highlight and cut. Then, back at your draft, you can paste it into your text.

Safeguarding Your Work on a Computer

As you enter text be sure that you SAVE the material every page or so. This command inscribes your writing onto the diskette or hard drive so that it will not be lost if the computer suddenly shuts down for any reason—a power failure or accidental unplugging of the machine.

When finished with your initial typing, do two things. First, copy the file onto two floppy diskettes. Second, have the computer print a copy of your paper in double or triple spacing. See also "Using the Computer to Edit Your Text," pages 148–50.

Transferring Graphics into the Text

You may create graphic designs and transfer them into your text. Some computers allow you to create bar, line, or pie graphs as well as spreadsheets and other original designs. Some computer software includes ready-made graphics. Such materials can enhance the quality of your presentation. After you create a table or locate a graphic design, transfer it to the body of your text and resize it to fit your space. Use four-color art if your printer will print in four colors.

Place a full-page graphic design on a separate sheet after making a textual reference to it on the previous page of text, such as "see Table 7." Place graphic designs in an appendix when you have several complex items that might distract the reader from your textual message. In all cases, conform to standard rules for numbering, labeling, and presenting tables and illustrations. (See pages 195–99 for rules and examples.) Finally, use graphic designs and tables *only* where appropriate. Do not substitute clip art for good, solid prose or use figures and text art to dazzle the reader when your information is shaky.

Writing in the Proper Tense

Verb tense often distinguishes a paper in the humanities from one in the natural and social sciences. MLA style and the footnote style both require the present tense to cite an author's work (e.g., "Johnson *explains*" or "the work of Elmford and Mills *shows*"). In contrast, APA style and CBE style both require the past tense or present perfect tense to cite an author's work (e.g., "Johnson *discovered* or "the work of Elmford and Mills *has demonstrated*").

MLA style requires that you use the present tense for comments by you and by the sources because the ideas and the words of the writers remain in print and continue to be true in the universal present. MLA usage demands

"Richard Ellmann argues" or "Eudora Welty writes" rather than past tense verb forms: "argued" or "wrote." Therefore, when writing a paper in the humanities, use the historical present tense, as shown here:

> "It was the best of times, it was the worst of times," writes Charles Dickens about the eighteenth century.

> Johnson argues that sociologist Norman Wayman has a "narrow-minded view of clerics and their role in the community" (64).

Use the past tense in a humanities paper only for reporting historical events. In the next example, past tense is appropriate for all sentences except the last:

> In 1876 Alexander Graham Bell invented the telephone. Signals, sounds, and music had been sent by wire before, but Bell's instrument was the first to transmit speech. Bell's story is a lesson in courage, one worthy of study by any would-be inventor.

See Chapters 10 and 11 for a full discussion of tense usage in scientific writing, as shown here:

> Matthews (1989) designed the experiment and, since that time, several investigators have used the method (Thurman, 1990; Jones, 1991).

Note: The scientific style *does* require present tense when you discuss the results, for example, *the results confirm* or *diuretic therapy helps control hypertension.*

Using the Language of the Discipline

Every discipline and every topic has its own vocabulary. Therefore, while reading and taking notes, jot down words and phrases relevant to the study. Get comfortable with them so you can use them effectively. For example, a child abuse topic requires the language of sociology, psychology, and medicine, thereby demanding an acquaintance with:

social worker	behavioral patterns	trauma
poverty levels	formative years	hostility
battered child	aggressive behavior	stress
maltreatment	incestuous relations	guardians

Similarly, a poetry paper might require *symbolism, imagery, rhythm, persona,* or *rhyme.* Many writers compose a terminology list to strengthen noun and verb usage. However, nothing will betray a writer's ignorance of the subject matter more quickly than awkward and distorted technical terminology. For example, the following sentence uses big words, but it distorts and scrambles the language:

> The enhancement of learning opportunities is often impeded by a pathological disruption in a child's mental processes.

The words may be large, but what does the passage mean? Probably this:

> Education is often interrupted by a child's abnormal behavior.

Writing in the Third Person

Write your paper with an impersonal effaced narration that avoids "I believe" or "It is my opinion." Rather than saying, "I think objectivity on television is nothing more than an ideal," just drop the opening two words and say, "Objectivity on television is nothing more than an ideal." Readers will understand that the statement is your thought. However, attribute human functions to yourself or other persons, not to nonhuman sources:

WRONG   The total study considered several findings.
CORRECT   This writer considered the findings of several sources.

Writing with Unity and Coherence

Unity gives writing a single vision; coherence connects the parts. Your paper has *unity* if it explores one topic in depth, with each paragraph carefully expanding upon a single aspect of the narrowed subject. It has *coherence* if the parts are connected logically by:

- repetition of key words and sentence structures,
- the judicious use of pronouns and synonyms,
- the effective placement of transitional words and phrases (e.g., *also, furthermore, therefore, in addition,* and *thus*).

The next passage moves with unity and coherence.

> Talk shows are spectacles and forms of ⌊dramatic⌋ entertainment; ⌊therefore⌋, members of the studio audience are ⌊acting⌋ out parts in the ⌊drama⌋, like a Greek chorus, just as the host, the guest, and the television viewers are ⌊actors⌋ as well. ⌊Furthermore⌋, some sort of interaction with the "characters" in this made-for-television ⌊"drama"⌋ happens all the time. If we read a book or attend a play, ⌊we question⌋ the text, ⌊we question⌋ the presentation, and ⌊we determine⌋ for ourselves what it means to us.

6e Writing the Introduction of the Paper

Use the first few paragraphs of your paper to establish the nature of your study. It should be long enough to establish the required elements described in this checklist.

Checklist for the Introduction

SUBJECT   Identify your specific topic, and then define, limit, and narrow it to one issue.

BACKGROUND   Provide relevant historical data. Discuss a few key sources that touch on your specific issue. If writing about a major figure, give relevant biographical facts, but not an encyclopedia-type survey. (See "Providing Background Information," page 134.)

PROBLEM   The point of a research paper is to explore or resolve a problem, so identify and explain the complications that you see. The examples shown on pages 134–37 demonstrate this technique.

THESIS SENTENCE   Within the first few paragraphs, use your thesis sentence to establish the direction of the study and to point your readers toward your eventual conclusions. (See "Opening with Your Thesis Statement," which follows below.)

How you work these essential elements into the framework of your opening will depend upon your style of writing. They need not appear in this order. Nor should you cram all these items into a short, opening paragraph. Feel free to write two or three paragraphs of the introduction, let it run over onto page two, if necessary. When crafting your introduction, use more than one of the techniques described in the following paragraphs.

Opening With Your Thesis Statement

Generally, the thesis statement will appear in the final paragraph of the general opening, although it sometimes begins a research paper. For example, this opening features the thesis first:

> Shoplifting in stores all over America has reached the point that all shoppers are suspects; each of us is photographed, followed, and watched. — **Thesis** The people who use the "five-finger discount" come from all walks of life --the unemployed, sure, but also doctors, lawyers, and even public officials. As a result, clerks in many retail stores look at us with ill will, not friendliness, and they treat us with suspicion, not trust.

Relating to the Well Known

This next opening suggests the significance of the subject as it appeals to the popular interest and knowledge of the reader:

Popular appeal —
| Television flashes images into our living rooms, radios invade the confines of our automobiles, and local newspapers flash their headlines to us daily. | However, one medium that has gained great popularity and influence within the past decade is the specialized magazine.

Providing Background Information

At times, it is important to trace the historical nature of your topic, give biographical data about a person, or provide general evidence. A summary of a novel, long poem, or other work can refresh a reader's memory about details of plot, character, and so forth.

Background —
| First published in 1915, *Spoon River Anthology* by Edgar Lee Masters gives readers candid glimpses into the life of a small town at the turn of the twentieth century. | Speaking from beyond the grave, the narrator gives a portrait of happy, fulfilled people or draws pictures of lives filled with sadness and melancholy.

This opening technique offers essential background matter, not information that is irrelevant to the thesis. For example, explaining that Eudora Welty was born in Jackson, Mississippi, in 1909 would contribute little to the following opening:

Background —
| In 1941 Eudora Welty published her first book of short stories, A Curtain of Green. That group of stories was followed by The Wide Net (1943) and The Bride of the Innisfallen (1955). | Each collection brought her critical acclaim, but taken together the three volumes established her as one of America's premier short story writers.

Reviewing the Literature

This opening procedure cites only books and articles relevant to the specific issue. It briefly introduces some of the literature connected with the topic. It gives distinction to your study because it establishes the scholarship on the subject. It also distinguishes your point of view by explaining the logical connections and differences between previous research and your work:

Review of literature —
| Billy Budd possesses many characteristics of the Bible. Melville's story depicts the "loss of Paradise" (Arvin 294); it serves as a gospel story (Weaver 37-38); and it hints at a moral and solemn purpose (Watson 319). | Throughout his tale, Melville

intentionally uses biblical references as means of portraying and distinguishing various characters, ideas, and symbols, and of presenting different moral principles by which people may govern their lives. The story explores the biblical passions of one man's confrontation with good and evil (Howard 327-328; Mumford 248).

Reviewing the History and Background of the Subject

This method reviews the scholarly history of the topic, usually with quotations from the sources, as shown below in APA style:

Autism, a neurological dysfunction of the brain which commences before the age of thirty months, was identified by Leo Kanner (1943). Kanner studied eleven cases, all of which showed a specific type of childhood psychosis that was different from other childhood disorders, although each was similar to childhood schizophrenia. Kanner described the characteristics of the infantile syndrome as:

1. Extreme autistic aloneness
2. Language abnormalities
3. Obsessive desire for the maintenance of sameness
4. Good cognitive potential
5. Normal physical development
6. Highly intelligent, obsessive, and cold parents

Background information

Ruter (1978) has reduced these symptoms to four criteria: onset within 30 months of birth, poor social development, late language development, and a preference for regular, stereotyped activity. In the United States, autism affects one out of 2,500 children, and is not usually diagnosed until the child is between two and five years of age (Koegel & Schreibman, 1981).

Taking Exception to Critical Views

This opening procedure identifies the subject, establishes a basic view taken by the literature, and then differs with or takes exception with the critical position of other writers, as shown in the following example:

Lorraine Hansberry's popular and successful <u>A Raisin in the Sun</u>, which first appeared on Broadway in 1959, is a problem play of a black family's determination to escape a Chicago ghetto to a better life in the suburbs. There is agreement that this escape theme explains the drama's conflict and its role in the black movement (e.g., Oliver, Archer, and especially Knight, who describes the Youngers as "an entire family that has become aware of, and is determined to combat, racial discrimination in a supposedly democratic land" [34]). Yet another issue lies at the

Exception to prevailing rules — heart of the drama. Hansberry develops a modern view of black matriarchy in order to examine both the cohesive and the conflict-producing effects it has on the individual members of the Younger family.

Challenging an Assumption

This opening technique establishes a well known idea or general theory in order to question and analyze it, challenge it, or refute it.

Challenge to an assumption — Christianity dominates the religious life of most Americans to the point that many assume that it dominates the world population as well. However, despite the denominational missionaries who have reached out to every corner of the globe, only one out of every four people on the globe is a Christian, and far fewer than that practice their faith (Walters 62).

Providing a Brief Summary

When the subject is a novel, long poem, book, or other work that can be summarized, a very brief summary refreshes the memory of the reader:

Summary — Ernest Hemingway's novel <u>The Old Man and the Sea</u> narrates the ordeal of an old Cuban fisherman, Santiago, who manages to endure a test of strength when locked in a tug of war with a giant marlin that he hooks and later when he fights sharks who attack his small boat. The heroic and stoic nature of this old hero reflects the traditional Hemingway code.

Or

Summary — Alice Walker's <u>The Color Purple</u> narrates the ordeal of a young black girl living in Georgia in the early years of the twentieth century. Celie writes letters to God because she has no one else to help her. The letters are unusually strong and give evidence of Celie's painful struggle to survive the multiple horrors

Defining Key Terms

Some opening methods explain difficult terminology, as shown with the following example:

Definition — Black matriarchy, a sociological concept with origins in slavery, is a family situation, according to E. Earl Baughman, in which no husband is present or, if he is present, in which the wife and/or mother exercises the main influence over family affairs (80–81). Hansberry develops a modern view of black matriarchy in order to examine the conflict-producing effects it has on the individual members of the Younger family.

Supplying Data, Statistics, and Special Evidence

This routine for the opening uses special evidence to attract the reader and establish the subject. For example, the opening about autism by Patti M. Bracy, see page 135, cites 11 cases studied by Kanner, it lists six characteristics of autism, and it mentions that one out of every 2,500 children are affected. A student working with demographics might compare the birth and death rates of certain sections of the world. In Europe, the rates are almost constant while the African nations have birth rates that are 30 percent higher than the death rates. Statistical evidence can be a useful tool in many papers, but complement it with clear, textual discussion.

Avoiding Certain Mistakes in the Opening

Avoid a purpose statement, such as "The purpose of this study is . . ." unless your writing reports empirical research, in which case you *should* explain the purpose of your study (see Chapter 10, "Writing in APA Style").

Avoid repetition of the title, which should appear on the first page of the text anyway.

Avoid complex or difficult questions that may puzzle the reader. However, general rhetorical questions are acceptable.

Avoid simple dictionary definitions, such as "Webster defines *monogamy* as marriage with only one person at a time." See page 140 for an acceptable opening that features definition, and for ways to define key terminology.

Avoid humor.

Avoid hand-drawn artwork but *do* use computer graphics, tables, and other designs that are appropriate to your subject.

Avoid a quotation that has no context; that is, you have not blended it into the discussion clearly and effectively.

6f Writing the Body of the Research Paper

When writing the body, you should trace, classify, compare, and analyze the various issues. Keep in mind three elements, as shown here:

Checklist for the Body of the Paper	
ANALYSIS	Classify the major issues of the study an[d] careful analysis of each in defense of you[r]
PRESENTATION	Provide well-reasoned statements at the [ ] your paragraphs, and supply evidence o[f] proper documentation.
PARAGRAPHS	Offer a variety of development to comp[lete the] process, narrate the history of the subje[ct] causes, and so forth.

Your paragraphs ought to be about one-half page in length or longer. You can accomplish this task only by writing good topic sentences and by developing them fully. Almost every paragraph you write in the body of the research paper is, in one way or another, *explanatory*. You must state your position in a good topic sentence and then list and evaluate your evidence.

The techniques described in the following paragraphs demonstrate how to build substantive paragraphs for your paper. The sample research papers presented on pages 214–18 and 218–31 may also prove helpful in demonstrating how several writers have built papers with well-developed paragraphs to explore their complex topics.

Relating a Time Sequence

Use *chronology* and *plot summary* to trace historical events and to survey a story or novel. You should, almost always, discuss the significance of the events. This first example traces historical events.

Quick — summary | Following the death of President Roosevelt in April 1945, Harry S. Truman succeeded to the Presidency. | Although he was an experienced politician, Truman "was ill prepared to direct a foreign policy," especially one that "called for the use of the atomic bomb to bring World War II to an end" (Jeffers 56). Consideration must be directed at the circumstances of the time, which lead up to Truman's decision that took the lives of over 100,000 individuals and destroyed four square miles of the city of Hiroshima. Consideration must be given to the impact that this decision had on the war, on Japan, and on the rest of the world. Consideration must be directed at the man who brought the twentieth century into the atomic age.

The next passage shows the use of plot summary.

Quick plot summary — | John Updike's "A & P" is a short story about a young grocery clerk named Sammy, who feels trapped by the artificial values of the small town where he lives and, in an emotional moment, quits his job. | The store manager, Lengel, is the voice of the conservative values in the community. For him, the girls in swimsuits pose a disturbance to his store, so he expresses his displeasure by reminding the girls that the A & P is not the beach (1088). Sammy, a liberal, believes the girls may be out of place in the A & P only because of its "fluorescent lights," "stacked packages," and "checkerboard green-and-cream-rubber-tile floor," all artificial things (1086).

> ***Note:*** Keep the plot summary short and relate it to your thesis, as shown by the first sentence in the passage above. Do not allow the plot summary to extend beyond one paragraph; otherwise, you may retell the entire story. Your task is to make a point, not retell the story.

Comparing or Contrasting Issues, Critics, and Literary Characters

Employ *comparison* and *contrast* to show the two sides of a subject, to compare two characters, to compare the past with the present, or to compare positive and negative issues. The next passage compares and contrasts the differences in forest conservation techniques.

> To burn or not to burn the natural forests in the national parks is the question. The pyrophobic public voices its protests while environmentalists praise the rejuvenating effects of a good forest fire. It is difficult to convince people that not all fire is bad. The public has visions of Smokey the Bear campaigns and mental images of Bambi and Thumper fleeting the roaring flames. Perhaps the public could learn to see beauty in fresh green shoots, like Bambi and Faline as they returned to raise their young. Chris Bolgiano explains that federal policy evolved slowly "from the basic impulse to douse all fires immediately to a sophisticated decision matrix based on the functions of any given unit of land" (22). Bolgiano declares that "timber production, grazing, recreation, and wilderness preservation elicit different fire-management approaches" (23).

— Comparison and contrast

Developing Cause and Effect

Write *cause and effect* paragraphs to develop the reasons for a circumstance or to examine the consequences. An example is shown here which not only explains with cause and effect but also uses the device of analogy, which is a metaphoric comparison of bread dough and the uniform expansion of the universe.

> To see how the Hubble Law implies uniform, centerless expansion of a universe, imagine that you want to make a loaf of raisin bread. As the dough rises, the expansion pushes the raisins away from each other. Two raisins that were originally about one centimeter apart separate more slowly than raisins that were about four centimeters apart. The uniform expansion of the dough causes the raisins to move apart at speeds proportional to their distances. Helen Write, in explaining the theory of Edwin Powell Hubble, says the farther the space between them, the faster two galaxies will move away from each other. This is the basis for Hubble's theory of the expanding universe (369).

— Analogy

Cause and effect

Defining Your Key Terminology

Use *definition* to explain and expand upon a complex subject. This next example defines "steroids" and briefly explains the consequences of consumption by athletes:

Definition —
Football players and weightlifters often use anabolic steroids to "bulk out." According to Oakley Ray, "Steroids are synthetic modifications of testosterone that are designed to enhance the anabolic actions and decrease the androgenic effects." He says the anabolic substance, which improves the growth of muscles, is an action caused by testosterone, a male sex hormone. Anabolism, then, increases the growth of muscle tissue (Ray 81).

Showing a Process

Draft a *process* paragraph that explains stage by stage the steps necessary to achieve a desired end:

Process —
Blood doping is a process for increasing an athlete's performance on the day of competition. To perform this procedure, technicians drain about one liter of blood from the competitor about 10 months prior to the event. This time allows the "hemoglobin levels to return to normal" (Ray 79). Immediately prior to the athletic event, the blood is reintroduced by injection to give a rush of blood into the athlete's system. Ray reports that the technique produces an "average decrease of 45 seconds in the time it takes to run five miles on a treadmill" (80).

Asking Questions and Providing Answers

Framing a question as a topic sentence gives you the opportunity to develop a thorough answer with specific details and evidence. Look at how a question and answer are used in this example:

Questions and answers —
Does America have enough park lands? The lands now designated as national and state parks, forest, and wildland total in excess of 33 million acres. Yet environmentalists call for additional protected land. They warn of imbalances in the environment. Dean Fraser, in his book, The People Problem, addresses the question of whether we have enough park land:

Yosemite, in the summer, is not unlike Macy's the week before Christmas. In 1965 it had over 1.6 million visitors; Yellowstone over 2 million. The total area of federal plus state-owned parks is now something like 33 million acres, which sounds impressive until it is divided by the total number of annual visitors of something over 400 million. . . . (33)

We are running short of green space, which is being devoured by highways, housing projects, and industrial development.

Citing Evidence from the Source Materials

Citing evidence from the various authorities in the form of quotations, paraphrases, and summaries to support your topic sentences is another excellent way to frame a paragraph. This next passage combines commentary by a critic and a poet to explore Thomas Hardy's pessimism in fiction and poetry.

Several critics reject the impression of Thomas Hardy as a pessimist. He is instead a realist who tends toward optimism. Thomas Parrott and Willard Thorp make this comment about Hardy in <u>Poetry of the Transition</u>:

> There has been a tendency in the criticism of Hardy's work to consider him as a philosopher rather than as a poet and to stigmatize him as a gloomy pessimist. This is quite wrong. (413)

Quotation of a secondary source

The author himself felt incorrectly labeled, for he writes:

> As to pessimism. My motto is, first correctly diagnose the complaint--in this case human ills-- and ascertain the cause: then set about finding a remedy if one exists. The motto of optimists is: Blind the eyes to the real malady, and use empirical panaceas to suppress the symptoms. (<u>Life</u> 383)

Quotation of a primary source

Hardy is dismayed by these "optimists" and has little desire to be lumped within such a narrow perspective.

Using a Variety of Other Methods

Use *classification* to identify several key issues of the topic, and then use *analysis* to examine each issue in detail. For example, you might classify several types of fungus infections and do an analysis of each, such as athlete's foot, dermatophytosis, and ringworm.

Use specific *criteria of judgment* to examine performances and works of art. For example, analyze the films of George Lucas by a critical response to story, theme, editing, photography, sound track, special effects, and so forth.

Use *structure* to control papers on architecture, poetry, fiction, and biological forms. For example, a short story might have six distinct parts that you can examine in sequence.

Use *location* and *setting* for arranging papers in which geography and locale are key ingredients. For example, examine the settings of several novels by William Faulkner or build an environmental study around land features (e.g., lakes, springs, or sinkholes).

Use *critical responses to an issue* to evaluate a course of action. For example, an examination of President Harry Truman's decision to use the atomic bomb at the end of World War II would invite you to consider several minor reasons and then to study Truman's major reason(s) for his decision.

Dividing the body by important *issues* is standard fare in many research papers. One student examined the major issues of automotive airbag safety. Another developed the major issues about radio and television talk shows.

Many other methods exist for developing paragraphs; among them are *description, statistics, symbolism, point of view, scientific evidence, history, character, setting,* and others. You must make the choices, basing your decision on your subject and your notes.

6g Writing the Conclusion of the Research Paper

The conclusion is not a summary; it is a discussion of beliefs based on your reasoning and on the evidence that has been presented. Select items from this next guide.

Checklist for the Conclusion

THESIS   Reaffirm the thesis sentence and the central mission of your study. If appropriate, give a statement in support or nonsupport of an original enthymeme or hypothesis.

JUDGEMENTS   Discuss and interpret the findings. Give answers. Now is the time to draw inferences, to emphasize a theory, and to find relevance in the details of the results.

DIRECTIVES   Based on the theoretical implications of the study, offer suggestions for action and for new research.

Restating the Thesis and Reaching Beyond It

As a general rule, restate your thesis sentence; however, do not stop and assume that your reader will generate final conclusions about the issues. Notice in the next example how one writer opened his conclusion with the thesis but then moved quickly to concluding judgments.

Thesis —
     Real or unreal, objectivity is something seldom, if ever, found on television. Ultimately, we must wonder why in the world 24% of the people surveyed watch talk shows on a regular basis, while 30% watch them sometimes (see Appendix, Table 2). We live the re-creations vicariously, briefly in 30 and 60 minute

Explanation of the thesis —
bites. According to one critic, the "programs provide instant, vivid, and easy to consume information about a wide and growing range of public affairs" (Kuklinski and Sigelman 810), but most of the guests appearing on these shows are not like us in any way.

Right? But we enjoy watching the freaks of our society or begrudging the super rich and their struggles with fame. We enjoy this "infotainment," as Wayne Edward Munson calls it (dissertation abstract). <u>The New Yorker</u> says that "Mostly, we just [become] more and more aware of our own voyeurism" (21). Nevertheless, tabloid television gives people a way to feel good about themselves. They become players in the virtual reality of the drama. They are helping to define their own subjective reality within the boundaries of the objective world and the symbolic reality of television.

Closing with an Effective Quotation

Sometimes a source may provide a striking commentary that deserves special placement, as shown by this example:

> W. C. Fields had a successful career that extended from vaudeville to musical comedy and finally to the movies. In his private life, he loathed children and animals, and he fought with bankers, landladies, and the police. Off screen, he maintained his private image as a vulgar, hard-drinking cynic until his death in 1946. On the screen, he won the hearts of two generations of fans. He was beloved by audiences primarily for acting out their own contempt for authority. The movies prolonged his popularity "as a dexterous comedian with expert timing and a look of bibulous rascality," but Fields had two personalities, "one jolly and one diabolical" (Kennedy 990).

—Quotation

Returning the Focus of a Literary Study to the Author

While the body of a literary paper should analyze the characters, images, and plot, the conclusion should explain the author's accomplishments. The following is how one writer accomplished this:

> By her characterization of Walter in <u>A Raisin in the Sun,</u> Lorraine Hansberry has raised the black male above the typical stereotype. Walter is not a social problem, nor a mere victim of matriarchy. Rather, Hansberry creates a character who breaks out of the traditional sociological image that dehumanizes the black male. By creating a character who struggles with his fate and rises above it, Hansberry has elevated the black male. As James Baldwin puts it, "Time has made some changes in the Negro face" (24).

Focus on author Hansberry

Comparing Past to Present

You can use the conclusion rather than the opening to compare past research to the present study or to compare the historic past with the contemporary

ple, after explaining the history of two schools of treatment
writer switched to the present, as shown in this excerpt:

Comparison of present and the future

e is hope in the future that both the cause and the cure
will be found. For the present, new drug therapies
and behavior modification offer some hope for the abnormal, SIB
action of autistics. Since autism is sometimes outgrown,
childhood treatment offers the best hope for the autistic person
who must try to survive in an alien environment.

Offering a Directive or Solution

After analyzing a problem and synthesizing issues, offer your theory or solution, as demonstrated immediately above in the example in which the writer suggests that "childhood treatment offers the best hope for the autistic person who must try to survive in an alien environment."

Discussing the Test Results

In scientific writing (see Chapter 10), your conclusion, labeled "discussion," will need to explain the ramifications of your findings and will identify any limitations of your scientific study, as shown:

Findings and limitations of the study

The results of this experiment were similar to expectations,
but perhaps the statistical significance, because of the small
subject size, was biased toward the delayed conditions of the
curve. The subjects were, perhaps, not representative of the total
population because of their prior exposure to test procedures.
Another factor that may have affected the curves was the
presentation of the data. The images on the screen were available
for five seconds, and that amount of time may have enabled the
subjects to store each image effectively. If the time period for each
image were reduced to one or two seconds, there could be lower
recall scores, thereby reducing the differences between the control
group and the experimental group.

Avoiding Certain Mistakes in the Conclusion

Avoid afterthoughts or additional ideas. Now is the time to end the paper, not begin a new thought. If new ideas occur to you as you write your conclusion, don't ignore them. Explore them fully in the context of your thesis and consider adding them to the body of your paper or modifying your thesis. Scientific studies often discuss options and possible alterations that might affect test results (see "Discussing the Test Results," page 144).

Avoid the use of "thus," "in conclusion," or "finally" at the beginning of the last paragraph. Readers will be able to see the end of the paper.

Avoid ending the paper without a sense of closure.

Avoid questions that raise new issues; however, rhetorical questions that restate the issues are acceptable.

6h   Revising the Rough Draft

Global Revision

Revision can turn a passable paper into an excellent one and can change an excellent one into a radiant one. First, revise the whole manuscript by performing these tasks:

Global Revision Checklist

1. Skim through the paper to check its unity. Does the paper maintain a central proposition from paragraph to paragraph?
2. Transplant paragraphs, moving them to more relevant and effective positions.
3. Delete sentences that do not further your cause.
4. Revise your outline to match these changes if you must submit the outline with the paper.

Revision of the Introduction

Examine your opening for the presence of several items:

Your thesis sentence
A clear direction or plan of development
A sense of involvement that invites the reader into your investigation
of a problem.

(For a full discussion, see Section 6f, pages 137–42.)

Revision of Your Paragraphs

Use the following checklist as a guide for revising each individual paragraph of the body of your paper.

Paragraph Revision Checklist

1. Cut out wordiness and irrelevant thoughts, even to the point of deleting entire sentences that contribute nothing to the dynamics of the paper.

2. Combine any short paragraphs with others or build the short paragraph into one of substance.

3. Revise long, difficult paragraphs by dividing them or by using transitions effectively (see "Writing with Unity and Coherence," page 132).

4. For paragraphs that seem short, shallow, or weak, omit them or add more commentary and more evidence, especially quotations from the primary source or critical citations from secondary sources.

5. Add your own input to paragraphs that rely too heavily on the source materials. In addition to these general activities, revise conscientiously the three main sections of the paper: the introduction, the body, and the conclusion.

6. Examine your paragraphs for transitions that move the reader effectively from one paragraph to the next.

Revision of the Conclusion

Examine the conclusion to show that you have (1) drawn from the evidence, (2) that you have developed ideas logically from the introduction and the body, and (3) that you have established your position on the issues (see also Section 6g, pages 142–45).

Using the Computer for Revision of the Whole Work

Once you have keyboarded the entire paper, you can redesign and realign sentences, paragraphs, and entire pages without bothering to cut the actual sheets and paste them back together. The computer cuts and pastes for you. You can add, delete, or rewrite material anywhere within the body. In like manner, you can delete and rewrite.

Depending on your software, the name for moving material will be MOVE, MOVE BLOCK, CUT, PASTE, COPY, and so forth. You will quickly learn the correct commands. After each move, remember to rewrite and blend the words into your text. Most software today will reformat your paragraph.

Use the FIND command to locate some words and phrases in order to eliminate constant scrolling up and down the screen. Use the FIND/REPLACE to change wording or spelling throughout the document.

When you are satisfied that the paper flows effectively point by point and fulfills the needs of your intended audience, you can begin editing with an exacting and demanding mood about correctness.

6i · Editing Before Typing or Printing the Final Manuscript

The cut and paste revision period is complemented by careful editing of paragraphs, sentences, and individual words. Travel through the paper to study your sentences and word choice. Look for ways to tighten and condense. Here is a checklist.

Editing Checklist

1. Cut phrases and sentences that do not advance your main ideas or that merely repeat what your sources have already stated.
2. Determine that coordinated, balanced ideas are appropriately expressed and that minor ideas are properly subordinated.
3. Change most of your "to be" verbs (is, are, was) to stronger active verbs.
4. Maintain the present tense in most verbs in MLA style manuscripts.
5. Convert passive structures to active if appropriate.
6. Confirm that you have introduced paraphrases and quotations so that they flow smoothly into your text.
7. Language should be elevated slightly in its formality, so be on guard against clusters of little monosyllabic words that fail to advance ideas. Examine your wording for its effectiveness within the context of your subject.
8. The first mention of a person requires the full name (e.g., Ernest Hemingway or Joan Didion) and thereafter requires only the use of the surname (e.g., Hemingway or Didion). At first mention, use Emily Brontë, but thereafter use Brontë, *not* Miss Brontë. In general, avoid formal titles (e.g., Dr., Gen., Mrs., Ms., Lt. or Professor). Avoid their equivalents in other languages (e.g., Mme, Dame, Monsieur).

Note the editing by one student in Figure 29.

In some cases   is   see
~~One critic calls~~ television "junk food" (Fransecky

717), and ~~I think~~ excessive viewing ~~does~~ distracts
                    (see esp. Paul Witty as qtd. in Postman 41)
from other activities, yet television can and does
                    and shows   of our best
bring cultural programs, some ~~good~~ novels. It does,
according to the evidence,
improve children's vocabularies, encourages their
                                    and school
reading, and inspires their writing. Television should
                    the traditional classroom curriculum should seek
not be ~~an~~ antagonist, ~~it should complement school~~
and find harmony with the preschool television curriculum.
~~work~~.

Figure 29
Example of editing on a manuscript page.

As shown above, the writer conscientiously edited the paragraph, deleting unnecessary material, adding supporting statements, relating facts to one another, rearranging data, adding new ideas, and rewriting for clarity. Review earlier sections of this text, if necessary, on matters of unity and coherence (page 132) and writing the body (pages 137–42).

Using the Computer to Edit Your Text

In some situations you may have a software program that examines the *style* of your draft. Such a program provides information on the total number of words, number of sentences, the average number of words per paragraph, and so forth. It provides a list of your most active words and may locate passive constructions, jargon words, and usage errors. Its analysis then suggests, for example, "Your short paragraphs suggest a journalistic style that may not be appropriate for scholarly writing" or "The number of words in your sentences exceeds the norm."

Readability Scores

The software program may provide a readability score. For example, the Flesch Reading Ease Score is based on the number of words in each sentence and also the average number of syllables per word. The highest score, 100, represents a 4th grade level. A Flesch score within the range of 40–50 would be acceptable for a research paper. Another program, the Gunning Fog index, examines sentence length, but it looks especially for words of three or more syllables. A score of six means an easy reading level, but research papers, because they use a specialized language, usually reflect a high level, one of 9–12.

Style Analysis

Some software programs will examine your grammar and mechanics, looking for some parentheses that you have opened but not closed, unpaired quotation marks, passive verbs, and other specific items that a computer can quickly mark and flag for your correction. Pay attention to the caution flags raised by this type of program. After a software program examines the style of your manuscript, you should revise and edit the text to improve certain stylistic weaknesses. However, you must edit and adjust your paper by *your* standards with due respect to the computer analysis. Remember, it is your paper, not the computer's. You may need to use some long words and write some long sentences, or you may prefer the passive voice in one particular sentence.

Spelling Checker

A spelling checker moves quickly through the text to flag misspelled words and words not in the computer dictionary, such as proper names. You must then move through the text to correct misspellings. Regardless of the availability of such sophisticated software, you should move through the text and make all necessary editorial changes.

Find and Search Functions

In particular, use the FIND or the SEARCH function of your computer system. It moves the cursor quickly to troublesome words and common grammatical errors. For example, if your experience with the use of *there, their,* and *they're* has been less than successful, search quickly all instances of these words. By concentrating on one problem and tracing it through the entire paper, you can edit effectively. If your writing history would suggest it, FIND and examine especially one or more of the following:

1. *Words commonly misused.* Do you sometimes use *alot* rather than *a lot* and *to* rather than *too?* If so, order a SEARCH or a FIND for *alot* and then for *to* and correct errors accordingly. You know your weaknesses, so search out usage problems that plague you:

accept/except	adapt/adopt
advice/advise	all ready/already
among/between	cite/site
criteria/criterion	data/datum
farther/further	its/it's
lay/lie	on to/onto
passed/past	suppose to/supposed to
use to/used to	

These are words the spelling checker will usually ignore, so the FIND or SEARCH is necessary.

2. *Contractions.* Research papers are formal, so avoid contractions (*it's, they're*). You can easily correct them by ordering a FIND for the apostrophe ('). But you will need the possessive form (*Hawthorne's novel*).

3. *Pronouns.* Troublesome words are *he, she, it, they, their* because referents can be unclear. For example, FIND each use of *he* to be sure you have a clear masculine referent, not ambiguity or bias:

> Stonewall Jackson served General Lee valiantly in the battles against Union forces. He was a man of raw courage.

The cursor, blinking as it pauses at *He,* encourages a change to:

> Stonewall Jackson served General Lee valiantly in the battles against Union forces. Jackson, like Lee, was a man of raw courage.

In the next example, the FIND command for the word *this* might uncover:

> Dr. Himmelwit stresses this point: "Book reading comes into its own, not despite television but because of it" (qtd. in Postman 33). This is not universally supported.

The first highlighted *this,* an adjective, is correct; however, the second, a pronoun, needs clarification, as with:

> This view by Himmelwit is not universally supported.

4. *Unnecessary negatives.* Use the FIND or SEARCH function to locate *no, not, never* in order to correct obtuse wording, as shown here:

> A not unacceptable reading of Hawthorne is Fogle's interpretation of <u>The Scarlet Letter.</u>

This correction turns the sentence into a positive assertion that is easily understood:

> Fogle's reading of <u>The Scarlet Letter</u> asserts Hawthorne's positive view of Hester's moral strength (15).

5. *Punctuation.* Use the FIND or SEARCH to locate all commas (,) and semicolons (;) to check your accuracy. Consult also Section 7j, pages 164–66, on punctuation of quotations. If you employ parentheses regularly, FIND or SEARCH for the opening parenthesis and check visually for a closing one.

6. *Abbreviations.* Use the FIND and REPLACE function to put into final form any abbreviated words or phrases employed in the early draft(s). For example, you might have saved time in drafting the paper by typing SL for *The Scarlet Letter.* Now is the time to REPLACE the abbreviation automatically with the full title.

Editing To Avoid Sexist and Biased Language

You must exercise caution against words that may stereotype any person, regardless of gender, race, nationality, creed, age, or disability. If your writing is not precise, readers might make assumptions about race, age, and disabilities. To many people, a reference to a doctor or governor may bring to mind a white male, while a similar reference to a teacher or homemaker may bring to mind a woman. In truth, no characteristic should be assumed for all members of a group. Therefore, do not freely mention sexual orientation, marital status, ethnic or racial identity, or a person's disability. The following are some guidelines to help you avoid discriminatory language:

1. **Age.** Review the accuracy of your statement.

   DISCRIMINATORY   Many elderly suffer senility.

   Avoid *elderly* as a noun; use *older persons*. *Dementia* is preferred over *senility.*

   NONDISCRIMINATORY   Fifteen older patients suffered senile dementia of the Alzheimer's type.

It is appropriate to use *boy* and *girl* for children of high school age and under. *Young man* and *young woman* or *male adolescent* and *female adolescent* can be appropriate.

2. **Gender.** *Gender* is a matter of our culture that identifies men and women within their social groups. *Sex* tends to be a biological factor (see below for a discussion of sexual orientation).

   a. Use plural subjects so that nonspecific, plural pronouns are grammatically correct. For example, do you intend to specify that Judy Jones maintains *her* lab equipment in sterile condition or to indicate that technicians, in general, maintain *their* own equipment? Do be careful, though, because the plural is easily overused and often inappropriate. For example, some people now use a plural pronoun with the singular *everybody, everyone, anybody, anyone, each one* in order to avoid the masculine reference (even though it is not correct grammar):

      SEXIST   Each author of the Pre-Raphaelite period produced *his* best work prior to 1865.

      COLLOQUIAL   Each author of the Pre-Raphaelite period produced *their* best work prior to 1865.

      FORMAL   *Authors* of the Pre-Raphaelite period produced *their* best *works* prior to 1865.

   b. Reword the sentence so that a pronoun is unnecessary:

      CORRECT   The doctor prepared the necessary surgical equipment without interference.

      CORRECT   Each technician must maintain the laboratory equipment in sterile condition.

   c. Use pronouns denoting gender only when necessary to specify gender or when gender has been previously established. A new pronoun, *s/he,* has gained popularity in some letters and memos. It has not yet become an acceptable choice in academic applications.

The use of a specifier (*the, this, that*) is often helpful. In directions and informal settings, the pronoun *you* is appropriate, but *it is not appropriate in research papers.* Note these sentences:

SPECIFY GENDER WITH A PRONOUN	Mary, as a new laboratory technician, must learn to maintain *her* equipment in sterile condition.
USE A DEMONSTRATIVE ADJECTIVE TO SPECIFY	The lab technician maintains *that* [not *his* or *hers*] equipment is in sterile condition.
USE SECOND PERSON	Each of you should maintain *your* equipment in sterile condition.

But avoid the use of second person in research papers.

   d. Usage varies on the use of *woman* and *female* as adjectives, as in *female athlete* or *woman athlete.* The suggestion is to use *woman* or *women* in most instances (e.g., a *woman's intuition*) and to use *female* for animals and statisitics, (e.g., *four female subjects, 10 males and 23 females,* or *a female chimpanzee*). The word *lady* has fallen from favor (i.e., avoid *lady pilot*).

   e. Avoid *man and wife* or *7 men and 16 females.* Keep them parallel by saying *husband and wife* or *man and woman* and *7 males and 16 females.*

3. **Sexual orientation.** The term *sexual orientation* is preferred over the term *sexual preference.* It is preferable to use the terms *lesbians* and *gay men* rather than *homosexuals.* The terms *heterosexual* and *bisexual* can be used to describe both the identity and the behavior of subjects.

4. **Ethnic and racial identity.** Some persons prefer the term *Black* and others prefer *African American.* The terms *Negro* and *Afro-American* are now dated and not appropriate. Use *Black* and *White,* not the lowercase *black* and *white.* In like manner, some individuals may prefer *Hispanic, Latino,* or *Chicano.* Use the term *Asian* or *Asian American* rather than *Oriental. Native American* is a broad term that includes Samoans, Hawaiians, and *American Indians.* A good rule of thumb is to use a person's nation when it is known (*Mexican* or *Korean* or *Nigerian*).

5. **Disability.** In general, place people first, not their disability. Rather than *disabled person* or *retarded child* say *person who has scoliosis* or *a child with Down's syndrome.* Avoid saying a *challenged person* or *a special child* in favor of *a person with* _____

or *a child with* _____. Remember that a *disability* is a physical quality while a *handicap* is a limitation that might be imposed by nonphysical factors, such as stairs or poverty or social attitudes.

Editing with an eye for the inadvertent bias should serve to tighten up the expression of your ideas. However, beware of the pitfalls of awkward wording, such as: "One must use one's judgment when he or she wishes to invest his or her money in the stock market." If such attempts to be unbiased draw more attention than the argument, it will ultimately detract from the paper.

6j Proofreading Before the Final Computer Printout

After you have edited the text to your satisfaction, print or type a hard copy of the manuscript. Check for double spacing, one-inch margins, running heads with page numbers, and so forth. Even if you used available software programs to check your spelling, grammar, and style, you must nevertheless proofread this final version for correctness of spelling, punctuation, alphabetizing of entries on the works cited page, and so forth. Errors in these areas might cause readers to question your attention to detail, which is a major failing in research.

> **Note:** Before and during final printing of the manuscript, consult 8b, "Glossary: Techniques for Preparing the Manuscript in MLA Style," pages 177–214, which provides tips on handling technicalities of the title page, margins, content notes, and many other matters.

If at all possible, print your final version on a laser printer or an inkjet printer. Such printers with sheet-fed paper or razor-cut continuous forms paper will produce a manuscript of the best typewriter quality. Perforated paper in continuous forms will leave the ragged edges along the top, sides, and bottom of sheets. A dot matrix printer will not give the black sharpness of detail that many instructors require. You can overcome that obstacle by using the double-strike feature available on most dot matrix printers. This feature commands the printer to strike each letter twice, with the second strike slightly off center, giving letters a darker quality.

You are ultimately responsible for the manuscript, whether you type it, produce it on a computer, or have somebody else type it. At this stage, be doubly careful; typographical errors often count against the paper just as heavily as other shortcomings. If necessary, make corrections neatly in ink; marring a page with a few handwritten corrections is better than leaving damaging errors in your text.

Specifically, use a few proofreading strategies, especially those geared to your particular style. Go through the paper several times to check for errors that plague your writing. You know which ones apply to you.

Proofreading Checklist

1. Check for errors in sentence structure, spelling, and punctuation.
2. Check for hyphenation and word division. Remember that **no** words should be hyphenated at the ends of lines. If you are using a computer, turn off the automatic hyphenation.
3. Read each quotation for accuracy of your own wording and of the words within your quoted materials. Look, too, for your correct use of quotations marks.
4. Double-check in-text citations to be certain that each one is correct and that each source is listed on your "Works Cited" page at the end of the paper.
5. Double-check the format: the title page, margins, spacing, content notes, and many other elements, as explained in Chapter 8, pages 173–231.

6k   Participating in Peer Review of Research Writing

Some instructors will ask you to participate in a peer review of a colleague's research paper. The task requires you to make judgments about another person's work. For this task, you need a set of criteria. You can use the following list as a bases for a peer review.

Checklist for Peer Review

1. Are the subject and the accompanying issues introduced early?
2. Is the writer's critical approach to the problem stated clearly in a thesis sentence or enthymeme? Is it placed effectively in the introduction?
3. Do the paragraphs of the body have individual unity? That is, does each one develop an important idea and *only* one idea?
4. Are sources introduced, usually with the name of the expert, and then cited by a page number within parentheses? Is it clear when a paraphrase begins and when it ends?
5. Are the sources relevant to the argument?
6. Does the writer depend too heavily upon source materials, especially long quotations that look like filler instead of substance?
7. Does the conclusion arrive at a resolution about the central issue?
8. Look now at the paper's title. Does it describe clearly what you have found in the contents of the research paper?

---

7 Blending Reference Material into Your Writing

Your in-text citations should conform to standards announced by your instructor. This chapter explains the MLA style, as established by the Modern Language Association. It governs papers in freshman composition, literature, English usage, and foreign languages. The MLA style puts great emphasis upon the writer, asking for the full name of the scholar whose words might endure through many years. Other styles emphasize the year of publication or use a number in order to emphasize the material and its timeliness (see Chapters 10 and 11).

In all styles, one of your primary tasks is to blend your source material into your writing with unity and coherence. First, the sources contribute to the **unity** of your paper if they are useful to the argument. That is, quotation, paraphrase, and summary must explain and support your paragraph's topic sentence. A collection of random quotations, even though they treat the same topic, is unacceptable. Second, the source material contributes to **coherence** only if you relate them directly to the matter at hand. Introductions, transitions, repetition of key words—these tie the paraphrase or the quotation to your exposition. (See also "Writing with Unity and Coherence," page 132.)

Notice how this next passage uses names and page numbers in two different ways. In the first sentence, the writer uses the name of the authority to introduce the quotation and places the page number after the quotation. In the second, the writer places both the name and the page number at the end:

According to John Hartley, 19th century scientists "discovered single cells that divided into two identical offspring cells" (56) . This finding eventually produced the cell theory, which asserts, "All organisms are composed of cells and all cells derive from other living cells" (Justice 431) .

> **Note:** In MLA style do not place a comma between the name and the page number.

7a   Blending a Reference into Your Text

An important reason for writing the research paper is to gather and present source material on a topic, so it only follows that you should display those sources prominently in your writing, not hide them or fail to cite them. As a general policy, provide just enough information within the text to identify a source. Remember, your readers will have full documentation to each source on the Works Cited page (see Chapter 9).

Making a General Reference Without a Page Number

Sometimes you will need no parenthetical reference.

> The women of Thomas Hardy's novels are the special focus of three essays by Nancy Norris, Judith Mitchell, and James Scott.

Keep your in-text citations as brief as possible because the Works Cited list will have full information.

Beginning with the Author and Ending with a Page Number

Introduce a quotation or a paraphrase with the author's name and close it with a page number, placed inside parentheses. Try always to use this standard citation because it informs the reader of the beginning and the end of borrowed materials, as shown here:

> Herbert Norfleet states that the use of video games by children improves their hand and eye coordination (45).

In the following example, the reader can easily trace the origin of the ideas.

> Video games for children have opponents and advocates. Herbert Norfleet defends the use of video games by children. He says it improves their hand and eye coordination and that it exercises their minds as they work their way through various puzzles and barriers. Norfleet states, "The mental gymnastics of video games and the competition with fellow players are important to young children and their physical, social, and mental development" (45).

Putting the Page Number Immediately after the Name

Sometimes, notes at the end of a quotation makes it expeditious to place the page number after the name of source.

> Boughman (46) urges carmakers to "direct the force of automotive airbags upward against the windshield" (emphasis added).

Putting the Name and Page Number at the End of Borrowed Material

As an alternative, you may put cited names with the page number within parentheses.

> "Each DNA strand provides the pattern of bases for a new strand to form, resulting in two complete molecules" (Justice, Moody, and Graves 462).

In the case of a paraphrase, you should give your reader a signal to show when the borrowing begins, as shown next:

> One source explains that the DNA in the chromosomes must be copied perfectly during cell reproduction (Justice, Moody, and Graves 462).

7b Citing a Source When No Author Is Listed

When no author is shown on a title page, cite the title of an article, the name of the magazine, the name of a bulletin or book, or the name of the publishing organization. Search for the author's name at the bottom of the opening page and at the end of the article.

Citing the Title of a Magazine Article

> Articles about the unusual names of towns, such as Peculiar, Missouri; Kinmundy, Illinois; and Frostproof, Florida, are a regular feature of one national magazine ("Name-Dropping" 63).

The Works Cited entry would read: "Name-Dropping." *Country* June/July 1994: 63. Shorten magazine titles to a key word for the citation, such as "Selling" rather than the full title, "Selling Products to Young Children." You would then give the full title in the Works Cited entry.

Citing the Title of a Report

> One bank showed a significant decline in assets despite an increase in its number of depositors (Annual Report 23).

Citing the Name of a Publisher or a Corporate Body

> The report by the school board endorsed the use of Channel One in the school system and said that "students will benefit by the news reports more than they will be adversely affected by advertising" (Clarion County School Board 3-4).

7c Identifying Unprinted Sources That Have No Page Number

On occasion you may need to identify unprinted sources, such as a speech, the song lyrics from a compact disc, an interview, or a television program. Since there is no page number, omit the parenthetical citation. Instead, introduce the type of source—i.e., lecture, letter, interview—so that readers do not expect a page number.

> Mrs. Peggy Meacham said in her ┌ phone interview ┐ that prejudice against young black women is not as severe as that against young black males.

7d Identifying Internet Sources

Currently, most Internet sources have no prescribed page numbers or numbered paragraphs. You cannot list a screen number because monitors differ. You cannot list the page numbers of a downloaded document because computer printers differ. Therefore, in most cases do not list a page number or a paragraph number. Here are basic rules.

1. **Omit a page or paragraph number.** The marvelous feature of electronic text is that its searchable, so your readers can find your quotation quickly with the FIND feature. Suppose that you have written the following:

> One source advices against making the television industry the "scapegoat for violence" by advocating a focus on "deadlier and more significant causes: inadequeate parenting, drugs, underclass rage, unemployment and availability of weaponry" (UCLA Television Violence Report 1996).

A reader who wants to investigate further will find your complete citation on your Works Cited page. There the reader will discover the Internet address for the article. After finding the article via a browser, (e.g., Netscape or Internet Explorer), the investigator can press EDIT, then FIND, and then type in a key phrase, such as *scapegoat for violence.* The software will immediately move the cursor to the passage shown above. That's much easier than counting through forty-six paragraphs.

2. **Provide a paragraph number.** Some academic societies are urging scholars who write on the Internet to number their paragraphs. So if you find an article on the Internet that has numbered paragraphs, by all means supply that information in your citation. Treat numbered screens in the same manner.

> The Insurance Institute for Highway Safety emphasizes restraint first, saying, "Riding unrestrained or improperly restrained in a motor vehicle always has been the greatest hazard for children" (par. 13).

3. **Provide a page number.** In a few instances, you will find page numbers buried within brackets here and there throughout an article. These refer to the page numbers of the printed version of the document. In this case, you should cite the page just as you would a printed source.

> The most common type of diabetes is non-insulin-dependent diabetes mellitus (NIDDM), which "affects 90% of those with diabetes and usually appears after age 40" (Larson 3).

7e Establishing the Credibility of the Source

In some instances, your instructors may expect you to indicate your best estimate of the scholarly value of a source. Consequently, Internet sources can be troublesome. For example, the citation on page 158 might be introduced in this way to verify the validity of the source:

> The UCLA Center for Communication Policy, which conducted an intensive study of television violence during 1995, has advised against making the television industry the "scapegoat for violence" by advocating a focus on "deadlier and more significant causes: inadequate parenting, drugs, underclass rage, unemployment and availability of weaponry" (UCLA Television Violence Report 1996).

Here's another example:

> John Armstrong, a spokesperson for Public Electronic Access to Knowledge (PEAK), states:
>
>> As we venture into this age of biotechnology, many people predict gene manipulation will be a powerful tool for improving the quality of life. They foresee plants engineered to resist pests, animals designed to produce large quantities of rare medicinals, and humans treated by gene therapy to relieve suffering.

Note: To learn more about the source of an Internet article, as in the case immediately above, learn to search out a home page. The address for Armstrong's article is:

⟨http://www.peak.org/[~]armstroj/america.html#Aims⟩

By truncating the address to ⟨http://www.peak.org/⟩ you can learn about the organization that Armstrong represents.

If you are not certain about the credibility of a source, that is, it seemingly has no scholarly or educational basis, do not cite it or describe the source so that readers can make their own judgments:

> An Iowa non-profit organization, the Mothers for Natural Law, says--but offers no proof--that eight major crops are affected by genetically engineered organisms--canola, corn, cotton, dairy products, potatoes, soybeans, tomatoes, and yellow crook-neck squash ("What's on the Market").

7f Citing Indirect Sources

Sometimes the writer of a book or article will quote another person from an interview or personal correspondence, and you will want to use that same quotation. For example, in a newspaper article in *USA Today,* page 9A, Karen S. Peterson writes this passage in which she quotes two other people:

> Sexuality, popularity, and athletic competition will create anxiety for junior high kids and high schoolers, Eileen Shiff says. "Bring up the topics. Don't wait for them to do it; they are nervous and they want to appear cool." Monitor the amount of time high schoolers spend working for money, she suggests. "Work is important, but school must be the priority." Parental intervention in a child's school career that worked in junior high may not work in high school, psychiatrist Martin Greenburg adds. "The interventions can be construed by the adolescent as negative, overburdening and interfering with the child's ability to care for himself." He adds, "Be encouraging, not critical. Criticism can be devastating for the teen-ager."

Suppose that you want to use the quotation above by Martin Greenburg. You will need to quote the words of Greenburg and also put Peterson's name in the parenthetical citation as the person who wrote the article, as shown in the following:

> After students get beyond middle school, they begin to resent interference by their parents, especially in school activities. They need some space from Mom and Dad. Martin Greenburg says, "The interventions can be construed by the adolescent as negative, overburdening and interfering with the child's ability to care for himself" (qtd. in Peterson 9A) .

On the Works Cited page, Peterson's name will appear on a bibliography entry, but Greenburg's name will not appear there because Greenburg is not the author of the article.

In other words, you need a double reference that introduces the speaker and includes a clear reference to the book or article where you found the quotation or the paraphrased material. Without the reference to Peterson, nobody could find the article. Without the reference to Greenburg, readers would assume that Peterson spoke the words.

Cite the original source if at all possible. If an author quotes from another writer's published essay or book, it is preferable to search for the original essay or book rather than use the double reference.

7g Citing Frequent Page References to the Same Work

When you make frequent references to the same book or novel, you need not repeat the author's name in every instance; a specific page reference is adequate, or you can provide act, scene, and line if appropriate. Note the following example:

> When the character Beneatha denies the existence of God in Hansberry's <u>A Raisin in the Sun,</u> Mama slaps her in the face and forces her to repeat after her, "In my mother's house there is still God" (37). Then Mama adds, "There are some ideas we ain't going to have in this house. Not long as I am at the head of the family" (37). Thus Mama meets Beneatha's challenge head on. The other mother in the Younger household is Ruth, who does not lose her temper, but through kindness wins over her husband (79-80).

> *Note:* If you are citing from two or more novels in your paper, let's say John Steinbeck's *East of Eden* and *Of Mice and Men,* provide both titles (abbreviated) and page(s) unless the reference is clear: (*Eden* 56) and (*Mice* 12–13).

7h Citing Material from Textbooks and Large Anthologies

Reproduced below is a small portion of a textbook:

METAPHOR
The Skaters
Black swallows swooping or gliding
In a flurry of entangled loops and curves;
The skaters skim over the frozen river.
And the grinding click of their skates as they impinge
     upon the surface,
Is like the brushing together of thin wing-tips of silver.

John Gould Fletcher

—From *Patterns in Literature,* ed. Edmund J. Farrell, Ouida H. Clapp, and Karen Kuehner. Glenview: Scott, 1991. 814

If you quote from Fletcher's poem, and if that is all you quote from the anthology, cite the author and page in the text and put a comprehensive entry in the Works Cited list.

Text

In "The Skaters" John Gould Fletcher compares "the grinding click" of ice skates to "the brushing together of thin wing-tips of silver" (814) .

Bibliography Entry

Fletcher, John Gould. "The Skaters." <u>Patterns in Literature</u>. Ed. Edmund J. Farrell, Ouida H. Clapp, and Karen Kuehner. Glenview: Scott, 1991. 814.

Suppose, however, that you also want to quote not only from Fletcher but also from the authors of the textbook and from a second poem in the book. You can make in-text citations to name and page, but your works cited entries can be shortened by cross references.

In the Text

In "The Skaters" John Gould Fletcher compares "the grinding click of ice skates to "the brushing together of thin wing-tips of silver" (814) . The use of metaphor is central to his poetic efforts. One source emphasizes Fletcher's use of metaphor, especially his comparison of "the silhouettes of a group of graceful skaters to a flock of black swallows" (Farrell et al. 814) . Metaphor gives us a fresh look, as when Lew Sarett in his "Requiem for a Modern Croesus" uses coins to make his ironic statement about the wealthy king of sixth century Lydia:

> To him the moon was a silver dollar, spun
> Into the sky by some mysterious hand; the sun
> Was a gleaming golden coin --
> His to purloin;
> The freshly minted stars were dimes of delight
> Flung out upon the counter of the night.
> In yonder room he lies,
> With pennies in his eyes. (814)

In addition, let's suppose that you also decide to cite a portion of Dickens's novel, *Great Expectations,* from this same anthology. Your Works Cited page will require four entries, mixed by alphabetical order with other entries. Dickens, in the example below, comes before Farrell et al. even though the anthology is the primary source. (See also "Cross-References," 245–46.)

Bibliography Entries

Dickens, Charles. <u>Great Expectations</u>. Farrell et al. 675–785.
Farrell, Edmund J., Ouida H. Clapp, and Karen Kuehner, eds. <u>Patterns in Literature</u>. Glenview: Scott, 1991.

Fletcher, John Gould. "The Skaters." Farrell et al. 814.
Sarett, Lew. "Requiem for a Modern Croesus." Farrell et al. 814.

7i Adding Extra Information to In-Text Citations

As a courtesy to your reader, add extra information within the citation. Show parts of books, different titles by the same writer, or several works by different writers. For example, your reader may have a different anthology than yours, so a clear reference "(*Great Expectations* 681; chap.4)," will enable the reader to locate the passage. The same is true with a reference to "(*Romeo and Juliet* 2.3.65–68)." The reader will find the passage in any edition of Shakespeare's play.

One of Several Volumes

These next two citations provide three vital facts: (1) an abbreviation for the title, (2) the volume used, and (3) the page number(s).

In a letter to his Tennessee Volunteers in 1812 General Jackson chastised the "mutinous and disorderly conduct" of some of his troops (Papers 2: 348–49).

Joseph Campbell suggests that man is a slave yet also the master of all the gods (Masks 1: 472).

Two or More Works by the Same Writer

In this next example the writer makes reference to two different novels, both abbreviated. Full titles are *Tess of the D'Urbervilles* and *The Mayor of Casterbridge*.

Thomas Hardy reminds readers in his prefaces that "a novel is an impression, not an argument" and that a novel should be read as "a study of man's deeds and character" (Tess xxii; Mayor 1).

The complete titles of the two works by Campbell that are referenced in the following example are *The Hero with a Thousand Faces* and *The Masks of God*, a four-volume work.

Because he stresses the nobility of man, Joseph Campbell suggests that the mythic hero is symbolic of the "divine creative and redemptive image which is hidden within us all . . ." (Hero 39). The hero elevates the human mind to an "ultimate mythogenetic zone--the creator and destroyer, the slave and yet the master, of all the gods" (Masks 1: 472).

Several Authors in One Citation

You may wish to make a citation to several different sources that treat the same topic. Put them in alphabetical order to match that of the Works Cited page, or place them in the order of importance to the issue at hand. That is, list first the source that you recommend to the reader.

> Several sources have addressed this aspect of gang warfare
> as a fight for survival, not just for control of the local turf
> (Robertson 98-134; Rollins 34; Templass 561–65).

Additional Information with the Page Number

> Horton (22, n. 3) suggests that Melville forced the symbolism,
> but Welston (199-248, esp. 234) reaches an opposite conclusion.

Classical prose works such as *Moby Dick* or *Paradise Lost* may appear in two or more editions. Courtesy dictates that you provide extra information to chapter, section, or part so that readers can locate a quotation in any edition of the work.

> Melville uncovers the superstitious nature of Ishmael by
> stressing Ishmael's fascination with Yojo, the little totem god of
> Queequeg (71; chap. 16).

> Homer takes great efforts in describing the shield of
> Achilles (18:558–709).

7j   Punctuating Citations Properly and with Consistency

Keep page citations outside quotation marks but inside the final period, as shown here:

> Smith says, "The benefits of cloning far exceed any harm that
> might occur" (34).

The exception occurs with long indented quotations, which do not use quotation marks at all. In MLA style, use no comma between the name and the page within the citation (for example, Jones 16–17 *not* Jones, 16–17). Do not use *p.* or *pp.* with the page number(s) in MLA style.

Commas and Periods

Place commas and periods inside quotation marks unless the page citation intervenes. The example below shows with (1) how to put the mark inside the quotation marks, (2) how to interrupt a quotation to insert the speaker,

(3) how to use single quotation marks within the regular quotation marks, and (4) how to place the period after a page citation.

> "Modern advertising⎡,⎤ says Rachel Murphy, "not only creates a marketplace, it determines values⎡.⎤ She adds, "I resist the advertiser's argument that they 'awaken, not create desires⎡'" (192).⎤

Suppose this is the original material:

> The Russians had obviously anticipated neither the quick discovery of the bases nor the quick imposition of the quarantine. Their diplomats across the world were displaying all the symptoms of improvisation, as if they had been told nothing of the placement of the missiles and had received no instructions what to say about them.—From: Arthur M. Schlesinger, Jr., *A Thousand Days* (New York: Houghton, 1965) 820.

Punctuate citations from this source in one of the following methods in accordance with MLA style:

> "The Russians," writes Schlesinger, "had obviously anticipated neither the quick discovery of the [missile] bases nor the quick imposition of the quarantine⎡" (820).⎤

> Schlesinger notes, "Their diplomats across the world were displaying all the symptoms of improvisation⎡. . ." (820).⎤

> Schlesinger observes that the Russian failure to anticipate an American discovery of Cuban missiles caused "their diplomats across the world" to improvise answers as "if they had been told nothing of the placement of the missiles . . ." (820).

Note that the last example correctly changes the capital "T" of "their" to lowercase to match the grammar of the restructured sentence, and it does not use ellipsis points before "if" because the phrase flows smoothly into the text.

Semicolons and Colons

Both semicolons and colons go outside the quotation marks, as illustrated by these three examples:

> Zigler admits that "the extended family is now rare in contemporary society⎡"; ⎤ however, he stresses the greatest loss as the "wisdom and daily support of older, more experienced family members" (42).

> Zigler laments the demise of the "extended family⎡": ⎤ that is, the family suffers by loss of the "wisdom and daily support of older, more experienced family members" (42).

Brian Sutton-Smith says, "Adults don't worry whether <u>their</u> toys are educational|" (64);| nevertheless, parents want to keep their children in a learning mode.

The third example shows how to place the page citation after a quotation and before a semicolon.

Question Marks and Exclamation Marks

When a question mark or an exclamation mark serves a part of the quotation, keep it inside the quotation mark. Put the in-text citation immediately after the name of the source, as shown below.

|Thompson (16)| passionately shouted to union members, "We can bring order into our lives even though we face hostility from every quarter!"

The philosopher |Thompson (16)| asks, "How should we order our lives?"

but

"How should we order our lives," asks |Thompson (16),| when we face "hostility from every quarter"?

Single Quotation Marks

When a quotation appears within another quotation, use single quotation marks with the shorter one.

George Loffler (32) confirms that |"|the unconscious carries the best of human thought and gives man great dignity, but it also has the dark side so that we cry, in the words of Shakespeare's Macbeth, |'|Hence, horrible shadow! Unreal mockery, hence|.'"|

Place the period inside the quotation marks

Remember that the period always goes inside quotation marks unless the page citation intervenes, as shown below:

George Loffler confirms that "the unconscious carries the best of human thought and gives man great dignity, but it also has the dark side so that we cry, in the words of Shakespeare's Macbeth, 'Hence, horrible shadow! Unreal mockery, hence |'" (32) .|

Place the period after the page citation

7k   Indenting Long Quotations

Set off long prose quotations of four lines or more by indenting one inch or 10 spaces with the Courier font. Do not use quotation marks with the indented material. If you quote only one paragraph or the beginning of one, do *not* indent the first line an extra five spaces. Double space between your text and the quoted materials. Place the parenthetical citation *after* the final mark of punctuation, as shown below:

> Television gives us symbolic reality but dresses it in the robes of "real" or "objective" reality. Two political commentators make this observation:
>
>> Every day the network news organizations face the task of reducing complex, multifaceted issues to simple, unambiguous stories that consume no more than a minute or two of precious air time. To avoid the accusation of being unfair, they also face the pressure to present "both sides" of the controversies they cover. (Kuklinski and Sigelman 814)
>
> Even Oprah has established a commercially viable structure that the show must squeeze into. Sometimes a little reality falls out when this squeezing occurs.

If you quote more than one paragraph, indent all paragraphs an extra three (3) spaces in Courier font or a quarter inch in other fonts. However, if the first sentence quoted does not begin a paragraph in the original source do not indent it an extra three spaces.

> Zigler makes this observation:
>
>> With many others, I am nevertheless optimistic that our nation will eventually display its inherent greatness and successfully correct the many ills that I have touched upon here.
>>
>> Of course, much remains that could and should be done, including increased efforts in the area of family planning, the widespread implementation of Education for Parenthood programs, an increase in the availability of homemaker and child care services, and a reexamination of our commitment to doing what is in the best interest of every child in America. (42)

71 Citing Poetry

Set off three or more lines of poetry by indenting 10 spaces in the Courier font or one inch in other fonts (usually two tabs), as shown below.

Courier Font:

```
The king cautions Prince Henry:
          Thy place in council thou has rudely lost,
          which by thy younger brother is supplied,
```

```
And art almost an alien to the hearts
Of all the court and princes of my blood.
                                    (3.2.32-35)
```

Arial Font:

The king cautions Prince Henry:

Thy place in council thou has rudely lost,
Which by thy younger brother is supplied,
And art almost an alien to the hearts
Of all the court and princes of my blood.
(3.2.32–35)

An alternative is to center the lines of poetry. Refer to act, scene, and lines only after you have established Shakespeare's *Henry IV. Part 1* as the central topic of your study; otherwise, write "(1H4 3.2.32–35)." (See also "Arabic Numerals," Section 8b, pages 186–89.)

Quoting Short Passages of Poetry

Incorporate short quotations of poetry (one or two lines) into your text.

Eliot's "The Waste Land" (1922) remains a springtime search for nourishing water: "Sweet Thames, run softly, for I speak not loud or long" (3.12) says the speaker in "The Fire Sermon" while in Part 5 the speaker of "What the Thunder Said" yearns for "a damp gust / Bringing rain" (5.73–74).

As the example demonstrates:

1. Set off the material with quotation marks
2. Indicate separate lines by using a virgule (/) with a space before and after the slash mark
3. Place line documentation within parentheses immediately following the final quotation mark and inside the period.
4. Use Arabic numerals for books, parts, volumes, and chapters of works; acts, scenes, and lines of plays; cantos, stanzas, and lines of poetry (see "Arabic Numerals," Section 8b, pages 186–89).

Signaling Turnovers for Long Lines of Poetry

When quoting a line of poetry that is too long for your right margin, indent the continuation line 3 spaces or a quarter inch more than the greatest indentation. See how one writer uses this format when quoting from a poem.

Plath opens her poem with these lines:

Love set you going like a fat gold watch.
The midwife slapped your footsoles, and
    your bald cry
Took its place among the elements.

(See also pages 169–71 for instructions on using ellipsis points to omit phrases and lines from poetry.)

7m Altering Initial Capitals in Some Quoted Matter

In general, you should reproduce quoted materials exactly, yet one exception is permitted for logical reasons. Restrictive connectors, such as *that* or *because,* create restrictive clauses and eliminate a need for the comma. Without a comma, the capital letter is unnecessary. In the following example, "The," which is capitalized as the first word in the original sentence, is changed to lowercase because it continues the grammatical flow of the student's sentence.

> Another writer argues that ⌐"the⌐ single greatest impediment to our improving the lives of America's children is the myth that we are a child-oriented society" (Zigler 39).

Otherwise, write:

> Another writer argues, ⌐"The⌐ single greatest . . . ."

7n Omitting Quoted Matter with Ellipsis Points

Here are rules for omitting portions of quoted material with ellipsis points (. . .).

1. **Context.** In omitting passages, be fair to the author. Do not change the meaning or take a quotation out of context.
2. **Correctness.** Maintain the grammatical correctness of your sentences; that is, avoid fragments and misplaced modifiers. You don't want your readers to misunderstand the structure of the original. When you quote only a phrase, readers will understand that you omitted most of the original sentence.

> Phil Withim recognizes the weakness in Captain Vere's "intelligence and insight" into the significance of his decisions regarding Billy Budd (118).

> However, if you quote most of a sentence but not all, you need to signify the omission because you are not reproducing completely the original sentence.

3. **Omission within a sentence.** Use three spaced ellipsis points (periods) to signal material omitted from *within* a sentence:

Three
spaced
ellipsis points

Phil Withim objects to the idea that "such episodes are intended to demonstrate that Vere $\boxed{. . .}$ has the intelligence and insight to perceive the deeper issue" (118).

4. **Omission at the end of a sentence.** If an ellipsis occurs at the end of your sentence, use four points with no space before the first.

Four
spaced
ellipsis points

R. W. B. Lewis (62) declares that "if Hester has sinned, she has done so an an affirmation of life, and her sin is the source of life$\boxed{. . . .}$"

But if a page citation also appears at the end in conjunction with the ellipsis, use three spaced ellipsis points, add the page citation, and then add the period.

R. W. B. Lewis declares that "if Hester has sinned, she has done so as an affirmation of life, and her sin is the source of life $\boxed{. . .}$" (62).

Ellipsis points
with period
after the
page citation

5. **Omission at the beginning of a sentence.** Most style guides discourage the use of ellipsis points for material omitted from the beginning of a source:

He states: $\boxed{\text{". . .}}$ the new parent has lost the wisdom and daily support of older, more experienced family members" (Zigler 34).

The passage would read better without the ellipsis points (see 7m):

He states that $\boxed{\text{"the}}$ new parent has lost the wisdom and daily support of older, more experienced family members" (Zigler 34).

6. **Omission of complete sentences and paragraphs.** When you omit an entire sentence or more, even a complete paragraph or more, use four ellipsis points with no space before the first. Just be sure that you maintain grammatical integrity with complete sentences before and after the ellipsis points.

Zigler reminds us that "child abuse is found more frequently in a single (female) parent home in which the mother is working$\boxed{. . . .}$ The unavailability of quality day care can only make this situation more stressful" (42).

7. **Omissions in poetry.** If you omit a word or phrase in your quotatation of poetry, indicate the omission with three or four ellipsis points just as you would with omissions in a prose passage. However, if you omit a complete line or more from the poem,

indicate the omission by a line of spaced periods that equals the average length of the lines.

Do ye hear the children weeping, O my brothers,
    Ere the sorrow comes with years?
They are leaning their young heads against their mothers,
And <u>that</u> cannot stop their tears.

> . . . .

They are weeping in the playtime of the others,
    In the country of the free. (Browning 382)

8. **Avoid excessive use of ellipsis points.** Many times you can be more effective if you incorporate short phrases rather than quote the whole passage sprinkled with many ellipsis points. Note how this next passage incorporates quotations without the use of ellipsis.

   The long-distance marriage, according to William Nichols, "works best when there are no minor-aged children to be considered," the two people are "equipped by temperament and personality to spend a considerable amount of time alone," and both are able to "function in a mature, highly independent fashion" (54).

7o Altering Quotations with Parentheses and Brackets

You will sometimes need to alter a quotation to emphasize a point or to make something clear. You might add material, italicize an important word, or use the word *sic* (Latin for *thus* or *so*) to alert readers that you have properly reproduced the material even though the logic or the spelling of the original might appear to be in error. Use parentheses or brackets according to these basic rules.

1. **Comment that follows the quotation.** Use parentheses to enclose comments or explanations that immediately follow a quotation as shown in this example:

   Boughman (46) urges carmakers to "direct the force of automotive airbags <u>upward</u> against the windshield" (emphasis added).

2. **Comment that goes inside the quotation.** Use brackets for interpolation, which means to insert new matter into a text or quotation. The use of brackets signals the insertion. Note the following rules.

a. **Use brackets to clarify:**

This same critic indicates that "we must avoid the temptation to read it [The Scarlet Letter] heretically" (118).

b. **Use brackets to establish correct grammar within an abridged quotation:**

"John F. Kennedy [was] an immortal figure of courage and dignity in the hearts of most Americans," notes one historian (Jones 82).

He states: "[The] new parent has lost the wisdom and daily support of older, more experienced family members" (Zigler 34).

c. **Use brackets to note the addition of underlining:**

He says, for instance, that the "extended family is now rare in contemporary society, and with its demise the new parent has <u>lost the wisdom</u> [my emphasis] and daily support of older, more experienced family members" (Zigler 42).

d. **Use brackets with *sic* to indicate errors in the original:**

Lovell says, "John F. Kennedy, assassinated in November of 1964 [sic], became overnight an immortal figure of courage and dignity in the hearts of most Americans" (62).

Note: The assassination occurred in 1963. However, do not burden your text with the use of "sic" for historical matter in which misspellings are obvious, as with: "Faire seemly pleasauance each to other makes."

8 Handling Format

This chapter addresses questions about margins, spacing, page numbers, and so forth. Section 8a shows you how to design the final manuscript, and section 8b explains matters of usage in an alphabetized glossary. Section 8c provides a short literary paper, and section 8d gives an example of a longer, more formal research paper.

8a Preparing the Final Manuscript in MLA Style

The format of a research paper consists of the following parts:

1. A title page
2. Outline
3. Abstract
4. The text of the paper
5. Content notes
6. Appendixes
7. Works Cited

Items 4 and 7 are required for a paper in the MLA style; use the other items to meet the needs of your research. *Note:* A paper in APA style (see Chapter 10) requires items 1, 3, 4, and 7, and the order differs for items 5–7.

Title Page or Opening Page

A research paper in MLA style does not need a separate title page unless you include an outline, abstract, or other prefatory matter. Place your identification in the upper left corner of your opening page, as shown on page 174.

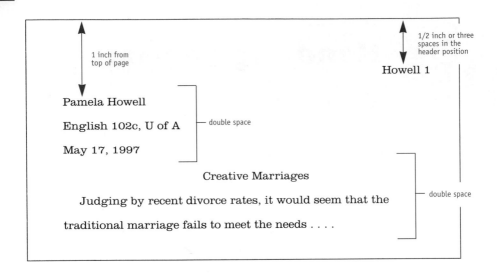

However, if you include prefatory matter, such as an outline, you need the title page with centered divisions for the title, the author, and the course identification.

An Interpretation of Melville's
Use of Biblical Characters
In <u>Billy Budd</u>

by
Doris Singleton

Freshman English II, Section 108b
Dr. Crampton
April 23, 1997

Follow these guidelines for writing a title page in MLA style:

1. Use an inverted pyramid to balance two or more lines.
2. Use capitals and lowercase letters without underlining and without quotation marks. Published works that appear as part of your title will require underlining (books) or quotation marks (short stories). Do not use a period after a centered heading.
3. Place your full name below the title, usually in the center of the page.

4. Employ separate lines, centered, to provide the course information, institution, instructor, date, or program (e.g., Honors Program).
5. Provide balanced, two-inch margins for all sides of the title page.
6. Use your computer to print a border on this page, if you so desire, but not on any other pages.

> **Note:** APA style requires a different setup for the title page; see page 292 for guidelines and an example.

Outline

Print your outline into the finished manuscript only if your instructor requires it. Place it after the title page on separate pages and number these pages with small Roman numerals, beginning with ii (for example, ii, iii, iv, v) at the top right-hand corner of the page just after your last name (e.g., Spence iii). For information on writing an outline, see Section 3c, pages 77–81 and the sample outline on pages 78–80.

Abstract

Include an abstract for a paper in MLA style only if your instructor requires it. (APA style requires the abstract; see Section 10h, pages 291–92). An abstract provides a brief digest of the paper's essential ideas in about 100 words. To that end, borrow from your introduction, use some of the topic sentences from your paragraphs, and use one or two sentences from your conclusion.

In MLA style, place the abstract on the first page of text (page 1) one double-space below the title and before the first lines of the text. Indent the abstract five spaces as a block, and indent the first line an additional five spaces. Use quadruple spacing at the end of the abstract to set it off from the text, which follows immediately after. You may also place the abstract on a separate page between the title page and the first page of text.

Remember that the abstract is usually read first and may be the *only* part read; therefore, make it accurate, specific, objective, and self-contained (i.e., so that it makes sense alone without references to the main text). Note the examples on pages 176 (MLA) and 293 (APA).

The Text of the Paper

Double-space throughout the entire paper except for the title page (page 174) and the separation of the abstract from the first line of text (page 176). In general, you should *not* use subtitles or numbered divisions for your

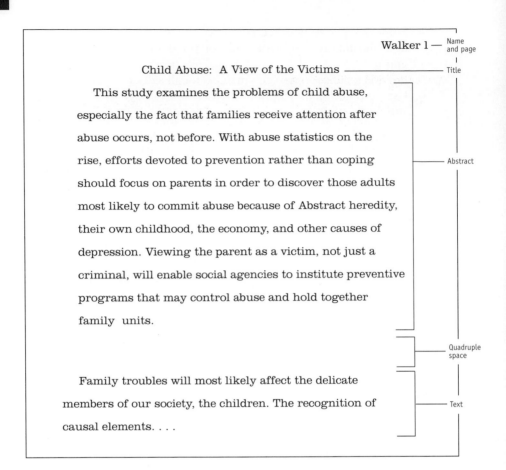

Walker 1 — Name and page

Child Abuse: A View of the Victims — Title

This study examines the problems of child abuse, especially the fact that families receive attention after abuse occurs, not before. With abuse statistics on the rise, efforts devoted to prevention rather than coping should focus on parents in order to discover those adults most likely to commit abuse because of Abstract heredity, their own childhood, the economy, and other causes of depression. Viewing the parent as a victim, not just a criminal, will enable social agencies to institute preventive programs that may control abuse and hold together family units. — Abstract

Quadruple space

Family troubles will most likely affect the delicate members of our society, the children. The recognition of causal elements. . . . — Text

paper, even if it becomes 20 pages long. Instead, use continuous paragraphing without subdivisions or headings. However, some scientific and business reports require subheads (see Chapters 10 and 11).

MLA style calls for present tense (see pages 273–75 for a discussion that compares tense for MLA and APA styles). If the closing page of your text runs short, leave the remainder of the page blank. Do not write "The End" or provide artwork as a closing signal. Do not start "Notes" or "Works Cited" on this final page of text. See also these sections:

1. Chapter 6 for a discussion of the three dominant parts of the text, introduction (Section 6e, pages 133–37), body (Section 6f, pages 137–41), and conclusion (Section 6g, pages 142–45).
2. "Drafting Your Paper" (Section 6d, pages 127–32) to learn more about such matters as tense, voice, and language.

    3. This section, pages 173–77, for details about name, page number, and course identification for your first page of text.

Content Endnotes Page

Label this page with the word "Notes," centered one inch from the top edge of the sheet and at least one double space below your page number. Double-space between the "Notes" heading and the first note. Number the notes in sequence with raised superscript numerals to match those within your text. Double-space all entries and double-space between them. See "Content Endnotes," pages 191–94, and see also the sample Notes page, found on page 229.

Appendix

Place additional material, if necessary, in an appendix preceding the Works Cited page. It is the logical location for numerous tables and illustrations, computer data, questionnaire results, complicated statistics, mathematical proofs, or detailed descriptions of special equipment. Double-space appendixes and begin each appendix on a new sheet. Continue your page numbering sequence in the upper right corner of the sheet. Label the page "Appendix," centered at the top of the sheet. If you have more than one appendix, use "Appendix A," "Appendix B," and so forth.

Works Cited

Center the heading "Works Cited" one inch from the top edge of the sheet. Continue the page numbering sequence in the upper right corner. Double-space throughout. Set the first line of each entry flush left and indent subsequent lines five spaces. If your software supports it, use the hanging indent. For samples and additional information see Chapter 9, "Works Cited," pages 233–72, and sample Works Cited on pages 234–35.

8b Glossary: Techniques for Preparing the Manuscript in MLA Style

The alphabetical glossary that follows will answer most of your miscellaneous questions about matters of form, such as margins, pagination, dates, and numbers. For matters not addressed below, consult the index, which will direct you to appropriate pages elsewhere in this text.

Abbreviations

Employ abbreviations often and consistently in notes and citations, but avoid them within sentences in the text.

> *Tip:* When drafting your text, abbreviate long titles, difficult names, or hard-to-spell terms (e.g., Tess for *Tess of the D'Urbervilles* or T for tourniquet), be certain that you expand the abbreviation with your software's FIND and REPLACE mode before printing the final copy.

In your Works Cited entries always abbreviate technical terms (anon., e.g., diss.), institutions (acad., assn., Cong.), dates (Jan., Feb.), states (OH or CA), and names of publishers (McGraw, UP of Florida). See also "Names of Persons," page 203, for comments on the correct abbreviations of honorary titles.

Abbreviations for Technical Terms and Institutions

abr.	abridged
AD	*anno Domini* ("in the year of the Lord"), precedes numerals with no space between letters, as in "AD 350"
anon.	anonymous
art., arts.	article(s)
assn.	association
assoc.	associate, associated
BC	Before Christ; follows numerals with no space between letters, as in "500 BC"
bk. bks.	book(s)
ca., c.	*circa* ("about"), used to indicate an approximate date, as in "ca. 1812"
cf.	*confer* ("compare" one source with another); not, however, to be used in place of "see" or "see also"
ch., chs.,	chapter(s); also shown as chap., chaps.
col., cols.	column(s)
comp.	compiled by or compiler
diss.	dissertation
doc.	document
ed., eds.	editor(s), edition or edited by
e.g.	*exempli gratia* ("for example"); preceded and followed by a comma
enl.	enlarged, as in enl. ed.
esp.	especially, as in "312–15, esp. 313"
et al.	*et alii* ("and others"); "John Smith et al." means John Smith and other authors
etc.	*et cetera* ("and so forth")
et pas.	*et passim* ("and here and there"); see *passim*
et seq.	*et sequens* ("and the following"); *9 et seq.* means "page nine and the following page"; compare *f.* and *ff.*
f., ff.	page or pages following a given page; *8f.* means page eight and the following page; but exact references are sometimes preferable, for example, "45–51, 55, 58" instead of "45ff." Acceptable also is "45+."

fig. figure

fl. *floruit* ("flourished"); which means a person reached greatness on these dates, as in "*fl.* 1420–50"; used when birth and death dates are unknown.

ibid. *ibidem* ("in the same place"); i.e., in the immediately preceding title, normally capitalized and underlined as in "Ibid., p. 34"

i.e. *id est* ("that is"); preceded and followed by a comma

illus. illustrated by, illustrations, or illustrator

infra "below"; refers to a succeeding portion of the text; compare *supra.* Generally, it is best to write "see below"

intro., introduction (by); also shown as introd.

loc. cit. *loco citato* ("in the place [passage] cited")

ms., mss. manuscript(s) as in "Cf. the mss. of Glass and Ford"

n., nn. note(s), as "23, n. 2" or "51 n."

narr. narrated by

n.d. no date (in a book's title or copyright pages)

no. nos. number(s)

n.p. no place (of publication)

ns new series

op. cit. *opere citato* ("in the work cited")

p., pp. page(s); do not use *ps.* for "pages"

passim "here and there throughout the work," for example, "67, 72, et passim," but also acceptable is "67+"

proc. proceedings

pseud. pseudonym

pt. pts. part(s)

rev. revised, revised by, revision, review, or reviewed by

rpt. reprint, reprinted

sec(s). section(s)

ser. series

sess. session

sic "thus"; placed in brackets to indicate an error has been made in the quoted passage and the writer is quoting accurately; see example on page 172

St., Sts. Saint(s)

st., sts. stanza(s)

sup. *supra* ("above"); used to refer to a preceding portion of the text; it is just as easy to write "above" or "see above"

supp. supplement(s)

s.v. *sub voce (verbo)* ("under the word or heading")

trans., tr. translator, translated, translated by, or translation

ts., tss. typescript, typescripts

viz. *videlicet* ("namely").

vol., vols. volume(s) (e.g., vol. 3)

vs., v. versus ("against"); used in citing legal cases

Abbreviations for Days and Months

Sun.	Jan.	Aug.
Mon.	Feb.	Sept.
Tues.	Mar.	Oct.
Wed.	Apr.	Nov.
Thurs.	May	Dec.
Fri.	June	
Sat.	July	

Abbreviations for States and Geographical Names

AL	Alabama	MT	Montana
AK	Alaska	NE	Nebraska
AZ	Arizona	NV	Nevada
AR	Arkansas	NH	New Hampshire
CA	California	NJ	New Jersey
CO	Colorado	NM	New Mexico
CT	Connecticut	NY	New York
DE	Delaware	NC	North Carolina
DC	District of Columbia	ND	North Dakota
FL	Florida	OH	Ohio
GA	Georgia	OK	Oklahoma
GU	Guam	OR	Oregon
HI	Hawaii	PA	Pennsylvania
ID	Idaho	PR	Puerto Rico
IL	Illinois	RI	Rhode Island
IN	Indiana	SC	South Carolina
IA	Iowa	SD	South Dakota
KS	Kansas	TN	Tennessee
KY	Kentucky	TX	Texas
LA	Louisiana	UT	Utah
ME	Maine	VT	Vermont
MD	Maryland	VI	Virgin Islands
MA	Massachusetts	VA	Virginia
MI	Michigan	WA	Washington
MN	Minnesota	WV	West Virginia
MS	Mississippi	WI	Wisconsin
MO	Missouri	WY	Wyoming

Abbreviations for Publishers' Names

Use the shortened forms below as guidelines. Some of these publishers no longer exist, but their imprints remain on copyright pages of the books.

Abrams	Harry N. Abrams, Inc.
Addison	Addison, Wesley, Longman
ALA	American Library Association
Allen	George Allen and Unwin Publishers, Inc.
Allyn	Allyn and Bacon, Inc.
Barnes	Barnes and Noble Books

Basic	Basic Books
Beacon	Beacon Press, Inc.
Bobbs	The Bobbs-Merrill Co., Inc.
Bowker	R. R. Bowker Co.
Cambridge UP	Cambridge University Press
Clarendon	Clarendon Press
Columbia UP	Columbia University Press
Dell	Dell Publishing Co., Inc.
Dodd	Dodd, Mead, and Co.
Doubleday	Doubleday and Co., Inc.
Farrar	Farrar, Straus, and Giroux, Inc.
Free	The Free Press
Gale	Gale Research Co.
GPO	Government Printing Company
Harcourt	Harcourt Brace Jovanovich, Inc.
Harper	Harper and Row Publishers, Inc.
HarperCollins	HarperCollins Publishers, Inc.
Harvard UP	Harvard UP
Heath	D. C. Heath and Co.
Holt	Holt, Rinehart, and Winston, Inc.
Houghton	Houghton Mifflin Co.
Indiana UP	Indiana University Press
Knopf	Alfred A. Knopf, Inc.
Lippincott	J. B. Lippincott Co.
Little	Little, Brown, and Co.
Longman	Addison, Wesley, Longman
Macmillan	Macmillan Publishing Co., Inc.
McGraw	McGraw-Hill, Inc.
MIT P	The MIT Press
MLA	Modern Language Association
Norton	W. W. Norton and Co., Inc.
Oxford UP	Oxford University Press
Prentice	Prentice-Hall, Inc.
Putnam's	G. P. Putnam's Sons
Random	Random House, Inc.
St. Martin's	St. Martin's Press, Inc.
Scott	Scott, Foresman and Co.
Scribner's	Charles Scribner's Sons
Simon	Simon and Schuster, Inc.
State U of New York P	State University of New York Press
U of Chicago P	University of Chicago Press
UP of Florida	University Press of Florida
Washington Square P	Washington Square Press

Abbreviations for Biblical Works

Use parenthetical documentation for biblical references in the text—that is, place the entry within parentheses immediately after the quotation, as in the example on page 182.

After the great flood God spoke to Noah, "And I will establish my covenant with you; neither shall all flesh be cut off any more by the waters of a flood; neither shall there any more be a flood to destroy the earth" (Gen. 9.11).

Do not italicize or underline titles of books of the Bible. Abbreviate books of the Bible except some very short titles, such as Ezra and Mark.

Acts	Acts of the Apostles
1 and 2 Chron.	1 and 2 Chronicles
Col.	Colossians
1 and 2 Cor.	1 and 2 Corinthians
Dan.	Daniel
Deut.	Deuteronomy
Eccles.	Ecclesiastes
Eph.	Ephesians
Exod.	Exodus
Ezek.	Ezekiel
Gal.	Galatians
Gen.	Genesis
Hab.	Habakkuk
Hag.	Haggai
Heb.	Hebrews
Hos.	Hosea
Isa.	Isaiah
Jer.	Jeremiah
Josh.	Joshua
Judg.	Judges
Lam.	Lamentations
Lev.	Leviticus
Mal.	Malachi
Matt.	Matthew
Mic.	Micah
Nah.	Nahum
Neh.	Nehemiah
Num.	Numbers
Obad.	Obadiah
1 and 2 Pet.	1 and 2 Peter
Phil.	Philippians
Prov.	Proverbs
Ps. (Pss.)	Psalm(s)
Rev.	Revelation
Rom.	Romans
1 and 2 Sam.	1 and 2 Samuel
Song of Sol.	Song of Solomon
1 and 2 Thess.	1 and 2 Thessalonians
1 and 2 Tim.	1 and 2 Timothy
Zech.	Zechariah
Zeph.	Zephaniah

Abbreviations for Literary Works

Shakespeare In parenthetical documentation, use italicized or underscored abbreviations for titles of Shakespearean plays once the full title is established, as shown in this example:

> Too late, Capulet urges Montague to end their feud, "O brother Montague, give me thy hand" (Rom. 5.3.296) .

Here is a complete list of abbreviations for Shakespeare's plays:

Ado	*Much Ado About Nothing*
Ant.	*Antony and Cleopatra*
AWW	*All's Well That Ends Well*
AYL	*As You Like It*
Cor.	*Coriolanus*
Cym.	*Cymbeline*
Err.	*The Comedy of Errors*
Ham.	*Hamlet*
1H4	*Henry IV, Part 1*
2H4	*Henry IV, Part 2*
H5	*Henry V*
1H6	*Henry VI, Part 1*
2H6	*Henry VI, Part 2*
3H6	*Henry VI, Part 3*
H8	*Henry VIII*
JC	*Julius Caesar*
Jn.	*King John*
LLL	*Love's Labour's Lost*
Lr.	*Lear*
Mac.	*Macbeth*
MM	*Measure for Measure*
MND	*A Midsummer Night's Dream*
MV	*Merchant of Venice*
Oth.	*Othello*
Per.	*Pericles*
R2	*Richard II*
R3	*Richard III*
Rom.	*Romeo and Juliet*
Shr.	*The Taming of the Shrew*
TGV	*Two Gentlemen of Verona*
Tim.	*Timon of Athens*
Tit.	*Titus Andronicus*
Tmp.	*Tempest*
TN	*Twelfth Night*
TNK	*The Two Noble Kinsmen*
Tro.	*Troilus and Cressida*
Wiv.	*The Merry Wives of Windsor*
WT	*Winter's Tale*

Use italics or underscoring for these abbreviations of Shakespeare's poems:

Luc.	*The Rape of Lucrece*
PhT	*The Phoenix and the Turtle*
PP	*The Passionate Pilgrim*
Son.	*Sonnets* (but "Sonnet 14")
Ven.	*Venus and Adonis*

Chaucer   Use the following abbreviations in parenthetical documentation. Italicize the book but not the individual tales:

CkT	The Cook's Tale
ClT	The Clerk's Tale
CT	*The Canterbury Tales*
CYT	The Canon's Yeoman's Tale
FranT	The Franklin's Tale
FrT	The Friar's Tale
GP	The General Prologue
KnT	The Knight's Tale
ManT	The Manciple's Tale
Mel	The Tale of Melibee
MerT	The Merchant's Tale
MilT	The Miller's Tale
MkT	The Monk's Tale
MLT	The Man of Law's Tale
NPT	The Nun's Priest's Tale
PardT	The Pardoner's Tale
ParsT	The Parson's Tale
PhyT	The Physician's Tale
PrT	The Prioress's Tale
Ret	Chaucer's Retraction
RvT	The Reeve's Tale
ShT	The Shipman's Tale
SNT	The Second Nun's Tale
SqT	The Squire's Tale
SumT	The Summoner's Tale
Th	The Tale of Sir Thopas
WBT	The Wife of Bath's Tale

Other Literary Works   Wherever possible in your in-text citations, use the initial letters of the title once the title is established. A reference to page 18 of Melville's *Moby Dick: The White Whale* could appear as: (*MD* 18). Use the following italicized abbreviations as guidelines:

Aen.	*Aeneid* by Vergil
Ag.	*Agamemnon* by Aeschylus
Ant.	*Antigone* by Sophocles
Bac.	*Bacchae* by Euripides
Beo.	*Beowulf*
Can.	*Candide* by Voltaire
Dec.	*Decameron* by Boccaccio

DJ	*Don Juan* by Byron
DQ	*Don Quixote* by Cervantes
Eum.	*Eumenides* by Aeschylus
FQ	*Faerie Queene* by Spenser
Gil.	*Gilgamesh*
GT	*Gulliver's Travels* by Swift
Il.	*Iliad* by Homer
Inf.	*Inferno* by Dante
MD	*Moby Dick* by Melville
Med.	*Medea* by Euripides
Nib.	*Nibelungenlied*
Od.	*Odyssey* by Homer
OR	*Oedipus Rex* by Sophocles
PL	*Paradise Lost* by Milton
SA	*Samson Agonistes* by Milton
SGGK	*Sir Gawain and the Green Knight*
SL	*Scarlet Letter* by Hawthorne

Accent Marks

When you quote, reproduce accents exactly as they appear in the original. You may need to use the character sets embedded within the computer software (see "Character Sets," page 191). Use ink if your typewriter or word processor does not support the marks.

> "La tradición clásica en españa," according to Romana, remains strong and vibrant in public school instruction (16).

Acknowledgments

Generally, acknowledgements are unnecessary. Nor is a preface required. Use a superscript reference numeral to your first sentence and then place any obligatory acknowledgements or explanations in a content endnote (see also page 191):

> [1]I wish here to express my thanks to Mrs. Horace A. Humphrey for permission to examine the manuscripts of her late husband.

> ***Note:*** Acknowledge neither your instructor nor typist for research papers, though such acknowledgments are standard with graduate theses and dissertations.

Ampersand

Avoid using the ampersand symbol (&) unless custom demands it (e.g., A & P). Use *and* for in-text citations in MLA style (e.g., Smith and Jones 213–14), *but do use* an ampersand in APA style references (e.g., Spenser & Wilson, 1994, p. 73).

Annotated Bibliography

An annotation describes the essential details of a book or article. Place it just after the facts of publication. Follow these suggestions:

1. Explain the main purpose of the work.
2. Briefly describe the contents.
3. Indicate the possible audience for the work.
4. Note any special features.
5. Warn of any defect, weakness, or suspected bias.

Provide enough information in about three sentences for a reader to have a fairly clear image of the work's purpose, contents, and special value. Turn to Section 4e, pages 97–99, to see a complete annotated bibliography.

Arabic Numerals

Both the MLA style and the APA style require Arabic numerals whenever possible: for volumes, books, parts, and chapters of works; acts, scenes, and lines of plays; cantos, stanzas, and lines of poetry.

Spell out whole numbers from one through ninety-nine. Use Arabic figures to express all numbers 100 and above (such as 154, 1,269). Write as Arabic numerals any numbers below 100 that cannot be spelled out in one or two words (e.g., 3¼ or 6.234).

For inclusive numbers that indicate a range, give the second number in full for numbers through 99 (e.g., 3–5, 15–21, 70–96). In MLA style, with three digits or more give only the last two in the second number unless more digits are needed for clarity (e.g., 98–101, 110–12, 989–1001, 1030–33, 2766–854). In APA style, with three digits or more give all numbers (e.g., 110–112, 1030–1033, 2766–2854).

Place commas between the third and fourth digits from the right, the sixth, and so on (e.g., 1,200 or 1,200,000). Exceptions are page and line numbers, addresses, the year, and zip codes (e.g., page 1620, at 12116 Nova Road, in 1985, or New York, NY 10012).

Use the number *1* in every case for numbers, not the lowercase *l* or uppercase *L,* especially if you are typing on a word processor or computer.

Numbers Expressed as Figures in Your Text

Use figures in your text according to the following examples:

1. All numbers 100 and above:

   a collection of 148 illustrations

2. Numbers that represent ages, dates, time, size, score, amounts of money, and numerals used as numerals:

   AD 200 *but* 200 BC
   in 1991–92 *or* from 1991 to 1992, *but not* from 1991–92
   32–34 *or* pages 32–34 *but not* pp. 32–34
   lines 32–34 *but not* ll. 32–34
   page 45, *but not* the forty-fifth page
   March 5, 1991 *or* 5 March 1991, *but not* both styles
   1990s *or* the nineties
   six o'clock *or* 6:00 p.m.
   6% *but* use "six percent" in discussions with few numbers
   $9.00 or $9
   scores in the 92–96 percentile
   from 1965 through 1970

3. Statistical and mathematical numbers:

   6.213
   0.5 *but not* .5
   consumed exactly 0.45 of the fuel

4. Numbers that precede units of measurement:

   a 5-milligram tablet
   use 7 centimeters of this fluid

5. Numbers below 100 grouped with higher numbers:

   3 out of 142 subjects
   tests 6 and 130
   but 150 tests in three categories (Tests and categories are different groups; they are not being compared.)

Numbers Expressed in Words in Your Text

Spell out numbers in the following instances:

1. Numbers less than 100 that are not used as measurements:

   three students
   he is one who should know
   a group of sixty-four professors
   six proposals
   three-dimensional renderings

2. Numbers less than 100 that are grouped with other numbers below 100:

   five sessions with six examinations in each session

the fifth of eight participants

3. Common fractions:

one fifth of the student population
eighty-eight errors
thirty-four times
a one-third majority

4. Any number that begins a sentence:

Thirty participants elected to withdraw.

5. The numbers *zero* and *one* when used alone:

zero-base budget planning
a one-line paragraph
one response *but* 1 of 155 responses

6. References to centuries:

twentieth century
twentieth-century literature

Numbers as Both Words and Figures

Combine words and figures in these situations:

1. Back to back modifiers:

twelve 6-year-olds or 12 six-year-olds,
   but not 12 6-year olds

2. Large numbers:

an operating budget of 4 million

Numbers in Documentation

Use numbers with in-text citations and works-cited entries according to the following examples:

(*Ham* 5.3.16–18)
(*Faust* 2.140)
(2 Sam. 2.1–8)
(Fredericks 23–24) (MLA style)
(Fredericks, 1995, pp. 23–24) (APA and CBE style)
2 vols.
Rpt. as vols. 13 and 14
MS CCCC 210
102nd Cong., 1st sess. S. 2411
16 mm., 29 min., color
Monograph 1962-M2

College English 15 (Winter 1995): 3–6 (MLA style)
Memory and Cognition, 3, 562–590 (APA style)
J. Mol. Biol. 1995;149:15–39 (CBE style)
Journal of Philosophy 29 (1995): 172–89 (footnote style)

Asterisks

Do not use asterisks (*) for tables, content notes, or illustrations (see Figures 34 and 35). Use numbers for tables and figures (e.g., Table 2 or Figure 3) and use letters for content notes (see Figure 34, page 199).

Bible

Use parenthetical documentation for biblical references in the text (e.g., 2 Chron 18.13). Do not underline the books of the Bible. For abbreviations, see page 182.

Borders

Computers offer you the opportunity for building borders around pages, paragraphs, and graphic designs. Use this feature with restraint. Place the title page within a full page border if you like, but *not* pages of your text. Use a border with a fill pattern, if desired, for graphs, charts, highlighted text, and other material that deserves special emphasis.

Bullets and Numbers

Computers will supply several bullet or number styles, which are indented lines that begin with a circle, square, diamond, triangle, number, or letter. Use this feature for a list:

- Observation 1: Kindergarten class
- Observation 2: First grade class
- Observation 3: Second grade class

Capitalization

Capitalizing Some Titles

For books, journals, magazines, and newspapers capitalize the first word, the last word, and all principal words, including words that that follow hyphens in compound terms (e.g., French-Speaking Islands). Do not capitalize articles, prepositions that introduce phrases, conjunctions, and the *to* in infinitives when these words occur in the middle of the title (for example, *The Last of the Mohicans*). For titles of articles and parts of books capitalize as for books (e.g., "Writing the Final Draft" or "Appendix 2"). If the first line of the poem serves as the title, reproduce it exactly as it appears in print (anyone lived in a pretty how town).

Note: Some scholarly styles capitalize only the first word and proper names of reference titles (including the first word of subtitles). Study the appropriate style for your field as found in Chapters 10 and 11.

Capitalizing After a Colon

When a *complete* sentence follows a colon, MLA style skips one space and does *not* capitalize the first word; APA style also skips one space but *does* capitalize the first word after the colon.

MLA style:

> The consequences of this decision will be disastrous: each division of the corporation will be required to cut twenty percent of its budget within this fiscal year.

APA style:

> They have agreed on the outcome: Informed subjects perform better than do uninformed subjects.

Do use a capital letter after the colon to introduce a rule or principle:

> Benjamin Franklin offers this maxim: "There never was a good war or bad peace."

Capitalizing Some Compound Words

Capitalize the second part of a hyphenated compound word only when it is used in a heading with other capitalized words:

> Low-Frequency Sound Equipment
> *but*
> Low-frequency sound distortion is caused by several factors.

Capitalizing Trade Names

Use capitals for trade names, such as: Pepsi, Plexiglass, Dupont, Dingo, Corvette, Xerox

Capitalizing Proper Names

Capitalize proper names used as adjectives *but not* the words used with them:

> Einstein's theory   Salk's vaccine

Capitalizing Specific Departments or Courses

Capitalize the specific names of departments or courses, but use lowercase when they are used in a general sense.

Department of Psychology *but* the psychology department
Psychology 314 *but* an advanced course in psychology

Capitalizing Nouns Used before Numerals or Letters

Capitalize the noun when the language denotes a place in a numbered series:

during Test 6	we observed Group C
as shown in Table 5	see Figure 2

However, do *not* capitalize nouns that make common references to books or tables followed by numerals:

chapter 12   page ix   column 14

Character Sets

Most computers provide characters that are unavailable on your keyboard. These are special letters, signs, and symbols, such as ♀, Σ, â, and ▶. The software instructions will help you find and utilize these marks and icons if you need them for your research writing.

Clip Art

Pictures, figures, and drawings are available on many computers, but avoid the temptation to embed them in your document. Clip art, in general, conveys an informal, sometimes comic effect, one that is inappropriate to the serious nature of most research papers.

Content Endnotes

As a general rule, put important matters in your text. Use a content note to explain research problems, conflicts in the testimony of the experts, matters of importance that are not germane to your discussion, interesting tidbits, credit to people and sources not mentioned in the text, and other tangential matters that you think will interest the readers. Therefore, after you have embedded most of your computer files into your draft, check the remaining files to find appropriate material for content endnotes.

Content notes should conform to these rules:

1. Content notes are *not* documentation notes. Use in-text citations to document your sources, not content notes. *Note:* Instructors in some fields, especially history, philosophy, and the fine arts, may ask for documentation footnotes; if so, see "Using the Footnote System," pages 324–32.
2. The content notes should be placed on a separate page(s) following the last page of text. Do not write them as footnotes at the

bottom of pages. See pages 324–32 for specifications on writing footnotes.

3. At a computer, use a word processing code to produce superscript numbers (e.g., ¹), or show them within slash marks after the period (e.g., /1/). *Note:* The computer superscript numerals often appear in a smaller size and a different font. At a typewriter, place superscript numerals within the text by turning the roller of the typewriter so that the Arabic numeral strikes about half a space above the line, like this.³ Each superscript numeral should follow immediately the material to which it refers, usually at the end of a sentence, with no space between the superscript numeral and a word or mark of punctuation, as show in this example:

> Third, a program to advise college students about politically correct language and campus attitudes¹ may incite demonstrations by both faculty and students against the censorship of free speech by both faculty and students.

Note: The superscript numeral above refers to note 1 under "Related Matters Not Germane to the Text," which follows. See also the sample paper on pages 218–31 for its use of superscript numerals and content endnotes.

---

4. Sources mentioned in endnotes must appear in your Works Cited even it they are not mentioned in the main body of text.

The samples below demonstrate various types of content notes.

Related Matters not Germane to the Text

¹The problems of politically correct language are explored in Adams, Tucker (4–5), Zalers, and also Young and Smith (583). These authorities cite the need for caution by administrators who would impose new measures on speech and behavior. Verbal abuse cannot be erased by a new set of unjust laws. Patrick German offers several guidelines for implementing an effective but reasonable program (170–72).

Blanket Citation

²On this point see Giarrett (3–4), de Young (579), Kinard (405–07), and Young (119).

³Cf. Campbell (<u>Masks</u> 1: 170–225; <u>Hero</u> 342–45), Frazer (312), and Baird (300–344).

Literature on a Related Topic

[4]For additional study of the effects of alcoholics on children, see especially the <u>Journal of Studies on Alcohol</u> for the article by Wolin et alii. and the bibliography on the topic by Orme and Rimmer (285–87). In addition, group therapy for children of alcoholics is examined in Hawley and Brown.

Major Source Requiring Frequent In-text Citations

[5]All citations to Shakespeare are to the Parrott edition.

[6]Dryden's poems are cited from the California edition of his <u>Works</u> and documented in the text with first references to each poem listing volume, page, and lines and with subsequent references citing only lines.

Reference to Source Materials

[7]Cf. James Baird, who argues that the whiteness of Melville's whale is "the sign of the all-encompassing God" (257). Baird states: "It stands for what Melville calls at the conclusion of the thirty-fifth chapter of <u>Moby-Dick</u> 'the inscrutable tides of God'; and it is of these tides as well that the great White Whale himself is the quintessential emblem, the iconographic representation" (257).

[8]On this point see also the essay by Patricia Chaffee in which she examines the "house" as a primary image in the fiction of Eudora Welty.

Explanation of Tools, Methods, or Testing Procedures

[9]Water samples were drawn from the identical spot each day at 8 a.m., noon, 4 p.m., and 8 p.m. with testing done immediately on site.

[10]The control group continued normal dietary routines, but the experimental group was asked to consume nuts, sharp cheeses, and chocolates to test acne development of its members against that of the control group.

[11]The initial sample was complete data on all twins born in Nebraska between 1920 and 1940. These dates were selected to provide test subjects 60 years of age or older.

> *Note:* A report of an empirical study in APA style would require an explanation of tools and testing procedures in the text under "Methods." See Chapter 10, pages 298–99.

Statistics

(See also "Figures and Tables," pages 195–99)

[12]Database results show 27,000 pupil-athletes in 174 high schools with grades 0.075 above another group of 27,000 non-athletes at the same high schools. Details on the nature of various <u>reward structures</u> are unavailable.

Acknowledgments for Assistance or Support

[13]Funds to finance this research were graciously provided by the Thompson-Monroe Foundation.

[14]This writer wishes to acknowledge the research assistance of Pat Luther, graduate assistant, Physics Department.

Variables or Conflicts in the Evidence

[15]Potlatch et al. included the following variables: the positive acquaintance, the equal status norm, the various social norms, the negative stereotypes, and sexual discrimination (415–20). However, racial barriers cannot be overlooked as one important variable.

[16]The pilot study at Dunlap School, where sexual imbalance was noticed (62 percent males), differed sharply from test results compared with those of other schools. The male bias at Dunlap thereby caused the writer to eliminate those scores from the totals.

Copyright Law

"Fair use" of the materials of others is permitted without the need for specific permission as long as your use is noncommercial for purposes of criticism, scholarship, or research. Under those circumstances, you can quote from sources and reproduce artistic works within reasonable limits. The law is vague on specific amounts that can be borrowed, suggesting only the "substantiality of the portion used in relation to the copyrighted work as a whole." In other words, you should be safe in reproducing the work of another as long as the portion is not substantial.

To protect your own work, keyboard in the upper right-hand corner of your manuscript, "Copyright © 19__ by _____." Fill the blanks with the proper year and your name. Then to register a work, order a form from the U. S. Copyright Office, Library of Congress, Washington, D.C. 20559.

Corrections

Because the computer can produce a printed copy quickly, you should make all proofreading corrections before printing a finished manuscript. With a typed paper, however, you may make corrections neatly using correction fluid, correction paper, or tape to cover and type over any errors. Add words or short phrases directly above a line, not in the margins. Keep such corrections to a minimum; retype pages that require four or more corrections. Do not strike over a letter, paste inserts onto the page, write vertically in the margins, or make handwritten notes on the manuscript pages.

Covers and Binders

Most instructors prefer that you submit manuscript pages with one staple in the upper left corner. Unless required, do not use a cover or binder.

Dates

See Arabic numerals, pages 186–89.

Definitions

For definitions and translations within your text, use single quotation marks without intervening punctuation, for example:

The use of <u>et alii</u> 'and others' has diminished in scholarly writing.

Endnotes for Documentation of Sources

An instructor or supervisor may prefer traditional superscript numerals within the text and documentation notes at the end of paper. If so, see Chapter 11, 324–32.

Etc. (*et cetera*)

Avoid using this abbreviation, which means "and so forth," by adding extra items to the list or by writing "and so forth."

Footnotes for Documentation

If your instructor requires you to use footnotes, see Chapter 11, pages 324–32, for discussion and examples.

Figures and Tables

A table is a systematic presentation of materials, usually in columns (see Figure 30). A figure is any nontext item that is not a table: blueprint, chart, diagram, drawing, graph, photo, photostat, map, and so on. Use graphs appropriately. A line graph serves a different purpose than a circle (pie) chart, and a bar graph plots different information than a scatter graph. Note the sample shown in Figure 31.

Table 1
Response by Class on Nuclear Energy Policy

	Freshmen	Sophomores	Juniors	Seniors
1. More nuclear power	150	301	75	120
2. Less nuclear power	195	137	111	203
3. Present policy is acceptable	87	104	229	37

Figure 30
Sample table in a paper.

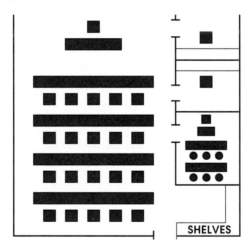

Figure 4: Audio Laboratory with Private
Listening Rooms and a Small Group Room

Figure 31
Sample illustration in a paper.

Your figures and tables, as shown above, should follow these guidelines:

1. Present only one kind of information in each one, and make it as simple and as brief as possible. Frills and fancy artwork may distract rather than attract the reader.
2. Place small figures and tables within your text; place large figures, sets of figures, or complex tables on separate pages in an appendix (see "Appendix," page 302).
3. Place the figure or table as near to your textual discussion as possible, but it should not precede your first mention of it.
4. In the text, explain the significance of the figure or table. Describe the figure or table so that your reader may understand your

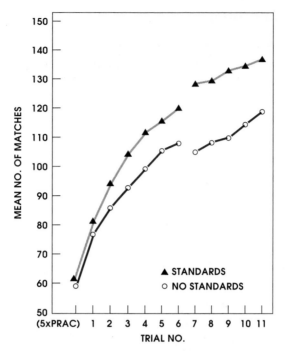

Figure 6: Mean Number of Matches by Subject
with and without Standard (by Trial). Source:
Lock and Bryan (289).

Figure 32
Sample illustration with clear labels and caption.

observations without reference to the figure or table, but avoid
giving too many numbers and figures in your text. Refer to figures and tables by number (for example, "Figure 5" or by number and page reference ("Table 4, 16"). Do not use vague references (such as "the table above," "the following illustration," or
"the chart below").

5. Write a caption for the figure or table so that your reader can understand it without reference to your discussion. Place the cap-
   tain *above* the table and *below* the figure, flush left, in full capital letters or in capitals and lowercase, but do not mix forms in
   the same paper. An alternative is to place the caption on the same
   line with the number (see Figure 32).

6. Number figures consecutively throughout the paper with Arabic
   numbers, preceded by *Fig.* or *Figure* (for example, "Figure 4").
   Place the figure number and the caption *below* the figure as
   shown in Figures 31, 32, and 33.

7. Number tables consecutively throughout the paper with Arabic
   numerals, preceded by "Table" (for example, "Table 2"). Place the

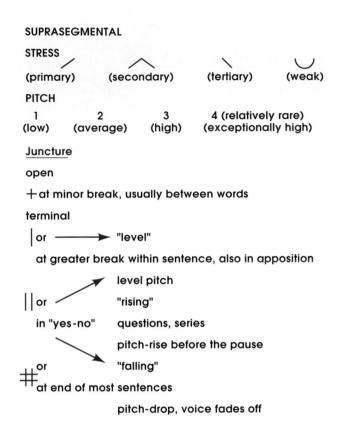

Figure 9: Phonemes of English. Generally this figure follows the Trager-Smith system, used widely in American linguistics. Source: Anna H. Live (1066).

Figure 33
Sample illustration with explanatory caption.

numbered designation one double-space flush left *above* the table, as shown in Figures 30, 34, and 35.

8. Insert a caption or number for each column of a table, centered above the column or, if necessary, inserted diagonally or vertically above it.

9. When inserting an explanatory or reference note, place it below both a table and an illustration; then use a lower case letter as the identifying superscript, not an Arabic numeral (see Figures 34 and 35).

10. Sources are abbreviated as in-text citations and full documentation must appear in the Works Cited.

Table 2[a]

Mean Scores of Six Values Held by College Students According to Sex

All Students		Men		Women	
Pol.	40.61	Pol.	43.22	Aesth.	43.86
Re.	40.51	Theor.	43.09	Rel.	43.13
Aesth.	40.29	Econ.	42.05	Soc	41.62
Econ.	39.45	Soc.	37.05	Econ.	36.85
Soc.	39.34	Aesth.	36.72	Theor.	36.50

[a]Carmen J. Finley, et al. (165).

Figure 34
Sample table with in-text citation.

Table 3

Inhibitory Effects of Sugars on the Growth of Clostribium Histoylticum (11 Strains) on Nutrient Agar

Sugar added 2%	Aerobic incubation (hr) 24	48	Anaerobic incubation (hr) 24	48
None	11[a]	11	11	11
Glucose	0	0	11	11
Maltose	0	0	11	11
Lactose	1	1	11	11
Sucrose	3	6	11	11
Arabinose	0	0	0	0
Inositol	0	0	11	11
Xylose	0	0	0	0
Sorbitol	2	7	11	11
Manitol	9	10	11	11
Rhamnose	0	0	11	11

Source: Nishida and Imaizumi (481).
[a]No. of strains that gave rise to colonies in the presence of the sugar.

Figure 35
Sample table with in-text citation and notes.

Fonts

Most computers offer a variety of typefaces. Courier (**Courier**), the typewriter font, is always a safe choice, but you may use others, such as a nonserif typeface like Arial (**Arial**) or a serif typeface like Times Roman (**Times Roman**). Use the same font consistently throughout for your text, but shift to different fonts if desired for tables, illustrations, and other matter.

Foreign Cities

In general, spell the names of foreign cities as they are written in original sources. However, for purposes of clarity, you may substitute an English name or provide both with one in parentheses:

Köln (Cologne)   Braunschweig (Brunswick)
München (Munich)   Praha (Prague)

Foreign Languages

Underscore or italicize foreign words used in an English text:

Like his friend Olaf, he is <u>aut Caesar</u>, <u>aut nihil</u>, either
overpowering perfection or ruin and destruction.

Do not underscore or italicize quotations of a foreign language:

Obviously, he uses it to exploit, in the words of Jean Laumon,
"une admirable mine de themes poetiques."

Do not underscore or italicize foreign titles of magazine or journal articles, but do underline the names of the magazines or journals:

Arrigoitia, Luis de. "Machismo, folklore y creación en Mario
Vargas Llosa." <u>Sin nombre</u> 13.4 (1983): 19–25.

Do not underscore or italicize foreign words of places, institutions, proper names, or titles that precede proper names:

Racine became extremely fond of Mlle Champmeslé, who
interpreted his works at the Hotel de Bourgogne.

For titles of French, Italian, and Spanish works, capitalize the first word, the proper nouns, but not adjectives derived from proper nouns:

La noche de Tlatelolco: Testimoniosde historia oral
Realismo y realidad en la narrativa argentina

Titles of German works: capitalize the first word, all nouns, and all adjectives derived from names of persons:

Über die Religion: Reden an die Gebildeten unter ihren Verächtern

Graphics

If they will contribute in a demonstrable way to your research study, you may create graphic designs and import them into your document. Computer software offers various methods for performing this task. See "Figures and Tables," pages 195–99, for basic rules; see also the paper by Patti M. Bracy, pages 292–302, for examples.

Headers and Footers

The software of your computer will automatically insert your name and the page number at the top, right margin of each page for MLA style (e.g., Morris 3). Use a numbering or header command to set an automatic numbering sequence. For APA style (see page 292) you will need a shortened title and page number with five spaces between the shortened title and the page number (see page 293 for an example). Footers are seldom used.

Headings

Begin every major heading on a new page of your paper (title page, opening page, notes, appendix, works cited). Center the heading in capital and lowercase letters one inch from the top of the sheet. Use a double-space between the heading and your first line of text. MLA papers do not require subheads, but see Section 10c (page 276) for an explanation of subheads in APA styles. (APA style also requires double-spaces between headings and text, but see Chapter 10, page 296, for use of a quadruple space above and below an equation or a figure or table.) Number *all* text pages, including those with major headings. (See also "Spacing," page 210.)

Hypertext Link

A hypertext link is simply a signal within your text that links a key word or phrase to another document. It assumes that your audience will read your document on the computer. Using your software appropriately, you can insert a "button" or a highlighted hypertext term. If the reader clicks the mouse on the word or touches certain keys (e.g., F2 or Ctrl-G), the reader will be automatically transported to another part of the text, perhaps an appendix, an endnote, or a spreadsheet. You may wish to use this technique for instructors who will read your work at their computer.

Hyphenation

Do not hyphenate words at the end of lines. If necessary, turn off your computer's automatic hyphenation command. See also "Punctuation," pages 205–09.

Indentation

Indent paragraphs 5 spaces or a half inch. Indent long quotations (4 lines or more) 10 spaces or one inch from the left margin. If you quote only one paragraph, do not indent the first line more than the rest. However, if you quote two or more paragraphs, indent the first line of each paragraph an extra three spaces or a quarter inch (see also Section 7k, pages 166–67). Indent entries of the Works Cited five spaces on the second and succeeding lines. Indent the first line of content footnotes five spaces. Other styles (APA or CBE) have different requirements (see Chapters 10 and 11, pages 273–332).

Italics

If your word-processing system and your printer will reproduce italic lettering, use it. Otherwise, show italics in a typed manuscript by underscoring (see also "Underscoring," pages 212–14).

Length of the Research Paper

A reasonable length is ten pages, but setting an arbitrary length for a research paper is difficult. The ideal length for your work will depend on the nature of the topic, the reference material available, the time allotted to the project, and your initiative as the researcher and writer. Your instructor or supervisor may set definite restrictions concerning the length of your paper. Otherwise, try to generate a paper of 2,000 to 3,000 words, about ten typewritten pages, excluding the title page, outline, endnotes, and Works Cited pages. *Tip:* When you run the spell checker, the final window will usually give the total number of words.

Margins

A basic one-inch margin on all sides is recommended. Place your page number one-half inch down from the top edge of the paper and one inch from the right edge. Your software will provide a ruler, menu, or style palette that allows you to set the margins. *Tip:* If you develop a header, the running head may appear one inch from the top, in which case your first line of text will begin 1½ inches from the top. Use a ragged right margin.

Monetary Units

In general, spell out monetary amounts only if you can do so in three words or less. Conform to the following:

ten dollars
$14.25 *but not* fourteen dollars and twenty-five cents
$4 billion *or* four billion dollars
$10.3 billion *or* $10,300,000,000

$63 *or* sixty-three dollars
The fee is one hundred dollars ($100) *or* the fee is one hundred (100)
 dollars
two thousand dollars *or* $2,000
thirty-four cents

In business and technical writing that frequently uses numbers, use numerals with appropriate symbols:

$99.45   6 @ 15.00   £92

Names of Persons

As a general rule, first mention of a person requires the full name (e.g., Emest Hemingway or Margaret Mead) and thereafter requires only usage of the surname, such as Hemingway or Mead. (*Note:* The Chicago footnote style conforms to these instructions, but APA style [Chapter 10] and CBE number style use *only* last names in the text in all cases.) Omit formal titles (Mr., Mrs., Dr., Hon.) in textual and note references to distinguished persons, living or dead. Convention suggests that certain prominent figures require the title (e.g., Lord Byron, Dr. Johnson, Dame Edith Sitwell) while others, for no apparent reason, do not (e.g., Tennyson, Browne, and Hillary rather than Lord Tennyson, Sir Thomas Browne, or Sir Edmund Hillary). Where custom dictates, you may employ simplified names of famous persons (e.g., use Dante rather than the surname Alighieri and use Michelangelo rather than Michelangelo Buonarroti). You may also use pseudonyms where custom dictates (e.g., George Eliot, Maxim Gorky, Mark Twain). Refer to fictional characters by names used in the fictional work (e.g., Huck, Lord Jim, Santiago, Capt. Ahab).

Numbering

Pagination

Use a header to number your pages in the upper right-hand corner of the page. Depending on the software, you can create the head with the numbering or the header feature. It may appear ½-inch or a full inch down from the top edge of the paper and one inch from the right edge. Precede the number with your last name unless anonymity is required, in which case you may use a shortened version of your title rather than your name, as in APA style (see page 293). Otherwise, type the heading and then triple-space to your text.

> *Note:* If your computer numbers pages automatically at the bottom of the sheet and you don't know how to change the configuration, leave the numbering at the bottom and put only your name in the upper right corner.

Use lowercase Roman numerals (ii, iii, iv) on any pages that precede your text. If you have a separate title page, count it as a page i, but do not type it on the page. You *should* put a page number on your opening page of text, even if you include course identification (see page 174).

Numbering a Series of Items

Within a sentence, incorporate a series of items into your text with parenthetical numbers or lower-case letters:

College instructors are usually divided into four ranks: (1) instructors, (2) assistant professors, (3) associate professors, (4) full professors.

Present a longer group of items in an enumerated list:

College instructors are divided into four ranks:

1. Full professors generally have 15 or more years of experience, have the Ph.D. or other terminal degree, and have achieved distinction in teaching and scholarly publications.
2. Associate professors. . . .

Paper

Print on one side of white bond paper, 16- or 20-pound weight, 8½ by 11 inches. If you write the final draft in longhand, use ruled theme paper. If you write the paper by word processor or computer, use the best quality paper available, and select letter quality if you have a dot matrix printer. Avoid erasable paper. Carefully strip continuous sheet forms of the side bars, separate the pages, and staple the manuscript. Do not enclose the manuscript within a cover or binder unless your instructor asks you to do so.

Percentages

Spell out percentages when they can be spelled out in three words or less:

percent *not* per cent
one hundred percent *but* 150 percent
a two-point average *but* a 2.568 average
one metric ton *but* 0.907 metric ton or 3.150 metric tons
forty-five percent *but* 45½ percent *or* 45½%

In business, scientific, and technical writing that requires frequent use of percentages, write all percentages as numerals with appropriate symbols:

100%   45½   12%   6 @ 15.00   £92 $99.45

Proofreaders' Marks

Be familiar with the most common proofreading symbols so that you can correct your own copy or mark your copy for a typist (see the inside back cover for a list of the standard symbols).

Punctuation

Consistency is the key to punctuation. Careful proofreading of your paper for punctuation errors will generally improve the clarity and accuracy of your writing.

Apostrophe

To form the possessive of singular nouns, add an apostrophe and *s* (e.g., the typist's ledger). Add only the apostrophe with plural nouns ending in *s* (e.g., several typists' ledgers). Use the apostrophe and *s* with singular proper nouns of people and places even if the noun ends in an *s* (e.g., Rice's story, Rawlings's novel, Arkansas's mountains, *but* the Rawlingses' good fortune). Exceptions are the names of *Jesus* and *Moses* (e.g., Jesus' scriptures, Moses' words and hellenized names of more than one syllable ending in *es* (e.g., Euripides' dramas). Use apostrophes to form the plurals of letters (e.g., a's and b's) but not to form the plural of numbers or abbreviations (e.g., ACTs in the 18s and 19s, the 1980s, sevens, three MDs).

Brackets

Use brackets to enclose words of the text. Use brackets to enclose phonetic transcription, mathematical formulas, and interpolations into a quotation. An interpolation is the insertion of your words into the text of another person (see Section 7o, pages 171–72, for examples).

Use brackets to enclose parenthetical material inside parentheses:

> The escape theme explains the drama's racial conflict (see esp. Knight, who describes the Younger family as one that opposes "racial discrimination in a supposedly democratic land" [34]).

or

> Consult the tables at the end of the report (i.e., the results for the experimental group [$\underline{n}$ = 5] are also listed in Figure 3, page 16.)

In addition, use brackets to present fractions:

> $\underline{a} = [(1 + \underline{b})/\underline{x}]^{1/2}$

To present fractions in a line of text, use a slash mark (/) and parentheses first ( ), then brackets [( )], and finally braces {[( )]}. Some typewriters do not have brackets or braces; therefore, leave extra space for the brackets and braces and write them in with ink.

Colons

Use colons to introduce examples or further elaboration on what has been said in the first clause. Semicolons join independent clauses. (For proper use of colons and semicolons within quotations see Section 7j, pages 165–66, and for usage within documentation see Section 9b, pages 237–50). Skip only one space after the colon or semicolon. Do not capitalize the first word after a colon or semicolon, but see page 190 for special applications. Do not use a colon where a semicolon is appropriate for joining independent clauses. Here a colon is used to introduce an elaboration or definition:

> Weathers reminds us of crucial differences in rhetorical profiles that no writer should forget: colloquial wording differs radically from formal wording and a plain texture of writing differs greatly from a rich texture.

Commas

Use commas between items listed in a series of three or more, including before the *and* and *or* that precedes the last item. For example:

> Reader (34), Scott (61), and Wellman (615–17) agree with Steinbeck on this point.

Never use a comma and a dash together. The comma follows a parenthesis if your text requires the comma:

> How should we order our lives, asks Thompson (22–23), when we face "hostility from every quarter"?

The comma goes inside single quotation marks as well as double quotation marks:

> Such irony is discovered in Smith's article, "The Sources of Franklin's 'The Ephemera,'" but not in most textual discussions.

Dashes

Use dashes to set off special parts of the text that require emphasis. On a computer, use the character set, which will give you an unbroken line. Otherwise, type two hyphens with no blank space before or after, as shown here:

> Two issues--slow economic growth and public debt--may prevent an early recovery for the banking industry.

Exclamation Marks

Exclamation marks make an emotional ending to a sentence. They should be avoided in research writing. A forceful declarative sentence is preferable.

Hyphens

Use hyphens to divide the syllables of words. Both MLA style and APA style discourage division of words at the end of a line, asking instead that you leave the lines short, if necessary, rather than divide a word. If you are using a word processing program with automatic hyphenation, you can usually disengage it.

If you must use hyphenation, always double-check word division by consulting a dictionary. Do not hyphenate proper names. Avoid separating two letters at the end or beginning of a line (for example, use "depend-able," not "de-pendable").

When using hyphenated words, follow a few general rules.

1. Do not hyphenate unless the hyphen serves a purpose: *a water treatment program* but *a water-powered turbine*.
2. Compound adjectives that *precede* a noun usually need a hyphen but those which follow do not: *same-age children* but *children of the same age*.
3. When a common base serves two or more compound modifiers, omit the base on all except the last modifier, but retain the hyphens on every modifier: *right- and left-hand margins* and *5-, 10-, and 15-minute segments*.
4. Write most words with prefixes as one word: *overaggressive, midterm, antisocial, postwar.* But there are exceptions: *self-occupied, self-paced, self-protection, post-1980.* Consult a dictionary regularly to resolve doubts on such narrow problems as *anti-Clinton* but *antisocial*.
5. Use a hyphen between pairs of coequal nouns: *scholar-athlete* or *trainer-coach*.

Parentheses

Use parentheses to enclose words and numbers in your text in the following situations:

1. In-text citations:

   Larson (23–25) and Mitchell (344–45) report. . . .

2. Independent matter:

   The more recent findings (see Figure 6) show. . . .

3. Headings for a series:

   The tests were (1) . . . (2) . . . and (3). . . .

4. First use of an abbreviation:

   The test proved reaction time (RT) to be. . . .

Periods

Use periods to signal the end of complete sentences of the text, endnotes, footnotes, and all bibliography entries. Use only one space after all periods. When periods are used between numbers indicate related parts (e.g., 2.4 for act 2, scene 4), use no space. The period normally follows the parenthesis. (The period is placed within the parenthesis only when the parenthetical statement is a complete sentence, as in this instance.) See also Section 7n, pages 169–71, for explanation of the period in conjunction with ellipsis points.

Quotation Marks

Use quotation marks to enclose all quotations used within your text. Long indented quotations need no marks because the indentation signals the use of a quotation. Quotations require proper handling to maintain the style of the original; they also require precise documentation (see examples and discussions in Chapter 7, pages 155–72).

In addition, use quotation marks for titles of articles, essays, short stories, short poems, songs, chapters of books, unpublished works, and episodes of radio and television programs.

Use quotation marks for words and phrases that you purposely misuse, misspell, or use in a special sense:

> The "patrons" turned out to be criminals searching for a way to
> launder their money.

However, use underscoring or italics for all linguistic forms (letters, words, and phrases) that are subjects of discussion (for example, "The word *patron*"). Use quotation marks around parenthetical translations of words or phrases from another language:

> Jose Donoso's El jardin de al lado "The Garden Next Door"
> dramatizes an artistic crisis that has ethical and political
> implications.

Use single quotation marks for definitions that appear without intervening punctuation (for example, *nosu* 'nose'). In other cases use quotation marks for foreign phrases and sentences and single quotation marks for your translation/definition.

> It was important to Bacon that the 1625 collection appear in
> France as "un oeuvre nouveau" 'a new work' (14:536).

Semicolons

Use semicolons to join two distinct independent clauses:

> Weathers reminds us of crucial differences in rhetorical profiles
> that no writer should forget; the writer who does forget may

substitute colloquial wording where formal is appropriate or may use a plain texture where rich texture is needed.

Roman Numerals

Use capital Roman numerals for titles of persons (Elizabeth II) and major sections of an outline (see pages 77–81). Use lowercase Roman numerals for preliminary pages of text, as for a preface or introduction (iii, iv, v). Otherwise, use Arabic numerals (e.g., Vol. 5, Act 2, Ch. 16, Plate 32, 2 Sam. 2.1–8, or *Iliad* 2.121–30), *except* when writing for some instructors in history, philosophy, religion, music, art, and theater, in which case you may need to use Roman numerals (e.g., III, Act II, I Sam. ii. 1–8, *Hamlet* I.ii.5–6). Here is a list of Roman numerals:

	Units	Tens	Hundreds
1	i	x	c
2	ii	xx	cc
3	iii	xxx	ccc
4	iv	xl	cd
5	v	l	d
6	vi	lx	dc
7	vii	lxx	dcc
8	viii	lxxx	dccc
9	ix	xc	cm

Thus, xxi equals 21, cx equals 110, and clv equals 155.

Running Heads

Repeat your last name in the upper right corner of every page just in front of the page number (see the sample paper, pages 214–18). APA style requires a short title at the top of each page just above the page number (see "Short Titles in the Text," immediately following.)

Short Titles in the Text

Use abbreviated titles of books and articles mentioned often in the text after a first, full reference. For example, after initial usage *Backgrounds to English as Language* should be shortened to *Backgrounds* both in the text, notes, and in-text citations (see also page 163) but not in the bibliography entry. Mention *The Epic of Gilgamesh* and thereafter use *Gilgamesh* (*Note*: Be certain to italicize it when referring to the work).

When keyboarding a manuscript according to APA style, shorten your own title to the first two or three words and place it at the top, right corner of each page for identification purposes (for example, "Discovering Recall

Differences of the Aged" should be shortened to "Discovering" or "Discovering Recall Differences"). See pages 293–302 for examples of the short title as page heading.

Slang

Avoid the use of slang. When using it in a language study, enclose in double quotation marks any words to which you direct attention. Words used as words, however, require underlining (see pages 213–14).

Spacing

As a general rule, double-space everything—the body of the paper, all indented quotations, and all reference entries. Footnotes, if used, should be single-spaced, but endnotes should be double-spaced (see pages 324–32). APA style (see pages 273–302) double-spaces after all headings and separates text from indented quotes or from figures by double-spacing; however, APA advocates quadruple-spacing above and below statistical and mathematical expressions.

Space after punctuation according to these stipulations:

1. Use one space after commas, semicolons, and colons (see also "Capitalizing After a Colon," page 190)
2. Use one space after punctuation marks at the end of sentences
3. Use one space after periods that separate parts of a reference citation (see page 208 or 237)
4. Do not use space before or after periods within abbreviations (i.e., e.g., a.m.)
5. Use one space between initials of personal names (M. C. Bone)
6. Do not use a space before or after a hyphen (a three-part test) *but* use 1 space before and after a hyphen used as a minus sign (e.g., $a - b + c$) and one space before but none after a hyphen for a negative value (e.g., -3.25)
7. Do not use a space before or after a dash (the evidence—interviews and statistics—was published)

Spelling

Spell accurately. Always use the computer to check spelling if the software is available. When in doubt, consult a dictionary. If the dictionary says a word may be spelled in two separate ways, be consistent in the form employed, as with *theater* and *theatre,* unless the variant form occurs in quoted materials. Use American (as opposed to English) spelling throughout.

Statistical and Mathematical Copy

Use the simplest form of equation that can be made by ordinary mathematical calculation. If an equation cannot be reproduced entirely by keyboard, type what you can and fill in the rest with ink. As a general rule, keep equations on one line rather than two:

$$\text{Acceptable:} \quad \frac{a + b}{x + y}$$

$$\text{Better:} \quad (a + b)/(x + y)$$

APA style requires quadruple line spacing above and below an equation.

Superscript Numerals in the Text

On a computer, use the appropriate keys as explained in the product manual or in the Help index. If necessary, place the number with slash marks (e.g, "the end of the sentence./3/"). At a typewriter, create a raised numeral by turning the roller of the typewriter so that the Arabic numeral strikes about half a space above the line, like this.[14] See also Section 11c, "Using the Footnote System."

Table of Contents

A table of contents is unnecessary for undergraduate research papers unless the instructor requests one, but *do* write a table of contents for a graduate thesis or dissertation (see "Theses and Dissertations," which follows). Many computers will develop a table of contents.

Theses and Dissertations

The author of a thesis or dissertation must satisfy the requirements of the college's graduate program. Therefore, even though you may use MLA style or APA style, you must abide by certain additional rules with regard to paper, typing, margins, and introductory matter such as title page, approval page, acknowledgment page, table of contents, abstract, and other matters. Use both the graduate school guidelines and this book to maintain the appropriate style and format.

Titles Within Titles

For a title to a book that includes another title indicated by quotation marks, retain the quotation marks.

O. Henry's Irony in "The Gift of the Magi"

For a title of an article within quotation marks that includes a title to a book, as indicated by underlining, retain the underlining or use italic lettering.

>   "*Great Expectations* as a Novel of Initiation"

For a title of an article within quotation marks that includes another title indicated by quotation marks, enclose the shorter title within single quotation marks.

>   "A Reading of O. Henry's 'The Gift of the Magi'"

For an underscored title to a book that incorporates another title that normally receives underscoring, do not underscore or italicize the shorter title nor place it within quotation marks.

>   *Interpretations of* Great Expectations
>   <u>Using Shakespeare's</u> Romeo and Juliet <u>in the Classroom</u>

Typing

Submit the paper in printed or typed form, although some instructors will accept handwritten manuscripts, if they are neat, legible, and written in blue or black ink on ruled paper. Print on only on one side of the page. In addition to the courier font (traditional with typewriters), you may use the clear, legible typefaces supported by computer software (Helvetica, Times Roman, Bodini, and others). Use no hyphens at the ends of lines. Avoid widows and orphans, which are single lines at the top or the bottom of the page; some computers will help you correct this problem. Use special features—boldface, italics, graphs, color—with discretion. The writing, not the graphics, will earn the credits and the better grades. You are ultimately responsible for correct pagination and accuracy of the manuscript. See also "Revising the Rough Draft," pages 145–47.

Underscoring

Titles

Use italics, not underscoring, if your computer will produce it. Otherwise, underscoring takes the place of italics in a keyboarded manuscript. Use a continuous line for titles of more than one word. Italicize or underline the titles of the following types of works:

Type of work	*Example*
aircraft	*Enola Gay*
ballet	*The Nutcracker*
book	*Earthly Powers*
bulletin	*Production Memo 3*
drama	*Desire Under the Elms*

film	*Treasure of the Sierra Madre*
Journal	*Journal of Sociology*
magazine	*Newsweek*
newspaper	*The Nashville Banner*
novel	*The Scarlet Letter*
opera	*Rigoletto*
painting	*Mona Lisa*
pamphlet	*Ten Goals for Successful Sales*
periodical	*Scientific American*
play	*Cat on a Hot Tin Roof*
poem	*Idylls of the King* (only if book length)
radio show	*Grand Ole Opry*
recording	*The Poems of Wallace Stevens*
sculpture	*David*
ship	*Titanic*
short novel	*Billy Budd*
symphony	Beethoven's *Eroica*
	but
	Beethoven's Symphony no. 3 in E-flat
	(to identify form, number, and key)
television	*Tonight Show* (program title, not a single episode)
yearbook	*The Pegasus*

In contrast, place quotation marks around: articles, essays, chapters, sections, short poems, stories, songs, lectures, sermons, reports, and individual episodes of television programs.

If separately published as a single book or booklet, underline titles of essays, lectures, poems, proceedings, reports, sermons, and stories. However, these items are usually published as an anthology of sermons or a collection of stories, in which cases you would underscore or italicize the title of the anthology or collection.

Do not underscore sacred writings (Genesis or Old Testament); series (The New American Nation Series); editions (Variorum Edition of W. B. Yeats); societies (Victorian Society); courses (Greek Mythology); divisions of a work (preface, appendix, canto 3, scene 2); or descriptive phrases (Nixon's farewell address or Reagan's White House years).

Individual Words for Emphasis

The use of underscoring to emphasize certain words or phrases is discouraged. A better alternative is to position the key word in such a way as to accomplish the same purpose. For example:

EXPRESSED EMPHASIS	Perhaps an answer lies in <u>preventing</u> abuse, not in makeshift remedies after the fact.
BETTER	Prevention of abuse is a better answer than makeshift remedies after the fact.

Some special words and symbols require underlining.

1. Species, genera, and varieties:

   <u>Penstemon caespitosus</u> subsp. <u>thompsoniae</u>

2. Letter, word, or phrase cited as a linguistic sample:

   the letter <u>e</u> in the word <u>let</u>

3. Letters used as statistical symbols and algebraic variables:

   trial <u>n</u> of the <u>t</u> test or <u>C</u>(3, 14) = 9.432

Word Division

Avoid dividing any word at the end of a line. Leave the line short rather than divide a word (see "Hyphens," page 207).

8c Sample Paper: A Short Essay with Documentation

The following paper demonstrates correct form for short papers that use only a few secondary sources. Keep in mind that a short paper, like the long formal research paper, requires correct in-text citations and a list of references. This paper is shown in Arial typeface, one of the fonts available on many computers. Most instructors will accept papers printed in Arial and other typefaces. You may also use italics rather than underscoring and other featurers of the computer.

Wickham 1

Jay Wickham

Professor Thompson

Heritage 1020

5 May 1997

Same Construction, Different Walls: Structural Similarities
in the Short Stories of Flannery O'Connor

Flannery O'Connor uses a recurring structural pattern in the development of the main characters in four short stories: "Greenleaf," "Good Country People," "Revelation," and "Everything That Rises Must Converge." The pattern consists of three stages: (1) the author makes use of the omniscient point of view, allowing the reader to be privy to all the characters' thoughts and motives; (2) then a disconcerting and jolting climax occurs, usually very harsh for the character; and (3) readers finally discover how this climax affects the characters.

The five main characters of these stories (Mrs. May, Hulga, Mrs. Turpin, Julian, and his mother) are all based on a common denominator in their character makeup--that of emotional contempt for the world they inhabit and, even more, contempt for themselves. O'Connor sets up these characters with inflated egos, then she pulls the rug out from under the characters in a climactic moment. Ironically, each character is smashed by something he or she held in contempt.

Critic Richard Poirer, writing on O'Connor's structure, argues that "she propels her characters towards the cataclysms where alone they can have a tortured glimpse of the need and chance for redemption" (qtd. in *CA* 721). The aftermath of those destructive moments is rather grim. The character dies or withdraws in shame and despair. David Havird goes so far as to say that O'Connor wants "to knock these proud female characters down a notch . . . by forcing upon them, in a sexually and often violent way, the humbling knowledge that they are after all women" (915).

In "Greenleaf" Mrs. May is (1) a woman with two lazy and ungrateful sons; (2) a woman who encourages her sons to go to church, even though she herself "did not, of course, believe any of [religion] was true" (*CS* 316); and (3) a woman who envies her despised neighbors, the Greenleafs, who become successful. Most frustrating to her is the fact that the Greenleafs succeed because she made it possible. The Greenleafs have made good in the wake of her failures.

Mrs. May is gored by the bull belonging to the Greenleafs, just as they have served as the thorn in her side. Mrs. May dies almost instantly, but not before O'Connor describes her as "leaning over . . . as if to whisper some final discovery into the bull's ear" (*CS* 334). This final

Annotations in right margin:

Use an inverted pyramid style for the title (see Section 8a, pages 173–74).

Identify the literary work early in the paper (see Section 6e, pages 133–37).

Use parenthetical numbers to list three or more ideas (see "Numbering a Series of Items," page 204).

Provide a thesis sentence to control the analysis of the literary works (see Sections 1d, pages 18–20, and 6a, pages 124–26).

The citation means that Poirer was quoted in *Contemporary Authors,* a book that the writer properly abbreviates in the text citations (see pages 184–85).

Introduce quotations with the speaker's name, and end them with the parenthetical citation (see Section 7a, pages 156–57).

The writer uses brackets to interpolate his own word, religion, into the quoted material (see Section 7o, pages 171–72).

Wickham 2

Use three ellipsis points to indicate the omission of words from a quotation (see Section 7n, pages 169–71).

sentence suggests that Mrs. May had learned something, but the story gives no hint as to what that might be, and just as well. Robert Drake calls it a "dark vision of modern damnation and redemption" (*CA* 721). Havird calls it a rape that brings a moment of grace to the masculine woman (15–26).

In "Good Country People," Hulga is a misanthropic Ph.D. with a wooden leg. Hulga is not satisfied with the quality of her life and perhaps justifiably so; a real leg would be nice, just as helpful sons would be nice for Mrs. May. Hulga takes her emotional pain out on others around her, scoffing at them for the miserable people they are, not realizing her own inadequacies.

Being a conceited intellectual, she has lived with the idea that the people around her, including her mother, are simpletons. Hulga regards her mother as a woman who refuses to use her mind, and would likely try to solve heartache with a peanut-butter and jelly sandwich; but when Manley Pointer pulls out his flask and his condoms, she is left with the realization that she, the self-acknowledged brilliant one, has been undone by a simple country boy who steals her wooden leg. He departs

Put a page citation in front of a quotation to avoid interfering with an exclamation point of a question mark (see pages 164–66).

and says (*CS* 291), "Hulga, you ain't so smart. I been believing in nothin' ever since I was born!" Her contempt does her no good now.

In "Revelation," Mrs. Turpin is a pious and prejudiced woman, yet she is another character who looks down on others around her. She takes comfort in the knowledge that people less important than herself exist so that she can look down on them, including the ugly girl in the waiting room.

At this point in the story, Mrs. Turpin has been prattling on for quite some time, to anyone in the waiting room who will converse with her, lauding all the while the many gifts a gracious God has given her. As she goes on and on, the ugly girl gets angry and finally explodes in a furious attack on Mrs. Turpin. The girl, finally restrained by orderlies, shouts to Mrs. Turpin, "Go back to hell where you came from, you old wart hog" (*CS* 500).

About this scene, Robert Brinkmeyer says, "Human pretensions are not merely undercut but utterly destroyed; they are shown to be worthless and insignificant if not terribly evil" (57). In "Revelation" the reader follows the main character home to see the long-term effects. Mrs. Turpin's self image has been destroyed. It causes her to scream and shake her fist at God, to question for the first time why she is what she is. Her answer is life-shattering, for she turns her high-powered and pious contempt on herself. She begins to feel her own worthlessness. Only by this grotesque initiation does she arrive at her revelation. (On

Wickham 3

this point see Rowley, who gives a Jungian reading on "individuation" to the story.)

Reference to an entire article, such as the one to Rowley, needs no in-text citation to a page number (see page 156).

Of her themes concerning piety, O'Connor writes:

> If other ages felt less, they saw more, even though they saw with the blind, prophetical, unsentimental eye of acceptance, which is to say, of faith. In the absence of this faith, now, we govern by tenderness. It is a tenderness which, long cut off from the person of Christ, is wrapped in theory. When tenderness is detached from the source of tenderness, its logical outcome is terror. (Qtd. in Morrow 145)

In "Everything That Rises Must Converge" Julian is a college graduate and, like Hulga, is overly proud of his intellect. He is misanthropic, especially toward his mother. Alienated from others, he has an insensitive personality, one that hates easier than it loves. His mother, on the other hand, is a friendly lady unaccustomed to questioning the feelings or impulses in her heart. She judges the right and wrong of situations by what Julian believes to be a worn-out set of values.

Leave a line short rather than use the hyphen to divide a word at the end of a line (see page 207).

Both Julian and his mother are also characterized by their racial prejudices. Julian is respectful of blacks, but he has no notion of how to interact. His mother, having grown up on a plantation, presumes to know how to treat blacks. However, a black woman strikes Julian's mother with a heavy purse when Julian's mother offers a penny to a black child. The blow causes Julian's mother to have a stroke, and she soon collapses. She has been destroyed by her own prejudices, in the sense that she could not anticipate that a black woman would be offended by her condescending offer. She never saw the blow coming.

In a domino effect, her stroke becomes Julian's moment of destruction. After taunting his mother, then realizing her serious condition, he runs from the scene into the night. The guilt of the moment follows close behind. The person he most condemned--his mother--has been eradicated. Perhaps that is why he ran; he cannot face the fact that he truly held his mother in contempt. He discovers "his own ignorance and cruelty" (Brinkmeyer 71). Thus "the tide of darkness seemed to sweep him back to her, postponing from moment to moment his entry into the world of guilt and sorrow" (*CS* 420).

Blend quotations into your sentence smoothly, as shown in these two examples (see Section 7a, pages 156–57).

The jolting climax of each story "produces a shock for the reader," says O'Connor, who adds, "and I think one reason for this is that it produced a shock for the writer" (qtd. in Brinkmeyer 39).

Wickham 4

Works Cited

Brinkmeyer, Robert. *The Art and Vision of Flannery O'Connor.* Baton
    Rouge: Louisiana State UP, 1989.

Contemporary Authors. Detroit: Gale, 1967.

Havird, David. "The Saving Rape: Flannery O'Connor and Patriarchal
    Religion." *The Mississippi Quarterly* 47 (1993): 15–26.

Morrow, Suzanne P. *Flannery O'Connor: A Study of the Short Fiction.*
    Boston: Twayne, 1988.

O'Connor, Flannery. *The Complete Stories.* New York: Farrar, 1962.

Rowley, Rebecca K. "Individuation and Religious Experience: A Jungian
    Approach to O'Connor's 'Revelation,'" *Southern Literary Journal*
    25 (1993): 92–103. Abstract. *InfoTrac* CD-ROM. Information
    Access 6 Mar. 1995.

Note the abbreviation for a university press (see pages 180–81).

Remember to include the primary source, the collection of stories, as well as the secondary sources (see Section 4d, pages 95–96).

8d   Sample Paper: A Formal Research Paper

The following paper illustrates the style and form of the fully developed research paper. It includes a title page, outline pages, a variety of in-text citations, superscript numerals to content endnotes, and a fully developed works cited page. Notations in the margins signal special circumstances in matters of form and style.

Show Me the Money:
The Inequality of Justice for Indigent Defendants

This title page is a three-part balance of title, author, and course information (see page 173).

by
Elizabeth L. Timpe

Composition 1020
Professor James D. Lester
7 August 1997

Outline

Thesis: The broader implication of the O.J. Simpson trial is that within the American justice system there exists a system for the rich and another for the poor.

I. Because of his wealth, O.J. Simpson's felony case was televised and commercialized in extreme proportions.
  A. Realities of the case were fogged.
  B. American public was misled about the criminal justice system.

II. Provisions are made for indigent defendants.
  A. Indigent defendants have been defined by law.
  B. The United States Code requires a plan for indigent representation.
  C. Legal representation is to be provided for indigents.

III. Equal justice is an illusion.
  A. The 1993 American Bar Association reports that the indigent defense system is in crisis.
  B. If O.J. had been represented by a public defender, it might have been an "open and shut" case.
  C. Division occurs by who can afford a private attorney and who cannot.

IV. Problems with the indigent defense system.
  A. Attorneys who represent indigents are often incompetent.
  B. The funding to public defenders offices is wholly inadequate.
  C. Time is not given to a public defender to prepare client's cases or do research.
  D. Proper defense involves proper funding.
  E. The system is failing to provide indigents with equal representation.
  F. While felony cases take time and money, defendants for lesser crimes are also being neglected.

V. Innocent men and women are going to jail because of poor representation.
  A. The kind of trial a man gets depends on how much money he has.
  B. The O.J. Simpson trial showed that freedom can be bought.

Use lowercase Roman numerals for preliminary pages (see pages 203–04).

This writer uses the topic outline (see pages 77–81).

Repeat your thesis at the beginning of the outline, although it may take a different form in the paper itself (see pages 124–26).

Use standard outline symbols (see page 78).

The headings for both the introduction (I) and conclusion (III) are content-oriented like other outline entries (see pages 77–81).

C. Until sufficient funding is allotted for these
    programs, the quality of defense will remain
    substandard, and unequal justice will escalate.

Show Me the Money: The
Inequality of Justice for
Indigent Defendants

Both running
head and page
number are giv-
en (but see page
209).

Repeat the title
on the first
pages of text.

On the morning of October 4, 1995, newspaper headlines
across the country donned the words "O.J. Simpson Found Not
Guilty." From the Bronco chase on June 17, 1994, to the
announcement of the verdict on October 3, 1995, Americans
watched the case's development in the most publicized and
televised trial in the century. Not only did Simpson have the
support of his family and friends, but more importantly, he had
the support of his money, enabling him to build a defense team
of monumental proportions with a wealth of experience to
contribute to getting an acquittal: F. Lee Bailey, Johnnie
Cochran, Jr., Robert Shapiro, Robert Blasier, Gerald Uelmen,
and Carl Douglas (Deutsch A12). While this decision was a
tremendous victory for Simpson, the broader implications of the
trial cast a dark shadow over the criminal justice system.
Ultimately, the entire trial demonstrated that the wealthy
defendant who has the money to hire "bigname" lawyers has a
greater chance of being acquitted than a poor, indigent
defendant whose fate lies in the hands of a public defender. In
spite of the landmark 1963 Supreme Court Decision, <u>Gideon v.
Wainwright</u>, that declared indigent defendants accused of
felonies must be provided with attorneys, the defendant who
cannot afford counsel often loses at trial due to inadequate
defense (Berry). The broader implication of the O.J. Simpson
trial is that within the American justice system there exists a
system for the rich and another for the poor.

For tips on
building
opening para-
graphs, see
Section 6e,
pages
133–37.

The thesis
comes late in
the opening; it
could also ap-
pear early (see
Section 6e,
page 133).

The reference to
Berry has no
page citation
because it is an
Internet source
(see pages
158–59).

The O.J. Simpson trial, while televised and commercialized
in extreme proportions, was a real felony case tried in the real
criminal justice system. The fact that O.J. Simpson was rich
transformed the case into a spectacle that went terribly off-
course, fogging the realities of the case and of the criminal
justice system. Special counsel to the National Legal Aid and
Defender Association, Scott Wallace, agrees with this position,
stating, "The O.J. case is fantasy land. It's not real life in the
criminal justice system" (qtd. in Gleick 42). In fact, the Simpson
trial ultimately misled the American public's view of the
criminal justice system overall:

This paragraph
blends personal
observation with
paraphrase;
short quotations;
and a long, in-
dented quotation
(see Chapter 7,
pages 155–72).

> It would be unfortunate if the public's avid
> consumption of this and other trials of the rich

Timpe 2

and famous--the Menendez brothers, Claus von
Bulow, William Kennedy Smith--left the general
impression that our criminal justice system
routinely allows defendants a thorough and
aggressive defense, in which no fact goes
unchallenged or theory unexplored. (Gleick 41)

Not only did the case leave an impression about the quality
of the defense allowed by the criminal justice system, but it also
left the impression that with the services of a high-powered
lawyers, minimal punishments could be avoided (Friend). The
reality of the matter is that the opposite occurs most often in
cases in which the fate of the indigent defendant relies on a
public defender. Prosecutor Christopher Darden, speaking with
disdain of the trial, commented that if "Simpson were poor and
unknown, it all would have been over months ago" (qtd. in
Gleick 40).

While the criminal justice system makes provisions for
indigent defenders on the books, in practice those too poor to
afford a defense team like that of Simpson often find themselves
behind bars or, in the worst case scenario, on death row. Here is
a definition of an indigent defendant:

> A person indicted or complained of who is without
> funds or ability to hire a lawyer to defend him is,
> in most instances, entitled to appointed counsel to
> represent him at every stage of criminal
> proceedings, through appeal, consistent with the
> protection of the Sixth and Fourteenth
> Amendments to the U.S. Constitution. (Black 532)

Within the United States Code, laws require the
establishment of a plan for providing legal representation to
impoverished criminal defendants in each federal district
(Markey 55). (See also the Appendix.) Legal representation is
provided to indigent defendants by court appointed counsel, by a
state or county public defender's office, or by contract public
defenders who have put in a bid to handle many cases in one
jurisdiction (Gleick 44).

While the appearance suggests that equal justice is
provided to all Americans, the truth of the matter is that equal
justice is an illusion. The 1993 American Bar Association's
report on indigent defense concluded that "the indigent defense
system was in 'crisis'" and that "far too many people are being

The writer shifts
to a new issue in
accordance with
her outline (see
Section 3c,
pages 77–81).

Use paren-
thetical cita-
tions to your
sources (see
Section 7a,
pages
156–57).

Long quotes are
generally intro-
duced by a
colon, indented,
without quota-
tion marks, dou-
ble-spaced, with
the source cited
at the end (see
Section 7k,
pages 166–70).

Use parentheses
to add clarifying
words to your
own text, but
use brackets to
insert your words
into a quotation
(see Section 7o,
pages 171–72).

The writer effectively summarizes the basic problem and them moves to the next issue.

tried and convicted and sentenced without even the rudimentary legal representation guaranteed by the Constitution" (qtd. in Gleick 41). Robert Spangenberg, co-author of the 1993 ABA report, said, "If O.J. were [represented by a public defender] in Jones County, Mississippi, it would be a two-day trial, an open-and-shut case" (qtd. in Gleick 41). Indigent defense coordinator for the National Association of Defense Lawyers, Paul Petterson, states, "There are two criminal justice systems in this country. There is a whole different system for poor people. It's in the same courthouse--it's not separate, but it's not equal" (qtd. in Gleick 41).

Blend quotations into your text smoothly (see Chapter 7, pages 156–57).

Some lines may appear extremely short but do not hyphenate words at the end of lines (see page 207).

This belief in the existence of a division in the criminal justice system between those who can afford a private defense attorney and those who cannot is voiced in an article entitled "Capital Punishment and the Poor" by Nick Dispoldo.

> If two suspects, one wealthy, one poor, are charged with capital crimes, the quality of justice immediately changes. The rich defendant may usually post bail, retain attorneys of choice, hire investigators and employ experts who will provide psychiatric testimony for the defense. The trial is often delayed for the benefit of the defense by legal maneuvers and multiple motions. . . . By way of contrast, the indigent defendant, unable to post bond, will remain in jail and will proceed to trial with a court-appointed attorney or, as is likely, a public defender who is generally either inexperienced or burdened with a staggering caseload. (Dispoldo 18)

Citations at the end of long quotations go outside this final period.

When the United States Supreme Court made the landmark ruling in <u>Gideon v. Wainright</u>, such a division in the criminal justice system was obviously unforeseen.

The fact is that in the 1990s eighty to ninety percent of all felony defendants in the United States fall under the category of "indigent" (Gleick 43).[1] Representation of these defendants is by court appointed lawyers who lack the resources to defend their clients adequately in capital cases, in spite of the fact that in 1989 the American Bar Association specified in its report to the House of Delegates:

Superscript numerals signal content endnotes (see page 191). Do not use superscript numerals and endnotes for documentation of sources unless you need to cluster several sources.

> . . . each federal district and circuit court to adopt and each federal circuit court judicial counsel to

Timpe 4

approve a plan for providing representation in
federal habeas corpus death penalty proceedings
which includes: 7) pre-assignment screening of
attorneys considered for appointment to such
cases to assure that only trained and experienced
attorneys are appointed. . . . (ABA)

Yet an article in the June 1994 issue of the <u>Harvard Law
Review</u> states that strict competency standards for an attorney
trying or appealing a capital case were once again demanded
and stated that the standard of <u>Strickland v. Washington</u> for the
effective assistance of counsel fails to provide the competence
and reliability warranted for the sentence of the death penalty.
In addition to inadequacy of the attorneys, there are numerous
other drawbacks to the program.

"The low level of funding provided in many jurisdictions"
is one of the major drawbacks to the indigent defender
programs offered by federal and state governments (Markey 57).
Because of this low level of funding, public defenders carry
"twice the caseload" they should under "national standards"
(Berry 2). For example, with a budget of only $32,000 a year,
which includes lawyers' salaries and expenses, two part-time
lawyers at the public defender's office in Jones County,
Mississippi, share "about 450 to 500 felony cases a year,
including death penalty cases" even though the ABA
recommends that "each public defender handle no more than
150 noncapital felonies a year" (Gleick 44). The lack of funding
for public defender's offices also contributes to the lack of office
support necessary to adequately prepare for trial; only three
percent of paralegals work in Legal Service/Legal Aid Offices
compared to twenty-six percent working in small private firms
and thirty percent working in large private firms (Statsky 58).
Noticing the lack of support provided to public defenders, as
well as other legal aid offices for the poor, the ABA Board of
Governors listed supporting legal aid to the poor as a "critical
priority" for its . . . legislative/governmental agenda (McMillion).

The lack of support and resources uncovers another
drawback--the lack of time provided to the public defender to
prepare for trial, for "the appointed attorney usually does not
enter the case until after the arrest or lodging of formal
charges" (Markey 57). David Ratcliff, one of the part-time
defenders in Jones County, Mississippi, explains that he has to

Internet sources
will not list a
page number nor
a paragraph
number (see
pages 158–59).

Even paraphrased
materials should
be introduced
and documented
in the text (see
Section 5d,
pages 112–14).

Use ellipsis
points for omit-
ted passages
(see pages
169–71).

The reference to
McMillion has no
page reference
because it is an
abstract, which
has no page
number.

Timpe 5

do all of his own research and witness finding, which leaves him "so worn out you just don't follow up on everything the way you should" before going to trial (qtd. in Gleick 44). However, such investigative work is not performed by many of the district attorney's offices in this country. Public defender Christopher Johns of Maricopa County, Arizona, states that the D.A.'s office does not perform the research, and does not pay for it.

> If the D.A. needs something investigated, they call
> the police department. If they need a DNA
> analysis, they call the FBI or they send samples off
> to the state lab. They don't get charged for that. If
> I need investigation done, [it] gets charged to this
> office. (Qtd. in Gleick 45)

With little funding, few resources, and little time for preparation, overworked and underpaid public defenders walk into courtrooms in this country everyday to defend their clients to the best of their ability, and often that defense is to no avail.

    What a proper defense boils down to in the end is money. Proof of this fact can be found in the story of Federico Martinez Macias which appeared in the June 19, 1995, issue of <u>Time</u> magazine entitled "The Difference a Million Makes." Macias was charged with a double murder arising from a burglary in El Paso, Texas, in 1993. The prime witness, also a suspect in the case, plead to a lesser charge for his testimony against Macias. When confronted with contradictory evidence to his testimony, including a failed polygraph test, the witness admitted that he had entered the victims' home and tied one of them up, but insisted that Macias murdered them. Based on this questionable testimony, the state sought the death penalty. Macias went to trial represented by two public defenders who made a number of errors in his defense, including the failure to call "an alibi witness who could have placed Macias miles away from the crime scene." Although Macias' trial lawyer contends that he devoted eight months to the case and that the lack of money was not a factor, the U.S. Court of Appeals for the Fifth Circuit disagreed. Taking the fact that the defense counsel was paid $11.84 an hour by the state, the U.S. Court of Appeals stated that "Unfortunately, the justice system got what it paid for" (Cohen 43).

    After spending almost ten years on death row in Texas, Macias got a break when his appeal case was assigned by the

---

Cross references to persons quoted in another source requires this form, "qtd. in" (see page 160).

Use brackets for interpretations (see pages 171–72).

Note the blend of paraphrase and quotation so that the text flows smoothly with proper introductions and in-text citations (see Section 7a, pages 156–59).

Timpe 6

American Bar Association to one of the largest and wealthiest corporate law firms in the country, Skadden, Arps, Slate, Meagher & Flom. A partner in the firm's Washington office, Douglas Robinson, and a team of Skadden lawyers and paralegals began work on Macias' case just as they would have for a rich private client. For expert psychological testimony, $11, 599 was spent. A partial eyewitness was found "who said Macias was not either of the two men she saw near the victims' house," and they brought in the alibi witness who had not been called in the first trial. After an investment of "about a million dollars" in billable hours and resources by the Skadden team, a 173-page petition convinced two federal courts that Macias had been wrongly convicted. A new grand jury was presented the case and found that "there was insufficient evidence to reindict." Macias was finally a free man after being wrongly convicted and subsequently spending ten years on death row (Cohen 43).

As the story of Macias illustrates, the criminal justice system is failing to provide equal representation to indigent defendants, leaving many to serve life sentences or even to face the death penalty. In his article on capital punishment, Dispoldo writes that in researching for his book on the 300-year history of the death penalty in the United States, he has discovered "only six cases in which those executed were individuals of influence or affluence." He contends, "It is primarily the poor and underprivileged whom the state is determined to kill." Dispoldo also recounts a horrifying story of Caryl Chessmann, a defendant "with no money in his pocket," convicted in 1949 of multiple counts of rape and sentenced to the death penalty under the Little Lindberg Law.[2] Of Chessmann, Dispoldo writes:

> A poor defendant without friends or family,
> Chessmann chose to defend himself rather than
> proceed to trial with a public defender who could
> not, in his opinion, adequately answer legal
> questions. (18)

Chessmann was executed on May 2, 1960.[3] This conviction and death penalty sentence occurred in the same courthouse in the state of California in which O. J. Simpson stood trial for two murders where the death penalty was not sought. The fact that the death penalty was not sought in the Simpson case only adds the question, "Does the death penalty apply only to those without money and affluence?" to the more vital question, "Is

The writer re-asserts her thesis. The conclusion now officially begins. Note how the writer develops a full judgment on the issue and does not merely summarize the paper.

For tips on writing paragraphs of the conclusion, (see Section 6g, pages 142–45).

Timpe 7

justice provided only to those who can afford it?"

According to Stephen Bright, a visiting lecturer at Yale
Law School, twenty-five men line up in an Atlanta court room
"to plead guilty and receive their sentences," about which he
comments: "The legal system is greatly over estimated in its
ability to sort out the innocent from guilty" (qtd. in Gleick 44).
To put this entire argument into the simplest of terms, a "level
playing field" must be created in order to insure equal justice
for every defendant:

> The tendency in talking about a level playing field
> is to focus on the starting line. But the fairness of
> the game cannot be determined without some
> reference to what happens at the finish line. There
> must be a sense that the winner somehow deserved
> to win, which in turn implies that the losers
> somehow deserved to lose. To a competitor who
> always loses, the playing field probably does not
> seem level, and the perpetual loser's complaint will
> sooner or later require a reevaluation of the game:
> Is there a flaw in the game that undermines its
> fairness and assures that this contestant always
> loses? (Foer 5)

There most certainly exists a flaw in the game of the criminal
justice system.

When the late Justice Hugo L. Black wrote in <u>Griffin v.
Illinois</u>, "There can be no equal justice when the kind of trial a
man gets depends on how much money he has in his pocket," he
did not know how true his statement was. If nothing else, the
trial of O.J. Simpson showed the United States of America, as
well as the world, that in the American criminal justice system a
person can buy their freedom regardless of whether he or she is
actually innocent or guilty.[4] Until every jurisdiction in this
country allots sufficient funding to the public defender offices
for salaries, resources, and office support, the quality of defense
provided to indigent defendants will remain substandard, and
unequal justice will continue to escalate for the poor, filling our
prisons with the innocent and our country clubs with the guilty.

Use superscript
numbers to sig-
nal a content
note (see
page 191).

Timpe 8
Notes

1. Current statistics on the number of indigent defendants could not be found at the time this paper was being written.

2. Chessman's guilt of the crime is of no significance to this study, but the fact that he chose to defend himself rather than have a public defender is significant.

3. In <u>Coker v. Georgia</u> in 1977, the U.S. Supreme Court decided that the death penalty for rape of an adult female was unconstitutional.

4. The O. J. Simpson case is used in this paper solely as an example of a case in which a defendant's financial means and status enabled the defendant to finance an extraordinary defense team. The outcome of the trial is irrelevant, and in no way should it be construed otherwise.

Content endnotes appear on a separate page. For tips on writing content endnotes (see pages 191–94).

Timpe 9

Appendix

See pages 175-76
for tips about
writing an
appendix.

Legal Representation to Impoverished Criminal Defendants,
as Established by the <u>United States Code</u> (18 *USC* 3006A)

Each United States district court, with the approval of the
judicial council of the circuit, shall place in operation
throughout the district a plan for furnishing representation for
any person unable to obtain adequate representation in
accordance with this section. Representation under each plan
shall include counsel and investigative, expert and other
services necessary for adequate representaion. Each plan shall
provide the following:

1. Representation shall be provided for any financially
   eligible person who--
   a. is charged with a felony or Class A misdemeanor;
   b. is a juvenile alleged to have committed an act of
      juvenile deliquency as defined in section 5031 of
      this title;
   c. is charged with a violation of probation;
   d. is under arrest when such representation is
      required by law;
   e. is charged with a violation of supervised release or
      faces modification, reduction, or enlargement of a
      condition or extension or revocation of a term of
      supervised release;

The writer enu-
merates specific
issues.

   f. is subject to a mental condition gearing under
      chapter 313 of this title;
   g. is in custody as a material witness;
   h. is entitled to appointment of counsel under the sixth
      amendment to the Consitution;
   i. faces loss of liberty in a case, and Federal law
      requires the appointment of counsel; or
   j. is entitled to the appointment of counsel under
      section 4109 of this title.

Source: <u>Criminal Law for Paralegals</u> 56

Timpe 10

Sources Cited

American Bar Association. <u>American Bar Association Standing Committee on Legal Aid and Indigent Defendants Section of Criminal Justice Section of litigation Report to the House of Delegates Recommendation</u>. February 1989. 6 Aug. 1997 ⟨http://www.abanet.org/irr/feb89a.html⟩.

Berry, Steve. "30 Years Ago, Gideon Won Freedom, Justice for the Poor." <u>Orlando Sentinel</u> 18 Jul. 1993: 1–5. <u>Sirs Researcher on the World Wide Web</u>. 6 Aug. 1997 ⟨http://researcher.sirs.com/cgi–bin . . . isplay?4HS002A+INDIGENT+DEFENDANTS⟩.

Black, Henry Campbell, Joseph R. Nolan, and Jacqueline M. Nolan-Haley. <u>Black's Law Dictionary</u>. 6th ed. St. Paul: West, 1991.

Cohen, Adam. "The Difference a Million Makes" <u>Time</u> 19 June 1995: 43.

Deutsch, Linda. "O.J. Vows to Find Real Killers." <u>The Leaf Chronicle</u> [Clarksville, TN] 4 Oct. 1995: A1+.

Dispoldo, Nick. "Capital Punishment and the Poor." <u>America</u> 11 Feb. 1995: 18–19.

"The Eighth Amendment and Ineffective Assistance of Counsel in Capital Trials." <u>Harvard Law Review</u> 107.8 (Jun. 1994): 1923–40. Abstract. <u>InfoTrac: Expanded Academic Index</u>. CD-ROM. Information Access. Aug. 1997.

Foer, Albert A. "American Idealism: Level Playing Fields." <u>Business and Society Review</u> 96.27 (Winter 1996): 27+. <u>InfoTrac: Expanded Academic Index</u>. CD-ROM. Information Access. Aug. 1997.

Friend, Tad. "The Untouchables." New York 28.41 (16 Oct. 1995): 26+. Abstract. <u>InfoTrac: Expanded Academic Index</u>. CD-ROM. Information Access. Aug. 1997.

Gleick, Elizabeth. "Rich Justice, Poor Justice." <u>Time</u> 19 Jun. 1995: 40–47.

Markey, Daniel J., Jr. and Mary Queen Donnelly, <u>Criminal Law for Paralegals</u>. Cincinnati: South-Western, 1994.

McMillion, Rhonda. "ABA Targets Legislative Priorites." <u>ABA Journal</u> 81 (May 1995): 106. Abstract. <u>InfoTrac: Expanded Academic Index</u>. CD-ROM. Information Access. Aug. 1997.

Statsky, William P. <u>Essentials of Paralegalism</u>. 2nd ed. St. Paul: West, 1993.

Start Works Cited on a new page.

For tips on writing the bibliographic entries, see Chapter 9, pages 233–72.

An electronic source (see pages 258–64).

An entry for three authors (see page 243).

Entry for a magazine (see page 253).

Entry for a newspaper (see pages 255–56).

An entry with no author (see page 242).

A typical entry for a journal article found on InfoTrac (see pages 261–63).

Entry for a source from CD-ROM (see pages 261–63).

Entry for a abstract found on InfoTrac (see pages 262–63).

Basic entry for a book, second edition (see page 239).

9 Works Cited: MLA Style

After writing your paper, you should prepare a Works Cited page to list your reference materials. List only the ones actually used in your manuscript, including works mentioned within content endnotes and in captions of tables and illustrations. If you carefully developed your working bibliography as a computer file (see pages 27–28), preparing the Works Cited will be relatively simple. Your list of sources, arranged alphabetically, can provide the necessary information.

Select a heading that indicates the nature of your list.

1. Label the page with the heading *Works Cited* if your list includes only the printed works quoted and paraphrased in the paper.
2. Use the label *Sources Cited* if your list includes nonprint items (e.g., an interview or speech or Internet sources) as well as printed works.
3. Reserve the heading *Bibliography* for a complete listing of *all* works related to the subject, an unlikely prospect for undergraduate papers.

(See also Annotated Bibliography, pages 97–99)
Works pertinent to the paper but not quoted or paraphrased, such as an article on related matters, can be mentioned in a content endnote (pages 191–94) and then listed in the Works Cited. On this point see especially the Notes page of the sample paper, page 229.

Keyboard your Works Cited page according to the MLA standards that follow. (For a variety of formats used in other disciplines, see Chapters 10 and 11).

9a Formatting the "Works Cited" Page

Arrange items in alphabetic order by the surname of the author using the letter-by-letter system. Ignore spaces in the author's surname. Consider the first names only when two or more surnames are identical. Note how the following examples are alphabetized letter by letter.

De Morgan, Augustus
Dempsey, William H.
MacDonald, Lawrence
McCullers, Carson
McPherson, James Alan
McPherson, Vivian M.
Saint-Exupéry, Antoine de
St. James, Christopher

When two or more entries cite coauthors that begin with the same name, alphabetize by the last names of the second authors:

Harris, Muriel, and David Bleich
Harris, Murial, and Stephen M. Fishman

When no author is listed, alphabetize by the first important word of the title. Imagine lettered spelling for unusual items. For example, "#2 Red Dye" should be alphebetized as though it were "Number 2 Red Dye."

The list of sources may also be divided into separate alphebetized sections for primary and secondary sources, for different media (film, books, CD-ROM diskettes), for differences in subject matter (biography, autobiography, letters), for different periods (Neoclassic period, Romantic period), and for different areas (German viewpoints, French viewpoints, American viewpoints). Place the first line of each entry flush with the left margin, and indent succeeding lines 5 spaces. Double-space each entry, and also double-space between entries. Use 1 space after periods and other marks of punctuation.

Set the title *Works Cited* or *Sources Cited* 1 inch down from the top of the sheet and double-space between it and the first entry. A sample page is illustrated below. (See also the sample Works Cited pages on pages 218 and 231.)

> **Note:** If you are writing the paper on a computer, you may italicize book titles rather than underscore them.

Sources Cited

Berg, Orley. <u>Treasures in the Sand: What Archaeology Tells Us about the Bible</u>. New York: Pacific Press, 1993.

The Bible. Revised Standard Version.

Bulfinch, Thomas. <u>Bulfinch's Mythology</u>. 2 vols. New York: Mentor, 1962.

Campbell, Joseph. <u>The Hero With a Thousand Faces</u>. Cleveland: Meridian, 1956.

---. <u>The Masks of God</u>. 4 vols. New York: Viking, 1970.

Chickering, H. "Hearing Ariel's Songs." <u>Journal of Medieval Renaissance Studies</u> 24 (1994): 131–72.

Dipert, Randall R. "The Mathematical Structure of the World as Graph." <u>Journal of Philosopy</u> 44.7 (1997): 329–58.

Henderson, Joseph L., and Maud Oakes. <u>The Wisdom of the Serpent: The Myths of Death, Rebirth, and Resurrection</u>. New York: Collier, 1971.

Homer. <u>The Iliad</u>. Trans. Richmond Lattimore. Chicago: U of Chicago P, 1951.

Laird, Charlton. "A Nonhuman Being Can Learn Language." <u>College Composition and Communication</u> 23 (1972): 142–54.

Lévi-Strauss, Claude. "The Structural Study of Myth." <u>Myth: A Symposium</u>. Ed. Thomas A. Sebeok. Bloomington: Indiana UP, 1958. 45–63.

"Mythology in Shakespeare's 'A Midsummer Night's Dream.'" 1 Aug. 1997 ⟨http://quarles.unbc.edu/midsummer/myth.html⟩.

Riccio, B. D. "Popular Culture and High Culture: Dwight MacDonald, His Critics and the Ideal of Cultural Hierarchy in Modern America." <u>Journal of American Culture</u> 16 (1993): 7–18.

Robinson, Lillian S. "Criticism--and Self-Criticism." <u>College English</u> 36 (1974): 436–45.

Index to Bibliographic Models: MLA Style

9b Bibliographic Form—Books

Enter information for books in the following order. Items 1, 3, and 8 are required; add other items according to the circumstances explained in the text that follows.

1. Author(s)
2. Chapter or part of book
3. Title of the book
4. Editor, translator, or compiler
5. Edition
6. Volume number of book
7. Name of the series
8. Place, publisher, and date
9. Page numbers
10. Total number of volumes

Name of the Author(s)

List the author's name, surname first, followed by given name or initials, and then a period:

> Alexander, Shoshana. <u>In Praise of Single Parents: Mothers and Fathers Embracing the Challenge</u>. New York: Houghton, 1994.

Always give authors' names in the fullest possible form, for example, "Cosbey, Robert C." rather than "Cosbey, R. C." unless, as indicated on the title page of the book, the author prefers initials. However, APA style (see Chapter 10, 273–302) requires last name and initials only (e.g., Cosbey, R. C.)

When an author has two or more works, do not repeat his or her name with each entry. Rather, insert a continuous three-hyphen line, flush with the left margin, followed by a period. Also, list the works alphabetically by the title (ignoring *a, an,* and *the*), not by the date of publication. In the following example, the *J* of *Just* precedes the *L* of *Later*.

> Paley, Grace. <u>Just As I Thought</u>. New York: Farrar, 1997.
> ---. <u>Later the Same Day</u>. New York: Farrar, 1985.

The three dashes stand for exactly the same name(s) as in the preceding entry. However, do not substitute three hyphens for an author who has two or more works in the bibliography when one is written in collaboration with someone else:

> Bizzell, Patricia. "Opportunities for Feminist Research in the History of Rhetoric." <u>Rhetoric Review</u> 11 (1992): 50–58.
> ---. "<u>The Praise of Folly</u>, The Woman Rhetorician, and Post-Modern Skepticism." <u>Rhetoric Society Quarterly</u> 22 (1992): 7–17.
> Bizzell, Patricia, and Bruce Herzberg. <u>The Rhetorical Tradition: Readings from Classical Times to the Present</u>. Boston: Bedford-St. Martin's, 1990.

If the person edited, compiled, or translated the work that follows on the list, place a comma after the three hyphens and write "ed.," "comp.," or "trans."

before you give the title. This label does not affect the alphabetic order by title.

> Finneran, Richard J. <u>Editing Yeat's Poems</u>. New York: St.
>   Martin's, 1983.
> ---, ed. <u>W. B. Yeats: The Poems</u>. New ed. New York: Macmillan,
>   1983.

Chapter or Part of the Book

List the chapter or part of the book on the Works Cited page only when it is separately edited, translated, or written, or when it demands special attention. For example, if you quote from a specific chapter of a book, let's say Chapter 11 of Brian Hall's book, the entry should read:

> Hall, Brian. <u>Madeleine's World: A Biography of a Three-Year-Old</u>.
>   New York: Houghton, 1997.

Your in-text citation will have listed specific page numbers, so there is no reason to mention a specific chapter, even though it is the only portion of Hall's book that you read.

However, if you cite from one work in a collection of works by the same author or from an anthology of works by many different authors, provide the specific name of the work and the corresponding page numbers. This next writer cites one story from a collection of stories by the same author:

> Kenan, Randall. "Run, Mourner, Run." <u>Let the Dead Bury Their</u>
>   <u>Dead</u>. San Diego: Harcourt, 1992. 163–91.

Edited anthologies supply the names of authors as well as editors. Almost always cite the author first. Conform to the rules given in these examples:

1. If you paraphrase or quote portions of an essay by Lonne Elder, write this entry:

> Elder, Lonne. "Ceremonies in Dark Old Men." <u>New Black</u>
>   <u>Playwrights: An Anthology</u>. Ed. William Couch, Jr.
>   Baton Rouge: Louisiana State UP, 1968. 55–72.

2. If you cite lines from Aristophanes' drama *The Birds* in your paper, write this entry:

> Aristophanes. <u>The Birds</u>. <u>Five Comedies of Aristophanes</u>.
>   Trans. Benjamin B. Rogers. Garden City, NY: Doubleday,
>   1955. 110–154.

3. If you cite material from a chapter of one volume in a multivolume set, write an entry like these:

> Child, Harold. "Jane Austen." <u>The Cambridge History of</u>
>   <u>English Literature</u>. Ed. A. W. Ward and A. R. Waller.
>   Vol. 12. London: Cambridge UP, 1927.

4. Although not required, you may also provide the total number of volumes:

> Saintsbury, George. "Dickens." <u>The Cambridge History of English Literature</u>. Ed. A. W. Ward and A. R. Waller. Vol. 13. New York: Putnam's, 1917. 14 vols.

In cases where you cite several different authors from the same anthology, you should make cross-references (see pages 245-46).

Title of the Book

Show the title of the work, underscored or italicized, followed by a period. Separate any subtitle from the primary title by a colon and one space even though the title page has no mark of punctuation or the card catalog entry has a semicolon:

> Hendrix, Harville, and Helen Hunt. <u>Giving the Love That Heals: A Guide for Parents</u>. New York: Pocket, 1997.

If a title includes the title of another article or book, special rules apply (see "Titles within Titles," pages 211–12). You may need to omit an underscore or italics on one of the titles, as in this next example:

> Schilling, Bernard N. <u>Dryden and the Conservative Myth: A Reading of</u> Absalom and Achitophel. New Haven: Yale UP, 1961.

Name of the Editor, Translator, or Compiler

Mention an editor, translator, or compiler of a collection after the title with the abbreviations "Ed.," "Trans.," or "Comp.," as shown here:

> Yeats, W. B. <u>The Poems of W. B. Yeats</u>. Ed. Richard J. Finneran. New ed. New York: Macmillan, 1983.

However, if your in-text citation refers to the work of the editor or translator (e.g., "The Ciardi edition caused debate among Dante scholars") use this form:

> Ciardi, John, trans. <u>The Purgatorio</u>. By Dante. New York: NAL, 1961.

Edition of the Book

Indicate the edition used, whenever it is not the first, in Arabic numerals (e.g., "3rd ed."), or as "Rev. ed.," "Abr. ed.," and so forth, without further punctuation:

> Schulman, Michael, and Eva Meckler. <u>Bringing Up a Moral Child</u>. Rev. ed. New York: Doubleday, 1994.

Name of the Series

If the book is one in a published series, show the name of the series, without quotation marks or underscoring, the number of this work in Arabic numerals (for example, "no. 3," or simply "3"), and a period:

> Brown, J. R., and Bernard Harris. <u>Restoration Theatre</u>. Stratford-upon-Avon Studies 6. London: Arnold, 1965.

Number of Volumes

If you are citing from two or more volumes of a multivolume work, show the number of volumes in Arabic numerals (e.g., "4 vols."), as shown here:

> Seale, William. <u>The President's House: A History</u>. 2 vols. Washington, DC: White House Historical Assn., 1986.

If you are citing from volumes that were published over a period of years, provide the inclusive dates at the end of the citation. Should the volumes still be in production, write "to date" after the number of volumes and leave a space after the hyphen which follows the initial date.

> Parrington, Vernon L. <u>Main Currrents in American Thought</u>. 3 vols. New York: Harcourt, 1927–32.
> Cassidy, Frederic, ed. <u>Dictionary of American Regional English</u>. 3 vols. to date. Cambridge: Belknap-Harvard UP, 1985–.

Handle the reprinting of volumes in this manner:

> Seivers, Harry J. <u>Benjamin Harrison: Hoosier Warrior</u>. 3 vols. 1952–68. Rpt. of vol. 1. Newtown CT: American Political Biography Press, 1997.

Volume Number

If you are citing from only one volume of a multivolume work, provide the number of that volume in the works cited entry with information for that volume only. In your text, you will need to specify only page numbers, for example, (Seale 45–46). See pages 249–50 for additional examples.

> Seale, William. <u>The President's House: A History</u>. Vol. 1. Washington, DC: White House Historical Assn., 1986.

Although additional information is not required, you may provide the inclusive page numbers, the total number of volumes, and the inclusive dates of publication.

> Daiches, David. "The Restoration." <u>A Critical History of English Literature</u>. 2nd ed. Vol. 2. New York: Ronald, 1970. 537–89. 2 vols.
> Wellek, René. <u>A History of Modern Criticism, 1750–1950</u>. Vol. 5. New Haven: Yale UP, 1986. 8 vols. 1955–92.

If you are using only one volume of a multivolume work and the volume has an individual title, you can cite the one work without mentioning the other volumes in the set.

> Crane, Stephen. <u>Wounds in the Rain</u>. <u>Stephen Crane: Tales of War</u>.
> Charlottesville: UP of Virginia, 1970. 95–284.

As a courtesy to the reader, you may include supplementary information about an entire edition.

> Crane, Stephen. <u>Wounds in the Rain</u>. <u>Stephen Crane: Tales of War</u>.
> Charlottesville: UP of Virginia, 1970. Vol. 6 of <u>The</u>
> <u>University of Virginia Edition of the Works of Stephen</u>
> <u>Crane</u>. Ed. Fredson Bowers. 95–284. 10 vols. 1069–76.

Place, Publisher, and Date

Indicate the place, publisher, and date of publication:

> Schmidgall, Gary. <u>Walt Whitman: A Gay Life</u>. New York: Dutton,
> 1997.

Include the abbreviation for the state or country only if necessary for clarity:

> Morgan, John A. <u>Drama at Stratford</u>. Manchester, Eng.: Wallace,
> 1995.

If more than one place of publication appears on the title page, the city mentioned first is sufficient. If successive copyright dates are given, use the most recent (unless your study is specifically concerned with an earlier, perhaps definitive, edition). A new printing does not constitute a new edition. For example, if the text has a 1940 copyright date and a 1975 printing, use 1940 unless other information is given, such as: "facsimile printing" or "1975 third printing rev."

> Bell, Charles Bailey, and Harriett P. Miller. <u>The Bell Witch: A</u>
> <u>Mysterious Spirit</u>. 1934. Facsim. ed. Nashville: Elder, 1972.

If the place, publisher, date of publication, or pages are not provided, use one of these abbreviations:

n.p.	No place of publication listed
n.p.	No publisher listed
n.d.	No date of publication listed
n.pag.	No pagination listed

> Lewes, George Henry. <u>The Life and Works of Goethe</u>. 1855. 2 vols.
> Rpt. as vols. 13 and 14 of <u>The Works J. W. von Goethe</u>. Ed.
> Nathan Haskell Dole. London: Nicolls, n.d. 14 vols.
> Perrine, Laurence. "A Monk's Allegory." <u>A Limerick's Always a</u>
> <u>Verse: 200 Original Limericks</u>. San Diego: Harcourt, 1990.
> N. pag.

Provide the publisher's name in a shortened form, such as "Bobbs" rather than "Bobbs-Merrill Co., Inc." (See pages 180–81 for a list of publishers' abbreviations.) A publisher's special imprint name should be joined with the official name, for example, Anchor-Doubleday, Jove-Berkley, Ace-Grossett, Del Rey-Ballantine, Mentor-NAL.

> Faulkner, William. "Spotted Horses." <u>Three Famous Short Stories</u>. New York: Vintage-Random, 1963.

Page Number(s) to a Section of a Book

Cite pages to help a reader find a particular section of a book.

> Knoepflmacher, U. C. "Fusing Fact and Myth: The New Reality of <u>Middlemarch</u>." <u>This Particular Web: Essays on</u> Middlemarch. Ed. Ian Adam. Toronto: U of Toronto P, 1975. 55–65.

See also "Chapter or Part of the Book," pages 238–39.

Sample Bibliographic Entries—Books

Author

> Welch, Evelyn. <u>Art and Society in Italy 1350–1500</u>. Oxford: Oxford UP, 1997.

Author, Anonymous

> <u>The Song of Roland</u>. Trans. Frederick B. Luquines. New York: Macmillan, 1960.

Author, Anonymous but Name Supplied

> [Madison, James.] <u>All Impressments Unlawful and Inadmissible</u>. Boston: William Pelham, 1804.

Author, Pseudonymous but Name Supplied

> Slender, Robert [Freneau, Philip]. <u>Letters on Various and Important Subjects</u>. Philadelphia: D. Hogan, 1799.

Author, Listed by Initials with Name Supplied

> A[lden], E[dmund] K. "Alden, John." <u>Dictionary of American Biography</u>. New York: Scribner's, 1928. 146–47.

Author, More Than One Work by the Same Author

> Michener, James A. <u>Centennial</u>. New York: Random, 1874.
> ---. <u>Chesapeake</u>. New York: Random, 1976.

Authors, Two

> Sulpy, Doug, and Ray Schweighardt. <u>Get Back: The Unauthorized Chronicle of the Beatles "Let It Be" Disaster</u>. New York: St. Martins, 1997.

Authors, Three

> Chenity, W. Carole, Joyce Takano Stone, and Sally A. Salisbury. <u>Clinical Gerontological Nursing: A Guide to Advanced Practice</u>. Philadelphia: Saunders, 1991.

Authors, More Than Three

Use "et al.," which means "and others," or list all the authors. See the two examples that follow:

> Lewis, Laurel J., et al. <u>Linear Systems Analysis</u>. New York: McGraw, 1969.
>
> Balzer, LeVon, Linda Alt Berene, Phyllis L. Goodson, Lois Lauer, and Irwin L. Slesnick. <u>Life Science</u>. Glenview, IL: Scott, 1990.

Author, Corporation or Institution

A corporate author can be an association, a committee, or any group or institution when the title page does not identify the names of the members.

> Committee on Telecommunications. <u>Reports on Elected Topics in Telecommunications</u>. New York: Nat. Acad. of Sciences, 1970.

List a committee or council as the author even when the organization is also the publisher, as in this example:

> American Council on Education. <u>Annual Report, 1997</u>. Washington, DC: ACE, 1991.

Alphabetized Works, Encyclopedias, and Biographical Dictionaries

Treat works arranged alphabetically as you would a collection, but omit the name of the editor(s), the volume number, place of publication, publisher, and page number(s). If the author is listed, begin the entry with the author's name; otherwise, begin with the title of the article. If the article is signed with initials, look elsewhere in the work for a complete name. Well-known works, such as the first two examples that follow, need only the edition and the year of publication.

> "Kiosk: Word History." <u>The American Heritage Dictionary of the English Language</u>. 3rd ed. 1992.

> Garrow, David J. "Martin Luther King, Jr." <u>The World Book Encyclopedia</u>. 1990 ed.

However, less-familiar reference works need a full citation, as shown in this next example:

> American Medical Association. "Infections and Infestations." <u>Guide to Prescription and Over-the-Counter Drugs</u>. Ed. Charles B. Clayman. New York: Random, 1988.

Place within quotation marks the titles to a synopsis or description of a novel or drama, even though the complete novel or drama would normally be underscored or italicized.

> "Antigone." <u>Masterpieces of World Literature</u>. Ed. Frank N. Magill. New York: Harper, 1989. 44–46.

The Bible

Do not underscore or italicize the word Bible or the books of the Bible. Common editions need no publication information. Do underscore or italicize special editions of the Bible.

> The Bible. [Denotes King James version]
> The Bible. The Old Testament. CD-ROM. Bureau Development, 1990.
> The Bible. Revised Standard Version.
> <u>The Geneva Bible</u>. 1560. Fascism. rpt. Madison: U of Wisconsin P, 1961.
> <u>The New Open Bible</u>. Large print ed. Nashville: Thomas Nelson, 1990.

A Book Published before 1900

For older books that are now out of print, you may omit the publisher. Use a comma, not a colon, to separate the place of publication from the year.

> Dewey, John. <u>The School and Society</u>. Chicago, 1899.

Classical Works

> Homer. <u>The Iliad</u>. Trans. Richmond Lattimore. Chicago: U of Chicago P, 1951.

Component Part of an Anthology or Collection

In general, works in an anthology have been published previously, but the prior publication data may not be readily available; therefore, use this form:

> Melville, Herman. "Bartleby the Scrivener." <u>The American Tradition in Literature</u>. 7th ed. Ed. George Perkins, Sculley

> Bradley, Richmond C. Beatty, E. Hudson Long. New York: McGraw, 1990. 818–42.

Provide the inclusive page numbers for the entire piece, not just the page or pages that you have cited in the text.

Use the following form if you can quickly identify original publication information:

> Scott, Nathan, Jr. "Society and the Self in Recent American Literature." <u>The Broken Center</u>. New Haven: Yale UP, 1966. Rpt. in <u>Dark Symphony: Negro Literature in America</u>. Ed. James A. Emanuel and Theodore L. Gross. New York: Free, 1968. 539–54.

If you use several works from the same anthology, you can shorten the citation by citing the short work and by making cross references to the larger one (see "Cross-References," immediately following, for specific details).

Cross-References

If you are citing several selections from one anthology or collection, provide a reference to the anthology and then provide individual references to the selections used from the anthology along with cross-references to the editor(s) of the anthology:

> Emanuel, James A., and Theodore L. Gross, eds. <u>Dark Symphony: Negro Literature in America</u>. New York: Free, 1968.
> Hughes, Langston. "Mulatto." Emanuel and Gross, 204–06.
> Scott, Nathan, Jr. "Society and the Self in Recent American Literature." Emanuel and Gross, 539–54.

Note also the following examples in which the first entry refers to the one that follows:

> Eliot, George. "Art and Belles Lettres." <u>Westminster Review</u>. USA ed. April 1856. Partly rpt. Eliot, <u>A Writer's Notebook</u>.
> ---. <u>A Writer's Notebook, 1854–1879, and Uncollected Writings</u>. Ed. Joseph Wiesenfarth. Charlottesville: UP of Virginia, 1981.

However, add an abbreviated title to the cross-reference if you list two or more works under the editor's name.

> Anson, David. "Searing, Nervy and Very Honest." Axelrod and Cooper, <u>Guide</u> 303–04.
> Axelrod, Rise B., and Charles R. Cooper. <u>Reading Critically, Writing Well</u>. New York: St. Martin's, 1987.
> Axelrod, Rise B., and Charles R. Cooper. <u>The St. Martin's Guide to Writing</u>. New York: St. Martin's, 1994.

Forster, E. M. "My Wood." Axelrod and Cooper, <u>Reading</u> 111–14.

Murayama, Veronica. "Schizophrenia: What It Looks Like, How It Feels." Axelrod and Cooper, <u>Guide</u> 181–84.

Edition

Cite any edition beyond the first, as shown below:

Keith, Harold. <u>Sports and Games</u>. 6th ed. Scranton: Crowell, 1976.

Indicate that a work has been prepared by an editor, not the original author:

Melville, Herman. <u>Moby Dick</u>. Ed. with Intro. by Alfred Kazin. Riverside ed. Boston: Houghton, 1956.

If you wish to show the original date of the publication, place the year immediately after the title, followed by a period.

Hardy Thomas. <u>Far from the Madding Crowd</u>. 1874. Ed. Robert C. Schweik. A Norton critical ed. New York: Norton, 1986.

Editor

List the editor first if your in-text citation refers to the work of the editor (for example, the editor's introduction or notes. "Bevington 316n)." The Works Cited entry should then be written as follows:

Bevington, David, ed. <u>The Complete Works of Shakespeare</u>. 4th ed. New York: Harper, 1992.

In other cases, you may wish to show the inclusive page numbers to a Foreword, Preface, Afterword, or some other commentary by an editor.

Bryant, Jennings, and Daniel R. Anderson, eds. Preface. <u>Children's Understanding of Television: Research on Attention and Comprehension</u>. New York: Academic, 1983. iv–xii.

Encyclopedia

Garrow, David J. "Martin Luther King, Jr." <u>The World Book Encyclopedia</u>. 1990 ed.

See also "Alphabetized Works, Encyclopedias, and Biographical Dictionaries" on pages 243–44 and "Citing Sources Found on CD-ROM," pages 261–63.

Introduction, Preface, Foreword, or Afterword

If you are citing the person who has written the introduction to a work by another author, use the following form:

Lowell, Robert. Foreword. <u>Ariel</u>. By Sylvia Plath. New York: Harper, 1966. vii–ix.

If the author has written the prefatory matter, not another person, use only the author's last name after *By*.

> Vonnegut, Kurt. Prologue. <u>Jailbird</u>. By Vonnegut. New York: Delacorte, 1979.

Note: Use the form above when you cite from the prologue only and not the main text.

Manuscript Collections in Book Form

> <u>Cotton Vitellius</u>. A.XV. British Museum, London. Chaucer, Geoffrey. <u>The Canterbury Tales</u>. Harley ms. 7334. British Museum, London.

See also "Manuscripts (ms) and Typescripts (ts)," page 268.

Play, Classical

> Shakespeare, William. <u>Macbeth</u>. <u>Shakespeare: Twenty-Three Plays and the Sonnets</u>. Ed. T. M. Parrott. New York: Scribner's, 1953.
> Racine, Jean. <u>Phaedra</u>. Trans. Robert Lowell. <u>World Masterpieces</u>. Ed. Maynard Mack et al. Continental ed. Vol. 2. New York: Norton, 1956. 102–46. 2 vols.

Play, Modern

> Greene, Graham. <u>The Complaisant Lover</u>. New York: Viking, 1959.
> Eliot, T. S. <u>The Cocktail Party</u>. <u>The Complete Poems and Plays: 1909–1950</u>. New York: Harcourt, 1952. 295–387.

Poem, Book Length

> Ciardi, John, trans. <u>The Purgatorio</u>. By Dante. New York: NAL, 1961.

Note: Use the form above only if the citation is to Ciardi's prefatory matter or notes to the text. Otherwise, cite Dante:

> Dante. <u>The Divine Comedy</u>. Trans. Lawrence G. White. New York: Pantheon, 1948.

Poem, Modern Collection

Use this form if you cite one short poem from a collection:

> Eliot, T. S. "The Love Song of J. Alfred Prufrock." <u>The Complete Poems and Plays 1909–1950</u>. New York: Harcourt, 1952. 3–7.

Use this next form if you cite one book-length poem:

> Eliot, T. S. <u>Four Quartets</u>. <u>The Complete Poems and Plays</u>
> <u>1909–1950</u>. New York: Harcourt, 1952. 115–45.

Do not cite specific poems and pages if you cite several different poems of the collection. Your in-text citations should cite the specific poems and page numbers (see pages 167–69). Your Works Cited entry would then look like this:

> Eliot, T. S. <u>The Complete Poems and Plays 1909–1950</u>. New York:
> Harcourt, 1952.

Republished Book

If you are citing from a republished book, such as a paperback version of a book published originally in hardback, provide the original publication date after the title and then provide the publication information for the book from which you are citing.

> Lowes, John Livingston. <u>The Road to Xanadu: A Study in the</u>
> <u>Ways of the Imagination</u>. 1930. New York: Vintage-Knopf,
> 1959.

Although it is not required, you may wish to provide supplementary information. Give the type of reproduction to explain that the republished work is, for example, a facsimile reprinting of the text:

> Hooker, Richard. <u>Of the Lawes of Ecclesiasticall Politie</u>. 1594.
> Fascism. rpt. Amsterdam: Teatrum Orbis Terrarum, 1971.

Give facts about the original publication. In this next example the republished book was originally published under a different title:

> Arnold, Matthew. "The Study of Poetry." <u>Essays: English and</u>
> <u>American</u>. Ed. Charles W. Eliot. 1886. New York: Collier,
> 1910. Rpt. of the General Introduction to <u>The English Poets</u>.
> Ed. T. H. Ward. 1880.

Series, Numbered and Unnumbered

> Commager, Henry Steele. <u>The Nature and the Study of History</u>.
> Soc. Sci. Seminar Ser. Columbus, OH: Merrill, 1965.
> Jefferson, D. W. "'All, all of a piece throughout': Thoughts on
> Dryden's Dramatic Poetry." <u>Restoration Theatre</u>. Ed. J. R.
> Brown and Bernard Harris. Stratford-upon-Avon Studies 6.
> London: Arnold, 1965. 159–76.
> Wallerstein, Ruth C. <u>Richard Crashaw: A Study in Style and</u>
> <u>Poetic Development</u>. U of Wisconsin Studies in Lang. and
> Lit. 37. Madison: U of Wisconsin P, 1935.

Sourcebooks and Casebooks

> Ellmann, Richard. "Reality." <u>Yeats: A Collection of Critical Essays</u>.
> Ed. John Unterecker. Twentieth Century Views. Englewood
> Cliffs: Prentice, 1963. 163–74.

If you can identify the original facts of publication, include that information also:

> Ellmann, Richard. "Reality." <u>Yeats: The Man and the Masks</u>. New
> York: Macmillan, 1948. Rpt. in <u>Yeats: A Collection of Critical</u>
> <u>Essays</u>. Ed. John Unterecker. Twentieth Century Views.
> Englewood Cliffs: Prentice, 1963. 163–74.

If you cite more than one article from a casebook, use cross references (see pages 245–46).

Title of a Book in Another Language

Use lowercase letters for foreign titles except for the first major word and proper names. Provide a translation in brackets if you think it necessary (e.g., Étranger [<u>The Stranger</u>] or Praha [Prague]).

> Brombert, Victor. <u>Stendhal et la voie oblique</u>. New Haven: Yale UP,
> 1954.
> Castex, P. G. Le rouge et le noir <u>de Stendhal</u>. Paris: Sedes, 1967.

See also "Titles within Titles," pages 211–12.

> Levowitz-treu, Micheline. <u>L'amour et la mort chez Standhal</u>. Aran:
> Editions due Grand Chéne, 1978.

Compare this form with that for a journal entry (see pages 254–55).

Translator

List the translator's name first only if the translator's work is the focus of your study.

> Condé, Maryse. <u>Segu</u>. Trans. Barbara Bray. New York: Ballantine,
> 1982.
> Shorey, Paul, trans. <u>The Republic</u>. By Plato. Cambridge: Harvard
> UP, 1937.

Volumes, a Work of Several Volumes

See page 240 for an explanation and additional examples to this bibliographic form:

> Ruskin, John. <u>The Works of Ruskin</u>. Ed. E. T. Cook and
> Alexander Wedderburn. 39 vols. London: Allen; New York:
> Longman, 1903.

Volumes, One of Several Volumes

> Dryden, John. <u>Poems 1649–1680</u>. <u>The Works of John Dryden</u>. Ed. Edward Niles Hooker et al. Vol. 1. Berkeley: U of California P, 1956.

Volumes, Component Part of One of Several Volumes

See pages 240–41 for an explanation and additional examples to this bibliographic form.

> Daiches, David. <u>A Critical History of English Literature</u>. 2nd ed. Vol. 2. New York: Ronald, 1970. 117–86.
>
> Hawthorne, Nathaniel. "My Kinsman, Major Molineaux." <u>The American Tradition in Literature</u>. Ed. Sculley Bradley, R. C. Beatty, and E. Hudson Long. 3rd ed. Vol. 1. New York: Norton, 1967. 507–22.

9c   Bibliographic Form—Periodicals

For journal or magazine articles, use the following order:

1. Author(s)
2. Title of the article
3. Name of the periodical
4. Series number (if it is relevant)
5. Volume number (for journals)
6. Issue number (if needed)
7. Date of publication
8. Page numbers

Name of the Author(s)

Show the author's name flush with the left margin, without a numeral and with succeeding lines indented five spaces. Enter the surname first, followed by a comma, followed by a given name or initials, followed by a period:

> Staten, Henry. "The Decomposing Form of Joyce's <u>Ulysses</u>." <u>PMLA</u> 112 (1997): 380–92.

Title of the Article

Show the title within quotation marks followed by a period inside the closing quotation marks:

> Baum, Rosalie Murphy. "Early-American Literature: Reassessing the Black Contribution." <u>Eighteenth Century Studies</u> 27 (1994): 533–49.

Name of the Periodical

Give the name of the journal or magazine, underscored or italicized, and with no following punctuation. Omit any introductory article to the title of the periodical or newspaper.

> Boose, Lynda E. "Othello's Handkerchief: 'The Recognizance and Pledge of Love.'" <u>English Literary Renaissance</u> 5 (1975): 360–74.

Volume, Issue, and Page Numbers for Journals

Most journals are paged continously through all issues of an entire year, so listing the month of publication is unnecessary. For example, page numbers and a volume number are sufficient for you to find an article in *Eighteenth Century Studies* or *English Literary Renaissance.* However, some journals have separate pagination for each issue. If that is the case, you will need to add an issue number following the volume number, separated by a period:

> Cann, Johnson, and Deborah Smith. "Volcanoes of the Mid-ocean Ridges and the Building of New Oceanic Crust." <u>Endeavor</u> 18.2 (1994): 61–66.

Add the month if more information would ease the search for the article:

> "20.5 (Nov. 1954): 4–6."

Specific Date, Year, and Page Numbers for Magazines

With magazines, the volume number offers little help for finding an article. For example, one volume of *Time* (52 issues) will have page 16 repeated 52 times. For this reason, you need to insert an exact date (month and day) for weekly and fortnightly publications:

> Lemonick, Michael D. "Adrift in Space." <u>Time</u> 28 July 1997: 47–48.

The month suffices for monthly and bimonthly publications:

> Levingston, Steven. "Steer Clear of These Dangerous Drivers." <u>Reader's Digest</u> July 1997: 50–55.

Supply inclusive numbers (202–09, 85–115, or 1112–24), but if an article is paged here and there throughout the issue (for example, pages 74, 78, and 81–88), write only the first page number and a plus sign with no intervening space:

> Gaylin, Jody. "Secrets of Marriages That Last." <u>Parents Magazine</u> Aug. 1991: 74+.

Sample Bibliographic Entries—Periodicals

Address, Published

> Humphries, Alfred. "Computers and Banking." Address to
> Kiwanis Club, Nashville, TN, 30 Feb. 1997. Rpt. in part
> <u>Tennessee Monthly</u> 31 Aug. 1997: 33–34.
> United States. President. "Address to Veterans of Foreign Wars."
> 19 Aug. 1974. Rpt. in <u>Weekly Compilation of Presidental
> Documents</u> 10 (26 Aug. 1974): 1045–50.

Author, Anonymous

> "Fiddling While Peace Burns." <u>Economist</u> 2 Apr. 1994: 14.

Interview, Published

> Safire, William. Interview. <u>Playboy</u> Nov. 1992: 63+.

Journal, with All Issues for a Year Paged Continuously

> Barnett, Pamela E. "Figurations of Rape and the Supernatural in
> <u>Beloved</u>." <u>PMLA</u> 112 (1997): 418–27.

Journal, with Each Issue Paged Anew

Add the issue number after the volume number because page numbers alone
are not sufficient to locate the article within a volume of 6 or 12 issues when
each issue has separate pagination.

> Naffziger, Douglas W., Jeffrey S. Hornsby, and Donald F. Kuralko.
> "A Proposed Research Model of Entrepreneurial Motivation."
> <u>Entrepreneurship: Theory and Practice</u> 18.3 (Spring 1994):
> 29–42.

If a journal uses only an issue number, treat it as a volume number:

> Wilson, Katharina M. "Tertullian's <u>De cultu foeminarum</u> and
> Utopia." <u>Moreana</u> 73 (1982): 69–74.

Journal, Volume Numbers Embracing Two Years

Some journals that publish only 4 or 6 issues a year will bind 8 issues or 12
issues, thereby putting two years together. Use the form shown in the following example.

> Callenbach, Ernest. "The Unbearable Lightness of Being." <u>Film
> Quarterly</u> 44–45 (Fall 1991): 2–6.

Magazine, Monthly

> Alleman, Richard. "Breaking Away on Bali." <u>Travel & Leisure</u> Feb.
> 1997: 94–105.

Magazine, Weekly

> France, David. "A Tree Dies in Manhattan: The Return of an
> Epidemic." <u>New York</u> 14 July 1997: 15–16.

Monograph

> Martin, Judith N., Michael L. Hecht, and Linda K. Larkey.
> "Conversational Improvement Strategies for Interethnic
> Communication: African American and European American
> Perspectives." <u>Communication Monographs</u> 61.3 (Sept.
> 1994): 236–55.

Notes, Queries, Reports, Comments, Letters

Magazine and journals publish many pieces that are not full-fledged articles.
Identify this type of material if the title of the article or the name of the journal does not make clear the nature of the material (e.g., "Letter" or "Comment").

> Brown, Amanda. "Comment and Response." <u>College English</u> 56
> (1994): 93–95.
> "Challenges to Intellectual Freedom Rise by Seven Percent."
> Bulletin. <u>Library Journal</u> 1 March 1994: 13.
> Holden, Michael. "Scholarship at Whose Service?" Letter. <u>PMLA</u>
> 109 (1994): 442–43.
> "Prioritizing the Powerless." Letter. <u>Library Journal</u> 1 March
> 1994: 3.

Reprint of a Journal Article

> Simonds, Robert L. "The Religious Right Explains the Religious
> Right." <u>School Administrator</u> 9 (Oct. 1993): 19–22. Rpt. in
> <u>Education Digest</u> Mar. 1994: 19–22.

If the article is reprinted in an information service that gathers together several articles on a common topic, such as Social Issues Resources Series
(SIRS), use the form shown in the following example (see also page 267).

> Edmondson, Brad. "AIDS and Aging." <u>American Demographics</u>
> Mar. 1990: 28+. <u>The AIDS Crisis</u>. Ed. Eleanor Goldstein. Vol.
> 2. Boca Raton: SIRS, 1991. Art. 24.

Review, in a Magazine or Journal

Name the reviewer and the title of the review. Then write *"Rev. of"* and the
title of the work being reviewed, followed by a comma, and the name of the
author or producer. If necessary, identify the nature of the work within
brackets immediately after the title.

> Seymour, Jim. "Push Back." Rev. of <u>Pointcast</u> and <u>Backweb</u>
> [computer software]. <u>PC Magazine</u> 16 (Aug. 1997): 93–94.

If the name of reviewer is not provided, begin the entry with the title of the review.

> "Recent Books." Rev. of <u>Writing as a Road to Self-Discovery</u>, by Barry Lane. <u>CCC</u> 45 (May 1994): 279.

If the review has no title, omit it from the entry.

> Rogers, Michael. Rev. of <u>Keats the Poet</u>, by Stuart Sperry. <u>Library Journal</u> 15 Mar. 1994: 105.

If the review is neither signed or titled, begin the entry with "*Rev. of*" and alphabetize the entry under the title of the work reviewed.

> Rev. of <u>Anthology of Danish Literature</u>, ed. F. J. Billeskov Jansen and P. M. Mitchell. <u>Times Literary Supplement</u> 7 July 1972: 785.

As shown in the example above, use an appropriate abbreviation (e.g., *ed., comp., trans.*) for the work of someone other than an author.

Series

Between the name of the publication and the volume number, identify a numbered series with an ordinal suffix (*2nd, 3rd*) followed by the abbreviation *ser.* For publications divided between the original series and a new series, show the series with *os* or *ns,* respectively.

> Hill, Christopher. "Sex, Marriage and the Family in England." <u>Economic History Review</u> 2nd ser. 31 (1978): 450–63.
>
> Terry, Richard. "Swift's Use of 'Personate' to Indicate Parody." <u>Notes and Queries</u> ns 41.2 (June 1994): 196–98.

Title, Omitted

> Berkowitz, David. <u>Renaissance Quarterly</u> 32 (1979): 396–493.

Title, Quotation within the Article's Title

> Ranald, Margaret Loftus. "'As Marriage Binds, and Blood Breaks': English Marriage and Shakespeare." <u>Shakespeare Quarterly</u> 30 (1979): 68–81.

Title, within the Article's Title

> Dundes, Alan. "'To Love My Father All': A Psychoanalytic Study of the Folktale Source of <u>King Lear</u>." <u>Southern Folklore Quarterly</u> 40 (1976): 353–66.

Title, Foreign

> Rebois, Charles. "Les effets du 12 juin." <u>Le Figaro Magazine</u> 2 juillet 1994: 42–43.

Stivale, Charles J. "Le vraisemblable temporel dans <u>Le Rouge et le noir</u>." <u>Stendhal Club</u> 84 (1979): 299–313.

See also "Title of a Book in Another Language," page 249.

9d Bibliographic Form—Newspapers

Provide the name of the author; the title of the article; the name of the newspaper as it appears on the masthead, omitting any introductory article (e.g., *Wall Street Journal,* not *The Wall Street Journal*); and the complete date—day, month (abbreviated), and year. Omit any volume and issue numbers.

Provide a page number as listed (e.g., 21, B-6, 14C, D3). For example, *USA Today* uses "6A" but *The New York Times* uses "A6." There is no uniformity among newspapers on this matter, so list the page accurately as an aid to your reader. If the article is not printed on consecutive pages (for example, if it begins on page 1 and skips to page 8), write the first page number and a plus (+) sign. If shown, give the edition (e.g., "late ed.") after the date and before the page number (see the Hoge citation on page 256).

Newspaper in One Section

Shields, Sharon. "Mothers March on Jail for 'Justice.'" <u>Chicago Defender</u> 13 May 1997: 7.

Newspaper with Lettered Sections

Cheaklos, Christina. "Grading Home-Schoolers." <u>Atlanta Journal-Constitution</u> 30 July 1997: B1.

Newspaper with Numbered Sections

Jones, Tim. "New Media May Excite, While Old Media Attract." <u>Chicago Tribune</u> 28 July 1997, sec. 4: 2.

Newspaper Editorial with No Author Listed

"Sales Tax Increase Is a Question of Priorities." Editorial. <u>Tennessean</u> [Nashville] 4 Sept. 1994: 4D.

Newspaper Article with City Added

In the case of locally published newspapers, add the city in square brackets (see also the sample entry immediately above).

Powers, Mary. "Finding Advances in the Search for Strep Vaccine." <u>Commercial Appeal</u> [Memphis] 7 July 1991: C3.

Newspaper Edition or Section for The New York Times

The Saturday edition of *The New York Times* is usually published as one complete section, so a lettered section is unnecessary. If you show the edition, place it after the year and before the page number, as shown in this next example.

> Hoge, William. "18th Century Bad Boy Who Fathered English Art." <u>New York Times</u> 14 June 1997, International ed.: 39+.

On Monday through Friday, *The New York Times* usually has four sections, *A, B, C, D.* You will need to show the section used.

> Levy, Clifford. "Do Words or Policies Protect Immigrants?" <u>The New York Times</u> 23 July 1997: B1, B4.

The Sunday edition of *The New York Times* has numbered sections, individually paged, to cover art, business, travel, and so forth. If you cite from one of these sections, provide the section number. Otherwise, cite the lettered section.

> Crossette, Barbara. "What Modern Slavery Is, and Isn't." <u>The New York Times</u> 27 July 1997, Sec. 4: 1+.

Newspaper in a Foreign Language

> Richard, Michel Bole, and Frédéric Fritscher. "Frederick DeKlerk, l'homme qui a aboli l'apartheid." <u>Le Monde</u> 3 juillet 1991: 1.

Serialized Article in a Newspaper or Periodical

A series of articles, published in several issues under the same general heading, requires indentification of the different issues. If each article that you cite has the same author and title, include the bibliographic information in one entry.

> Meserole, Harrison T., and James M. Rambeau. "Articles on American Literature Appearing in Current Periodicals." <u>American Literature</u> 52 (1981): 688–705; 53 (1981): 164–80, 348–59.

If each article that you cite has different authors and/or different titles, list each one separately. Indicate the number of this article in the series and give the name of the series. If the series features the same author(s), alphabetize by the first letters of the titles.

> Thomas, Susan, and Brad Schmitt. "Kids Find Their Fun in Danger." <u>Tennessean</u> [Nashville] 1 Sept. 1994: 1A+. Pt. 5 of a 30-day journal. Taking Back Our Kids: An Inner City Diary, begun 28 Aug. 1994.
> ---. "Little Love, Less Hope, Lost Lives." <u>Tennessean</u> [Nashville] 28 Aug. 1994: 1A+. Pt. 1 of a 30-day journal. Taking Back Our Kids: An Inner City Diary.
> ---. "This Is a Horrible Street." <u>Tennessean</u> [Nashville] 29 Aug. 1994: 1A+. Pt. 2 of a 30-day journal. Taking Back Our Kids: An Inner City Diary, begun 28 Aug. 1994.

9e Bibliograpic Form—Government Documents

Since the nature of public documents is so varied, the form of the entry cannot be standardized. Therefore, you should provide sufficent information so that the reader can easily locate the reference. As a general rule, place information in the bibliographic entry in this order:

> Government
> Body or agency
> Subsidiary body
> Title of document
> Identifying numbers
> Publication facts

When you cite two or more works by the same government, substitute three hyphens for the name of each government or body that you repeat:

> United States. Cong. House.
> ---. ---. Senate.
> ---. Dept. of Justice.

Congressional Papers

Senate and House sections are identified by an *S* or an *H* with document numbers (e.g., S. Res. 16) and page numbers (e.g., H2345–47).

> United States. Cong. Senate. Subcommittee on Juvenile Justice of the Committee on the Judiciary. <u>Juvenile Justice: A New Focus on Prevention</u>. 102nd Cong., 2nd sess. S. Hearing 102–1045. Washington, DC: GPO, 1992.
> ---. ---. ---. <u>Violent Crime Control Act 1991</u>. 102d Cong., 1st sess. S. 1241. Washington, DC: GPO, 1991.

If you provide a citation to the *Congressional Record,* you should abbreviate it and provide only the date and page numbers.

> <u>Cong. Rec</u>. 25 Aug. 1994: S12566-75.

Executive Branch Documents

> United States. Dept. of State. <u>Foreign Relations of the United States: Diplomatic Papers, 1943</u>. 5 vols. Washington, DC: GPO, 1943–44.
> ---. President. <u>Health Security: The President's Report to the American People</u>. Pr Ex 1.2:H34/4. Washington, DC: GPO, 1993.

Documents of State Governments

Publication information on state papers will vary widely, so provide provide sufficient data for your reader to find the document.

> Tennessee. Tennessee Board of Regents. <u>1992–1993 Statistical Report</u>. TBRA-001-92. Nashville: State of Tennessee, 1994.
> Tennessee. Tennessee State Library and Archives. <u>Tennessee Election Returns: 1796–1825</u>. Microfilm JK 5292. Nashville: State of Tennessee, n.d.
> Tennessee. State Department of Education. "Giles County." <u>1993–94 Directory of Schools</u>. Nashville: State of Tennessee, 1995.

Legal Citations and Public Statutes

Use the following examples as guidelines for developing your citations.

> California. Const. Art. 2, sec. 4.
> Environmental Protection Agency et al. v. Mink et al. US Reports, CDX. 1972.
> 15 US Code. Sec. 78h. 1964.
> Illinois. Revised Statutes Annotated. Sec. 16-7-81. 1980.
> Noise Control Act of 1972. Pub. L. 92–574. 1972. Stat. 86.
> People v. McIntosh. California 321 P.3d 876, 2001–6. 1970.
> State v. Lane. Minnesota 263 N. W. 608. 1935.
> U.S. Const. Art 2, sec. 1.

9f   Electronic Sources (CD-ROM, Internet, E-Mail, Databases)

New technology makes it possible for you to have access to information at your computer that was only a dream five years ago. The Internet, in particular, opens a cornucopia of information from millions of sources.

Citing Sources Found on the Internet

Include these items as appropriate to the source:

1. Author/editor name, followed by a period
2. Title of the article or short article (story or poem) within quotation marks
3. Name of the book, journal, or complete work, italicized
4. Publication information, followed by a period

   Place, publisher, and date for books
   Volume and year of a journal
   Exact date of a magazine
   Date and description for government documents

5. Date of your access, *not* followed by a period
6. URL (Uniform Resource Locator), within angle brackets, followed by a period; in MLA style break URLs only after a virgule (/).

Note: Do not include page numbers unless the Internet article shows original page numbers from the printed version of the journal or magazine. Do not include the total number of paragraphs nor specific paragraph numbers.

World Wide Web Sites

Online Journal

> Banning, E. B. "Herders or Homesteaders? A Neolithic Farm in Wadi Ziqlab, Jordan." *Biblical Archaeologist* 58.1 (1995). 9 Apr. 1997 ⟨http://scholar.cc.emory.edu/scripts/ASOR/BA/Banning.html⟩.

Abstract of a Journal Article

> Kassim, Saul M. "The Psychology of Confession Evidence." *American Psychologist* 52 (1997). Abstract. 10 Apr. 1997 ⟨http://www.apa.org/journals/amp397tc.html⟩.

Online Magazine

> Cohoon, Sharon, Jim McCausland, and Lauren Bonar Swezey. "Secrets of the Garden Masters: Heims's Secrets." *Sunset* Sept. 1996. 4 Mar. 1997 ⟨http://pathfinder.com@AiRYiAYAC5LGsKR/ . . . Sunset/1996/September/features/heims.html⟩.
>
> Fahcy, Todd Brendan. "Beach House." *Kudzu* Autumn 1995. 10 Mar. 1997 ⟨http://www.etext.org/Zines/K954/Fahey-Beach.html⟩.

Online Magazine, No Author Listed

> "Health-Care Inflation: It's Baaack!" *Business Week* 17 Mar. 1997. 18 Mar. 1997 ⟨http://www.businessweek.com/1997/11/b351852.htm⟩.

Government Document

> United States. Cong. Senate. *Superfund Cleanup Acceleration Act of 1997.* 21 Jan. 1997. 105th Cong. Senate Bill 8. 4 Mar. 1997 ⟨http.thomas.loc.gov/egi-bin/query/2?C105:S.8⟩.

Gopher Sites

> D'Agour, Amand. Review of *Classical Women Poets* by Josephine Balmer, ed. and trans. Newcastle-upon-Tyne: Bloodaxe Books, 1996. 10 Mar. 1997 ⟨gopher://gopher.lib.virginia.edu:70/alpha/bmer/v97/97-I-4⟩.

Diamond, Richard. "Seeing Ones Way: The Image and Action of 'Oidipous Tyrannos.'" *Electronic Antiquity* 1 (1993). 6 Mar. 1997 ⟨gopher://gopher.info.edu.au⟩.

"No One Scientific Study Can Tell All." 10 Mar. 1997 ⟨gopher:// gopher.fhcrc.org:70/Owaisdocid%3 . . . mer_Quest_1994/ SciNews⟩.

E-mail

Clemmer, Jim. "Writing Lab." E-mail to the author. 15 Jan. 1998.

Online Posting for E-mail Discussion Groups

If you cite from E-mail discussion groups, such as Listserv, add the description *Online Posting* and the name of the group. The address might be an Internet site or an E-mail address.

Camilleri, Rosemary. "Narrative Bibliography." 10 Mar. 1997. Online Posting. H-Rhetoric. 11 Mar. 1997 ⟨H-RHETOR@msu.edu⟩.

Merrian, Joanne. "Spinoff: Monsterpiece Theatre." 30 Apr. 1994. Online Posting. Shaksper: The Global Electronic Shakespeare Conference. 27 Aug. 1997 ⟨http://www.arts.ub.ca/ english/iemls/shak/MONSTERP_SPINOFF.txt⟩.

Linkage Data (a File Accessed from Another File)

"What Happens to Recycled Plastics?" 1996. Online Posting. Lkd. Better World Discussion Topics at Recycling Discussion Group. 18 June 1997 ⟨http://www.betterworld.com/BWZ/9602/ learn.htm⟩.

Newsgroups

Link, Richard. "Territorial Fish." 11 Jan. 1997. Online Posting. Environment Newsgroup. 11 Mar. 1998 ⟨rec.aquaria.freshwater.misc⟩.

HyperNews

Ochberg, Abigail. "Algae-based Paper." 9 Oct. 1996. Online Posting. Recycling Discussion Group. 18 June 1997 ⟨http:// www.betterworld.com/BWDiscuss/get/recycleD.html?embed=2⟩.

Telnet Site

U. S. Naval Observatory. "The Mercury Ion Frequency Standard." 24 Feb. 1997. Online Posting. 6 Mar. 1997 ⟨telnet:duke.ldgo.columbia.edu/ port=23 login ads, set terminal to 8/N/1⟩.

FTP Site

Kranidiotis, Argiris A. "Human Audio Perception Frequently Asked Questions." 7 June 1994. Online Posting. Human Audio

Perception Discussion Group. 11 Mar. 1997 ⟨ftp://
svr-ftp.eng.cam.ac.uk/pub/com.speech/info/
HumanAudio Perception⟩.

Article in a Reference Database

"Florida." *Britannica Online.* Vers. 97.1.1. Mar. 1997.
Encyclopaedia Britannica. 11 Jan. 1998
⟨http://www.eb.com:1754⟩.

Personal Site

Lester, James D. Home page. 11 Jan. 1998 ⟨http://
www.apsu01.apsu.edu/~lesterj/lester.htm⟩.

Scholarly Project and Professional Sites

Victorian Women Writers Project. Ed. Perry Willett. Apr. 1997.
Indiana U. 4 Jan. 1998 ⟨http://www.indiana.edu/~letrs/vwwp/⟩.
Portuguese Language Page. U of Chicago. 4 Jan. 1998 ⟨http://
humanities.uchicago.edu/romance/port/⟩.

Miscellaneous Internet Sources

List the type of work for such items as a cartoon, map, chart, advertisement,
and so forth, as shown in this example.

Toles, Tom. "What Americans Don't Want to See in Iraq." Cartoon.
US News Online. 26 Jan. 1998. 30 Jan. 1998 ⟨http://
www.usnews.com/usnews/issue/980126/26tole.htm⟩.

Citing Sources Found on CD-ROM

CD-ROM technology provides information in four different ways, and each
method of transmission requires an adjustment in the form of the entry for
your works cited page.

   1. **CD-ROM, full-text articles with publication information for the
printed source.** Full-text articles are available from national distributors,
such as Information Access Company (InfoTrac), UMI-Proquest (Proquest),
Silverplatter, or SIRS CD-ROM Information Systems. Conform to the examples that follow.

DePalma, Antony. "Mexicans Renew Their Pact on the
Economy, Retaining the Emphasis on Stability." New
York Times 25 Sept. 1994: 4. New York Times Ondisc.
CD-ROM. UMI-Proquest. Jan. 1995.
Mann, Thomas E., and Norman J. Ornstein. "Shipshape? A
Progress Report on Congressional Reform." Brookings
Review Spring 1994: 40–45. SIRS Researcher. CD-
ROM. Boca Raton: SIRS, 1994. Art. 57.

See also page 267 for citing SIRS in its loose-leaf form.

Silver, Daniel J. "The Battle of the Books." Rev. of The
    Western Canon: The Books and Schools of the Ages, by
    Harold Bloom. Commentary 98.6 (1994): 60–63.
    Resource/One. CD-ROM. UMI-Proquest. Feb. 1995.

Wessel, David. "Fed Lifts Rates Half Point, Setting Four-Year
    High." Wall Street Journal. 2 Feb. 1995: A2+. Wall
    Street Times Ondisc. CD-ROM. UMI-Proquest. Feb.
    1995.

Note: When you cite from electronic sources, complete information may not
be readily available—for example, the original publication data may be
missing. In such cases, provide what is available:

Silver, Daniel J. "The Battle of the Books." Rev. of The
    Western Canon: The Books and School of the Ages, by
    Harold Bloom. Resource/One. CD-ROM. UMI-Proquest.
    Feb. 1995.

   2. **CD-ROM, full-text articles with no publication information for
a printed source.** Sometimes the original printed source of an article or report will not be provided by the distributor of the CD-ROM database. In such
a case, conform to the examples that follow:

"Faulkner Biography." Discovering Authors. CD-ROM.
    Detroit: Gale, 1993.

"U.S. Population by Age: Urban and Urbanized Areas." 1990
    U.S. Census of Population and Housing. CD-ROM. US
    Bureau of the Census. 1990.

   3. **Texts of complete books and other publications on CD-ROM.**
Cite this type of source as you would a book, and then provide information
to the electronic source that you accessed.

The Bible. The Old Testament. CD-ROM. Parsippany, NJ:
    Bureau Development, 1990.

English Poetry Full-Text Database. Rel. 2. CD-ROM.
    Cambridge, Eng.: Chadwyck, 1993.

"John F. Kennedy." InfoPedia. CD-ROM. n.p.: Future Vision,
    n.d.

Poe, Edgar Allan. "Fall of the House of Usher." Electronic
    Classical Library. CD-ROM. Garden Grove, CA: World
    Library, 1993.

Williams, T. Harry. The Military Leadership of the North and
    the South: US History on CD-ROM. 1960. Parsippany,
    NJ: Bureau Development, 1990.

Wilson, Gohan. The Ultimate Haunted House. CD-ROM.
    Redman, WA: Microsoft, 1992.

   4. **Abstracts on CD-ROM to books and articles provided by the national distributors.** As a service to readers, the national distributors have

members of their staff write abstracts of articles and books if the original authors have not provided such abstracts. As a result, an abstract that you find
on Info Trac and ProQuest may not be written by the original author, so you
should not quote such abstracts. You may quote from abstracts that say, "Abstract written by the author." Silverplatter databases *do* have abstracts written by the original authors.

In either case, you need to show in the works cited entry that you have
cited from the abstract, so conform to the examples that follow:

> Figueredo, Aurelio J., and Laura Ann McCloskey. "Sex,
> Money, and Paternity: The Evolutionary Psychology of
> Domestic Violence." Ethnology and Sociobiology 14
> (1993): 353–79. Abstract. PsychLit. CD-ROM.
> Silverplatter. 12 Jan. 1997.
> O'Keefe, Maura. "Linking Marital Violence, Mother-
> Child/Father-Child Aggression, and Child Behavior
> Problems." Journal of Family Violence 9.1 (1994):
> 63–79. Abstract. InfoTrac: Expanded Academic Index.
> CD-ROM. Information Access. 6 Dec. 1997.
> Silver, Daniel J. "The Battle of the Books." Rev. of The
> Western Canon: The Books and School of the Ages, by
> Harold Bloom. Abstract. UMI-Proquest. 23 Feb. 1995.
> Steele, Janet. "TV's Talking Headaches." Columbia
> Journalism Review 31.2 (1992): 49–52. Abstract.
> InfoTrac: Expanded Academic Index. CD-ROM.
> Information Access. 16 July 1996.

5. **Encyclopedia article on CD-ROM.** Use the following form:

> "Abolitionist Movement." Compton's Interactive
> Encyclopedia. CD-ROM. Softkey Multimedia. 1996.

Citing a Source That You Access in More Than One Medium

Some distributors issue packages that include different media, such as CD-
ROM and accompanying microfiche or a diskette and an accompanying
videotape. Cite such publications as you would a nonperiodical CD-ROM (see
item 3 above) with the addition of the media available with this product.

> Franking, Holly. Negative Space: A Computerized Video Novel.
> Vers. 1.0. Diskette, videocassette. Prairie Village: Diskotech,
> 1990.
> Jolly, Peggy. "A Question of Style." Exercise Exchange 26.2
> (1982): 39–40. ERIC. CD-ROM, microfiche. Silverplatter. Feb.
> 17, 1995. ED236601, fiche 1.
> Silver, Daniel J. "The Battle of the Books." Rev. of The Western
> Canon: The Books and School of the Ages, by Harold Bloom.
> Resource/One. CD-ROM, microfiche S-637. UMI-Proquest.
> Feb. 1995.

Citing a Source Found on a Diskette

Cite a diskette as you would a book with the addition of the word *Diskette.* Conform to the examples that follow:

> Lester, James D. Grammar: Computer Slide Show. 10 lessons on 4 diskettes. Clarksville, TN: Austin Peay State U, 1997.
> "Nuclear Medicine Technologist." Guidance Information System. 17th ed. Diskette. Cambridge: Riverside-Houghton, 1992.

Citing a Source Found on a Magnetic Tape

Write this entry as you would for a book with the addition of the words *Magnetic tape.* If relevant, show edition (3rd ed.), release (Rel. 2), or version (Ver. 3). Conform to this example:

> Statistics on Child Abuse--Montgomery County, Tennessee. Rel. 2. Magnetic tape. Clarksville, TN: Harriett Cohn Mental Health Center, 1997.

Citing a Source Found on a Database

To access a database, such as DIALOG, conform to the style shown in these samples:

> Bronner, E. "Souter Voices Concern over Abortion Curb." Boston Globe 31 Oct. 1990: 1. Dialog. 22 Nov. 1997.
> Priest, Patricia Joyner. "Self-Disclosure on Television: The Counter-Hegemonic Struggle of Marginalized Groups on 'Donahue.'" Diss. New York U, 1990. DAI 53.7 (1993): 2147A. Dissertation Abstracts Online. Dialog. 10 Feb. 1994.

Material Accessed through E-mail

Electronic mail may be treated as a letter or memo (see page 260). Provide the name of the sender, a title or subject if one is listed, a description of the mail (e.g., "E-mail to Greg Norman"), and the date of transmission.

> Taylor, Stephanie. "Mail How-To #1." E-Mail to Harned users. 26 Sept. 1994.
> Morgan, Melvin S. E-Mail to the author. 16 Feb. 1995.

9g   Bibliographic Form—Other Sources

Advertisement

Provide the name of the advertisement or the name of the product, the label *Advertisement,* and publication information.

> You've Got Some Royal Caribbean Coming. Advertisement. New Yorker 20 Feb. 1995: 163.
> Delta Faucets. Advertisement. ESPN. 16 Feb. 1995.

Jenkins & Wynne Ford/Mercury. Billboard advertisement.
Clarkville, TN. Aug. 1994.

Art Work

If you actually experience the work itself, use the form shown by the next
two entries:

Remington, Frederic. <u>Mountain Man</u>. Metropolitan Museum of
Art, New York.
Wyeth, Andrew. <u>Hay Ledge</u>. Private Collection of Mr. and Mrs.
Joseph E. Levine, New York.

If the art work is a special showing at a museum, use the form of these next
examples. You may show the date of your viewing.

"Gertrude Vanderbilt Whitney: Printmakers' Patron." Whitney
Museum of American Art, New York. 22 Feb. 1995.
Mortenson, Ray. "Photographs of Lakes and Ponds in the Hudson
Highlands." Borden Gallery, New York. 26 Feb. 1995.

Use this next form to cite reproductions in books and journals.

Lee-Smith, Hughie. <u>Temptation</u>. 1991. <u>A History of African-
American Artists: From 1792 to the Present</u>. Ed. Romare
Bearden and Harry Henderson. New York: Pantheon, 1993.
Raphael. <u>School of Athens</u>. The Vatican, Rome. <u>The World Book-
Encyclopedia</u>. 1976 ed.

If you can indicate the date of the original, place the date immediately after
the title.

Raphael. <u>School of Athens</u>. 1510–1511. The Vatican, Rome. <u>The
World Book-Encyclopedia</u>. 1976 ed.

Broadcast Interview

Dole, Robert, Senate Majority Leader. Interview with David
Brinkley. <u>This Week with David Brinkley</u>. ABC. WKRN,
Nashville. 19 Feb. 1995.
Wolfe, Tom. Interview. <u>The Wrong Stuff: American Architecture</u>.
Dir. Tom Bettag. Videocassette. Carousel, 1983.

Bulletin

Economic Research Service. <u>Demand and Price Situation</u>. Bulletin
DPS-141, 14 pp. Washington, DC: Department of
Agriculture, Aug. 1994.
French, Earl. <u>Personal Problems in Industrial Research and
Development</u>. Bulletin No. 51. Ithaca: New York State School
of Industrial and Labor Relations, 1993.

Cartoon

Danzig. Cartoon. <u>The Christian Science Monitor</u> 1 Sept. 1994: 6.

If you cannot decipher the name of the cartoonist, use this form:

Cartoon. <u>New Yorker</u> 12 Sept. 1994: 92.

Computer Software

<u>Aldus Pagemaker 5.0</u>. Computer software. Seattle: Aldus, 1994.
Matthews, Martin S., and Carole B. Matthews. <u>Corel!5 Made Easy:</u>
<u>The Basics and Beyond</u>. Berkeley: Osborne McGraw-Hill,
1994.

Conference Proceedings

Miller, Wilma J., ed. <u>Writing across the Curriculum</u>. Proceedings
of the Fifth Annual Conference on Writing across the
Curriculum, Feb. 1995, U of Kentucky. Lexington: U of
Kentucky P, 1995.

Dissertation, Published

Nykrog, Per. <u>Les Fabliaux: Etude d'histoire littéraire et de</u>
<u>stylistique mediévale</u>. Diss. Aarhus U, 1957. Copenhagen:
Munksgaard, 1957.

Dissertation, Unpublished

Burks, Linda Carol. "The Use of Writing as a Means of Teaching
Eighth-Grade Students to Use Executive Processes and
Heuristic Strategies to Solve Mathematics Problems." Diss. U
of Michigan, 1992.

Dissertation, Abstract Only

Use this form when you cite from *Dissertation Abstracts International (DAI)*.
The page number features *A, B,* or *C* to designate the series used: A Humanities, B Sciences, C European dissertations.

Burks, Linda Carol. "The Use of Writing as a Means of Teaching
Eighth-Grade Students to Use Executive Processes and
Heuristic Strategies to Solve Mathematics Problems." Diss. U
of Michigan. 1992. <u>DAI</u> 54 (1993): 4019A.

See also "Abstracts on CD-ROM," pages 262–63, and "Citing a Source Found
on a Database," page 264.

Film or Video Recording

Cite title, director, distributor, and year.

<u>Scent of a Woman</u>. Dir. Martin Brest. Universal Pictures, 1992.

If relevant to your study, add the names of performers, writers, or producers after the name of the director.

<u>Mask</u>. Dir. Charles Russell. Perf. Jim Carey. New Line Prod. 1994.

If the film is a videocassette, filmstrip, slide program, or videodisc, add the type of medium before the name of the distributor. Add the date of the original film, if relevant, before the name of the medium.

> <u>Mask</u>. Dir. Charles Russell. Perf. Jim Carey. 1994. Videocassette. New Line Home Video, 1995.

If you are citing the accomplishments of the director or a performer, begin the citation with that person's name.

> Pacino, Al. <u>Scent of a Woman</u>. Dir. Martin Brest. 1992. Videocassette. MCA Universal, 1993.

If you cannot find certain information, such as the original date of the film, cite what is available.

> Altman, Robert, dir. <u>The Room</u>. Perf. Julian Sands, Linda Hunt, Annie Lennox. Videocassette. Prism, 1987.

Interview, Unpublished

For an interview that you conduct, name the person interviewed, the type of interview (e.g., telephone interview, personal interview, E-Mail interview), and the date.

> Safire, William. Telephone interview. 5 Mar. 1995.

See also "Interview Published," page 252 and "Broadcast Interview," page 265.

Letter, Personal

> Weathers, Walter. Letter to the author. 5 Mar. 1997.

Letter, Published

> Eisenhower, Dwight. Letter to Richard Nixon. 20 April 1968. <u>Memoirs of Richard Nixon</u>. By Richard Nixon. New York: Grosset, 1978.

Loose-Leaf Collections

If you cite an article from SIRS. *Opposing Viewpoints,* or other loose-leaf collections, provide both the original publication data and then add information for the loose-leaf volume, as shown in this next example:

> Hodge, Paul. "The Adromeda Galaxy." <u>Mercury</u> July/Aug. 1993: 98+. <u>Physical Science</u>. Ed. Eleanor Goldstein. Vol. 2. Boca Raton: SIRS, 1994. Art. 24.

Manuscripts (ms) and Typescripts (ts)

Glass, Malcolm. Journal 3, ms. M. Glass Private Papers, Clarksville, TN.

Tanner. Ms. 346. Bodleian Library, Oxford, Eng.

Williams, Ralph. Notebook 15, ts. Williams Papers. Vanderbilt U., Nashville.

Map

County Boundaries and Names. United States Base Map GE-50, No. 86. Washington, DC: GPO, 1987.

Virginia. Map. Chicago: Rand, 1987.

Microfilm or Microfiche

Chapman, Dan. "Panel Could Help Protect Children." Winston-Salem Journal 14 Jan. 1990: 14. Newsbank: Welfare and Social Problems 12 (1990): fiche 1, grids A8–11.

Jolly, Peggy. "A Question of Style." Exercise Exchange 26.2 (1982): 39–40. ERIC ED2336601, fiche 1.

Tuckerman, H. T. "James Fenimore Cooper." Microfilm. North American Review 89 (1859): 298–316.

Mimeographed Material

Smith, Jane L. "Terms for the Study of Fiction." Mimeographed material. Athens: Ohio U. 1998.

Miscellaneous Materials (Program, Leaflet, Poster, Announcement)

"Earth Day." Poster. Louisville. 23 Mar. 1998.

"Gospel Arts Day." Program. Nashville: Fisk U. 18 June 1997.

Monograph

Tennessee Teachers Group. Kindergarten Practices, 1995. Monograph 1995–M2. Knoxville: Author, 1995.

See also "Monograph," page 253, for a monograph published in a journal.

Musical Composition

Mozart, Wolfgang A. Jupiter. Symphony No. 41.

Wagner, Richard. Lohengrin.

Treat a published score as you would a book.

Legrenzi, Giovanni. "La Buscha." Sonata for Instruments. Historical Anthology of Music. Ed. Archibald T. Davison and Willi Apel. Cambridge, MA: Harvard UP, 1950. 70–76.

Pamphlet

Treat pamphlets as you would a book.

> Federal Reserve Board. <u>Consumer Handbook to Credit Protection
>   Laws</u>. Washington, DC: GPO, 1993.
> Westinghouse Advanced Power Systems. <u>Nuclear Waste
>   Management: A Manageable Task</u>. Madison, PA: Author, n.d.

Performance

Treat a performance (e.g., play, opera, ballet, or concert) as you would a
film, but include the site (normally the theatre and city) and the date of the
performance.

> <u>Lakota Sioux Indian Dance Theatre</u>. Symphony Space, New York.
>   18 Feb. 1995.
> <u>Oedipus at Colonus</u>. By Sophocles. Trans. Theodore H. Banks.
>   Pearl Theatre, New York. 8 Feb. 1995.
> <u>Sunset Boulevard</u>. By Andrew Lloyd Webber. Dir. Trevor Nunn.
>   Perf. Glenn Close, George Hearn, Alan Campbell, and Alice
>   Ripley. Minskoff Theatre, New York. 7 Feb. 1995.

If your text emphasizes the work of a particular individual, begin with the
appropriate name.

> Cytron, Sara. "Take My Domestic Partner--Please," Conf. on Coll.
>   Composition and Communication Convention. Grand Hyatt
>   Hotel, Washington, DC. 24 Mar. 1995.
> Gregory, Dick, comedian. Village Vanguard, New York. 22 Feb.
>   1995.
> Marcovicci, Andrea, cond. "I'll Be Seeing You: Love Songs of
>   World War II." American Symphony Orchestra. Avery Fisher
>   Hall, New York. 15 Feb. 1995.

Public Address or Lecture

Identify the nature of the address (e.g., Lecture, Reading), include the site
(normally the lecture hall and city), and the date of the performance.

> Evans, Nekhena. Lecture. Brooklyn Historical Soc., New York. 26
>   Feb. 1995.
> Freedman, Diane P. "Personal Experience: Autobiographical
>   Literary Criticism." Address. MLA Convention. Marriott
>   Hotel, San Diego. 28 Dec. 1994.
> Kinnel, Galway. Reading of Smart, Rilke, Dickinson, and others.
>   Manhattan Theatre Club, New York. 20 Feb. 1995.

Recording on Record, Tape, or Disc

If you are not citing a compact disc, indicate the medium (e.g., audiocassette, audiotape [reel-to-reel tape], or LP [long-playing record]).

> "Chaucer: The Nun's Priest's Tale." <u>Canterbury Tales</u>. Narr. in Middle English by Robert Ross. Audiocassette. Caedmon, 1971.
>
> John, Elton. "This Song Has No Title." <u>Goodbye Yellow Brick Road</u>. LP. MCA, 1974.
>
> Reich, Robert B. <u>Locked in the Cabinet: A Political Memoir</u>. 4 cassettes abridged. New York: Random Audio, 1997.
>
> Sanborn, David. "Soul Serenade." <u>Upfront</u>. LP. Elektra, 1992.
>
> Tchaikovsky. <u>Romeo and Juliet</u>. Fantasy-Overture after Shakespeare. New Philharmonia Orchestra. London. Cond. Lawrence Siegel. Audiotape. Classical Masters, 1993.

Do not underscore, italicize, or enclose within quotation marks a private recording or tape. However, you should include the date, if available, as well as the location and the identifying number.

> Walpert, Wanda A. Folk Stories of the Smokey Mountains. Rec. Feb. 1995. Audiotape. U of Knoxville. Knoxville, TN. UTF. 34.82.

Cite a libretto, liner notes, or booklet that accompanies a recording in the form shown in the following example.

> Brooks, Garth. Booklet. <u>No Fences</u>. By Garth Brooks. Capital Nashville, 1990.

Report

Unbound reports are placed within quotation marks; bound reports are treated as books:

> Coca-Cola Company. <u>1994 Annual Report</u>. Atlanta: Author, 1994.
>
> Linden, Fabian. "Women: A Demographic, Social and Economic Presentation." Report. The Conference Board. New York: CBS/Broadcast Group, 1973.

Reproductions and Photographs

> Blake, William. <u>Comus</u>. Plate 4. Photograph in Irene Taylor. "Blake's <u>Comus</u> Designs." <u>Blake Studies</u> 4 (Spring 1972): 61.
>
> Michener, James A. "Structure of Earth at Centennial, Colorado." Line drawing in <u>Centennial</u>. By Michener. New York: Random, 1974. 26.
>
> Snowden, Mary. <u>Jersey Pears</u>. 1982. <u>American Realism: Twentieth Century Drawings and Watercolors</u>. New York: Abrams, 1986. 159.

Table, Illustration, Chart, or Graph

Tables or illustrations of any kind published within works need a detailed citation:

> Abken, Peter A. "Over-the-Counter Financial Derivatives: Risky Business?" Chart No. 2. <u>Economic Review</u> 79.2 (Mar.–Apr. 1994): 7.
> Alphabet. Chart. Columbus: Scholastic, 1994.
> Corbett, Edward P. J. Syllogism graph. <u>Classical Rhetoric for the Modern Student</u>. New York: Oxford UP, 1965.

Television or Radio Program

If available or relevant, provide information in this order: the episode (in quotation marks), the title of the program (underscored or italicized), title of the series (not underscored nor in quotation marks), name of the network, call letters and city of the local station, and the broadcast date. Add other information (such as narrator) after the episode or program narrated or directed or performed. Place the number of episodes, if relevant, before the title of the series.

> "<u>Frankenstein</u>: The Making of the Monster." <u>Great Books</u>. Narr. Donald Sutherland. Writ. Eugenie Vink. Dir. Jonathan Ward. Learning Channel. 8 Sept. 1993.
> "News Headlines." Narr. Sadie Sakleford. <u>Weekend Edition</u>. NPR. WPHN, Nashville. 19 Feb. 1995.
> <u>Middlemarch</u>. By George Eliot. Adapt. Andrew Davies. Dir. Anthony Pope. Perf. Juliet Aubrey and Patrick Malahide. 6 episodes. Masterpiece Theatre. Introd. Russell Baker. PBS. WCDN, Nashville. 10 Apr.–15 May 1994.
> <u>Nutrition & Aids</u>. Narr. Carolyn O'Neil. CNN. 19 Feb. 1995.
> <u>Prairie Home Companion</u>. NPR. WPHN, Nashville. 18 Feb. 1995.
> "Some of Our Planes Are Missing." Narr. Morley Safer. Prod. David Fitzpatrick. <u>60 Minutes</u>. CBS. WTVF, Nashville. Feb. 19 1994.

Thesis

See "Dissertation, Unpublished," page 266.

Transparency

> Sharp, La Vaughn, and William E. Loeche. <u>The Patient and Circulatory Disorders: A Guide for Instructors</u>. 54 transparencies, 99 overlays. Philadelphia: Lippincott, 1969.

Unpublished Paper

> Elkins, William R. "The Dream World and the Dream Vision: Meaning and Structure in Poe's Art." Unpublished paper. Little Rock, AR, 1995.

Videotape

Cronkite Remembers. Videocassette. CBS Video, 1997.

The Gate to the Mind's Eye. A Computer Animation Odyssey. Dir. Michael Boydstein. Music by Thomas Dolly. Videocassette. BMG Video, 1994.

A Portrait of the Artist as a Young Man. By James Joyce. Dir. Joseph Strick. Perf. Bosco Hogan. Videocassette. Mystic Fire Video, 1989.

Thompson, Paul. "W. B. Yeats." Lecture. Videocassette. Memphis U, 1995.

Sevareid, Eric, narr. CBS News. 11 Mar. 1975. Media Services Videocassette. Vanderbilt U, 1975.

Voice Mail

Warren, Vernon. "Memo to Lester." Voice mail to the author. 6 Jan. 1995.

10 Writing in APA Style

Your instructor may require you to write the research paper in APA style, which is governed by *The Publication Manual of the American Psychological Association*. This style has gained wide acceptance in academic circles. APA style is used in the social sciences, and versions similar to it are used in the biological sciences, business, and the earth sciences. This chapter conforms to the stipulations of the fourth edition of the APA style manual, published in 1994, with adjustments based on APA's Web page.

You need to understand two basic ideas that govern this style. First, a scientific paper attempts to show what has been proven true by research in a narrowly defined area, so it requires the past tense when you cite the work of scientists (Johnson stipulated *or* the work of Elmford and Mills showed). Second, the scientific community considers the year of publication as vital information, so they feature it immediately after any named source in the text, like this: (Johnson & Marshall, 1991). These two primary distinctions, and others, are explained below.

10a Writing in the Proper Tense for an APA Styled Paper

Verb tense is an indicator that distinguishes papers in the humanities from those in the natural and social sciences. MLA style, as shown in previous chapters, requires you to use present tense when you refer to a cited work (Johnson stipulates *or* the work of Elmford and Mills shows). In contrast, APA style requires you to use past tense or present perfect tense (Marshall stipulated *or* the work of Elmford and Mills has demonstrated). The APA style does require present tense when you discuss the results (e.g., the results confirm *or* the study indicates) and when you mention established knowledge (e.g., the therapy offers some hope *or* salt contributes to hypertension).

A paper in the humanities (MLA style) makes universal assertions, so it uses the historical present tense:

"It was the best of times, it was the worst of times," writes Charles Dickens about the eighteenth century.

Johnson argues that sociologist Norman Manway has a "narrow-minded view of clerics and their role in nineteenth century fiction" (64).

A scientific study makes a specific claim and requires the past tense or the present perfect tense with your citations to a scientist's work:

Matthews (1994) designed the experiment, and since that time several investigators have used the method (Thurman, 1996; Jones, 1998).

Note the differences in the verbs of these next two passages whenever the verbs refer to a cited work.

MLA style	*APA style*
The scholarly issue at work here is the construction of reality. Cohen, adoni, and Bantz label the construction a social process "in which human beings act both as the creators and products of the social world" (34). These writers identify three categories (34–35).	The scholarly issue at work here is the construction of reality. Cohen, Adoni, and Bantz (1994) have labeled the construction a social process "in which human beings act both as the creators and products of the social world" (p. 34). These writers have identified three categories.

As illustrated in the preceding example on the left, MLA style requires that you use the present tense both for personal comments and for introducing sources. In MLA style the ideas and words of the authorities, theoretically, remain in print and continue to be true in the universal present. APA style, shown on the right, requires that you use the present tense for generalizations and references to stable conditions, but it requires the present perfect tense or the past tense for sources cited (e.g., the sources have tested a hypothesis *or* the sources reported the results of a test). This next sentence uses tense correctly for APA style:

> The danger of steroid use ⌞ exists ⌟ for every age group, even youngsters. Lloyd and Mercer (1997) ⌞ reported ⌟ on six incidents of liver damage to 14-year-old swimmers who used steroids.

As shown above in the example, use the present tense (*exists*) for established knowledge and the present perfect or the past tense (*reported*) for a citation.

10b Establishing a Critical Approach

In scientific writing, the thesis (see pages 18–20) usually takes a different form. It appears as a *hypothesis, statement of principle,* or an *enthymeme.*

The hypothesis is a theory that needs testing and analysis, which you will do as part of your research. It is an idea expressed as a truth for the purpose of argument and investigation. It makes a prediction based upon the theory. Here is an example:

> It was predicted that patients who suffer a compulsive bulimic disorder would have a more disrupted family life.

In a similar fashion, the statement of principle makes a declarative statement in defense of an underlying but unstated theory, as shown here:

> The most effective recall cue is the one that is encoded within the event that is to be remembered.

Your work would attempt to prove this principle. An enthymeme is an incomplete logical structure that depends on one or more unstated assumptions to be complete. It serves as the beginning position for an argument. Most enthymemes include a *because* clause. Here is an example:

> Little league sports are good for children because they promote discipline.

Unstated is the assumption that discipline is good for children. Most of your scientific investigations will use one of these controlling devices.

10c Using Subheads

Most papers will need only major headings (A-level), but the advent of desktop publishing makes it possible for some research papers to gain the look of professional typesetting. Use the following guideline for writing subheads in your paper.

Writing a Research Paper ◄— A heading, centered

Writing the First Draft ◄——————— B heading, flush left with capital letters on each major word

Revising and editing the manuscript ◄——— C heading, flush left with only the first word capitalized

　　Proofreading. Every researcher . . ◄——— D heading, run-in side head, underscored or italicized, that begins a paragraph

10d Using In-Text Citations in APA Style

APA style uses these conventions for in-text citations.

1. Cites last names only.
2. Cites the year, within parentheses, immediately after the name of the author. That is, give a page number to a paraphrase of a passage in a long work as a courtesy to the reader. However it is not required.
3. Cites page numbers always with a direct quotation, seldom with a paraphrase.
4. Uses "p." or "pp." before page numbers.

Citing Last Name Only and the Year of Publication

An in-text citation in APA style requires the last name of the author and the year of publication.

> Devlin (1997) has advanced the idea of combining the social sciences and mathematics to chart human behavior.

If you do not use the author's name in your text, place the name(s) within the parenthetical citation, followed by a comma and the year.

> One study has advanced the idea of combining the social sciences and mathematics to chart human behavior (Devlin, 1997).

Providing a Page Number

If you quote the exacts words of a source, provide a page number and *do* use "p." or "pp." Place the page number in one of two places: after the year or at the end of the quotation.

> Devlin (1997) has advanced the idea of "soft mathematics," which is the practice of "applying mathematics to study people's behavior" (p. B4).

Citing a Block of Material

Write a quotation of 40 words or more as a separate block, indented 5 spaces from the left margin. (*Note:* MLA style uses 10 spaces). Because it is set off from the text in a distinctive block, do not enclose it with quotation marks. Do not indent the first line an extra 5 spaces; however, do indent the first line of any additional paragraphs that appear in the block an extra 5 spaces, that is, 10 spaces from the left margin. Set parentehtical citations outside the last period.

Albert (1997) reported the following:

> Whenever these pathogenic organisms attack the human body and begin to multiply, the infection is set in motion. The host responds to this parasitic invasion with efforts to cleanse itself of the invading agents.
>
> When rejection efforts of the host become visible (fever, sneezing, congestion), the disease status exists. (pp. 314–315)

Citing a Work with More than One Author

When one work has two or more authors, use *and* in the text but use *&* in the citation.

> Werner [and] Throckmorton (1998) offered statistics on the toxic levels of water samples from six rivers.

but

> It has been reported (Werner [&] Throckmorton, 1998) that toxic levels exceeded the maximum allowed each year since 1983.

For three to five authors, name them all in the first entry (e.g., Torgerson, Andrews, Smith, Lawrence, & Dunlap, 1989), but thereafter use "et al." (e.g., Torgerson et al., 1989). For six or more authors, employ "et al." in the first and in all subsequent instances (e.g., Fredericks et al., 1989).

Citing More than One Work by an Author

Use small letters (a, b, c) to identify two or more works published in the same year by the same author, for example, (Thompson, 1996a) and (Thompson, 1996b)." Then use "1996a" and "1996b" in your "List of References" (see page 285 for an example). If necessary, specify additional information:

> Horton (1996; cf. Thomas, 1997a, p. 89, and 1997b, p. 426) suggested an intercorrelation of these testing devices. But after multiple-group analysis, Welston (1998, esp. p. 211) reached an opposite conclusion.

Citing Indirect Sources

Use a double reference to cite somebody who has been quoted in a book or article. That is, use the original author(s) in the text and cite your source for the information in the parenthetical citation.

> In other research, Massie and Rosenthal (1996) studied home movies of children diagnosed with autism, but determining criteria was difficult due to the differences in quality and dating of the available videotapes (cited in Osterling & Dawson, 1998, p. 248).

Citing from a Textbook or Anthology

If you make an in-text citation to an article or chapter of a textbook, case-book, or anthology, use the in-text citation to refer only to the person(s) you cite:

> One writer stressed that two out of every three new Jobs in the 1990s will go to women (Bailey, 1992).

The list of references will clarify the nature of this reference to Bailey (see "Part of a Book," page 285).

Citing Classical Works

If an ancient work has no date of publication, cite the author's name in the text followed by *n.d.* within parentheses.

> Sophocles (n.d.) saw psychic emotions as . . . .

Cite the year of a translation you used, preceded by *trans.,* and give the date of a version used, followed by *version.*

> Plato (trans. 1963) offered a morality that . . . .
> Plato's <u>Phaedrus</u> (1982 version) explored . . . .

If you know the original date of publication, include it before the date of the translation or version you have used.

> In his "The Poetic Principle," Poe (1850/1967) announced the doctrines upon which he built his canon.

Note: Entries on your References page need not cite major classical works and the Bible. Therefore, identify in your textual citations the version used and the book, chapter, line, verse, or canto. That is, the textual reference is all your reader will have to identify the source.

> Exodus 24:3–4 (King James Version)
> The Epic of Gilgamesh shows, in part, the search for everlasting life (Part 4).
> Homer takes great efforts in describing the shield of Achilles (18:558–709).

Abbreviating Corporate Authors in the Text

Corporate authors may be abbreviated after a first, full reference:

> One source has questioned the results of the use of aspirin for arthritis treatment in children (American Medical Association [AMA], 1991).

Thereafter, refer to the corporate author by initials: (AMA, 1991).

Citing an Anonymous Work

When a work has no author listed, cite the title as part of the in-text citation (or use the first few words of the material.

> The cost per individual student has continued to rise rapidly ("Money Concerns," 1998, p. 2).

Citing Personal Communications

E-Mail, telephone conversations, memos, interviews, and conversations do not provide recoverable data, so APA style excludes them from the list of references. Consequently, you should cite personal communications in the text only. In so doing, give the initials as well as the last name of the source, provide the data, and briefly decribe the nature of the communication.

> A. C. Eaves (personal communication, August 24, 1997) described the symptoms of Wilson's disease.

10e   Citing Internet Sources

As in MLA style, material from electronic sources presents special problems when you are writing in APA style. Currently, most Internet sources have no prescribed page numbers or numbered paragraphs. You cannot list a screen number because monitors differ. You cannot list the page numbers of a downloaded document because computer printers differ. Therefore, in most cases do not list a page number or a paragraph number. Here are basic rules.

1. **Omit a page or paragraph number.** The marvelous feature of electronic text is that its searchable, so your readers can find your quotation quickly with the FIND feature. Suppose that you have written the following:

> The UCLA Television Violence Report (1996) advices against making the television industry the "scapegoat for violence" by advocating a focus on "deadlier and more significant causes: inadequeate parenting, drugs, underclass rage, unemployment and availability of weaponry."

A reader who wants to investigate further will find your complete citation on your Works Cited page. There the reader will discover the Internet address for the article. After finding the article via a browser, (e.g., Netscape or Internet Explorer), the investigator can press EDIT, then FIND, and then type in a key phrase, such as "scapegoat for violence." The software will immediately move the cursor to the passage shown above. That's much easier than counting through forty-six paragraphs.

2. **Provide a paragraph number.** Some scholars who write on the Internet number their paragraphs. Therefore, if you find an article on the Internet that has numbered paragraphs, by all means supply that information in your citation.

The Insurance Institute for Highway Safety (1997) emphasizes restraint first, saying, "Riding unrestrained or improperly restrained in a motor vehicle always has been the greatest hazard for children" (par. 13).

The most common type of diabetes is non-insulin-dependent-diabetes mellitus (NIDDM), which "affects 90% of those with diabetes and usually appears after age 40" (Larson, 1996, par. 3).

3. **Provide a page number.** In a few instances, you will find page numbers buried within brackets here and there throughout an article. These refer to the page numbers of the printed version of the document. In these cases, you should cite the page just as you would a printed source. Note this example:

Source: De-nationalizing does not mean abolishing difference but abolishing the myth of identity that regulated and policed difference upholds. Thus, what is required is a reading of the frontiers and borders that are at ⌐/pp 17–18/⌐ work within and against the pretensions to "greatness," to majority, of any national literature. That is to say, a finding of the minor and the evocation of its difference where it is not expected—R. C. Readings

Readings (1991) has argued that each literary culture should identify the minor literature as a part of its national identity, not just elevate its majority literature as its "greatness" (pp. 17–18).

World Wide Web Site

Dove (1997) has made the distinction between a Congressional calendar day and a legislative day, noting, "A legislative day is the period of time following an adjournment of the Senate until another adjournment."

"Psychologically oriented techniques used to elicit confessions may undermine their validity" (Kassin, 1997, abstract).

Commenting on Neolithic sites of the Southern Levant in <u>Biblical Archaeologist,</u> Banning (1995) has argued that the "Natufians set the stage for the development of large villages with an increasing reliance on cereal grains and legumes that could be cultivated." Banning's work has shown that small villages often existed for a time only to disappear mysteriously, perhaps because of plagues, invaders, or--most likely--a nomadic way of life.

E-Mail

The Publication Manual of the American Psychological Association stipulates that personal communications, which others cannot retrieve, should be cited in the text only and not mentioned at all in the bibliography. However, electronic chat groups have gained legitimacy in recent years, so in the text give an exact date and provide the E-mail address *only* if the citation has scholarly relevance and *only* if the author has made public the E-mail address with the expressed wish for correspondence.

> One technical writing instructor (March 8, 1997) has bemoaned the inability of hardware developers to maintain pace with the ingenuity of software developers. In his E-mail message, he indicated that educational institutions cannot keep pace with the hardware developers. Thus, "students nationwide suffer with antiquated equipment, even though it's only a few years old" (Clemmer J@APSU01.APSU.EDU).

If the E-mail is part of a network or online journal, it *should be* listed in the bibliography. In such cases, use the form shown next under "Listserv" and see the bibliography form on page 290.

Listserv (E-mail Discussion Group)

> Camilleri (May 7, 1997) has identified the book <u>Storyteller</u> for those interested in narrative bibliography.

> Funder (April 5, 1997) has argued against the "judgmental process."

HyperNews Posting

> Ochberg (1996) has commented on the use of algae in paper that "initially has a green tint to it, but unlike bleached paper which turns yellow with age, this algae paper becomes whiter with age."

Gopher Site

> In an essay in <u>Electronic Antiquity,</u> Diamond (1993) has explored the issue of psychological blindness in Oedipus Rex:
>> Thus Sophokles has us ask the question, who is blind? We must answer that Teiresias is physically blind, yet he sees himself and Oidipous' nature. Oidipous is physically sighted, but he is blind to himself, to his own nature.

Online Magazine

> In <u>Kudzu</u> Fahey (1995) described one of his characters in "Beach House" as a psychological wreck:
>> Johnny was, by my estimation, a Casualty, though a functional one. He walked everywhere, and everywhere

he walked, a bright, pleasant grin stretched his facial muscles, and he looked like a carpenter who had plied his trade well.

BusinessWeek (1997) reported that health-care inflation seems determined to climb because medical costs are increasing and could "hit double digits."

Government Document

The Web site *Thomas* (1997) has provided the four-page outline to the *Superfund Cleanup Acceleration Act of 1997,* which will provoke community participation, enforce remedial actions, establish liability, and protect natural resources.

FTP Sites

Kranidiotis (1994) has shown in the following graph that perceptually "all the sounds corresponding to the points on the curve have the same intensity: this means that the ear has a large range where it is nearly linear (1000 to 8000 Hz), achieving better results on a little domain."

CD-ROM

Compton's Interactive Encyclopedia (1996) has explained that the Abolition Society, which originated in England in 1787, appears to be the first organized group in opposition to slavery. Later, in 1823 the Anti-Slavery Society was formed by Thomas Fowell Buxton, who wielded power as a member of Parliament.

10f   Preparing a Working Draft or Publishing the Manuscript

The American Psychological Association has established a website that, among other things, explains its method for citing Internet sources. Consult this URL:

http://www.apa.org/journals/webref.html

At this site, Leslie Cameron, Director of APA Journals, provides instructions that supercede those in the 1994 *Publication Manual of the American Psychological Association,* 4th edition. Also available from APA is a site that answers frequently asked questions about APA style. Consult this URL:

http://www.apa.org/journals/faq.html

The APA style manual is very clear about the margins for bibliography entries. If you are preparing a draft to go to a journal for publication, you should use a paragraph indention and underlining, as shown:

> Banning, E. B. (1995). Herders or homesteaders? A neolithic farm in Wadi Ziqlab, Jordan. <u>Biblical Archaeologist, 58.</u> Retrieved March 9, 1997 from the World Wide Web: http://scholar.cc.emory. edu/scripts/ASOR/BA/Banning.html

However, if your research paper is being printed as a final document for your instructor or if your research paper will be published on a Web site, you should use the hanging indention of three (3) spaces and, if you so desire, use the italics font for titles and volume numbers, as shown in the next example. That is, you are "publishing" the paper for the instructor or you are publishing the paper on a Web site. Thus, you should use this next form on most occasions as a student:

> Banning, E. B. (1995). Herders or homesteaders? A neolithic farm in Wadi Ziqlab, Jordan. *Biblical Archaeologist, 58.* Retrieved March 9, 1997 from the World Wide Web: http://scholar.cc. emory.edu/scripts/ASOR/BA/Banning.html

This form, with hanging indention, will serve as the default form throughout this chapter.

10g   Preparing the List of References

Use the title "References" for your bibliography page. Alphabetize the entries and double-space throughout. Every reference used in your text should appear in your alphabetical list of references at the end of the paper. Type the first line of each entry flush left, and indent succeeding lines three (3) spaces (note: MLA style uses five spaces). You may italicize or underscore names of books, periodicals, and volume numbers. Use the hanging indention, as explained immediately above, for your undergraduate research papers.

Books

Book (Basic Form)

Indent the second line three spaces. An alternative is to use the tab key for whatever indention the font provides; be consistent.

> Carter, J. (1988). <u>An outdoor journal: Adventures and reflections.</u> New York: Bantam.

List the author (surname first with initials for given names), year of publication within parentheses, title of the book italicized or underscored and with only first word of the title and any subtitle capitalized (but do capitalize proper nouns), place of publication, and publisher. In the publisher's name omit the words *Publishing, Company,* or *Inc.,* but otherwise give a full name: Florida State University Press; Addison, Wesley, Longman; HarperCollins.

List chronologically, not alphabetically, two or more works by the same author, for example, Fitzgerald's 1989 publication would precede his 1991 publication.

> Fitzgerald, R. F. (1997). Water samples. . . .
> Fitzgerald, R. F. (1998). Controlling. . . .

References with the same author in the same year are alphabetized and marked with lowercase letters—a, b, c—immediately after the date:

> Cobb, R. A. (1990a). Circulating systems. . . .
> Cobb, R. A. (1990b). Delay valves. . . .

Entries of a single author precede multiple-author entries beginning with the same surname without regard for the dates:

> Fitzgerald, R. F. (1990). Controlling. . . .
> Fitzgerald, R. F., & Smithson, C. A. (1988). Mapping . . .

References with the same first author and different second or third authors should be alphebetized by the surname of the second author:

> Fitzgerald, R. F., & Smithson, C. A. (1988). Mapping . . .
> Fitzgerald, R. F., & Waters, W. R. (1989). Microcarbons . . .

Part of a Book

List author(s), date, chapter or section title, editor (with name in normal order) preceded by "In" and followed by "(Ed.)" or "(Eds.)," the name of the book (underscored or italicized), page numbers to the specific section of the book cited (placed with parentheses), place of publication, and publisher.

> Hartley, J. T., Harker, J. O., & Walsh, D. A. (1980). Contemporary issues and new directions in adult development of learning and memory. In L. W. Poon (Ed.), Aging in the 1980s: Psychological issues (pp. 239–252). Washington, DC: American Psychological Association.

Textbook, Casebook, Anthology

Make a primary reference to the anthology.

> Vesterman, W. (Ed.) (1991). Readings for the 21st century. Boston: Allyn & Bacon.

Thereafter, make cross references to the primary source, in this case to Vesterman. *Note:* these entries should be mingled with all others on the reference page in alphabetical order so that cross references may appear before or after the primary source. The year cited should be the date when the cited work was published, not when the Vesterman book was published; such information is usually found in a headnote, footnote, or list of credits at the front or back of the anthology.

> Bailey, J. (1988). Jobs for women in the nineties. In Vesterman, pp. 55–63.
>
> Fallows, D. (1982). Why mothers should stay home. In Vesterman, pp. 69–77.
>
> Steinem, G. (1972). Sisterhood. In Vesterman, pp. 48–53.
>
> Vesterman, W. (Ed.). (1991). <u>Readings for the 21st century.</u> Boston: Allyn & Bacon.

The alternative to the style shown above is to provide a complete entry for every one of the authors cited from the casebook (in which case you do not need a separate entry to Vesterman):

> Bailey, J. (1988). Jobs for women in the nineties. In W. Vesterman (Ed.), (1991), <u>Readings for the 21st century</u> (pp. 55–63). Boston: Allyn & Bacon.
>
> Fallows, D. (1982). Why mothers should stay home. In W. Vesterman (Ed.), (1991), <u>Readings for the 21st century</u> (pp. 69–77). Boston: Allyn & Bacon.
>
> Steinem, G. (1972). Sisterhood. In W. Vesterman (Ed.), (1991), <u>Readings for the 21st century</u> (pp. 48–53). Boston: Allyn & Bacon.

Book with Corporate Author, Third Edition

List author, year, title of the article, title of the encyclopedia (underlined), place, and publisher.

> American Psychiatric Association. (1980). <u>Diagnostic statistical manual of mental disorders</u> (3rd ed.). Washington, DC: Author.

If no author is listed, begin with the title of the article.

> Brazil. (1970). <u>Harper Encyclopedia of the Modern World.</u> New York: Harper.

Periodicals

Journal

List author(s), year, title of the article without quotation marks and with only the first word capitalized, name of the journal underscored or italicized and with all major words capitalized, volume number underscored or italicized, inclusive page numbers *not* preceded by "p." or "pp."

> Mielke, K. W. (1988). Television in the social studies classroom. <u>Social Education, 52,</u> 362–365.

Full-Text Article Retrieved From CO-ROM Servers Such as InfoTrac, Silverplatter, ProQuest, and Other Servers

> Wakschlag, L. S. & Leventhal, B. L. (1996). Consultation with young autistic children and their families. <u>Journal of the American Academy of Child and Adolescent Psychiatry, 35,</u> 963–65. Retrieved August 8, 1997 from <u>Expanded Academic Index,</u> No. A18486937.

Magazine

List author, the date of publication (year, month without abbreviation, and the specific day for weekly and fortnightly magazines), title of the article without quotation marks and with only the first word capitalized, name of the magazine underlined with all major words capitalized, and inclusive page numbers not preceded by "p." or "pp."

> Kluger, Jeffrey. (1997, August 4). Beyond cholestrol. <u>Time, 150,</u> 46.

Newspaper

List author, date (year, month, and day), title of article with only first word and proper nouns capitalized, complete name of newspaper in capitals and underlined, and the section with all discontinuous page numbers, preceded by p. or pp.

> Devlin, K. (1997, August 8). "Soft" mathematics can help us understand the human mind <u>Chronicle of Higher Education,</u> pp. B4–B5.

Abstract of a Published Article

> Misumi, J., & Fujita, M. (1982). Effects of PM organizational development in supermarket organization. <u>Japanese Journal of Experimental Social Psychology, 21,</u> 93–111. (From <u>Psychological Abstracts,</u> 1982, <u>68,</u> Abstract No. 11474).

Abstract of an Unpublished Work

> Havens, N. B. (1982) Verbalized symbolic play of pre-school children in two types of play environments. Abstract of doctoral dissertation, Temple University. (From <u>Dissertation Abstracts International, 42,</u> 5058A.)

Abstract Retrieved from CD Servers, Such as InfoTrac, Silverplatter, or ProQuest

> Rapin, I. (1997) Autism [rev. article] <u>The New England Journal of Medicine, 337,</u> 97–104. Retrieved August 4, 1997 from <u>Expanded Academic Index,</u> Abstract No. A19615909.

Note: Do not quote from an abstract unless the server stipulates that the author wrote the abstract.

Review

Jones, S. L. (1991, January 6). The power of motivation [Review of Body Heat]. Contemporary Film Review, p. 18.

Report

Lance, J. C. (1990). Housing regulations (KU No. 90–16). Lawrence, KS: Media Center.

Nonprint Material

Corborn, W. H. (1990, November 3). "On facing the fears caused by nightmares" [Interview.] Lexington, KY.

Purple, W. C. (Producer). (1990). Hitting the backhand [Videotape]. Nashville: Sports Network.

Landers, J., Woolfe, R. T., & Balcher, C. (1990). Geometry games: Level two [Computer program]. Emporia, KS: Mediaworks.

Citing Internet Sources in APA Style

The following information conforms to the instructions of APA. When citing sources in the References of your APA-style paper, provide this information if available:

1. Author/editor last name, followed by a comma and the initials
2. Year of publication, followed by a comma, then month and day for magazines and newspapers, within parentheses
3. Title of the article, not within quotations and with only major words capitalized, followed by the total number of paragraphs within brackets only if that information is provided (for an example, see the Trehin citation, below). *Note:* You need not count the paragraphs yourself; in fact, it's better that you don't.
4. Name of the book, journal, or complete work, italicized, if one is listed
5. Volume number, if listed, italicized
6. Page numbers only if you have that data from a printed version of the journal or magazine. If the periodical has no volume number, use "p." or "pp." before the numbers; if the journal has a volume number, omit "p." or "pp.")
7. The word "Retrieved," followed by the date of access, followed by the source (e.g., World Wide Web or Telnet) and a colon
8. The URL (URLs can be quite long, but you will need to provide the full data for other researchers to find the source.)

World Wide Web Sites

Online Journal

Trehin, P. (1994). Computer aided teaching. [6 paragraphs]. Computer Technology and Autism, 15. Retrieved April 28,

1997 from the World Wide Web: http://web.syr.edu/~jmwobus/
autismLINK.htm#Section_1.0.1

Abstract from an Online Journal

Kassim, S. M. (1997). The psychology of confession evidence.
[Abstract] American Psychologist, 52. Retrieved April 10,
1997 from the World Wide Web: http://www.apa.org/journals/
amp397tc.html

Online Magazine

Cohoon, S., McCausland, J., & Swezey, L. B. (1996, September).
Secrets of the garden masters: Heims's secrets. Sunset.
Retrieved March 4, 1997 from the World Wide Web: http/
pathfinder.com@AiRYiAYAC5LGs KR/ . . . Sunset/1996/
September/features/heims.html

Fahey, T. B. (1995, Autumn). Beach house. Kudzu, 3. Retrieved
March 10, 1997 from the World Wide Web: http://www.etext.
org/Zines/K954/Fahey-Beach.html

Online Magazine, No Author Listed

Health-care inflation: It's baaack! (1997, March 17). Business
Week, 56–62. Retrieved March 18, 1997 from the World Wide
Web: http://www.businessweek.com/1997/11/b351852.html

Online Newspaper Article

Raver, A. (1997, August 5) Qualities of an animal scientist: Cow's
eye view and autism. New York Times Online. Retrieved
August 6, 1997 from the World Wide Web: http://search.
nytimcs.com/search/daily/bi . . . m%29%26OR%28treatment%
29%26OR%26%28%29

Bulletins and Government Documents

Edelson, S. B. (1995). Autism: An environmental maladaptation.
Environment and Preventive Health Center of America.
Retrieved March 10, 1998 from the World Wide Web: http://
www.envprevhealthctratl.com/env-mal.htm

U.S. Cong. Senate. (1997, January 21). Superfund cleanup
acceleration act of 1997. Senate Bill 8. Retrieved March 9,
1998 from the World Wide Web: http.thomas.loc.gov/
egi-bin/query/2?C105:S.8

Hypernews Posting

Ochberg, A. (Oct. 9, 1996). Algae-based paper. Recycling
Discussion Group. Retrieved June 18, 1997, from the World
Wide Web: http://www.betterworld.com/BWDiscuss/get/
recycleD.html?embed=2

Gopher Site

D'Agour, A. (1996). Classical women poets. [Review of the book <u>Classical women poets</u>]. Retrieved March 10, 1997 from gopher://gopher.lib.virginia.edu:70/alpha/bmer/v97/97-I-4

Diamond, R. (1993). Seeing one's way: The image and action of <u>Oidipous Tyrannos</u> [13 paragraphs]. <u>Electronic Antiquity, 1.</u> Retrieved March 6, 1997 from gopher: gopher//gopher.info.edu. au

No one scientific study can tell all. (1997, March 10). Retrieved March 10, 1998 from gopher:gopher.fhcrc.org:70/0waisdocid% 3 . . . mer_Quest_1994/SciNews

Linkage Data (a File Accessed from Another File)

What happens to recycled plastics? (1996). Lkd. Better world discussion topics at recycling discussion group. Retrieved June 18, 1997 from http://www.betterworld.com/BWZ/9602/learn.htm

Listserv (E-Mail Discussion Group)

Camilleri, R. (1997, March 10). Narrative bibliography. Retrieved March 11, 1997 from E-Mail: H-RHETOR<@>msu.edu

Newsgroups

Anders, J. (1997, February 21). Global warming/climate change: A new approach. Institute of Marine Research. Retrieved March 11, 1997 from Usenet: cgi-bin/news?msg@44430/sci. environment/330DE368.4CC8@imr.no

Link, R. (1997, January 11). Territorial fish. Southwest Research Institute. Retrieved March 10, 1997 from Usenet: cgi-bin . . . @10016/rec.aquaria.freshwater.misc/5b9u9p$kod<@>pemrac.s pace.swri.edu

Telnet Site

U. S. Naval Observatory. The mercury ion frequency standard. Retrieved March 6, 1997 from Telnet 192.5, 41.239/duke.ldgo. columbia.edu/port=23 login ads, set terminal to 8/N/1

FTP Site

Kranidiotis, A. A. (1994, June 7). Human audio perception frequently asked questions. Retrieved March 11, 1997 from FTP:svr-ftp.eng.cam.ac.uk/pub/comp.speech/info/ HumanAudioPerception

CD-ROM

Material cited from a CD-ROM requires different forms. If you are citing from an abstract on CD-ROM, use this form:

> Figueredo, A. J., & McCloskey, L.A. (1993). Sex, money, and paternity: The evolutionary psychology of domestic violence [CD-ROM]. Ethnology and Sociobiology, 14, 353–79. Abstract from Silverplatter File: PsychLIT item: 81–3654.

For an encyclopedia article on CD-ROM, use this form:

> Abolitionist movement [CD-ROM]. (1996). Compton's interactive encyclopedia. New York: Softkey Multimedia.

For a full-text article found on CD-ROM, use the following form:

> Wessel, D. (1995, February 2). Fed lifts rates half point, setting four-year high [CD-ROM]. Wall Street Journal, p. A2+. Article from UMI-ProQuest file: Wall Street Journal Ondisc. Item 34561.

10h   Writing the Abstract

You should provide an abstract with every paper written in APA style. An abstract is a quick but thorough summary of the contents of your paper (see Précis, pages 115–17, and the sample on page 293). It is read first and may be the only part read, so it must be:

1. *Accurate* in order to reflect both the purpose and content of the paper.
2. *Self-contained* so that it (a) explains the precise problem and defines terminology, (b) describes briefly both the methods used and the findings, and (c) may give an overview of your conclusions (but see item 4 immediately below).
3. *Concise and specific* in order to remain within a range of 80 to 150 words.
4. *Nonevaluative* in order to report information, not to appraise or assess the value of the work.
5. *Coherent and readable* in a style that uses an active, vigorous syntax and that uses the present tense to describe results (e.g., the findings confirm) but the past tense to describe testing procedures (e.g., I attempted to identify).

For theoretical papers, the abstract should include:

- The topic in one sentence, if possible
- The purpose, thesis, and scope of the paper
- The sources used (e.g., published articles, books, personal observation)

- Your conclusions and the implications of the study

For a report of an empirical study, the abstract should include:

- The problem and hypothesis in one sentence if possible
- The subjects (e.g., species, number, age, type)
- The method, including procedures and apparatus
- The findings
- Your conclusions and the implications of the study

10i Sample Paper in APA Style

The following paper demonstrates the format and style of a paper written to the standards of the published form in APA style.

The **published form** gives you more freedom with regard to fonts, margins, borders, hanging indentions, and other desk-top publishing features. Check with your instructor if you want to present your paper in the published form. In either case, the paper requires a title page that establishes the running head, an abstract, in-text citations to name and year of each source used, and a list of references.

A **working draft** is the more traditional form as produced by a typewriter with the courier typeface, with underlining for italics, with a ragged right margin, and with references indented as paragraphs, the idea being that the typesetting system at a publishing house will convert the manuscript to a published form. Your instructor may require a working draft.

The general paradigm for a scientific study has four parts:

Introduction:	The problem
	The background
	The purpose and rationale
Method:	Subjects
	Apparatus
	Procedure
Results	
Discussion	

The Bracy paper that follows uses a variation on this paradigm. Hers gives an introduction followed by examination of the cause, the typical behavior, the early behavior indications, retrospective research, web sites, results, and the discussion.

Your paper may need to find its own headings, but stay as close to the original paradigm as possible. See pages 73–77 for other types of paradigms for academic papers.

Marginal notations, on the pages that follow, explain specific requirements.

Running Head: AUTISM

The running head will appear at the top of each page.

Autism: Early Intervention
in Diagnosing and Educating
the Autistic Child

Patti M. Bracy

Austin Peay State University

Abstract

Place the abstract separately on page 2.

Autism has been reported as a neurological dysfunction of the brain that afflicts infants before age 30 months. Theories about the causes and the necessary treatment have differed ever since Kanner (1943) reported his findings that autism differed from other childhood disorders. Attempts to treat and detect autism have resulted in new classifications of the term <u>autism</u> and the discovery that many children may benefit from early behavioral training. By diagnosing autism in infants and toddlers, some autistic children may be trained to live more independent, normal lives. In recent years, an attempt has been made to diagnose children with autism earlier than the standard 4 years by using home movies to determine early behavioral characteristics of autism in infants and toddlers.

Do not use a paragraph indentation for the abstract.

The abstract should not exceed 120 words in length.

Autism: Early Intervention in Diagnosing
and Educating the Autistic Child

Autism, a neurological dysfunction of the brain, which commences before the age of 30 months, was discovered by Leo Kanner (1943), who studied 11 cases, all of which showed a specific type of childhood psychosis that was different from other childhood disorders, although each was similar to childhood schizophrenia. He described the syndrome as:

- Extreme autistic aloneness
- Language abnormalities
- Obsessive desire for the maintenance of sameness
- Good cognitive potential
- Normal physical development
- Highly intelligent, obsessive, and cold parents

Rutter (1978) reduced these symptoms to four criteria: onset within 30 months of birth, poor social development, late language development, and a preference for regular, stereotyped activity. The American Psychiatric Association (1987) has limited the definition of autism to three primary characteristics which must be present before the age of 3 years:

1. Qualitative impairment in reciprocal social interaction
2. Impairment in communication and imaginative activity
3. Markedly restricted repertoire of activities and interests

In the United States, autism affects one out of 2,500 children and is not usually diagnosed until the child is between 2 and 5 years of age (Koegel & Schreibman, 1981). The study of twins has shown that autism "has a genetic component" (Rapin, 1997, abstract). Typically, the child is diagnosed around the age of 4 years (Siegel, Pliner, Eschler, & Elliott, 1988). The remarkable story of one father's ordeal with an autistic child has been recorded (Martin, 1994).

In recent years, studies have focused on infantile and preschool characteristics of autism in order to detect children with autism earlier. Many children with autism, if detected early enough and if enrolled in intensive early intervention programs, may be admitted into the mainstream of regular education without any special services (Lovaas, 1987; Strain & Hoyson, 1988, cited in Powers, 1992). Early intervention seems to be the preferred action, especially since the "facilitated

---

Margin notes:

Cite the year immediately after the name of the source.

Use the past tense or present perfect tense when citing sources.

Use arabic numbers in the text.

Use ampersand in citations, not in the text.

communication" technique was condemned with vitriolic criticism in 1994. Facilitated communication requires a person to guide the autistic's hand over a computer keyboard, but the person doing the guiding may have more input than the autistic person (see esp. Berger, 1994).

Accordingly, special qualifying characteristics have been devised in order to successfully identify infants with autism. A public policy directive (PL99–457) has provided money to fund the design of programs geared especially for the infant or toddler with disabilities and for their families (Powers, 1992).

Cause

Rutter (1978) listed three possible causes: behavioral syndrome, organic brain disorder, or a range of biological and psychosocial factors. Rutter, Bailey, Bolton, and LeCouteur (1994, p. 311) acknowledged that the "organic basis of autism" was generally agreed upon.

Gallagher, Jones, and Byrne (1990) surveyed professionals in the mental health field for opinions about the causes of autism. Gallagher et al. explained the study in this manner:

> The results of the segment of the analysis exhibited in Table 1 [shown on the next page] can be summarized straightforwardly: Biogenic factors clearly dominate psychiatrists' current attitudes toward etiological theories of infantile autism. Among the biogenic factors, by far the prominent choice is "biochemical imbalance," with a perceived strength-of-relationship mean value about midway between "related" and "strongly-related." (p. 936)

Behavior

The behavior of the autistic child has been reported (Fay, 1986; Happé, 1994; Osterling & Dawson, 1994; Rimland, 1984; Vandershaf, 1987). A typical autistic child withdraws into self-imposed privacy, avoids social contact, and avoids the touching hands of others. The child often rocks rhythmically and silently. He or she cannot or will not answer questions, and many autistics cannot or will not speak. Some of them senselessly copy the voices of others, a syndrome called echolalia. Others only emit a few sounds.

Use underscored headings to mark divisions within a paper in APA style.

For three to five authors, list all authors at first use; thereafter use et al. with the lead author's name.

Explain tables in the text.

Indent long quotations of 40 words or more 5 additional spaces, and omit the quotation marks.

Page numbers go outside the final period after a long quotation.

Table 1

See pages 195–99 for information on using illustrations and tables.

Psychiatrists' Attitudes Toward Etiological Theories of Infantile Autism

Etiological theory	Mean value	Rank
Biochemical imbalance	3.491	1
Genetic inheritance	3.078	2
Brain lesion	3.014	3
Metabolic dysfunction	2.832	4
Prenatal factors	2.821	5
Chromosomal mutation	2.623	6
Maternal deprivation	1.933	7
Cold "intellectualized" parenting	1.752	8
Immune system deficiency	1.718	9
Maternal age	1.714	10

Use this form to cite the source of a table.

Note. From "A National Survey of Mental Health Professionals Concerning the Causes of Early Infantile Autism," by B. J. Gallagher, B. J. Jones and M. Byrne, 1990, Journal of Clinical Psychology, 46, p. 936.

Establish abbreviations before you use them alone.

They speak "at" people, not "to" them, and they usually avoid eye contact. Many autistic children are hyperactive. They fling their hands, flick their fingers, blink their eyes repeatedly, and commit self-injurious behavior (SIB), especially when placed in an unfamiliar area. Rutter (1978) has reported four ritualistic behaviors commonly seen with autism:

1. Autistic children may select toys of a specific shape or structure and play.
2. An autistic child may become overattached to a certain toy. The child will want that toy with him or her at all times. Should it be taken away, the child will usually throw a tantrum.
3. The child may have unusual concern for numbers, geometric shapes, bus routes, and colors.
4. The child maintains a specific routine and order, and the child gets perturbed if it is changed. (pp. 139–140)

Early Behavior Indications

Use the past tense to cite the work of a scientist.

In an effort to identify autistic children earlier, Osterling and Dawson (1994) studied videotapes of autistic children's first birthdays. In almost every instance, the studied videotape correctly identified the autistic child under 13 months old. The conclusive behaviors observed by Osterling and Dawson's study consisted of pointing, showing objects, looking at others, and orienting to name. How often a child looked at others was determined to be the best predictor of autism (see the Appendix for a bar graph that depicts differences in infants judged to be normal or autistic).

Summarize experiments and testing procedures in your text.

Retrospective Research

In an effort to determine autism as quickly as possible in infants and toddlers, several studies have been performed based on a parent's remembrances before a child was diagnosed with autism (Dahlgren & Gillberg, 1989). The problem with these studies was that a parent's memories after a 4-year interlude were generally unreliable (Osterling & Dawson, 1994). In an effort to substantiate the claim that parents generally suspected a problem long before their children reached diagnosis, another means of assessment was deemed to be necessary to record objectively earlier behaviors of infants and toddlers.

In other research, Massie and Rosenthal (1975) studied home movies of children diagnosed with autism, but determining criteria was difficult due to the differences in quality and dating of the available videotapes (cited in Osterling & Dawson, 1994, p. 248). In some instances, dating was difficult to establish with any close degree of accuracy.

In other studies (Adrien et al., 1991, 1992) infants with and without behavioral abnormalities in social, affective, motor, and attentional abilities were studied using home movies. Using an infant behavior checklist, differences were detected during the infants' first year that corresponded to the childrens' current diagnoses (cited in Osterling & Dawson, 1994, p. 248).

For six or more authors, use et al. in the first and all subsequent instances.

Videotapes of first birthdays were used (Osterling & Dawson, 1994) to determine the differences in behavior of normal and autistic children. Eleven diagnosed autistic children, and 11 normal children were studied. Four questions were used:

1. Are differences between autistic and normal children's behavior apparent at 1 year of age?
2. Can specific behaviors be identified that distinguish autism?

3. Does the early development of children with autism differ between those with and without later documented cognitive delay?

4. Is there any evidence to support the existence of late-onset autism?

Web Sites

Keeping an up-to-date profile on autism is now easier with the Internet sites that offer vast amounts of information. For example, the Autism Treatment Guide provides a vast list of books on the topic, which was prepared by a parent of a 12-year-old son with autism. It features such texts as Bachrach, Mosley, Swindle, and Wood, Development Therapy for Young Children with Autistic Characteristics.

Of more importance, perhaps, the Internet itself serves as therapy for some autistics, according to Blume (1997), who says, "The impact of the Internet on autistics may one day be compared in magnitude to the spread of sign language among the deaf." Blume adds, "By filtering out the sensory overload that impedes communication among autistics, the Internet opens vast new opportunities for exchange."

Also available on the Internet are case studies by professionals, parents, and others who share ideas, especially therapy that works well (see, for example, Raver, the various FEAT sites [Families for Effective Autism Treatment], and the Home Pages devoted to autism).

Methods

The videotapes of 11 children with autism and 11 children with normal development were used to determine whether there were differences that could be noted in the tapes. Although differences were noted in the settings and quality of the birthday tapes, factors such as number of people (adults and children) in groupings, and number of minutes the child was alone on the tape were factored in to provide consistency.

Established autistic-like and behaviorally appropriate characteristics were assigned codes, and the presence or absence of these characteristics during a 1-minute period were identified by raters who did not know which children were autistic or not. The behaviors coded included:

Social behaviors consist of looking at another's face, looking at the face of another while smiling, seeking

contact with an adult, and imitating the behavior of
another. Affective behaviors consisted of distress and
tantrums. Joint attention behaviors consisted of
pointing, vague pointing (reaching for something in
a communicative way), showing an object to another.
Communicative behaviors included babbling, saying a
word, using a conventional gesture such as waving
goodbye, and following the verbal directions of
another. Specific autistic behaviors included self-
stimulatory behavior, covering ears, failing to orient
to name being called, staring blankly into space, and
blunt affect. (Osterling & Dawson, 1994, p. 251)

The results of frequencies in the behaviors of the children
are shown in Figure 1 of the Appendix, page 11. Social and joint
attention behaviors show a marked difference between normal
and autistic children. Communicative behaviors show a
difference but are not as statistically viable as the first two
behaviors.

Discussion

Early intervention has proven to be beneficial in educating
and assisting children with autism, especially if the home
environment is not adequate to provide social, physical,
cognitive, or emotional development (Berkson, 1993). Many
times, children that are not diagnosed until school age will not
respond as well to treatment; their defects may have caused
further delay in their normal progress. Therefore, every effort
should be made to identify infants and preschoolers at risk for
autism.

The study of the parent, as well as the child, is mandatory.
The unusual pattern of the disorder destroys a parent's feelings
of control, so the parents resist clinical help at the same time as
the child (see esp. Wakschlag & Leventhal, 1996).

There is hope in the future that both the cause and the
cure for autism will be found. For the present, early
identification and intervention offer some hope for the children
at risk for autism and their families. Since autism is sometimes
outgrown, childhood treatment offers the best hope for the
autistic person who must try to survive in an alien environment.

The discussion should evaluate and interpret the implications of your study.

Autism   9

References

Adrien, J., Faure, M., Perrot, A., Hameury, L., Garreau, B.,
Barthelemy, C., & Sauvage, D. (1991). Autism and family
home movies: Preliminary findings. Journal of Autism and
Developmental Disorders, 21, 43–49.

Adrien, J., Perrot, A., Sauvage, D., Leddet, I., Larmande, C.,
Hameury, L., & Barthelemy, C. (1992). Early symptoms in
autism from family home movies. Acta Paedopsychiatrica,
55, 71–75.

American Psychiatric Association. (1987). Diagnostic and
statistical manual of mental disorders (3rd ed., rev.).
Washington, DC: Author.

Autism Treatment Guide. (1997). Family Resource Services.
Retrieved August 6, 1997 from the World Wide Web:
http://frs-inc.com/autism2.htm1

Berger, J. (1994 February 12). Shattering the silence. New York
Times, p.21.

Berkson, G. (1993). Children with handicaps: A review of
behavioral research. Hillsdale, NJ: Lawrence Erlbaum
Associates.

Blume, H. (1997, June 30). Autistics are communicating in
cyberspace. Cybertimes [New York Times]. Retrieved August
8, 1997 from the World Wide Web: http://search.nytimes.
com/search/daily/bi . . . m%29%26OR%26%28treatment

Dahlgren, S., & Gillberg, C. (1989). Symptoms in the first two
years of life: A preliminary population study of infantile
autism. European Archives of Psychiatry and Neurological
Sciences, 238, 169–174.

Fay, M. (1986, September). Child of silence. Life, 9, 84–89.

Gallagher, B., Jones, B., & Byrne, M. (1990). A national survey
of mental health professionals concerning the causes of early
infantile autism. Journal of Clinical Psychology, 46,
934–939.

Happé, G. (1994). Annotation: Current psychological theories of
autism: The "theory of mind" account and rival theories.
Journal of Child Psychology and Psychiatry, 35(2), 215–229.

Kanner, L. (1943). Autistic disturbances of affective contact.
Nervous Child, 2, 217–250.

Koegel, R., & Schreibman, L. (1981). Teaching autistic and other
severely handicapped children. Austin: Pro-ed.

Journal article.

Indent three spaces.

Book.

Magazine article.

Issue number is not underscored.

Lovaas, O. I. (1987). Behavioral treatment and normal educational and intellectual functioning in young autistic children. Journal of Consulting and Clinical Psychology, 55, 3–9.

Martin, R. (1994) Out of silence: A journey into language. New York: Holt.

Osterling, J., & Dawson, G. (1994). Early recognition of children with autism: A study of first birthday home videotapes. Journal of Autism and Developmental Disorders, 24, 247–257.

Powers, M. (1992). Early intervention for children with autism. In D. Berkell, pp. 225–252.

Rapin, I. (1997) Autism [rev. article]. The New England Journal of Medicine, 337, 97–104. Retrieved August 4, 1997 from InfoTrac: Expanded Academic Index, Abstract No. A19615909.

Raver, A. (1997, August 5). Qualities of an animal scientist: Cow's eye view and autism. New York Times Online. Retrieved August 6, 1997 from the World Wide Web: http://search. nytimes.com/ search/daily/bi . . . m%29%26OR%28treatment%29%26OR%26%28%29

Rimland, B. (1984). Infantile autism. New York: Appleton-Century-Crofts.

Rutter, M. (1978). Diagnosis and definition of childhood autism. Journal of Autism and Childhood Schizophrenia, 8, 139–161.

Rutter, M. (1983). Cognitive deficits in the pathogenesis of autism. Journal of Child Psychology and Psychiatry, 26, 513–531.

Rutter, M., Bailey, A. Bolton, P., & Le Couteur, A. (1994). Autism and known medical conditions: Myth and substance. Journal of Child Psychology and Psychiatry, 35(2), 311–322.

Siegel, B., Pliner, C., Eschler, J., & Elliott, G. R. (1988). How children with autism are diagnosed: Difficulties in identification of children with multiple developmental delays. Developmental and Behavioral Pediatrics, 9(4), 199–204.

Vandershaf, S. (1987, March). Autism: A chemical excess? Psychology Today, 21, 15–16.

Wakschlag, L. S. & Leventhal, B. L. (1996). Journal of the American Academy of Child and Adolescent Psychiatry, 35, 963–65. Retrieved August 8, 1997 from InfoTrac: Expanded Academic Index, No. A18486937.

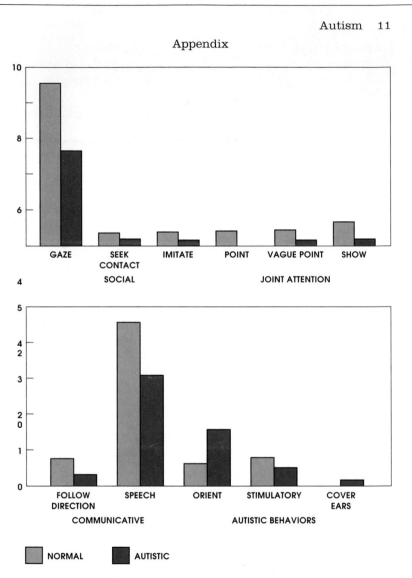

Appendix

<u>Figure 1</u> Mean frequency of social, joint attention, communicative, and autistic behaviors shown by 1-year-old infants later judged to be normal or autistic. From "Early recognition of children with autism: A study of first birthday home videotapes," by J. Osterling and G. Dawson, 1994, <u>Journal of Autism and Developmental Disorders, 24,</u> 255.

11 Form and Style for Other Disciplines

Every academic discipline has distinctive forms for displaying scholarship, as shown in Chapters 1–9 for literature and modern languages and in Chapter 10 for psychology. When writing papers in physics, biology, music, and other fields, you may need to cite works according to one of these additional formats:

1. The **name and year system** for use in the social sciences, biological and earth sciences, education, linguistics, and business.
2. The **number system** for use in the applied sciences, such as chemistry, computer science, mathematics, physics, and medicine.
3. The **footnote system** for use with papers in the fine arts (art, theater, and music) and humanities (history, philosophy, and religion, but excluding language and literature, which use the MLA style).

Guide by Discipline

11a   Using the Name and Year System

When writing research papers by the name and year system, conform to the following rules (see also Section 10d):

1. Place the year within parentheses immediately after the authority's name:

   Smith (1997) ascribes no species-specific behavior to human beings. However, Adams (1997) presents data that tend to be contradictory.

2. If you do not mention the authority's name in your sentence, insert the name, year, and even page number(s) in parentheses:

   Hopkins (1997) found some supporting evidence for a portion of the questionable data (Marr & Brown, 1997, pp. 23–32) through point bi-serial correlation techniques.

3. For two authors, employ both names (Torgerson & Andrews, 1998). For three to six authors, name them all in the first entry (Torgerson, Andrews, & Dunlap, 1998), but thereafter use "et al." (Torgerson et al., 1998). For seven or more authors, employ "et al." in the first and all subsequent instances (Fredericks et al., 1998).

4. Use small letters (*a, b, c*) to identify two or more works published in the same year by the same author (e.g., Thompson [1994a] and Thompson [1994b]). Then use "1994a" and "1994b" in your References page (see the Dubinskas entry on page 309 for an example).

5. If necessary, specify additional information. For example:

   Horton (1995; cf. Thomas, 1993, p. 89) suggests an intercorrelation of these testing devices. But after multiple-group analysis, Welston (1998, esp. p. 211) reached an opposite conclusion.

6. In the case of a direct quotation or paraphrase to a specific page, you must include the author(s), year, and page number(s), as follows:

   a. A quotation or paraphrase in the middle of a sentence:

   He stated, "These data of psychological development suggest that retarded adolescents are atypical in maturational growth" (Jones, 1998, p. 215), but he failed to clarify which data were examined.

b. A quotation or paraphrase at the end of a sentence:

Jones (1998) found that "these data of psychological development suggest that retarded adolescents are atypical in maturational growth" (p. 215).

c. A long quotation set off from the text in a block (and therefore without quotation marks):

Albert (1994) found the following:
> Whenever these pathogenic organisms attack the human body and begin to multiply, the infection is set in motion. The host responds to this parasitic invasion with efforts to cleanse itself of the invading agents. When rejection efforts of the host become visible (fever, sneezing, congestion), the disease status exists. (pp. 314–315)

7. Every reference used in your text should appear in your alphabetic list of references at the end of the paper. Because the format differs by discipline, consult the list on pages 303–04 to find the instructions appropriate for your discipline.

Using the Name and Year System for Papers in the Social Sciences

Education	**Geography**
Linguistics	**Physical Education**
Political Science	**Home Economics**
Psychology	**Sociology and Social Work**

The disciplines of the social sciences employ the name and year system. In general, the stipulations of the *Publication Manual of the American Psychological Association* (see Chapter 10) have gained wide acceptance, but variations exist by discipline.

Education

In-Text Citation Use the name and year system as explained on pages 304–05, or Section 10d, pages 277–80.

List of References Use the APA style with hanging indentation as described in Chapter 10, pages 284–91.

Geography

See the form and style for Sociology and Social Work, page 307.

Home Economics

Use the name and year system as explained on pages 304–05 or in Section 10d, pages 277–80.

Linguistics: LSA (Linguistic Society of America) Style

In-Text Citation In-text citations for linguistic studies almost always include a specific page reference to the work along with the date, separated by a colon. For example:

> Gifford's recent reference (1998: 162) disagrees with that of Jores (1998: 12–18).

Therefore, follow basic standards for the name and year system (see pages 304–05) with a colon to separate the year and page number(s).

List of References As shown in the following example, label the list "References" and alphabetize the entries. Place the year immediately after the name of the author(s). For journal entries, use a period rather than a colon or comma to separate the volume and page. There is *no* use of italics or underscoring except for words used as words. Linguistic journals are abbreviated; others are not. A sample list of references follows:

References

Aristar, Allen. 1994. Review of typology and universals, by
    William Croft. Lg. 70.172–175.

Beal, Carole R., and Susan L. Belgrad. 1990. The development of
    message evaluation skills in young children. Child
    Development 61.705–713.

Birner, Betty J. 1994. Information status and word order: An
    analysis of English inversion. Lg. 70.233–259.

Burnam, Tom. 1988. A misinformation guide to grammar.
    Writer's Digest 68.36–39.

Chomsky, Noam. 1965. Aspects of the theory of syntax.
    Cambridge, MA: MIT Press.

------. 1975. Reflections on language. New York: Pantheon.

De Boysson-Bardies, Bénédicte, and Marilyn M. Vihman. 1991.
    Adaptation to language: Evidence from babbling and first
    words in four languages. Lg. 67.287–319.

Jacobsson, Bengt. 1988. Should and would in factual that clauses.
    English Studies 69.72–81.

Ross, John R. 1967. Constraints on variables in syntax. MIT
    dissertation.

Singer, Murry, Arthur C. Graesser, and Tom Trabasso. 1994.
    Minimal or global interference during reading. Journal of
    Memory and Language 33.421–441.

> ***Note:*** The form of the entries on page 306 conforms in general to that advocated by the Linguistic Society of America, *LSA Bulletin,* No. 71 (December 1976), 43–45; the annual December issue; and the form and style practiced by the journal *Language.*

Physical Education

In-Text Citation Use the name and year system as explained on pages 304–05 or in Section 10d, pages 277–80.

List of References Follow the APA form and style pages 284–91.

Political Science

In-Text Citation Use the name and year system as explained on pages 304–05, or in Section 10d, pages 277–80.

List of References Follow the form and style for Sociology, see below, this page.

Psychology: APA Style

See Chapter 10.

Sociology and Social Work

In-Text Citation Use the name and year system as explained on pages 304–05 or in Section 10d, pages 277–80.

List of References Use APA style (see Chapter 10) or the format shown here, which duplicates the style of the *American Journal of Sociology.*

References

Berezin, Mabel. 1994. "Cultural Form and Political Meaning: State-Subsidized Theater, Ideology, and the Language of Style in Fascist Italy." <u>American Journal of Sociology</u> 99:1237–86.

Dowrick, Stephanie. 1994. <u>Intimacy and Solitude</u>. New York: Norton.

Epstein, Edwin M. 1980. "Business and Labor under the Federal Election Campaign Act of 1971." Pp. 107–151 in <u>Parties, Interest Groups, and Campaign Finance Laws</u>, edited by Michael J. Malbin. Washington, DC: American Enterprise Institute for Public Policy Research.

Gest, Ted. 1994. "Crime's Bias Problem." <u>U.S. News & World Report</u> July 25:31–32.

Using the Name and Year System for Papers in the Biological and Earth Sciences

Agriculture	**Biology**
Anthropology	**Botany**
Archaeology	**Geology**
Astronomy	**Zoology**

The disciplines of this major grouping employ the name and year system. In general, the rules of APA style (see Chapter 10) match the documentation standards of these disciplines, especially for the in-text citations. However, stylistic variations do exist for the reference lists, as explained and demonstrated below.

Agriculture

In-Text Citation Use the name and year system as explained on pages 304–05 or in Section 10d, pages 277–80.

List of References In general, the form and style follows that for other disciplines using the name and year system. In this field, use hanging indentions of 5 spaces, abbreviations, journal titles, and no spaces between volume, issue, and page numbers.

References

Akayezu, J. M., et al. 1994. Evaluation of calf starters containing different amounts of crude protein for growth of Holstein calves. J. of Dairy Sci. 77.7:1882–89.

Benson, D. 1994. Dirt: The lowdown on growing a garden with style. New York: Dell.

Brotherton, I. 1990. On the voluntary approach to resolving rural conflict. Environ. & Plan Ag. 64:923.

Celis, W. 1988. Tax changes hit groups in land conservation. Wall Street J. Jan. 26:38.

Corring, T., A. Aumaitre, and G. Durand. 1978. Development of digestive enzymes in the piglet from birth to 8 weeks. Nutr. Metab. 22:231.

> ***Note:*** The form of these entries conforms, in general, to that found in numerous agriculture journals, especially *Animal Science, Journal of Animal Science,* and *Journal of the American Society for Horticultural Science.*

Anthropology and Archaeology

In-Text Citation Use the name and year system as explained on pages 304–05 or in Section 10d, pages 277–80.

List of References Set the author's name and the date to the left, as shown in the style of *The American Anthropologist:*

References Cited

Anderson, Jonathan W.

1994   Review of Spiritual Discourse: Learning with an Islamic Master, by Frances Trix. American Anthropologist 96:480–481.

Bastien, Joseph

1978   Mountain of the Condor: Metaphor and Ritual in an Andean Ayllu. American Ethnological Society Monograph 64. St. Paul, MN: West Publishing Co.

Binford, Louis R.

1962   Archaeology as Anthropology. American Antiquity 28:217–225.

Briody, Elizabeth K., and Marietta L. Baba

1991   Explaining Differences in Repatriation Experiences: The Discovery of Coupled and Decoupled Systems. American Anthropologist 93:322–344.

Dubinskas, Frederick A.

1988a   [ed.] Making Time: Ethnographies of High-Technology Organizations. Philadelphia, PA: Temple University Press.

1988b   Janus Organizations: Scientists and Managers in Genetic Engineering Firms. In Making Time: Ethnographies of High-Technology Organizations. pp. 170–232. Philadelphia, PA: Temple University Press.

Dye, Daniel S.

1949   A Grammar of Chinese Lattice. 2nd ed. Harvard-Yenching Monograph Series VI. Cambridge: Harvard University Press.

Jennings, J. D.

1978   Origins. In J. D. Jennings, ed. Ancient Native Americans. Pp. 1–41. San Francisco: Freeman.

McLaren, Peter L.

1988   The Liminal Servant and the Ritual Roots of Critical Pedagogy. Language Arts 65:164–180.

Astronomy

See format and style for geology, pages 311–12.

Biology/Botany/Zoology: CBE (Council of Biology Editors) Style

Writers in these disciplines should follow the advice of The Council of Biology Editors style manual, *Scientific Style and Format: The CBE Manual for Authors. Editors, and Publishers* (1994). This guide advocates two citation and reference styles: (1) the name and year system for general biological studies (shown following) and (2) the number system for bio-medical papers (see "Using the Number System for Papers in the Medical Sciences," pages 318–19, especially the list of references on page 319).

In-Text Citation Use a variation of the name and year system as explained on pages 304–05 or in Section 10d, pages 277–80, but do not use a comma between the name and year, as demonstrated with this example:

> This investigation (Logan 1994) has broken new ground in its findings on the herb as a medicinal agent. Walker and Tidwell (1995, pp. 45–56) suggest that "many other herbs may have these same effects, but research remains limited." Caution has been advised (Morgan 1994) because one herb has been identified as a potential poison if misapplied (Borders and Funderberg 1994).

Note: Do use a comma to distinguish between same-year (Smith 1994a, 1994b) or different-year citations (Johnson 1994, 1995).

List of References Alphabetize the list, and label it "Cited References." Keyboard the first line of each entry flush left; indent the second line and other succeeding lines 2 spaces. For books, list the author(s) with initials jammed together (JM.), year of publication, title, place, publisher, and total number of pages (optional). For articles, list the author(s), year of publication, article title, journal title, volume number, and inclusive pages. Add the issue number and/or a specific date for magazines and journals paged anew with each issue.

Cited References

Argyres, A., Schmitt, J. 1991. Microgeographic structure of morphological and life history traits in a natural population of <u>Impatients capensis</u>. Evolution 45:178–89.

Atwell, J. 1994. Characterization of pilin genes from seven serologically defined prototype strains of <u>moraxella boyis.</u> Journal of Bacteriology 176:4875–82.

Bateson, P. 1978. Sexual imprinting and optimal out-crossing. Nature 273:659–660.

Bertin, RI. 1982. Paternity and fruit production in trumpet creeper (<u>Campsis radicans</u>). American Naturalist 119:694–709.

Ephron, B. 1982. The jackknife, the bootstrap, and other resampling plans. Philadelphia: Society for Industrial and Applied Mathematics.

Edelson, SB. Autism: An environmental maladaptation [bulletin online] 1995; 3 pars. Available from: http://www. envprevhealthctratl.comj/env_mal.htm Accessed 1997 Apr. 26.

Handel, S. 1983. Pollination ecology, plant population structure, and gene flow. <u>In</u>: Real, L., editor. Pollination biology. Orlando: Academic Press. pp. 163–211.

Trehin, P. Computer aided teaching. Computer Technology and
Autism [serial online] 1994, No. 15; 6 par. Available from:
http://web.syr.edu/-jmwobus/autism/LINK.html Section 1.0.1
Accessed 1997 Apr. 26.

> ***Note:*** The form of the entries on pages 310–11 conforms in general to the
> style of *Scientific Style and Format: The CBE Manual for Authors, Editors,
> and Publishers.* 6th ed. (New York: Cambridge University Press, 1994).

Geology

The United States Geological Survey sets the standards for geologic papers,
as explained in the following.

In-Text Citation Use the name and year system as explained on pages
304–05 or in Section 10d, pages 277–80, and as demonstrated with this
example:

> In view of Niue's position as a former volcanic island rising from
> a submarine plateau (Schowater, 1994), it might be further
> speculated that it has a late stage, silicic, peralkaline phase
> (Thomas, 1994, pp. 344–345). Such melts readily lose significant
> amounts of uranium and other elements on crystallization (Holt
> et al., 1991; Haffty and Nobel, 1992; Day and Webber, 1994),
> which are available to contemporary or later hydrothermal
> systems (Wallace, 1992).

List of References Label the bibliography "Literature Cited," and list only
those works mentioned in the paper. If you list references not used in the paper, label the page "Selected Bibliography." Alphabetize the list. For books,
list the author(s), followed by a comma; the year of publication, followed by
a comma; the title of the work with only the first word, proper names, and
first word after a colon capitalized, followed by a colon; the place of publication, followed by a comma; the publisher, followed by a comma; total
pages, followed by a period. For journals, list the author, followed by a comma; the year of publication, followed by comma; the title of the article with
only the first word, proper nouns, and first word after a colon capitalized, followed by a colon; the name of the journal, abbreviated but not italicized or
underscored, followed by a comma; the volume number with lower case v.
(e.g., v. 23), followed by a comma; the inclusive page numbers preceded by
one p. Add other notations for issue number, maps, illustrations, plates, and
so forth (see the Mattson entry in the following list of references).

Literature Cited

Banner, J. L., and Kaufman, J., 1994, The isotopic record of ocean
chemistry and diagenesis preserved in non-luminescent
brachiopods from Mississippian carbone rocks, Illinois and
Missouri: Geo. Soc. of Amer. Bull., v. 106, p. 1074–1082.

Bowler, S., 1990a, Unprecedented damage as earthquake occurs
    close to surface: New Sci., v. 126, 30 June, p. 31.
--- 1990b, When will a big quake hit eastern US?: New Sci., v. 127,
    29 Sept., p. 26.
--- 1991, Alaska quake spurs huge wave: New York Times, 22
    Feb., p. A18.
Donath, F. A., 1963, Strength variation and deformational
    behavior in anisotropic rock, p. 281–297 <u>in</u> Judd, Wm. R.,
    Editor, State of stress in the earth's crust: New York,
    American Elsevier Publishing Co., Inc., 732 p.
Friedlander, G., Kennedy, J. W., and Miller, J. M., 1964, Nuclear
    and radiochemistry: New York, John Wiley and Sons, 585 p.
Heard, H. C., Turner, F. J., and Weiss, L. E., 1965, Studies of
    heterogeneous strain in experimentally deformed calcite,
    marble, and phyllite: Univ. of Calif. Pub. in Geol. Sci., v. 46,
    p. 81–152.
Hill, M. L., and Troxel, B. W., 1966, Tectonics of Death Valley
    region, California: Geol. Soc. of Amer. Bull., v. 77, p.
    435–438.
Mattson, Peter H., 1979, Subduction, buoyant braking, flipping,
    and strike-slip faulting in the northern Caribbean: J. of
    Geol., v. 87, no. 3, p. 293–304, 3 figs., map.

Note: The form of these geology entries conforms to the style of *Geological Society of America Bulletin* and to *Suggestions to Authors of the Reports of the United States Geological Survey,* 6th ed. (Washington, DC: Dept. of the Interior, 1991), and to the *Journal of Geology* and *Journal of Geological Education.*

Using the Name and Year System for Papers in Business and Economics

In-Text Citation Use the name and year system as explained on pages 304–05 or in Section 10d, pages 277–80.

List of References Consult with your instructor. Many business instuctors endorse APA style (see Section 10d, pages 277–80) because it is used in many business journals, such as *Journal of Marketing Education, Applied Financial Economics,* and *Applied Economics.* For other instructors, you may need to modify APA style to conform with another set of business journals, such as *Journal of Marketing* or *Journal of Marketing Research.* If modification is required, do so in this manner:

1. Separate two authors with *and,* not *&.*
2. Use capitals for all major words in titles of books and articles.
3. Enclose the title of an article within quotation marks.

4. Use commas to separate items in a journal reference.
5. Do not italicize or underscore the volume number.

References

Addison, J. T., and Hirsch, B. T. (1989), "Union Effects on Productivity, Profits and Growth: Has the Long Run Arrived?" Journal of Labor Economics, 7, 72–105.

Anderson, J. E. (1981), "Cross-Section Tests of the Heckscher-Ohlin Theorem: Comment," American Economic Review, 71, 1037–1039.

Antyoulatos, A. A. (1994), "Credit Rationing and Rational Behavior," Journal of Money, Credit and Banking, 26, 182–202.

Carter, A. (1970), Structural Change in the American Economy. Cambridge: Harvard University Press.

Celis, W. (March 1, 1991), "Study Urges a Preschool Role for Businesses," New York Times, A2.

Chirls, S. B. (Jan. 7, 1988), "Yule Workout Leaves Retailers in Good Shape," Daily News Record, 1–2.

Deardorff, A. V. (1979), "Weak Links in the Chain of Comparative Advantage," Journal of International Economics, 9, 197–209.

Deardorff, A. V. (1980), "The General Validity of the Law of Comparative Advantage," Journal of Political Economy, 88, 941–957.

Dooley, M., and Isard, P. (May 1979), "The Portfolio-Balance Model of Exchange Rates," International Finance Discussion Paper No. 141, Federal Reserve Board.

Doti, J. (Jan. 1978), "An Economic Theory of Shopping Behavior," Center for Economic Research Report No. 3, Chapman College.

Ellis, J. (June 1985), "Starting a Small Business Inside a Big One," Money, 85–86, 88, 90.

"An Updated Yardstick for GNP Growth," Business Week, (10 June 1985), 18.

> ***Note:*** The form of these economics entries is based in general upon the style and format of *Applied Economics* and the *Economics Journal.*

11b Using the Number System

The number system is used in the applied sciences (chemistry, computer science, engineering, mathematics, and physics) and in the medical sciences (bio-medicine, health, medicine, and nursing). In simple terms, it requires an in-text number, rather than the year, and references at the end of the paper are numbered to correspond to the in-text citations. Writers in these fields conform to several general regulations that apply to all applied sciences.

After completing a list of references, assign a number to each entry. Use one of two methods for numbering the list: (1) arrange references in alphabetic order, and number them consecutively (in which case, of course, the numbers will not appear in consecutive order in the text); or (2) forego an alphabetic arrangement, and number the references consecutively as they appear in the text, interrupting that order when entering references cited earlier.

When writing a rough draft, use the appropriate numbers as in-text citations. The number serves as a key reference to the source, as listed at the end of the paper. If you quote a source, add specific page numbers to the bibliographic entry (see examples in the reference lists that follow) or add page numbers to your in-text citations. Conform to the following guidelines:

1. Place the number within parentheses (1) or brackets [2] alone or with the name(s) of the source:

   In particular, the recent paper by Hershel, Hobbs, and Thomason (1) has raised many interesting questions related to photosynthesis, some of which were answered by Skelton (2).

   An alternative, used by several disciplines and their journals, is to use a raised superscript number:

   In particular, the recent paper by Hershel, Hobbs, and Thomason[1] has raised many interesting questions related to photosynthesis, some of which were answered by Skelton.[2]

2. If you do not mention the authority's name in your text, employ one of the following two methods:

   a. Insert the number only, enclosing it within parentheses or brackets, or using a superscript number:

      It is known (1) that the DNA concentration of a nucleus doubles during interphase.

      It is known[1] that the DNA concentration of a nucleus doubles during interphase.

   b. Insert both name and number:

      Additional observations include alterations in carbohydrate metabolism (Evans, 3), changes in ascorbic acid incorporation into the cell (Dodd and Williams, 11) and adjoining membranes (Holt and Zimmer, 7).

3. If necessary, add specific data, such as page numbers, to the entry:

"The use of photosynthesis in this application is crucial to the environment" (Skelton,[8] p. 732).

The results of the respiration experiment published by Jones (3, Table 6, p. 412) had been predicted earlier by Smith (5, Proposition 8).

Using the Number System for Papers in the Applied Sciences

Chemistry	**Computer Science**	**Engineering**
Mathematics	**Physics**	

The disciplines of the applied sciences employ the number system, but variations by field exist both in text citations and in entries of the list of references.

Chemistry: ACS (American Chemical Society) Style

In-Text Citation You may use one of two styles. Check with your chemistry instructor for his or her preference.

1. Use raised superscript numerals as references occur:

The stereochemical features of arene molecules chemisorbed on metal surfaces cannot be assessed precisely.[3-5]

2. Place the reference numbers within parentheses:

However, composite statistics from theoretical calculations (6) and chemical studies (7–10) indicate that benzene is often chemisorbed.

Number your references in consecutive order as used, *not* in alphabetic order. If a reference is repeated, use the original number, not a new one.

List of References Label the list "References." List entries as they occur in the text, not in alphabetic order. The basic forms for chemical entries are demonstrated in the following example. Titles of journal articles are not listed at all. Dates of journal articles are placed in boldface (**1994**) or marked for boldface (1994), but dates of books are not. A sample list follows:

References

1. Mouscadet, J., et al. <u>J. Biol. Chem.</u> 1994, <u>269</u>, 21635–21643.
2. Duffey, J. L.; Kurth, M. L. <u>J. Organ. Chem.</u> 1994, <u>59</u>, 3783–3785.
3. "Selected Values of Chemical and Thermodynamic Properties." <u>Natl. Bur. Stand. (U.S.) Circ.</u> 1950, No. 500.

4. Humphries, R. B. In <u>High School Chemistry</u>, 3rd ed.; Lamm, Nancy, Ed.; Lumar Press: New York, 1984; Vol. III, Ch. 6.
5. Terrel, L. <u>J. Chem.</u> 1960, 34, 256; <u>Chem. Abstr.</u> 1961, 54, 110a.
6. Cotton, F. A. <u>J. Am. Chem. Soc.</u> 1968, 90, 6230.
7. (a) Sievert, A. C.; Muetterties, E. L. <u>Inorg. Chem.</u> 1981, 20, 489. (b) Albright, T. A., unpublished data, 1984.

Note: The in-text citation may refer to 7, 7a, or 7b.

Note: The form of these chemistry entries conforms to the *ACS Style Guide: A Manual for Authors and Editors.* Ed. Janets S. Dodd. (Washington, DC: American Chemical Society, 1986).

Computer Science

In-Text Citation   Use raised superscript numerals (as shown for Chemistry, page 315) and then number them in consecutive order by appearance in the paper, not in alphabetic order.

List of References   Label the list "Works Cited." Number the references according to their appearance in the text, not by alphabetic order. For books, titles are italicized or underscored; the publisher precedes the city of publication; and specific page(s) of books need not be listed, but in-text citations should specify pages for paraphrases and direct quotations. For journals, the title of the article is provided within quotation marks, with first word, title, proper nouns, and first word after a colon capitalized; the title of the journal and volume number are italicized or underscored; and the issue number is provided whenever available, preceding the date and page number(s). A sample follows:

Works Cited

1. Globus, A.; and Raible, E. "Fourteen ways to say nothing with scientific visualization." <u>Computer 27</u> (July 1994), 73–83.

2. Stonebraker, M. "Future trends in database systems." <u>IEEE Trans. Knowledge and Data Eng. 1</u> (Mar. 1989), 33–44.

3. Aho, A. V.; Hopcroft, J. E.; and Ullman, J. D. <u>The Design and Analysis of Computer Algorithms</u>. Addison-Wesley, Reading, Mass., 1974.

4. Gligor, V. D.; and Shattuck, S. H. "On deadlock detection in distributed systems." <u>IEEE Trans. Softw. Eng. SE-6</u> (5) (Sept. 1980), 435–40.

5. Sklansky, J.; and Wassel, G. N. <u>Pattern Classifiers and Trainable Machines</u>. Springer-Verlag, New York, 1981.

6. Holt, R. C. "Some deadlock properties of computer systems." Computer Surv. 4 (3) (Sept. 1972), 179–96.

7. Nelson, T. "On the Xanadu project." Byte 15 (Sept. 1990), 298–99.

Engineering

See the form and style for Physics, page 318.

Mathematics: AMS (American Mathematical Society) Style

In-Text Citation   First alphabetize and then number the list of references. Label the list "References." All in-text citations are then made to the reference number, which you should place in your text within brackets as boldface or marked as boldface (wavy line). For example:

> In addition to the obvious implications it is already known from [8] that every d-regular Lindelof space is D-normal. Further results on D-normal spaces will appear in [8], which is in preparation. The results obtained here and in [2], [3], and [5] encourage further research.

List of References   For books, the titles are italicized or underscored, the publisher precedes the city of publication, and the specific page(s) of books need not be listed. For journals, the title of the article is italicized or underscored, the journal title is *not* italicized or underscored, the volume is placed in boldface or marked for boldface (wavy line), the year of publication follows within parentheses, and the complete pagination of the article comes last. A sample list follows:

References

1. R. Artzy, Linear geometry, Addison-Wesley, Reading, Mass., 1965.

2. H. Colonius and D. Vorberg, Distribution inequalities for parallel models with unlimited capacity, J. Math. Psy. 38 (1994), 35–58.

3. I. M. Isaacs and D. S. Passman, Groups with representations of bounded degree, Canad. J. Math. 16 (1964), 299–309.

4. ---, Characterization of groups in terms of the degrees of their characters, Pacific J. Math. 15 (1965), 877–903.

5. L. J. Meconi, Number bases revisited, Sch. Science & Math. 90 (1990), 396–403.

6. O. Solbrig, Evolution and systematics, Macmillan, New York, 1966.

> **Note:** The form of these entries conforms to *A Manual for Authors of Mathematical Papers,* rev. ed. (Providence, RI: American Mathematical Society, 1990).

Physics: AIP (American Institute of Physics) Style

In-Text Citation Use raised superscript numerals, like this.[12] Number the list of references in consecutive order of in-text usage, not in alphabetic order.

List of References For books, titles are italicized or underscored, the name of the publisher precedes the place of publication, and specific page references should be provided. For journals, the title of the article is omitted entirely, the title of the journal is abbreviated and *not* italicized or underscored, the volume is placed in boldface or marked for boldface (wavy line), and the year within parentheses follows the pagination. A sample list follows:

References

[1]T. Fastie, W. G., Physics Today 44, 37–44 (1991).

[2]C. D. Motchenbacher and F. C. Fitchen, <u>Low-Noise Electronic Design</u> (Wiley, New York, 1973), p. 16.

[3]L. Monchick, S., Chem. Phys. 71, 576 (1979).

[4]F. Riesz and B. Nagy, <u>Functional-Analysis</u> (Ungar, New York, 1955), Secs. 121 and 123.

[5]G. E. Brown and M. Rho, Phys. Lett. 82B, 177 (1979); G. E. Brown, M. Rho, and V. Vento, Phys. Letts. 84B, 383 (1979); Phys Rev D22, 2838 (1980); Phys Rev. D24, 216 (1981).

[6]Marc D. Levenson, Phys. Today 30 (5), 44–49 (1977).

> *Note:* The Form of these entries conforms to the *Style Manual for Guidance in the Preparation of Papers for Journals Published by the American Institute of Physics,* 3rd ed. (New York: American Institute of Physics, 1978).

Using the Number System for Papers in the Medical Sciences

Health   Medicine   Nursing   Bio-Medicine

Like other applied sciences, the medical sciences, as a general rule, employ the number system. Variations among medical journals do exist, so consult your instructor about the proper format. *Note:* The number system shown below is the second style advocated by the *CBE Style Manual* (see pages 309–11 for the CBE name and year system).

In-Text Citation For citations that occur in the text, use numbers in parentheses or superscript numerals. See the explanation and examples in Section 11b, pages 313–18.

List of References Label the list "References." Do not alphabetize the list; rather, number it to correspond to sources as you cite them in the text. For books, list the author(s); the title, italicized or underscored and with all major words capitalized; the place; the publisher; and the year of publication. For journals, list the author; the title of the article without quotation marks and with proper nouns, first words, and the first word after a colon capitalized; the name of the journal, italicized or underscored and with major words capitalized and abbreviated *without* periods (but followed by a period); the year followed by a semicolon; the volume followed by a colon; and the page number(s). A sample list follows:

References

1. Tardiff, K., et al. Homicide in New York City: Cocaine use and firearms. <u>JAMA</u> 1994;272:43–52.
2. Miner, K. J., Baker, J. A. Media coverage of suntanning and skin cancer: Mixed messages of health and beauty. <u>J Health Ed</u>. 1994;25:234–238.
3. Antonovsky, A. <u>Health, Stress, and Coping</u>. San Francisco, Jossey-Bass, 1979.
4. Ayman, D. The personality type of patients with arteriolar essential hypertension. <u>Am J Med Sci</u>. 1983;186:213–233.
5. Nash, P. <u>Authority and Freedom in Education</u>. New York, Wiley, 1966.
6. Green, M. I., Haggery, R. J. (eds). <u>Ambulatory Pediatrics</u>. Philadelphia, W. B. Saunders, 1968.

Note: The form of these entries represents a general standard as established by (1) the American Medical Association, *Style Book: Editorial Manual,* 6th ed. (Acton, Mass.: Publishing Sciences Group, Inc., 1976); (2) *Scientific Style and Format: The CBE Manual for Authors, Editors, and Publishers;* and by numerous medical journals, such as *JAMA, Nutrition Reviews, Journal of American College Health,* and others.

Sample Paper Using the Number System

The following paper demonstrates the format for a paper in the applied sciences and the medical sciences. It is recommended that you use numbers within parentheses rather than raised superscript numbers in order to simplify the task of keyboarding the paper. However, your instructor may require the superscript numbering.

Autism 1

Patti M. Bracy
May 8, 1994

Autism: Early Intervention in Diagnosing
and Educating the Autistic Child

Autism, a neurological dysfunction of the brain which
commences before the age of thirty months, was discovered by
Leo Kanner (1), who studied 11 cases, all of which showed a
specific type of childhood psychosis that was different from
other childhood disorders, although each was similar to
childhood schizophrenia. He described the characteristics of the
early infantile syndrome as:

- Extreme autistic aloneness
- Language abnormalities
- Obsessive desire for the maintenance of sameness
- Good cognitive potential
- Normal physical development
- Highly intelligent, obsessive, and cold parents

Further investigation (2) reduced these symptoms to four
criteria: onset within 30 months of birth, poor social
development, late language development, and a preference for
regular, stereotyped activity. Autism's characteristics have been
identified (3):

1. Qualitative impairment in reciprocal social interaction
2. Impairment in communication and imaginative activity
3. Markedly restricted repertoire of activities and interests

In the United States, autism affects one out of 2,500
children, and is not usually diagnosed until the child is between
two and five years of age (4). Typically, the child is diagnosed
around the age of 4 years (5). The remarkable story of one
father's ordeal with an autistic child has been recorded (6).

In recent years, studies have focussed on infantile and
preschool characteristics of autism in order to detect children
with autism earlier. Many children with autism, if detected early
enough and if enrolled in intensive early intervention programs,
may be admitted into the mainstream of regular education
without any special services (7, 8). Early intervention seems to
be the preferred action, especially since the "facilitated
communication" technique was condemned with vitriolic
criticism in 1994 (9). Facilitated communication requires a

Cite a number immediately after the name of the source.

Refer to several sources in one citation by citing more than one number

Separate two sources by a comma.

Autism 2

person guiding the autistic's hand over a computer keyboard, but the person doing the guiding may have more input than the autistic person.

Accordingly, special qualifying characteristics have been devised in order to successfully identify infants with autism. A public policy directive (PL99-457) has provided money to fund the design of programs geared especially for the infant or toddler with disabilities and their families (8).

Cause

Rutter (10) listed three possible causes: behavioral syndrome, organic brain disorder, or a range of biological and psychosocial factors. In 1994, it was acknowledged (11, p. 311) that the "organic basis of autism" was generally agreed upon. . . .

Add a page number if you quote the source.

Note: Omitted pages of this essay can be found in the full essay in APA style in Chapter 10, pages 293–302.

Social and joint attention behaviors show a marked difference between normal and autistic children. Communicative behaviors show a difference but are not as statistically viable as the first two behaviors. Also the autistic children showed more autistic symptoms than the normal children. The study showed that there are identifiable traits associated with infant autism.

Discussion

Early intervention has proved beneficial (22) in educating and assisting children with autism, especially if the home environment is not adequate to provide social, physical, cognitive, or emotional development. Many times, a child that is not diagnosed until school age will not respond as well to treatment; their defects may have caused further delay in their normal progress. Therefore, every effort should be made to identify infants and preschoolers at risk for autism.

There is hope in the future that both the cause and the cure for autism will be found. For the present, early identification and intervention offers some hope for the children at risk for autism and their families. Since autism is sometimes outgrown, childhood treatment offers the best hope for the autistic person who must try to survive in an alien environment.

Autism 3

References

1. Kanner, L. Autistic disturbances of affective contact. Nervous Child. 1943;2:217–250.

2. Rutter, M. Diagnosis and definition of childhood autism. J of Autism and Childhood Schizophrenia. 1978;8:139–161.

3. American Psychiatric Association. Diagnostic and statistical manual of mental disorders. 3rd ed., rev. Washington, DC: Author; 1987.

4. Koegel, R., & Schreibman, L. Teaching autistic and other severely handicapped children. Austin: Pro–ed; 1981.

5. Siegel, B., Pliner, C., Eschler, J., & Elliott, G. R. How children with autism are diagnosed: Difficulties in identification of children with multiple developmental delays. Dev and Behav Pediatrics. 1988;9(4):199–204.

6. Martin, R. Out of silence: A journey into language. New York: Holt; 1994.

7. Lovaas, O. I. Behavioral treatment and normal educational and intellectual functioning in young autistic children. J of Consult and Clin Psy. 1987;55:3–9.

8. Powers, M. Early intervention for children with autism. In D. Berkell, Autism: Identification, education, and treatment. Hillsdale, NJ: Erlbaum; 1992, pp. 225–252.

9. Berger, J. Shattering the silence. New York Times. 1994 Feb. 12;Sect L:21.

10. Rutter, M. Cognitive deficits in the pathogenesis of autism. J of Child Psy and Psy. 1983;26:513–531.

11. Rutter, M., Bailey, A. Bolton, P., & Le Couteur, A. Autism and known medical conditions: Myth and substance. J of Child Psy and Psych. 1994;35, vol.2:311–322.

12. Gallagher, B., Jones, B., & Byrne, M. A national survey of mental health professionals concerning the causes of early infantile autism. J of Clin Psy. 1990;46:934–939.

13. Fay, M. Child of silence. Life 1986 Sept:84–89.

14. Happé, G. Annotation: Current psychological theories of autism: The "theory of mind" account and rival theories. J of Child Psy and Psy. 1994;35(2):215–229.

15. Osterling, J., & Dawson, G. Early recognition of children with autism: A study of first birthday home videotapes. J of Autism and Dev Disorders. 1994;24:247–257.

16. Rimland, B. Infantile autism. New York: Appleton-Century-Crofts; 1984.

The reference list is numbered by appearance of the source in the text, not by alphabetic order.

The citations on this page conform to the style of the CBE Style Manual.

Autism 4

17. Vandershaf, S. Autism: A chemical excess? Psy Today 1987 Mar:15–16.
18. Dahlgren, S., & Gillberg, C. Symptoms in the first two years of life: A preliminary population study of infantile autism. European Archives of Psych and Neuro Sciences. 1989;238:169–174.
19. Ornitz, E., Guthrie, D., & Farley, A. The early development of autistic children. J of Autism and Childhood Schizophrenia. 1977;7:207–229.
20. Adrien, J., Faure, M., Perrot, A., Hameury, L., Garreau, B., Barthelemy, C., & Sauvage, D. Autism and family home movies: Preliminary findings. J of Autism and Dev Disorders. 1991;21:43–49.
21. Adrien, J., Perrot, A., Sauvage, D., Leddet, I., Larmande, C., Hameury, L., & Barthelemy, C. Early symptoms in autism from family home movies. Acta Paedopsychiatrica. 1992;55:71–75.
22. Berkson, G. Children with handicaps: A review of behavioral research. Hillsdale, NJ: Erlbaum, 1993.

11c Using the Footnote System

The fine arts and some fields in the humanities (not literature) employ traditional footnotes, which should conform to standards set by the *The Chicago Manual of Style,* 14th ed., 1993. With this system, you must employ superscript numerals within the text, (like this[15]) and place documentary footnotes on corresponding pages. Although no Works Cited page is usually necessary, some instructors may ask for one at the end of the paper; if so, see pages 331–32. The discussion in this section assumes that notes will appear as footnotes. However, some instructors accept endnotes, that is, the grouping of all notes together at the end of the paper, not at the bottom of individual pages (see pages 328 and 191–94).

If available on your software, use the footnote or endnote feature. It will not only insert the raised superscript numbers but also keep your footnotes arranged properly at the bottom of each page. In most instances, the software will first insert the superscript numeral in the text and then skip to the bottom of the page so that you can write the footnote. However, it will not, of course, write the note automatically; you must type in the essential data in the correct style.

In-Text Citation: Superscript Numerals Use arabic numerals typed slightly above the line (like this[12]). Place this superscript numeral at the end of quotations or paraphrases, with the number following immediately without a space after the final word or mark of punctuation, as in this sample:

> Colonel Warner soon rejoined his troops despite severe pain. He wrote in September of 1864: "I was obliged to ride at all times on a walk and to mount my horse from some steps or be helped on. My cains [sic] with which I walked when on foot were strapped to my saddle."[6] Such heroic dedication did not go unnoticed, for the <u>Washington Chronicle</u> cited Warner as "an example worthy of imitation."[7] At Gettysburg, Warner's troops did not engage in heavy fighting and suffered only limited casualties of two dead and five wounded.[8]

The use of "[sic]" indicates exact quotation, even to the point of typing an apparent error. Avoid placing one superscript numeral at the end of a long paragraph because readers will not know whether it refers to the final sentence only or to the entire paragraph. A better strategy is to introduce borrowed materials with an authority's name and then place a superscript numeral at the end. By doing this, you direct the reader to the full extent of the borrowed material.

Footnotes

Place footnotes at the bottom of pages to correspond with superscript numerals. Some papers require footnotes on almost every page. Follow these conventions:

1. *Spacing.* Single-space each footnote, but double-space between footnotes.
2. *Indentation.* Indent the first line 5 spaces.
3. *Numbering.* Number the footnotes consecutively throughout the entire paper.
4. *Placement.* Collect at the bottom of each page all the footnotes to citations made on that page.
5. *Distinguish footnotes from text.* Separate footnotes from the text by triple spacing or, if you prefer, by a 12-space line beginning at the left margin.
6. *Footnote form.* Basic forms of footnotes should conform to the following:

For a Book

    1. James K. Greer, <u>Texas Ranger: Jacks Hays in the Frontier Southwest</u> (Bryan: Texas A & M University Press, 1994), 28.

For a Journal Article

    2. Peter Hedstrom, "Contagious Collectivities: On the Spatial Diffusion of Swedish Trade Unions, 1890–1940," <u>American Journal of Sociology</u> 99 (1994): 1157–79.

For a Collection

    3. Lonne Elder, "Ceremonies in Dark Old Men," in <u>New Black Playwrights: An Anthology</u>, ed. William Couch, Jr. (Baton Rouge: Louisiana State University Press, 1968), 62–63.

For an Edition with More than Three Authors

    4. Albert C. Baugh et al., <u>A Literary History of England</u>. 2d ed. (New York: Appleton, 1967), 602–11.

For a Magazine Article

    5. Ken Auletta, "Free Speech," <u>The New Yorker</u>, 12 September 1994, 40–43.

For a Newspaper Article

    6. Karen Grassmuck, "More Small Colleges Merge with Larger Ones, but Some Find the Process Can Be Painful," <u>The Chronicle of Higher Education</u>, 18 September 1991, sec. A, pp. A37–A39.

    Note: Use "p." or "pp." to distinguish pages from sections or columns.

For a Review Article

    7. Michael Rogers, review of <u>Keats the Poet</u>, by Stuart Sperry, <u>Library Journal</u>, 15 March 1994, 105.

Electronic Sources

Cite electronic sources in this general order:

> author
> title of article
> the text in which the article appears, preceded by *in*
> the type of online source, within brackets [database online]
> publication data within parentheses; that is, the place, publisher, volume, and date, as appropriate, with the date that *you* cited the source within brackets *inside* the parentheses, followed by a semicolon
> the address, preceded by *available from*

Online Journal

10. E. B. Banning, "Herders or Homesteaders? A Neolithic Farm in Wadi Ziqlab, Jordan," in <u>Biblical Archaeologist</u>, par. 6 [online journal] (vol. 58.1, March 1995 [cited 9 April 1997]); available from World Wide Web @ http://scholar.cc.emory.edu/scripts/ASOR/BA/Banning.html

Online Magazine

11. Jon Guttman, "Constitution: The Legendary Survivor," in <u>Military History</u>, par. 46 [online magazine] (1997 [cited 28 April 1997]); available from World Wide Web @ http://www:thehistorynet.ccm/M . . . ry/articles/1997/0297-text.htm

Government Document

12. United States Congress, Senate, <u>Superfund Cleanup Acceleration Act of 1997</u> [database online] (105th Cong., Senate Bill 8, 21 January 1997 [cited 4 March 1997]); available from World Wide Web @ http.thomas.loc.gov/egi-bin/query/ 2?C105:S.8:

Gopher Site, Review

13. Armand D'Agour, review of <u>Classical Women Poets</u>, by Josephine Balmer, ed. and trans. [electronic bulletin board] (Newcastle-upon-Tyne: Bloodaxe Books, 1996 [cited 10 March 1997]); available from gopher @ gopher.lib.virginia.edu:70/alpha/hmer/v97/97-I-4

Listserv (E-mail Discussion Group)

14. Rosemary Camilleri, "Narrative Bibliography" [electronic bulletin board] (10 March 1997 [cited 11 March 1997]); available from listserv @ H-RHETOR@msu.edu

Newsgroups

15. Richard Link, "Territorial Fish," [electronic newsgroup] (11 Jan. 1997 [cited 14 March 1997]); available from listserv@rec.aquaria.freshwater.misc

Telnet Site
   16. United States Navel Observatory, "The Mercury Ion Frequency Standard," par. 3 [electronic bulletin board] (cited 6 March 1997); available from Telnet @ duke.ldgo.columbia.edu/port=23 login ads, set terminal to 8/N/1

FTP Site
   17. Argiris A. Kranidiotis, "Human Audio Perception Frequently Asked Questions," par. 2 [electronic bulletin board] (7 June 1994 [cited 11 March 1997]); available from ftp://svrftp.eng.cam.ac.uk/pub/comp. speech/info/HumanAudioPerception

HyperNews
   18. Abigail Ochberg, "Algae-based Paper." [Recycling Discussion Group] (9 Oct. 1996 [cited 18 June 1997]); available from HyperNews posting http://www.betterworld.com/BWDiscuss/get/recycleD. html?embed=2

Linkage Data (a File Accessed from Another File)
   19. "What Happens to Recycled Plastics?" [Lkd. Better World Discussion Topics at Recycling Discussion Group] (1996 [cited 18 June 1997]); available from World Wide Web @ http://www.betterworld.com/BWZ/9602/learn.htm

CD-ROM
   20. "Abolitionist Movement," in <u>Compton's Interactive Encyclopedia</u> [CD-ROM] (Softkey Multimedia, 1996 [cited 11 March 1996]).

   21. David Wessel, "Fed Lifts Rates Half Point, Setting Four-Year High," in <u>Wall Street Journal</u> [CD-ROM] (<u>Wall Street Journal Ondisc</u> 2 February 1995: A2+ [cited 6 February 1996]); available from UMI-ProQuest.

   22. Aureliio J. Figueredo and Laura Ann McCloskey, "Sex, Money, and Paternity: The Evolutionary Psychology of Domestic Violence," in <u>Ethnology and Sociobiology</u>, abstract (vol. 14, 1993: 353–79 [cited 12 March 1997]); available from <u>PsychLIT</u> Silverplatter.

Subsequent Footnote Reference

After a first full reference subsequent footnotes should be shortened to the name of the author(s) and the page number. When an author has two works mentioned, employ a shortened version of the title (e.g., [3]Jones, <u>Paine</u>, 25). In general, avoid Latinate abbreviations such as *loc. cit.* or *op. cit.;* however, whenever a note refers to the source in the immediately preceding note, you may use "Ibid." with a page number a shown below. (Note especially the difference between footnotes 4 and 6.)

   3. Jerrold Ladd, <u>Out of the Madness: From the Projects to a Life of Hope</u> (New York: Warner, 1994), 24.

4. Ibid., 27.

5. Michael Schulman and Eva Meckler, <u>Bringing Up a Moral Child</u>, rev. ed. (New York: Doubleday, 1994), 221.

6. Ladd, <u>Out of the Madness</u>, 24.

7. Ibid., 27.

Endnotes

With permission of your instructor, put all your notes together as a single group of endnotes to make keyboarding your paper easier. Most computer software programs help you with this task by inserting the superscript numerals in the text and by allowing you to keyboard the endnotes consecutively at the end of the text, not at the bottom of each page. Follow these conventions:

a. Begin notes on a new page at the end of the text.
b. Entitle the page "Notes," centered, and placed 2 inches from the top of the page.
c. Indent the first line of each note 5 spaces, number the note followed by a period, begin the note, and use the left margin for succeeding lines.
d. Double-space the notes, and double-space between the notes.
e. Triple-space between the heading and the first note.

Conform to the following sample:

Notes

1. Jerrold Ladd, <u>Out of the Madness: From the Projects to a Life of Hope</u> (New York: Warner, 1994), 24.

2. Ibid., 27.

3. Michael Schulman and Eva Meckler, <u>Bringing Up a Moral Child</u>, rev. ed. (New York: Doubleday, 1994), 221.

4. W. V. Quine, <u>Word and Object</u> (Cambridge, Mass.: MIT Press, 1966), 8.

5. Schulman and Meckler, 217.

6. Abraham J. Heschel, <u>Man Is Not Alone: A Philosophy of Religion</u> (New York: Farrar, Straus, and Young, 1951), 221.

7. Ladd, <u>Out of the Madness</u>, 24.

8. Ibid., 27.

9. Quine, <u>Word and Object</u>, 9–10.

10. Ladd, <u>Out of Madness</u>, 28.

Using the Footnote System for Papers in the Humanities

History   Philosophy   Religion   Theology

In-Text Citation Use the form of raised superscript numerals as explained on pages 324–25.

List of References Place the references at the bottom of each page on which a citation occurs. See explanation above, pages 324–28, and duplicate the form and style of the following footnotes:

Footnotes for a Paper on Religion

1. Stephanie Dowrick, <u>Intimacy and Solitude</u> (New York: Norton, 1994), 23–27.

2. Jo Ann Hackett, "Can a Sexist Model Liberate Us? Ancient New Eastern 'Fertility' Goddesses," <u>Journal of Feminist Studies in Religion</u>, 5 (1989): 457–58.

3. Claude Levi-Strauss, <u>The Savage Mind</u> (Chicago: University of Chicago Press, 1966), 312.

4. Ibid., 314.

5. Edward Evans-Pritchard, <u>Theories of Primitive Religion</u> (Oxford: Clarendon Press, 1965), 45.

6. Evans-Pritchard, <u>Nuer Religion</u> (Oxford: Clarendon Press, 1956), 84.

7. Evans-Pritchard, <u>Primitive Religion</u>, 46.

8. Patrick T. Humphries, "Salvation Today, Not Tomorrow," Sermon (Bowling Green, KY: First Methodist Church, 1994).

9. Rom. 6:2.

10. 1 Cor. 13:1–3.

11. Report of a Commission Appointed by the Archbishops of Canterbury and York in 1949, <u>The Church and the Law of Nullity of Marriage</u> (London: Society for Promoting Christian Knowledge, 1995), 12–16.

Footnotes for a History Paper

1. Richard Zacks, <u>History Laid Bare: Love, Sex, and Perversity from the Ancient Etruscans to Warren G. Harding</u> (New York: HarperCollins, 1994), 34.

2. Thomas Jefferson, <u>Notes on the State of Virginia</u> (1784), ed. William Peden (Chapel Hill: University of North Carolina Press, 1955), 59.

3. Ralph Lerner, <u>Revolutions Revisited: Two Faces of the Politics of Enlightenment</u> (Chapel Hill: University of North Carolina Press, 1994), 56–60.

4. <u>Encyclopedia Britannica: Macropaedia</u>, 1974 ed., s.v. "Heidegger, Martin."

Note: The abbreviation s.v. stands for sub verbo, which means "under the word."

5. Henry Steele Commager, <u>The Nature and Study of History</u>, Social Science Seminar Series (Columbus, Ohio: Merrill, 1965), 10.

6. Department of the Treasury, "Financial Operations of Government Agencies and Funds," <u>Treasury Bulletin</u> (Washington, D.C.: GPO, June 1974), 134–41.

7. U. S. Constitution, art. 1, sec. 4.

8. United Kingdom, <u>Coroner's Act, 1954</u>, 2 & 3 Eliz. 2, ch. 31.

9. <u>State v. Lane</u>, Minnesota 263 N. W. 608 (1935).

10. Papers of Gen. A. J. Warner (p-973, Service Record and Short Autobiography), Western Reserve Historical Society.

11. Ibid., clipping from the <u>Washington Chronicle</u>.

12. Gregory Claeys, "The Origins of the Rights of Labor: Republicanism, Commerce, and the Construction of Modern Social Theory in Britain, 1796–1805." <u>The Journal of Modern History</u> 66 (1994): 249–90.

13. Lerner, 54–55.

Using the Footnote System for Papers in the Fine Arts

Art   Dance   Music   Theater

Documentation for a research paper in the fine arts uses superscript numerals in the text (see pages 324–25).

Endnotes for a Paper in the Fine Arts

Notes

1. Natasha Staller, "Melies's 'Fantastic' Cinema and the Origins of Cubism," <u>Art History</u> 12 (1989): 202–39.

2. There are three copies of the papal brief in the archives of the German College, now situated on Via S. Nicola da Tolentino. The document is printed in Thomas D. Culley, <u>Jesuits and Music</u> (Chicago: Jesuit Historical Institute Press, 1970), I, 358–59.

3. Staller, "Cubism," 214.

4. Denys Hay, ed., <u>The Age of the Renaissance</u>, 2nd ed. (London: Guild, 1986), 286.

5. Aristophanes, <u>The Birds</u>, in <u>Five Comedies of Aristophanes</u>, trans. Benjamin B. Rogers (Garden City, N.Y.: Doubleday, 1955), 1.2. 12–14.

6. Jean Bouret, <u>The Life and Work of Toulouse Lautrec</u>, trans. Daphne Woodward (New York: Abrams, n.d.), 5.

7. Cyrus Hoy, "Fathers and Daughters in Shakespeare's Romances," in <u>Shakespeare's Romances Reconsidered</u>, ed. Carol McGinnis Kay and Henry E. Jacobs (Lincoln: University of Nebraska Press, 1978), 77–78.

8. Lionello Venturi, <u>Botticelli</u> (Greenwich, Conn.: Fawcett, n.d.), p. 214, plate 32.

Note: Add "p." for page only if needed for clarity.

9. Cotton Vitellius MSS, A., 15. British Museum.

10. <u>Hamlet</u>, 2.3.2.

11. George Henry Lewes, review of "Letters on Christian Art," by Friedrich von Schlegel, <u>Athenaeum</u> 1117 (1849): 296.

12. Ron Stoppelmann, "Letters," <u>New York</u>, 23 August 1982, 8.

13. <u>The World Book Encyclopedia</u>, 1976 ed., s.v. "Raphael."

14. <u>The Last Tango in Paris</u>, United Artists, 1972.

15. Wolfgang A. Mozart, <u>Jupiter, Symphony No. 41</u>.

16. William Blake, <u>Comus, photographic reproduction in Irene Taylor</u>, "Blake's <u>Comus</u> Designs," <u>Blake Studies</u> 4 (spring 1972): 61, plate 4.

17. Lawrence Topp, <u>The Artistry of Van Gogh</u> (New York: Matson, 1983), transparency 21.

18. Eric Sevareid, <u>CBS News</u> (New York: CBS-TV, 11 March 1975); Media Services Videotape 1975–142 (Nashville: Vanderbilt University, 1975).

19. Daniel Zipperer, "The Alexander Technique as a Supplement to Voice Production," <u>Journal of Research in Singing</u> 14 (June 1991): 1–40.

Writing a Bibliography for a Paper That Uses Footnotes

In addition to footnotes or endnotes, you may need to supply a separate bibliography that lists sources used in developing the paper. Use a heading that represents its contents, such as "Selected Bibliography," "Sources Consulted," or "Works Cited."

If you write completely documented footnotes, the bibliography is redundant. Check with your instructor before preparing one because it may not be required. Separate the title from the first entry with a triple space. Keyboard the first line of each entry flush left; indent the second line and other succeeding lines 5 spaces. Alphabetize the list by last names of authors. List alphabetically by title two or more works by one author. The basic forms are shown here.

For a Book
Mapp, Alf J., Jr. <u>Thomas Jefferson: A Strange Case of Mistaken Identity</u>. New York: Madison, 1987.

For a Journal Article
Aueston, John C. "Altering the Course of the Constitutional Convention." <u>Yale Law Journal</u> 100 (1990): 765–783.

For a Newspaper
Stephenson, D. Grier, Jr. "Is the Bill of Rights in Danger?" <u>USA Today</u>, 12 May 1991, sec. 3, p. 83.

See also the bibliographies that accompany the sample papers, pages 322–23 and 231.

APPENDIX A*
Reference Sources

Index to List of Reference Sources, by Discipline

---

*Revised and annotated by Anne May Berwind, head of Library Information Services, Austin Peay State University.

333

List of Reference Sources, by Discipline

The double asterisk (**) before an entry signals a particularly important source within a discipline. A brief annotation explains the nature of these special reference works.

Art

Basic Sources and Guides to Art Literature

American Art Directory. New York: Bowker, 1952–present.

American Graphic Design, A Guide to the Literature. Westport, CT: Greenwood, 1992.

Art Research Methods and Resources: A Guide to Finding Art Information. Ed. L. S. Jones. Dubuque, IA: Kendall/Hunt, 1985.

Artwords: A Glossary of Contemporary Theory. Westport: CT: Greenwood, 1997.

A Biographical Dictionary of Women Artists in Europe and America Since 1850. Ed. P. Dunford. Philadelphia: U of Pennsylvania P, 1990.

Britannica Encyclopedia of American Art. Ed. M. Rugoff. Chicago: Encyclopedia Britannica, 1973.

Contemporary Architects. 2nd ed. Chicago: St. James, 1987.

Contemporary Artists. 4th ed. New York: St. James, 1995.

Contemporary Designers. 2nd ed. Chicago: St. James, 1990.

Contemporary Photographers. 3rd ed. Detroit: Gale, 1995.

**Dictionary of Art.* 34 vols. Ed. J. Turner. New York: Grove's, 1996.
The definitive encyclopedia of the visual arts. Includes definitions and biographies as well as longer articles on geographical regions and forms of art. Also includes illustrations and bibliographies.

Dictionary of Contemporary American Artists. 6th ed. New York: St. Martin's, 1994.

Dictionary of Symbols in Western Art. New York: Facts on File, 1995.

Encyclopedia of Architecture: Design, Engineering, and Construction. Ed. S. A. Wilkes and R. T. Packard. 5 vols. New York: Wiley, 1988–1990.

**Encyclopedia of World Art.* 15 vols. New York: McGraw, 1959–1968. Supplements, 1983 and 1987.
An international, scholarly encyclopedia covering all aspects of art. Articles

are historical (e.g., baroque art), conceptual (e.g., biblical subjects), and geographic (e.g., Americas), so it's best to use the index volume to locate information on a particular subject or artist.

Fletcher, B. *A History of Architecture.* 18th ed. New York: Scribner's, 1975.
Lists vital information on every important building.

Focal Encyclopedia of Photography. 3rd ed. Ed. L. Stroebel and R. Zakia. Stoneham, MA: Focal P, 1993.

A Glossary of Art, Architecture, and Design Since 1945. 3rd ed. Ed. J. A. Walker. Boston: Hall, 1992.

A Guide to Art. Ed. S. Sproccati. Bergenfield, NJ: Abrams, 1992.

**Guide to the Literature of Art History.* Ed. E. Arntzen and R. Rainwater. Chicago: ALA, 1980.
A comprehensive listing of sources in art history worldwide. A section on general reference sources is followed by sections on individual arts (e.g., sculpture), which are organized by time period and by country. Has a subject index.

Hall, J. *Illustrated Dictionary of Symbols in Eastern and Western Art.* New York: IconEditions, 1994.

Historical Art Index A.D. 400–1650: People, Places, and Events Depicted. Jefferson City, NC: McFarland, 1989.

International Dictionary of Art and Artists. 2 vols. Ed. J. Vinson. Detroit, MI: St. James, 1990.

Mayer, R. *HarperCollins Dictionary of Art Terms and Techniques.* 2nd ed. New York: Harper Perennial, 1991.

Oxford Illustrated Encyclopedia of the Arts. New York: Oxford UP, 1990.

Pelican History of Art. 50 vols. Baltimore: Penguin, 1953–1989 and New Haven: Yale UP, 1990–present.

Print Index: A Guide to Reproductions. Comp. P. J. Parry and K. Chipman. Westport, CT: Greenwood, 1983.

Research Guide to the History of Western Art. Chicago: ALA, 1982.

Rosenfeld, L.B. et al. *Internet Compendium: Subject Guides to Humanities Resources.* New York: Neal-Schuman, 1995.

Who's Who in American Art. New York: Bowker, 1935–present. Annually.

Bibliographies to Art Books and Other Sources

Applied and Decorative Arts: A Bibliographic Guide. ed. D. L. Ehresmann.

3rd ed. Littleton, CO: Libraries Unlimited, 1993.

Arts in America: A Bibliography. Ed. B. Karpel. 4 vols. Washington, DC: Smithsonian, 1979–1980.

Bibliographic Guide to Art and Architecture. Boston: Hall, 1977–present (annually).

Fine Arts: A Bibliographic Guide. Ed. D. L. Ehresmann. 3rd ed. Littleton, CO: Libraries Unlimited, 1990.

Electronic Sources to Art Literature

ARCHITECTURE DATABASE (RILA)
ARTBIBLIOGRAPHIES MODERN
ART LITERATURE INTERNATIONAL (RILA)
ARTS & HUMANITIES SEARCH
EXPANDED ACADEMIC INDEX
WILSONDISC: ART INDEX

Indexes to Articles in Art Journals

ARTbibliographies Modern. Santa Barbara, CA: ABC Clio, 1969–present.

***Art Index.* New York: Bowker, 1929–present.
Indexes most art journals, such as American Art Journal, Art Bulletin, Artforum, Design, Sculpture Review, and many others.

RILA. Repetoire international de le littérature de l'art. Williamstown, MA: RILA, 1975–date.

Biological Sciences

Basic Sources and Guides to Biological Sciences Literature

Agriculture: Illustrated Search Strategy and Sources. Ann Arbor, MI: Pierian P. 1992.

Biolexicon: A Guide to the Language of Biology. Springfield, IL: Thomas, 1990.

Davis, E. B. and D. Schmidt. *Using the Biological Literature, A Practical Guide.* 2nd ed. New York: Dekker, 1995.

Encyclopedia of Bioethics. Rev. ed. 5 vols. New York: Macmillan, 1995.

Encyclopedia of Human Biology. 8 vols. Ed. R. Dulbecco. New York: Academic P, 1991.

Grzimek's Encyclopedia of Mammals. 2nd ed. 5 vols. New York: McGraw, 1996.

Henderson's Dictionary of Biological Terms. Ed. E. Lawrence. 11th ed. New York: Wiley, 1995.

***Information Sources in the Life Sciences.* Ed. H. V. Wyatt. 4th ed. London: Bowker-Saur, 1994.
Consists of in-depth bibliographic essays on the literature of biology. Includes chapters focusing on subspecialties such as microbiology.

Magill's Survey of Science: Life Science Series. Ed. F. Magill. 6 vols. Englewood Cliffs, NJ: Salem, 1991.

Rosenfeld, L.B. et al. *Internet Compendium: Subject Guides to Health and Science Resources.* New York: Neal-Schuman, 1995.

Bibliographies to Biological Sciences Books and Other Sources

Bibliography of Bioethics. 9 vols. Ed. L. Walters. Detroit: Gale, 1984.
Annual update volumes published since 1984 by Georgetown University Kennedy Institute.

Biological Abstracts. Philadelphia: Biological Abstracts, 1926–date.

Electronic Sources to Biological Sciences Literature

ACRICOLA
AGRIS INTERNATIONAL
AQUACULTURE
BIOSIS PREVIEWS
LIFE SCIENCES COLLECTION
SCISEARCH
WILSONDISC: BIOLOGICAL & AGRICULTURAL INDEX
ZOOLOGICAL RECORD

Indexes to Articles in Biological Sciences Journals

***Biological Abstracts.* Philadelphia: Biological Abstracts, 1926–present.
Indexes and gives brief descriptions of books and journal articles, especially to journals such as American Journal of Anatomy, *American Zoologist, Biochemistry, Journal of Animal Behavior, Quarterly Review of Biology, Social Biology,* and many others.

Biological and Agricultural Index. New York: Wilson, 1964–date.

General Science Index. New York: Wilson, 1978–present.

Business

See also Economics, page 339.

Basic Sources and Guides to Business Literature

Business Information Desk Reference. New York: Macmillan, 1991.

***Business Information Sources.* Ed. L. M. Daniells. 3rd ed. Berkeley: U of California p, 1993.

A selective guide to business sources, arranged by subject area (e.g., insurance). Within each subject area are listed several recommended reference sources by type (e.g., handbooks).

Businesss Rankings Annual. Detroit: Gale, 1994–present. Annually.

Dictionary for Business and Finance. 2nd ed. Fayetteville: U of Arkansas P, 1990.

Dictionary of Business and Management. New York: Wiley, 1992.

Encyclopedia of American Industries. Vol. 1: Manufacturing; Vol. 2: Service & Non-Manufacturing. Detroit: Gale, 1994.

Encyclopedia of American Business History and Biography. 9 vols. Ed. W. H. Baker. New York: Facts on File, 1987–1994.

Encyclopedia of Banking and Finance. 10th ed. New York: Irwin, 1993.

Encyclopedia of Business. Ed. J. G. Mauer et al. Detroit: Gale, 1996.

Encyclopedia of Business Information Sources. 11th ed. Ed. J. Woy. Detroit, MI: Gale, 1996.

The History of Accounting: An International Encyclopedia. New York: Garland, 1996.

Hoover's Handbook of American Business. Austin, TX: Reference P. Annually.

International Bibliography of Business History. New York: Routledge, 1997.

International Directory of Company Histories. Detroit, MI: St. James, 1990–present (in progress).

Irwin Business and Investment Almanac. New York: Irwin. 1977–Annually.

Maier, E. L. and H. W. Johnson. *The Business Library and How to Use It: A Guide to Sources and Research Strategies for Information on Business and Management* Detroit: Omnigraphics, 1996.

Pagell, R. A. and M. Halperin. *International Business Information: How to Find It, How to Use It.* Phoenix, AZ: Oryx, 1994.

Portable MBA Desk Reference. New York: Wiley, 1993.

Prentice Hall Encyclopedic Dictionary of Business Terms. Englewood Cliffs, NJ: Prentice Hall, 1995.

Rosenfeld, L.B. et al. *Internet Compendium: Subject Guides to Social Sciences, Business, and Law Resources.* New York: Neal-Schuman, 1995.

Small Business Sourcebook. 10th ed. Detroit, MI: Gale, 1996.

Thunderbird Guide to International Business Resources on the World Wide Web. New York: Wiley, 1997.

World Market Share Reporter. Detroit: Gale, 1995.

Bibliographies to Business Books and Other Sources

Bibliographic Guide to Business and Economics. 3 vols. Boston: Hall, 1975–present. Annually.

Business Publications Index and Abstracts. Detroit: Gale, 1983–present. Annually.

Core Collection. Cambridge, MA: Harvard UP, 1971–present. Annually.

Electronic Sources to Business Literature

ABI/INFORM
AGRIBUSINESS U.S.A.
CENDATA
D&B DUN's FINANCIAL RECORDS
D&B ELECTRONIC YELLOW PAGES
DISCLOSURE
ECONOMIC LITERATURE INDEX
EXPANDED ACADEMIC INDEX
EXPANDED BUSINESS INDEX
FINIS (Financial Industry National Information Service)
LABORLAW
MANAGEMENT CONTENTS
MOODY's CORPORATE NEWS
PTS F&S INDEXES
PTS PROMPT
STANDARD & POOR's NEWS
TRADE AND INDUSTRY INDEX
WILSONDISC: BUSINESSS PERIODICALS INDEX

Indexes to Articles in Business Journals

**Accountants' Index* (1921–1991) and *Accounting and Tax Index* (1992–present). New York: AICPA. Indexes accounting and tax subjects in journals such as *Accountants' Digest, Accounting Review, Banker's Magazine, CA Magazine, Journal of Finance, Tax Adviser,* and many others.

**Business Periodicals Index.* New York: Wilson, 1958–date. Indexes journals such as *Business Quarterly, Business Week, Fortune, Journal of Business, Journal of Marketing, Personnel Journal,* and many others.

Personnel Literature. Washington, DC: OPM Library, 1942–present.

The Wall Street Journal Index. New York: Dow Jones, 1958–present.

Chemistry and Chemical Engineering

Basic Sources and Guides to Chemistry and Chemical Engineering Literature

ACS Style Guide: A Manual for Authors & Editors. Ed. J. S. Dodd. Washington, DC: ACS, 1985.

Chemical Engineers' Handbook. 6th ed. New York: McGraw, 1984.

CRC Handbook of Chemistry and Physics. Boca Raton, FL: CRC. Annually.

Encyclopedia of Chemical Technology. 4th ed. 27 vols. Ed. J. I. Kroschwitz and M. Howe-Grant New York: Wiley, 1991–present (in progress).

Hawley's Condensed Chemical Dictionary. 13th ed. New York: Reinhold, 1996.

***How to Find Chemical Information: A Guide for Practicing Chemists, Teachers, and Students.* Ed. R. E. Maizell. 2nd ed. New York: Wiley, 1987.
A detailed overview of selected sources in chemistry. Good explanations of how to use major sources (e.g., Chemical Abstracts). Also covers online searching and patents.

Information Sources in Science and Technology. 2nd ed. Englewood, CO: Libraries Unlimited, 1994.

Lange's Handbook of Chemistry. 14th ed. Ed. J. A. Dean. New York: McGraw, 1992.

Macmillan Encyclopedia of Chemistry. 4 vols. Ed. J J. Lagowski. New York: Macmillan, 1997.

Noether, D. *Encyclopedic Dictionary of Chemical Technology.* New York: VCH, 1993.

Riegel's Handbook of Industrial Chemistry. 9th ed. New York: Reinhold, 1992.

Ridley, D. D. *Online Searching: A Scientist's Perspective, A Guide for the Chemical and Life Sciences.* New York: Wiley, 1996.

Rosenfeld, L.B. et al. *Internet Compendium: Subject Guides to Health and Science Resources.* New York: Neal-Schuman, 1995.

Bibliographies to Chemistry and Chemical Engineering Books and Other Sources

Chemical Abstracts. Easton, PA: ACS, 1907–present. Weekly.

Chemical Titles. Easton, PA: ACS, 1960. Bi-weekly.

Selected Titles in Chemistry. 4th ed. Washington, DC: ACS, 1977.

Electronic Sources to Chemistry and Chemical Engineering Literature

BEILSTEIN ONLINE
CA SEARCH
CHEMICAL INDUSTRY NOTES
CHEMNAME
CHEMSIS
Claims/U.S. PATENTS ABSTRACTS
COMPENDEX
HEILBRON
INSPEC
NTIS
SCISEARCH
WILSONDISC: GENERAL SCIENCE INDEX

Indexes to Articles in Chemistry and Chemical Engineering Journals

***Chemical Abstracts: Key to the World's Chemical Literature.* Easton, PA: American Chemical Society, 1907–present. Weekly.
Indexes such journals as *Applied Chemical News, American Chemical Society Journal, Chemical Bulletin, Chemist, Journal of the Chemical Society,* and many more. Provides a good abstract even if your library does not house the journal.

General Science Index. New York: Wilson, 1978–present.

Computer Science

Basic Sources and Guides to Computer Science Literature

Computer Glossary. 6th ed. New York: AMACOM, 1993.

Dictionary of Computing. 3rd ed. New York: Oxford, UP 1990.

Encyclopedia of Computer Science. 4th ed. New York: VNR, 1997

Encyclopedia of Computer Science and Technology. Ed. J. Belzer. 22 vols. New York: Dekker, 1975–1991. And supplements 1991–present.

IBM Dictionary of Computing. Ed. G. McDaniel. New York: McGraw, 1994.

Macmillan Encyclopedia of Computers. 2 vols. Ed. G. G. Biter. New York: Macmillan, 1992.

Software Encyclopedia 1996: A Guide for Personal, Professional, and Business

Users. 2 vols. New Providence, NJ: Bowker, 1996

Bibliographies to Computer Science Books and Other Sources

ACM Guide to Computing Literature. 1978–present. Annually.

Bibliographic Guide to the History of Computing, Computers, and the Information Processing Industry. Westport, CT: Greenwood, 1990.

Computer-Readable Bibliographic Data Bases: A Directory and Data Sourcebook. Washington, DC: ASIS, 1976–present.

Electronic Sources to Computer Science Literature

BUSINESS SOFTWARE DATABASE
COMPENDEX PLUS
COMPUTER DATABASE
COMPUTER-READABLE DATABASES
INSPEC
MICROCOMPUTER INDEX
WILSONDISC: APPLIED SCIENCE AND TECHNOLOGY

Indexes to Articles in Computer Science Journals

**Applied Science and Technology Index.* New York: Wilson, 1958–date. Indexes articles in *Byte, Computer Design, Computers in Industry, The Computer Journal, Computer Methods, Computer, Data Processing,* and *Microcomputing.*

Computer Abstracts. West Yorks, UK: Technical Information, 1957–date.

Computer Literature Index. Phoenix, AZ: ACR, 1971–present.

Microcomputer Index (1980–94) and *Microcomputer Abstracts* (1994–present). Medford, NJ: Information Today.

Ecology

Basic Sources and Guides to Ecology Literature

Atlas of United States Environmental Issues. New York: Macmillan, 1991.

Conservation and Environmentalism, An Encyclopedia. New York: Garland, 1995.

Cooper's Comprehensive Environmental Desk Reference. New York: VNR, 1996.

Encyclopedia of Environmental Biology. 3 vols. San Diego: Academic Press, 1995.

Energy Information Guide. Ed. D. R. Weber. Rev. ed. 3 vols. San Carlos, CA: Energy Info P, 1994.

Environment and the Law: A Dictionary. Santa Barbara, CA: ABC-Clio, 1995.

Environment Information Access. New York: EIC, 1971–present.

The Green Encyclopedia. New York: Prentice-Hall, 1992.

The Last Rain Forest: A World Conservation Atlas. New York: Oxford UP, 1990.

Recycling in America: A Reference Handbook. Santa Barbara, CA: ABC-Clio, 1992.

Rosenfeld, L. B. et al. *Internet Compendium: Subject Guides to Health and Science Resources.* New York: Neat-Schuman, 1995.

Toxics A to Z: A Guide to Everyday Pollution Hazards. Berkeley: U of California P, 1991.

***World Resources.* Oxford: Oxford UP, 1986–present. Annually. Contains chapters on conditions and trends in the environment worldwide (e.g., energy). Also provides statistical tables (e.g., Net Additions to the Greenhouse Heating Effect).

Bibliographies to Ecology Books and Other Sources

Environment Abstracts. New York: EIC, 1971–present.

Pollution Abstracts. Washington, DC: Cambridge Scientific Abstracts, 1970–present.

Selected Water Resources Abstracts. Springfield, VA: NTIS, 1968–present.

Electronic Sources to Ecology Literature

BIOSIS PREVIEWS
COMPENDEX
ENVIRONLINE
ENVIRONMENTAL BIBLIOGRAPHY
EXPANDED ACADEMIC INDEX
GEOBASE
POLLUTION ABSTRACTS
TOXLINE
WATER RESOURCES ABSTRACTS
WILSONDISC: APPLIED SCIENCE AND TECHNOLOGY
WILSONDISC: BIOLOGICAL AND AGRICULTURAL INDEXES

Indexes to Articles in Ecology Journals

**Biological Abstracts.* Philadelphia: Biological Abstracts, 1926–present.

Indexes articles on environmental issues in journals such as *American Forests. The Conservationist, Sierra, Ambio, Ecology,* and others.

**Biological and Agricultural Index. New York: Wilson, 1964–present.
Includes coverage of *Ecology, Environmental Pollution,* and *Journal of Environmental Biology,* as well as others.

Ecological Abstracts. Norwich, UK: Geo Abstracts, 1974–present.

Environment Abstracts Annual. New York: Bowker, 1970–present.

The Environmental Index. Ann Arbor, MI: UMI, 1992–present.

General Science Index. New York: Wilson, 1978–present.

Economics

See also Business, page 335.

Basic Sources and Guides to Economics Literature

Basic Statistics of the European Communities. New York: Unipub. Annually.

Bibliographic Guide to Business and Economics. Boston: Hall, annually.

Emory, C. W., and D. R. Cooper. *Business Research Methods.* 5th ed. Homewood, IL: Irwin, 1994.

**Information Sources in Economics. Ed. J. Fletcher. 2nd ed. London: Saur, 1984. Covers research sources by type (e.g., databases) and also by subject areas (e.g., macroeconomics). Describes and evaluates the sources listed.

McGraw-Hill Encyclopedia of Economics. 2nd ed. New York: McGraw Hill, 1994.

**The New Palgrave: A Dictionary of Economics. Ed. J. Fletcher. 3 vols. New York: Stockton, 1992.
A scholarly, thoroughly documented work that covers all aspects of economic theory and thought. The bibliographies following each article are very helpful.

Rosenfeld, L. B. et al. *Internet Compendium: Subject Guides to Social Sciences, Business, and Law Resources.* New York: Neal-Schuman, 1995.

Rutherford, D. *Dictionary of Economics.* New York: Routledge, 1992.

Survey of Social Science: Economics Series. 5 vols. Ed. F. Magill. Englewood Cliffs, NJ: Salem, 1991.

Who's Who in Finance and Industry. New Providence, NJ: Marquis. Biennially.

Bibliographies to Economics Books and Other Sources

Bibliographic Guide to Business and Economics. Boston: Hall, 1975–present. Annually.

Brealey, R., and H. Edwards. *A Bibliography of Finance.* Cambridge, MA: MIT, 1991.

Business and Economics Book Guide. 2 vols. Boston: Hall, 1974. Supplements.

Business and Economics Books, 1876–1983. 5 vols. New Providence, NJ: Bowker, 1985.

Economics Books. Clifton, NJ: Kelley, 1974–present. Annually.

Electronic Sources to Economics Literature

ECONBASE: TIME SERIES AND FORECASTS

ECONOMIC LITERATURE INDEX

EXPANDED ACADEMIC INDEX

EXPANDED BUSINESS INDEX

FOREIGN TRADE AND ECONOMIC ABSTRACTS

PTS INTERNATIONAL FORECASTS

PTS U.S. FORECASTS

Indexes to Articles in Economics Journals

Index of Economic Articles. Homewood, IL: Irwin, 1961–present.

**Journal of Economic Literature. Nashville, TN: American Economics Assn., 1964–present.
Indexes such journals as *American Economist, Applied Economics, Business Economics,* and many more.

The Wall Street Journal Index. New York: Dow Jones, 1958–present.

Education

Basic Sources and Guides to Education Literature

American Educators' Encyclopedia. Westport, CT: Greenwood, 1991.

Education: A Guide to Reference and Information Sources. Englewood, CO: Libraries Unlimited, 1989.

Educator's Desk Reference. New York: Macmillan, 1989.

Encyclopedia of American Education. 3 vols. Ed. H. G. Unger. New York: Facts on File, 1996.

Encyclopedia of Early Childhood Education. Ed. L. R. Williams et al. New York: Garland, 1992.

The Encyclopedia of Education. Ed. L. C. Deighton. 10 vols. New York: Macmillan, 1971.

Encyclopedia of Educational Research. Ed. M. C. Alkin. 6th ed. 4 vols. New York: Free P, 1992.

Handbook of Research on Teaching. Ed. M. C. Wittrock. 3rd ed. New York: Macmillan, 1986.

Handbook of World Education. Houston, TX: American Collegiate Service, 1991.

International Encyclopedia of Education. 2nd ed. Ed. T. Husen and T. N. Postlethwaite. 12 vols. Elmsford, NY: Pergamon, 1994. Supplements 1988 and 1990.

International Yearbook of Education. Paris: UNESCO, 1948–present.

Miller, E. B. *The Internet Directory for K-2 Teachers and Librarians.* Englewood, CO: Libraries Unlimited, 1997.

Multicultural Education: A Source Book. New York: Garland, 1989.

The Philosophy of Education, An Encyclopedia. New York: Garland, 1996.

Place, R. et al. *Educator's Internet Yellow Pages.* Upper Saddle River, NJ: Prentice Hall, 1996.

World Education Encyclopedia. 3 vols.. New York: Facts on File, 1988.

Bibliographies to Education Books and Other Sources

Bibliographic Guide to Education. Boston: Hall, 1978–date.

Bibliographic Guide to Educational Research. Ed. D. M. Berry. 3rd ed. Metuchen, NJ: Scarecrow, 1990.

Resources in Education (formerly *Research in Education*). Washington, DC: ERIC, 1956–present.

Subject Bibliography of the History of American Higher Education. Westport, CT: Greenwood, 1984.

Electronic Sources to Education Literature

A-V ONLINE (nonprint educational materials)

ERIC

EXCEPTIONAL CHILD EDUCATION RESOURCES

EXPANDED ACADEMIC INDEX

WILSONDISC: EDUCATION INDEX

Indexes to Articles in Education Journals

Current Index to Journals in Education. Phoenix, AZ: Oryx, 1969–present.

***Education Index.* New York: Wilson, 1929–date.

Indexes articles in such journals as *Childhood Education, Comparative Education, Education Digest, Educational Forum,* and many more.

Exceptional Child Education Resources. Reston, VA: CEC, 1968–present.

State Education Journal Index. Westminster, CO: SEJI, 1963–present.

Electronics

Basic Sources and Guides to Electronics Literature

Advances in Electronics and Electron Physics. New York: Academic P, 1948–present (continuous).

Buchsbaum's Complete Handbook of Practical Electronics Reference Data. 2nd ed. Englewood Cliffs, NJ: Prentice-Hall, 1987.

Dictionary of Electronics. Ed. S. W. Amos and S. R. Amos. 3rd ed. Woburn, MA: Butterworth, 1996.

Electronics Style Manual. Ed. J. Markus. New York: McGraw, 1978.

Encyclopedia of Computer Science and Technology. Ed. J. Belzer. 21 vols. New York: Dekker, 1975–1989, and supps. to date.

Encyclopedia of Electronics. 2nd ed. Ed. E. S. Gibilisco and N. Sclater. Blue Ridge Summit, PA: TAB Books, 1990.

Information Sources in Engineering. Ed. K.W. Mildren and P.J. Hicks. New Providence, NJ: Bowker-Saur, 1996.

International Encyclopedia of Robotics: Applications and Automation. 3 vols. New York: Wiley, 1988.

Rosenfeld, L. B. et al. *Internet Compendium: Subject Guides to Health and Science Resources.* New York: Neal-Schuman, 1995.

Scientific and Technical Information Sources. Ed. C. Chen. 2nd ed. Boston: MIT P, 1987.

Bibliographies to Electronics Books and Other Sources

Bibliography of the History of Electronics. Ed. G. Shiers. Metuchen, NJ: Scarecrow, 1972.

Electronics: A Bibliographical Guide. Ed. C. K. Moore and K. J. Spencer. 3 vols. New York: Plenum, 1961–1973.

Electronic Sources to Electronics Literature
COMPENDEX
INSPEC
SCISEARCH
SUPERTECH
WILSONDISC: APPLIED SCIENCE AND
TECHNOLOGY

Indexes to Articles in Electronics Journals
**Applied Science and Technology Index.*
New York: Wilson, 1958–date.
Indexes electronics articles in journals
such as *Electrial Communication, Electrical Engineer, Electrical Review,* and
many more.
Engineering Index. New York: Engineering
Information, 1906–present.

Ethnic Studies

Basic Sources and Guides to Ethnic Studies Literature
Dictionary of American Immigration History. Ed. F. Cordasco. Metuchen, NJ:
Scarecrow, 1990.
Encyclopedia of Multiculturalism. 6 vols.
Ed. S. Auerbach. New York: Marshall
Cavendish, 1994.
Ethnic Periodicals in Contemporary America: An Annotated Guide. Ed. S. Ireland.
Westport, CT: Greenwood, 1990.
Gale Encyclopedia of Multicultural America. 2 vols. Ed. J. Galens et al. Detroit:
Gale, 1995.
Guide to Multicultural Resources, 1995/1996. Ed. A. Boyd. Ft. Atkinson,
WI: Highsmith, 1995.
Kinloch, G. *Race and Ethnic Relations: An Annotated Bibliography.* New York:
Garland, 1984.
Minority Organizations: A National Directory. 4th ed. Garrett Park, MD: Garrett
Park P, 1992.
Multiculturalism in the United States: A Comparative Guide. Westport, CT:
Greenwood, 1992.
Racism in Contemporary America. Ed. M.
Weinberg. Westport, CT: Greenwood,
1996.
Rosenfeld, L. B. et al. *Internet Compendium: Subject Guides to Humanities Resources.* New York: Neal-Schuman,
1995.
_____. *Internet Compendium: Subject Guides to Social Sciences, Business,*

and Law Resources. New York: Neal-Schuman, 1995.
Stevens, G. I. *videos for Understanding Diversity: A Core Selection and Evaluative Guide.* Chicago: ALA,
1993.
Voices of Multicultural America, Notable Speeches Delivered by African, Asian, Hispanic, and Native Americans. Ed.
D. G. Straub. Detroit: Gale, 1996.

Guides and Bibliographies to Native American Studies
Chronology of Native North American History From Pre-Columbian Times to the Present. Ed. D. Champagne. Detroit:
Gale, 1994.
Dictionary of Native American Literature.
Ed. A. Wiget. New York: Garland, 1994.
**Guide to Research on North American Indians.* Ed. A. Hirschfelder. Chicago:
ALA, 1983.
Lists basic sources of information for
researching Native Americans. Chapters
cover a variety of aspects, including
history, economics, society, religion,
the arts, and literature.
Handbook of North American Indians. 20
vols. Washington, DC: Smithsonian,
1978–present (in progress).
Indians of North America: Methods and Sources for Library Research. New
Haven, CT: Library Professional Pubs.,
1983.
Native American Issues: A Reference Handbook. Santa Barbara, CA: ABC-Clio,
1996.
Native American Women: A Biographical Dictionary. Ed. G. Bataille. New York:
Garland, 1993.
Native Americans: An Annotated Bibliography. Englewood Cliffs, NJ: Salem,
1991.
Notable Native Americans. Detroit: Gale,
1995.
Peck, D. R. *American Ethnic Literatures: Native American, African American, Chicano/Latino, and Asian American Writers and Their Backgrounds, An Annotated Bibliography.* Englewood
Cliffs, NJ: Salem, 1992.
Reference Encyclopedia of the American Indian. Ed. B. Klein. 7th ed. West Nyack, NY: Todd, 1995.
Ruoff, L. *American Indian Literatures: An Introduction, Bibliographic Review, and Selected Bibliography.* New York:
MLA, 1990.

Statistical Record of Native North Americans. 2nd ed. Ed. M. A. Reddy. Detroit, MI: Gale, 1995.

White, P. M. *American Indian Studies: A Bibliographic Guide.* Englewood, CO: Libraries Unlimited, 1995.

Guides to Asian-American Studies

Asian American Encyclopedia. 6 vols. Ed. F. Ng. New York: Marshall Cavendish, 1995

**Asian American Studies.* Ed. H. Kim. Westport, CT: Greenwood, 1989.
A bibliography of books and articles about Asian Americans. Includes historical and cultural and sociological studies as well.

Cheung, K. *Asian American Literature.* New York: MLA, 1988.

Japanese-American History: An A to Z Reference from 1868 to the Present. Ed. B. Niiya. New York: Facts on File, 1993.

Melendy, H. B. *Asians in America: Filipinos, Koreans, and East Indians.* New York: Hippocrene, 1981.

Montero, D. *Vietnamese Americans: Patterns of Resettlement and Socioeconomic Adaptation in the United States.* Boulder, CO: Westview, 1979.

Notable Asian Americans. Detroit: Gale, 1995.

Statistical Record of Asian Americans. Detroit, MI: Gale, 1993.

Wilson, R. A., and B. Hosokawa. *East to America: A History of the Japanese in the United States.* New York: Quill, 1980.

Guides and Bibliographies to African-American Studies

See also African-American Literature, page 352.

The African American Almanac. 7th ed. Detroit, MI: Gale, 1997.

African American Biographies: Profiles of 558 Current Men and Women. Jefferson, NC: McFarland, 1992; vol. 2, 1994.

**African American Encyclopedia.* 6 vols. North Bellmore, NY: Marshall Cavendish, 1993. And supp. 1997.
A thorough alphabetic listing of Afro-American issues, personalities, and events.

**Afro-American Reference.* Ed. N. Davis. Westport, CT: Greenwood, 1985.
A selective listing of sources on all aspects of the Afro-American experience. Lists other reference sources as well as

recommends individual books on particular subjects (e.g., Afro-Americans in motion pictures).

The African American Resource Guide to the Internet and Online Services. New York: McGraw Hill, 1996.

Bibliographic Guide to Black Studies. Boston: Hall, 1975–present.

Black Women in America: An Historical Encyclopedia. 2 vols. Ed. D. C. Hine. Brooklyn, NY: Carlson, 1993.

Blacks in the Humanities, 1750–1984. Ed. D. F. Joyce. Westport, CT: Greenwood, 1986.

Blacks in Science and Medicine. Ed. V. O. Sammons. New York: Hemisphere, 1989.

Contemporary Black Biography. Ed. M. L. LaBlanc. Detroit, MI: Gale, 1992–present (in progress).

Contributions of Black Women to America. 2 vols. Ed. M. W. Davis. Columbia, SC: Kenday, 1982.

Dictionary of American Negro Biography. Ed. R. W. Logan and M. R. Winton. New York: Norton, 1982.

Distinguished African American Scientists of the 20th Century. Phoenix, AZ: Oryx, 1996.

Encyclopedia of African American Culture and History. 5 vols. New York: Macmillan, 1996.

Encyclopedia of African-American Education. Westport, CT: Greenwood, 1996.

Encyclopedia of African-American Civil Rights. Westport, CT: Greenwood, 1992.

Encyclopedia of Black America. Ed. W. A. Low. New York: McGraw, 1981.

**Glover, D. M. *Voices of the Spirit: Sources for Interpreting the African American Experience.* Chicago. ALA, 1994.
A good starting point for the beginning researcher. Glover points you in the right direction for a multitude of scholarly projects.

Index to Periodical Articles by and About Blacks. Boston: Hall, 1973–present. Annually.

The Kaiser Index to Black Resources, 1948–1986. 5 vols. Brooklyn, NY: Carlson, 1992.

Notable Black American Women. Ed. J. C. Smith. Detroit, MI: Gale, 1992. And book 2, 1996.

Statistical Record of Black America. 4th ed. Detroit: Gale, 1996.

Who's Who Among Black Americans. Northbrook, IL: WWABA, 1976–present.

*Guides and Bibliographies
to Hispanic-American Studies*

Chicano Literature: A Reference Guide. Ed.
J. A. Martinez and F. A. Lomeli. Westport, CT: Greenwood, 1985.

Handbook of Hispanic Cultures in the U.S.
Houston, TX: Arte Publico, 1993.

Hispanic-American Almanac. 2nd ed. Ed.
N. Kanellos. Detroit, MI: Gale, 1996.

Hispanic American Periodicals Index. Los
Angeles: UCLA Latin American Center,
1974–present.

*Hispanic Americans Information Directo-
ry.* 3rd ed. Detroit, MI: Gale, 1993.

The Hispanic Presence in North America.
New York: Facts on File, 1991.

*Hispanics in the United States: A New So-
cial Agenda.* Ed. P. S. J. Cafferty and W.
McCready. New Brunswick, NJ: Trans-
action, 1984.

Kanellos, N. *Chronicle of Hispanic-American History from Pre-Columbian Times
to the Present.* Detroit: Gale, 1995.

Latino Encyclopedia. 6 vols. New York:
Marshall Cavendish, 1996.

Literature Chicana. Comp R. G. Trujillo.
Encino, CA: Floricanto P, 1985.

Masterpieces of Latino Literature. New
York: HarperCollins, 1994.

Notable Hispanic American Women. Ed. D.
Telgen and J. Kamp. Detroit, MI: Gale,
1993.

*Notable Latino Americans, A Biographical
Dictionary.* Ed. M.S. Meier et al. Westport, CT: Greenwood, 1997.

***Sourcebook of Hispanic Culture in the
United States.* Chicago: ALA, 1982.
Essays surveying Mexican-American,
Puerto Rican-American, Cuban-Ameri-
can, and Hispanic-American literature,
education, sociolinguistics, and music.
Each essay concludes with lengthy,
evaluative bibliographies of recommended books and periodical articles,
many in English.

*Spanish-American Women Writers: A Bibli-
ographical Research Checklist.* Ed. L. E.
R. Cortina. New York: Garland, 1982.

Statistical Record of Hispanic Americans.
2nd ed. Ed. M. A. Reddy. Detroit, MI:
Gale, 1995.

Who's Who Among Hispanic Americans.
3rd ed. Detroit, MI: Gale, 1994.

Zimmerman, M. *U. S. Latino Literature: An
Essay and Annotated Bibliography.*
Chicago: March Abrazo, 1992.

*Electronic Sources to Ethnic Studies
Literature*

AMERICA: HISTORY AND LIFE
EXPANDED ACADEMIC INDEX
POPULATION BIBLIOGRAPHY
SOCIAL SCISEARCH
SOCIOLOGICAL ABSTRACTS
WILSONDISC: SOCIAL SCIENCES AND
    HUMANITIES INDEXES

*Indexes to Articles in Ethnic Studies
Journals*

MLA International Bibliography. New
York: MLA, 1921–present.

Sage Race Relations Abstracts. London and
Beverly Hills, CA: 1976–present.

***Social Sciences Index.* New York: Wilson,
1974–present.
Indexes articles on many minority topics in journals such as *American Journal of Physical Anthropology, Aztlan,
Black Scholar, Ethnic Groups, Ethnic
and Racial Studies,* and others.

Sociological Abstracts. La Jolla, CA: Sociological Abstracts, 1952–present.

Foreign Language Studies

*Basic Sources and Guide to Foreign
Language Studies Literature*

French

Coleman, K. *Guide to French Poetry Explication.* Boston: Hall, 1993.

Critical Bibliography of French Literature.
Syracuse, NY: Syracuse UP, 1947–1985
(in progress).

*Dictionnaire Étymologique de la langue
française.* 10th ed. New York: French
and European, 1994.

***French Language and Literature: An Annotated Bibliography.* Ed. F. Bassan et
al. 2nd ed. New York: Garland, 1989.
A listing of reference books, periodicals, and other books to consult when
researching French. Includes historical
and cultural aspects of French language
and literature in France and other
French-speaking countries.

*French Twenty Bibliography: Critical and
Biographical References for the Study of
French Literature Since 1885.* Ed. D. W.
Alden. New York: French Institute,
1969–present. Annually.

Grand larousse encyclopedique. 12 vols.
Elmsford, NY: Maxwell, 1964. Supplements.

Larousse Dictionnaire Général. Paris: Larousse, 1993.

Levi, *A. Guide to French Literature. Volume 1:1789 to the Present; Volume 2: Beginnings to 1789.* Detroit, MI: St. James, 1992 and 1994.

New History of French Literature. 2 vols. Cambridge: Harvard UP, 1989.

New Oxford Companion to Literature in French. New York: Oxford, 1995.

German

Collins German-English, English-German Dictionary, Unabridged. 2nd ed. New York: HarperCollins, 1993.

Der Grosse Duden. Ed. R. Duden. 10 vols. New York: Adler's, 1971.

Deutsches Woerterbuch. Ed. J. Grimm and W. Grimm. 32 vols. New York: Adler's, 1973.

Duden Worterbuch. 8 vols. Maspeth, New York: Langenscheidt, 1996.

The Friendly German-English Dictionary: A Guide to German Language, Culture and Society through Faux Amis, Literary Illustration and Other Diversions. London: Libris, 1996.

***Introduction to Library Research in German Studies.* Ed. L. Richardson. Boulder, CO: Westview, 1984.
A listing of reference sources for research on German language, literature, art, and civilization (history, folklore, philosophy and religion, music, and cinema). Includes descriptive and evaluative comments.

Oxford Companion to German Literature. Ed. H. Garland. 2nd ed. New York: Oxford UP, 1986.

Wer Ist Wer. 20th ed. New York: IPS, 1973. Supplements.

Latin

Jenkins, F. *Classical Studies, A Guide to the Reference Literature.* Englewood, CO: Libraries Unlimited, 1996.

***Ancient Writers: Greece and Rome.* Ed. T. J. Luce. 2 vols. New York: Scribner's, 1982.
Detailed information on 47 classical authors and their works. Each article is followed by a selective listing of recommended reading.

Cambridge History of Classical Literature. New York: Cambridge UP, 1982–present (in progress).

Classical Greek and Roman Drama, An Annotated Bibliography. Englewood Cliffs, NJ: Salem, 1989.

Jenkins, F. *Classical Studies, A Guide to the Reference Literature.* Englewood, CO: Libraries Unlimited, 1996.

Oxford Companion to Classical Literature. 2nd ed. Ed. M. C. Howatson. New York: Oxford UP, 1989.

Oxford Latin Dictionary. Ed. P. G. Glare. New York: Oxford UP, 1982.

Wagenvoort, H. *Studies in Roman Literature, Culture and Religion.* New York: Garland, 1978.

Russian

Bibliography of Russian Literature in English Translation to 1945. Ed. M. B. Line. 1963; rpt. Totowa, NJ: Rowman, 1972.

Corten, I. H. *Vocabulary of Soviet Society & Culture: A Selected Guide to Russian Words, Idioms, and Expressions of the Post-Stalin Era, 1953–1991.* Durham, NC: Duke UP, 1992.

Dictionary of Russian Literature Since 1917. New York: Columbia UP, 1988.

Elsevier's Dictionary of Science and Technology: Russian-English. Comp. G. Chakalov. New York: Elsevier, 1993.

Elsevier's Russian English Dictionary. 4 vols. New York: Elsevier, 1990.

Guide to Bibliographies of Russian Literature. Ed. S. A. Zenkovsky and D. L. Armbruster. Nashville, TN: Vanderbilt UP, 1970.

Guide to Russian Reference Books. Ed. K. Maichel. 5 vols. Stanford, CA: Hoover, 1962–1967.

***Introduction to Russian Language and Literature.* Ed. R. Auty and D. Obolensky. New York: Cambridge UP, 1977.
A survey of the history of Russian, with chapters on linguistics, printing, prose, poetry, and theater.

Modern Encyclopedia of Russian and Soviet Literature. Gulf Breeze, FL: Academic International, 1971–present (in progress).

Russia, the USSR, and Eastern Europe: A Bibliographic Guide to English Language Publications, 1975–1980. Littleton, CO: Libraries Unlimited, 1982. Supplements, 1981–1985, 1987.

Who Was Who in the U.S.S.R. Metuchen, NJ: Scarecrow, 1972.

Spanish

Encyclopedia of Latin American Literature. NY: Fitzroy Dearborn, 1997.

Bibliography of Old Spanish Texts. 3rd ed. Ed. A. Cardenas et al. Madison, WI: Hispanic Seminary, 1984.

Biographical Dictionary of Hispanic Literature in the United States. Westport, CT: Greenwood, 1989.

**Bleznick, D. W. A *Sourcebook for Hispanic Literature and Language.* 3rd ed. Metuchen, NJ: Scarecrow, 1995.
Lists a selection of reference sources and other recommended reading on the literatures of Spain and Spanish America. Includes some sources written in English.

Chandler, R. E., and K. Schwartz. *New History of Spanish Literature.* Baton Rouge, LA: LSU, 1991.

Collins Spanish-English, English-Spanish Dictionary. 3rd ed. New York: Harper-Collins, 1992.

Contemporary Spanish American Poets. A Bibliography of Primary and Secondary Sources. Ed. J. Sefami. Westport, CT: Greenwood, 1992.

Encyclopedia of Latin American Literature. NY: Fitzroy Dearborn, 1997.

Flores, A. *Spanish American Authors, The Twentieth Century.* New York: Wilson, 1992.

Handbook of Latin American Literature. 2nd ed. Comp. D. W. Foster. New York: Garland, 1992.

Handbook of Latin American Studies. Gainesville: UP of Florida, 1935–date.

Historia de la literature espanola y hispanoamerica. Spain: Aguilar, 1983.

The Latin American Short Story: An Annotated Guide to Anthologies and Criticism. Ed. D. Balderston. Westport, CT: Greenwood, 1992.

Latin American Writers. Ed. C. A. Solé. 3 vols. New York: Scribner's, 1989.

Modern Spanish and Portuguese Literatures. Ed. M. J. Schneider and I. Stern. New York: Ungar, 1988.

Oxford Companion to Spanish Literature. Ed. F. Ward. Oxford: Clarendon, 1978.

Spanish American Women Writers. Ed. D. Marting. Westport, CT: Greenwood, 1990.

Spanish and Spanish-American Literature: An Annotated Guide to Selected Bibliographies. Ed. H. C. Woodbridge. New York: MLA, 1983.

Electronic Sources to Foreign Language Studies Literature

ARTS AND HUMANITIES SEARCH
EXPANDED ACADEMIC INDEX
LLBA (Linguistics and Language Behavior Abstracts)
MLA BIBLIOGRAPHY

WILSONDISC: HUMANITIES INDEX

Indexes to Articles in Foreign Language Studies Journals

Humanities Index. New York: Wilson, 1974–present.

***MLA International Bibliography.* New York: MLA, 1921–present.
Indexes articles in journals such as *Yale French Studies, German Quarterly, Philological Quarterly, Journal of Spanish Studies,* and many others.

Geography

Basic Sources and Guides to Geography Literature

America's Top-Rated Cities, 1996. 4 th ed. Boca Raton, FL: Universal Reference, 1996.

America's Top-Rated Smaller Cities, 1996–97. 2nd ed. Boca Raton, FL: Universal Reference, 1996.

Dictionary of Global Culture. New York: Knopf, 1997

Encyclopedia of Climate and Weather. 2 vols. Ed. S. H. Schneider. New York: Oxford, 1996.

Encyclopedia of the Peoples of the World. Ed. A. Gonen. New York: Holt, 1993.

Encyclopedia of Sub-Saharan Africa. 4 vols. Ed. J. Middleton. New York: Scribner, 1997.

Encyclopedia of the Modern Middle East. 4 vols. New York: Macmillan, 1996.

Encyclopedia of the Third World. 4th ed. 3 vols. New York: Facts on File, 1990.

Encyclopedia of World Cultures. 10 vols. Boston: Hall, 1994.

Facts About the Cities. 2nd ed. New York: Wilson, 1996.

Goode's World Atlas. Ed. B. Rodner. 19th ed. Chicago: Rand McNally, 1995.

Guide to the Republics of the Former Soviet Union. Westport, CT: Greenwood, 1993.

***Illustrated Encyclopedia of Mankind.* 22 vols. Freeport, NY: Marshall Cavendish, 1989.
Good starting place for background information on the cultures of 500 different peoples of the world.

***The Literature of Geography: A Guide to Its Organization and Use.* 2nd ed. New Haven, CT: Shoe String, 1978.
An introductory overview of geographic research methods and materials. Includes chapters on specific areas of geography (e.g., regional) with lists of sources for research.

Modern Geography: An Encyclopedic Survey. Ed. G. S. Dunbar. New York: Garland, 1991.

Oxford Dictionary of the World. New York: Oxford, 1996.

Rosenfeld, L. B. et al. *Internet Compendium: Subject Guides to Social Sciences, Business, and Law Resources.* New York: Neal-Schuman, 1995.

The Times Atlas of the World. 10th ed. New York: Oxford, 1996.

Weather America: The Latest Climatological Data for Over 4,000 Places, With Rankings. Ed. A.N. Garwood. Milpitas, CA: Toucan Valley Pubs., 1996.

Weather Almanac. 7th ed. Detroit, MI: Gale, 1996.

Bibliographies to Geography Books and Other Sources

Geographers: Bio-Bibliographical Studies. Ed. T. W. Freeman et al. London: Mansell, 1977–present. Annually.

Geographical Bibliography for American Libraries. Ed. C. D. Harris. Washington, DC: Assn. of American Geographers, 1985.

International List of Geographical Serials. 3rd ed. Chicago: U of Chicago P, 1980.

Electronic Sources to Geography Literature

EXPANDED ACADEMIC INDEX
GEOBASE
SOCIAL SCISEARCH
WILSONDISC: SOCIAL SCIENCES INDEX

Indexes to Articles in Geography Journals

Geo Abstracts. Norwich, UK: Geo Abstracts, 1966–present.

***Social Sciences Index.* New York: Wilson, 1974–present.
Indexes articles in journals such as *American Cartographer, Cartographic Journals, Cartography, Economic Geography, Geographical Analysis,* and others.

Geology

Basic Sources and Guides to Geology Literature

Challinor's Dictionary of Geology. 6th ed. New York: Oxford UP, 1986.

Encyclopedia of Earth Sciences. 2 vols. Ed. E. J. Dasch. New York: Macmillan, 1996.

***Encyclopedia of Field and General Geology.* Ed. C. W. Finkle. New York: Reinhold, 1982.
One volume of the Encyclopedia of Earth Sciences series. Gives technical, documented information and references to other sources.

The Encyclopedia of the Solid Earth Sciences. Ed. P. Kearey et al. London: Blackwell, 1993.

Glossary of Geology. Ed. R. L. Bates and J. A. Jackson. 3rd ed. Falls Church, VA: AGI, 1987.

Information Sources in the Earth Sciences. Ed. J. Hardy et al. 2nd ed. New Providence, NJ: Bowker-Saur, 1990.

McGraw-Hill Encyclopedia of the Geological Sciences. 2nd ed. New York: McGraw, 1988.

Magill's Survey of Science: Earth Science Series. 5 vols. Englewood Cliffs, NJ: Salem, 1990.

Rosenfeld, L. B. et al. *Internet Compendium: Subject Guides to Health and Science Resources.* New York: Neal-Schuman, 1995.

***Use of Earth Sciences Literature.* Ed. D. N. Wood. New York: Archon, 1973.
Discusses types of information sources (e.g., maps and review publications) and then provides extensive bibliographies in specific areas of geology (e.g., stratigraphy).

Bibliographies to Geology Books and Other Sources

Bibliography and Index of Geology. Alexandria, VA. Monthly with annual indexes, 1969–present.

Catalog of the U. S. Geological Survey Library. Boston: Hall, 1964. Supplements.

Geological Reference Sources: A Subject and Regional Bibliography. Ed. D. Ward, M. Wheeler, and R. Bier. Metuchen, NJ: Scarecrow, 1981.

Publications of the Geological Survey. Washington, DC: GPO, 1979. Supplements.
An annual listing of USGS publication, updated by their monthly New Publications of the Geological Survey.

Electronic Sources to Geology Literature

APILIT (American Petroleum Institute)
COMPENDEX
GEOARCHIVE
GEOBASE

GEOREF
INSPEC
WILSONDISC: APPLIED SCIENCE AND
TECHNOLOGY and GENERAL
SCIENCE

Indexes to Articles in Geology Journals

**Bibliography and Index of Geology.* Boulder, CO: AGA, 1933–present.
Indexes geology journals, such as *American Journal of Science, American Mineralogist, Chemical Geology,* and others.

Bibliography and Index of Geology. Boulder, CO: GSA. Monthly with annual indexes.

**General Science Index.* New York: Wilson, 1978–present.
Covers about 100 science periodicals, including *Earth Science, Geological Society of America Bulletin,* and *Mineralogical Record.*

Health and Physical Education

See also Education, page 339, and Medical Studies, page 356.

Basic Sources and Guides to Health and Physical Education Literature

**Biographical Dictionary of American Sports.* Westport, CT: Greenwood, 1987–1989. Supplements, 1992 and 1995.
Features four separate volumes on baseball, basketball, football, and other outdoor sports.

Chronicle of the Olympics, 1896–1996. New York: DK Pubs., 1996.

Columbia Encyclopedia of Nutrition. New York: Putnam, 1988.

Consumer Health Information Source Book. 4th ed. Phoenix, AZ: Oryx, 1994.

Dictionary of American Food and Drink. New York: Hearst, 1994.

Dictionary of the Sport and Exercise Sciences. Champaign, IL: Human Kinetics, 1991.

Encyclopedia of Health Information Sources. 3rd ed. Ed. P. Wasserman. Detroit, MI: Gale, 1996.

**Encyclopedia of Sports Science.* 2 vols. Ed. H. Zumerchik. New York: Macmillan, 1996.
Provides information on the physics of individual sports (e.g., resistive forces in skiing) and the physiological aspects of sports and exercise (e.g., overuse injuries).

Encyclopedia of Sports. New York: Barnes and Noble, 1978. Supplements.

Foundations of Physical Education and Sport. 12 ed. Ed. W. Vest and C. A. Bucher. St. Louis, MO: Mosby, 1994.

International Handbook of Public Health. Ed. K. Hurrelman & U. Laaser. Westport, CT: Greenwood, 1996.

**Introduction to Reference Sources in Health Sciences.* Ed. F. Roper and J. Boorkman. 2nd ed. Metuchen, NJ: Scarecrow, 1984.
Discusses and lists health science reference materials, bibliographic sources, and other specialized sources (e.g., statistical). Explains how to use many of the sources described.

Key Guide to Electronic Resources: Health Sciences. Medford, NJ: Learned Information, 1995.

Kirby's Guide to Fitness and Motor Performance Tests. Cape Girardeau, MO: BenOak, 1991.

Magill's Medical Guide: Health and Illness. 3 vols. Englewood Cliffs, NJ: Salem, 1995; three supplementary volumes, 1996.

Merck Manual of Medical Information-Home Edition. Rahway, NJ: Merck, 1997.

Rosenfeld, L. B. et al. *Internet Compendium: Subject Guides to Health and Science Resources.* New York: Neal-Schuman, 1995.

**Sports and Physical Education: A Guide to the Reference Resources.* Ed. B. Gratcher et al. Westport, CT: Greenwood, 1983.
Lists biographical, statistical, and other sources on physical education and many individual sports. Briefly describes each source.

Bibliographies to Health and Physical Education Books and Other Sources

Annotated Bibliography of Health Economics. Ed. A. J. Culyer et al. New York: St. Martin's, 1977.

Electronic Sources to Health and Physical Education Literature

ERIC
EXPANDED ACADEMIC INDEX

MEDLINE
SOCIAL SCISEARCH
SPORT
WILSONDISC: EDUCATION and
    GENERAL SCIENCE INDEXES

Indexes to Articles in Health and Physical Education Journals

See also Education, page 000, and Medical Studies, page 000.

Current Index to Journals in Education.
    Phoenix, AZ: Oryx, 1969–present.
**Education Index.* New York: Wilson,
    1929–present.
    Both preceding titles index articles on
    physical education and health educa-
    tion in such journals as *Journal of
    Physical Education and Recreation,
    Journal of School Health, Physical Edu-
    cator, Research Quarterly for Exercise
    and Sport,* plus many others.
**General Science Index.* New York: Wil-
    son, 1978–present.
    Indexes 100 science journals including
    *American Journal of Public Health,
    Health, JAMA, The Physician,* and
    Sportsmedicine.
Physical Education Index. Cape Giradeau,
    MO: BenOak, 1978–present.
Physical Fitness and Sports Medicine.
    Washington, DC: GPO, 1978–present.

History

Basic Sources and Guides to History Literature

*American Historical Association's Guide to
    Historical Literature.* 3rd ed. 2 vols.
    New York: Oxford, 1995.
Barzun, J., and H. Graff. *The Modern Re-
    searcher.* 5th ed. New York: Harcourt,
    1992.
Britannica Book of the Year. Chicago: En-
    cyclopaedia Britannica, 1938–present.
Civilizations of the Ancient Near East. 4
    vols. Ed. J. Sasson et al. New York:
    Scribner, 1995.
A Companion to American Thought. Cam-
    bridge, MA: Blackwell, 1995.
**Dictionary of American History.* 8 vols.
    New York: Scribner's, 1976, supp. 1996.
    Although dated, this encyclopedia is a
    well-documented, scholarly source for
    background information on the people,
    places, and events in U.S. history.
Dictionary of the Middle Ages. Ed. J. R.
    Strayer. 13 vols. New York: Scribner's,
    1982–1989.

Encyclopedia of American History. 7th ed.
    Ed. R. Morris. 6th ed. New York: Harp-
    er, 1996.
Encyclopedia of American Social History. 3
    vols. Ed. Cayton, Gorn, and Williams.
    New York: Scribner's, 1993.
Encyclopedia of Asian History. 4 vols. New
    York: Scribner's, 1988.
*Encyclopedia of Colonial and Revolution-
    ary America.* New York: Facts on File,
    1989.
Encyclopedia of the Renaissance. New
    York: Facts on File, 1987.
Explorers and Discoverers of the World. Ed.
    D. B. Baker. Detroit, MI: Gale, 1993.
Facts on File Yearbook. New York: Facts on
    File, 1946–present.
Grum, B. *Timetables of History.* 3rd ed.
    New York: Simon & Schuster, 1991.
*Harper Encyclopedia of Military History:
    From 3500 BC to Present.* 4th ed. New
    York: HarperCollins, 1993.
**History: Illustrated Search Strategy and
    Sources.* 2nd ed. Ed. E. Frick. Ann Ar-
    bor, MI: Pierian P, 1995.
    Step-by-step guide to using reference
    sources in American history. Does not
    list many sources but thoroughly ex-
    plains and analyzes all of the major
    tools in history.
Jenkins, F. *Classical Studies, A Guide to the
    Reference Literature.* Englewood, CO:
    Libraries Unlimited, 1996.
Oxford Classical Dictionary. 3rd ed. New
    York: Oxford, 1996.
**Prucha, F. P. *Handbook for Research in
    American History.* 2nd ed. Lincoln: U
    of Nebraska P, 1994.
    Lists sources of information, arranged
    by type of material and then by subject.
    A good resource for comprehensive re-
    search in American history when the
    basic sources are exhausted.
*The Reader's Companion to Military Histo-
    ry.* New York: Houghton Mifflin, 1996.
Rosenfeld, L. B. et al. *Internet Compendi-
    um: Subject Guides to Humanities Re-
    sources.* New York: Neal-Schuman,
    1995.
_____. *Internet Compendium: Sub-
    ject Guides to Social Sciences, Business,
    and Law Resources.* New York: Neal-
    Schuman, 1995.
Trinkle, D. A. *The History Highway: A
    Guide to Internet Resources.* Armonk,
    New York: M.E. Sharpe, 1997.
Williams, N. *Chronology of the Modern
    World, 1763 to 1992.* 2nd ed. New
    York: Simon & Schuster, 1995.

Times Atlas of World History. Ed. G. Parker.
4th ed. Maplewood, NJ: Hammond,
1993.

Bibliographies to History Books and Other Sources

Bibliographer's Manual of American History. 5 vols. Philadelphia: Henkels,
1907–1910; rpt. Gordon Press, 1993.
Bibliography of British History. Oxford:
Clarendon, 1928–1977.
Combined Retrospective Indexes to Journals in History: 1838–1974. 11 vols. Arlington, VA: Carroliton, 1977.
The English Historical Review. Harlow, Essex, England: Longman, 1886–present.
This journal regularly features valuable
bibliographies.
Goldentree Bibliographies in History.
A series of books published in different
years by different publishers on specific
time period in American history (e.g.,
*Manifest Destiny and the Coming of the
Civil War, 1840–1861*).
Historical Abstracts. Santa Barbara, CA:
ABC-Clio, 1955–present.
*International Bibliography of Historical
Sciences.* New York: Wilson, 1930–present.
Wars of the United States. New York: Garland, 1984–present.
A series of annotated bibliographies.
Writings on American History. Washington,
DC: AHA, 1902–present.

Electronic Sources to History Literature

AMERICA: HISTORY AND LIFE
EXPANDED ACADEMIC INDEX
HISTORICAL ABSTRACTS
WILSONDISC: HUMANITIES INDEX

Indexes to Articles in History Journals

***America: History and Life.* Santa Barbara,
CA: ABC-Clio, 1964–present.
Well indexed and provides both articles
and bibliographies.
***American Historical Association.* Recently
Published Articles. 1976–present.
Indexes articles on American history in
journals such as *American Historical
Review, Civil War History, Journal of
American History,* and many others.
Historical Abstracts. Santa Barbara, CA:
ABC-Clio, 1955–present.
***Humanities Index.* New York: Wilson,
1974–present.

Indexes world history and American
history in *Canadian Journal of History,
English Historical Review, European
Historical Quarterly, Journal of Modern
History,* and many others.

Journalism and Mass Communications

Basic Sources and Guides to Journalism and Mass Communications Literature

*The Associated Press Stylebook and Libel
Manual.* 4th. ed. New York: AP, 1994.
Black, E. S., and J. K. Bracken. *Communication and the Mass Media, A Guide to
the Reference Literature.* Englewood,
CO: Libraries Unlimited, 1991.
Broadcasting Cablecasting Yearbook.
Washington, DC: Broadcasting Publications, 1982–present. Annually.
**Cates, J. A. *Journalism: A Guide to the
Reference Literature.* Englewood, CO:
Libraries Unlimited, 1990.
**An extensive listing of sources of use
in researching print and other mass
media. Provides evaluative, descriptive
comments on each of the 700 sources
included.
Encyclopedia of Twentieth-Century Journalists. Ed. W. H. Taft. New York: Garland, 1984.
Halliwell's Film Guide. New York: Harper,
1996.
*Information Sources in the Press and
Broadcast Media.* Ed. S. Eagle. New
Providence, NJ: Bowker-Saur, 1991.
***International Encyclopedia of Communications.* Ed. E. Barnouw et al. 4 vol.
New York: Oxford UP, 1989.
**A very scholarly, thorough treatment
of a great variety of subjects. Includes
articles on key people in mass communications (e.g., Charlie Chaplin) as well
as concepts and issues (e.g., copyright,
cybernetics).
Les Brown's Encyclopedia of Television. 3rd
ed. Detroit, MI: Gale, 1992.
MacDonald, R. *A Broadcast News Manual
of Style.* 2nd ed. New York: Longman,
1994.
Nelson, H. L., D. L. Teeter, Jr, and R. D.
LeDuc. *Law of Mass Communications.*
8th ed. Mineola, NY: Foundation, 1995.
Supp., 1996.
Pruett, B. *Popular Entertainment Research:
How to Do It and How to Use It.*
Metuchen, NJ: Scarecrow, 1992.

The Reporter's Handbook. 3rd ed. New
York: St. Martin's, 1995.

Rosenfeld, L.B. et al. *Internet Compendi-
um: Subject Guides to Social Sciences,
Business, and Law Resources*. New
York: Neal-Schuman, 1995.

**Rubin, R. B., et al. *Communication Re-
search*. 4th ed. Belmont, CA:
Wadsworth, 1996.
Along with chapters providing guidance in library research plans and the
sources needed for them, also contains
useful information on conducting formal research studies.

**Variety's Film Reviews*. New Providence,
NJ: Bowker, 1983–present.
Already comprising more than 20 volumes, this set reprints all film reviews
that have appeared in Variety since
1907.

Bibliographies to Journalism and Mass Communications Books and Other Sources

Annotated Media Bibliography. Ed. B.
Congdon. Washington, DC: ACC, 1985.

*Black Media in America: A Resource
Guide*. Ed. G. H. Hill. Boston: Hall,
1984.

*Broadcasting Bibliography: A Guide to the
Literature of Radio and Television*. Rev.
ed. Washington, DC: National Association of Broadcasters, 1989.

Journalism Biographies: Master Index. Detroit, MI: Gale, 1979. Supplements.

*Law of Mass Communications: Freedom
and Control of Print and Broadcast
Media*. Mineola, NY: Foundation, 1995.

Manchel, F. *Film Study: An Analytical Bibliography*. 4 vols. Madison, NJ: Farleigh
Dickinson, 1990.

Mass Media Bibliography. Ed. E. Blum et
al. Champaign: U of Illinois P, 1990.

*Mass Media and the Constitution: An Ency-
clopedia of Supreme Court Decisions*.
Ed. R. F. Hixson. New York: Garland,
1989.

McCoy, R. E. *Freedom of the Press: An Annotated Bibliography*. Carbondale:
Southern Illinois University Press, 1968.
And supplements for 1968–1977 and
1978–1992.

*Radio and Television: A Selected, Annotat-
ed Bibliography*. Metuchen, NJ: Scarecrow, 1978. Supplements to 1986.

*Violence and Terror in the Mass Media: An
Annotated Bibliography*. Westport, CT:
Greenwood, 1988.

Electronic Sources to Journalism and Mass Communications Literature

AP NEWS
ARTS AND HUMANITIES SEARCH
EXPANDED ACADEMIC INDEX
MAGAZINE INDEX
NATIONAL NEWSPAPER INDEX
NEWSEARCH
REUTERS
UPI NEWS
WILSONDISC: BUSINESS,
HUMANITIES, and the READERS'
GUIDE INDEXES

Indexes to Articles in Journalism and Mass Communications Journals

**Business Periodicals Index*. New York:
Wilson, 1958–present.
Indexes such industry periodicals as
*Broadcasting, Communications News,
Television/Radio Age,* and *Telecommu-
nications*.

Communications Abstracts. Beverly Hills,
CA: Sage, 1978–present.
Indexes approximately 100 journals
and selected books.

**Humanities Index*. New York: Wilson,
1974–present.
Indexes journalism articles in such journals as *Journalism History, Journalism
Quarterly, Columbia Journalism Review,* and others.

**Readers' Guide to Periodical Literature*.
New York: Wilson, 1900–date.
Indexes news and general interest mag-
azines, such as *Nation, Newsweek, New
York Review of Books, New Republic,
Saturday Review, U.S. News and World
Report,* and others.

Law

See also Political Science, pages 360–61.

Basic Sources and Guides to Law Literature

American Jurisprudence. 2nd ed.
Rochester, NY: Lawyers Cooperative,
1962–present (continuously revised and
supplemented).

American Justice. 3 vols. Ed. J.M. Bessette.
Pasadena, CA: Salem, 1996.

Black's Law Dictionary. 6th ed. St. Paul,
MN: West, 1990.

Cohen, M., and K. C. Olson. *Legal Research in a Nutshell.* 6th ed. Minneapolis, MN: West, 1996.

Corpus Juris Secundum. New York: American Law Book, 1936–present (continuously revised and supplemented).

Dictionary of Modern Legal Usage. 2nd ed. New York: Oxford UP, 1995.

Encyclopedia of American Prisons. New York: Garland, 1996.

Encyclopedia of Constitutional Amendments, Proposed Amendments, and Amending Issues. Santa Barbara: ABC-Clio, 1996.

Encyclopedia of Legal Information Sources. 3rd ed. Ed. P. Wasserman et al. Detroit, MI: Gale, 1996.

Fox, J. R. *Dictionary of International and Comparative Law.* Dobbs Ferry, NY: Oceana, 1992.

Gibson, J.S. *Dictionary of International Human Rights Law.* Lanham, MD: Scarecrow, 1996.

**Guide to American Law.* 12 vols. and annual yearbooks. St. Paul, MN: West, 1985.

An encyclopedia of law written for the nonspecialist. Provides background and explanations of legal topics and issues (e.g., abortion, civil rights).

Guide to the Supreme Court. 3rd ed. Washington, DC: Congressional Quarterly, 1997.

Hill, G. N. and K. T. Hall. *Real Life Dictionary of the Law: Taking the Mystery Out of Legal Language.* LA: General Publishing Group, 1996.

Historic U.S. Court Cases, 1690–1990: An Encyclopedia. Ed. J. W. Johnson. New York: Garland, 1992.

How to Research the Supreme Court. Washington, DC: Congressional Quarterly, 1992.

Legal Research in a Nutshell. 6th ed. St. Paul, MN: West, 1996.

Legal Research and Writing. 4th ed. St. Paul, MN: West, 1992.

MacLeod, D. *The Internet Guide for the Legal Researcher.* Teaneck, NJ: Infosources Pubs., 1995.

Modern Dictionary for the Legal Profession. 2nd ed. Buffalo, NY: Hein, 1996.

National Survey of State Laws. 2nd ed. Detroit, MI: Gale, 1995.

Rosenfeld, L. B. et al. *Internet Compendium: Subject Guides to Social Sciences, Business, and Law Resources.* New York: Neal-Schuman, 1995.

Bibliographies to Law Books and Other Sources

Index to Legal Books. 6 vols. New York: Bowker, 1989.

The U.S. Supreme Court: A Bibliography. Washington, DC: Congressional Quarterly, 1990.

Electronic Sources to Law Literature

CRIMINAL JUSTICE PERIODICALS INDEX

LABORLAW

LEGAL RESOURCE INDEX

LEXIS

NCJRS (National Criminal Justice Reference Service)

WILSONDISC: INDEX TO LEGAL PERIODICALS

Indexes to Articles in Law Journals

***Index to Legal Periodicals.* New York: Wilson, 1909–present.

Indexes such journals as the *American Bar Association Journal, Harvard Law Review,* and *Trial.*

***PAIS International in Print* (formerly *PAIS Bulletin*). New York: PAIS, 1915–present.

Indexes government publications and other books, as well as such journals as *High Technology Law Journal, Labor Law Journal, Law and Contemporary Problems,* and *Real Estate Law Journal.*

Literature and Language Studies

Basic Sources, Guides, and Bibliographies to Literature

Abrams, M. H. *A Glossary of Literary Terms.* 6th ed. New York: Harcourt, 1993.

Bracken, J. K. *Reference Works in British and American Literature.* Vol. 1: Literature; Vol. 2: Writers. Englewood, CO: Libraries Unlimited, 1990–1991.

Cambridge Guide to Literature in English. 2nd ed. New York: Cambridge UP, 1994.

Contemporary Authors. Detroit, MI: Gale, 1962–present.

Contemporary Literary Criticism. Detroit, MI: Gale, 1973–present.

***Dictionary of Literary Biography.* Series. Detroit, MI: Gale, 1978–present (in progress).

Already comprising more than 130 volumes, this excellent, well-documented encyclopedia is the best source for finding background information and selected bibliographies on individual authors.

Essay and General Literature Index. New York: Wilson, 1900–present.

**Harner, J. L. *Literary Research Guide.* 2nd ed. New York: MLA, 1993.
A comprehensive guide to major literary reference tools and other sources for literature worldwide.

Hawthorn, J. *A Glossary of Contemporary Literary Theory.* 2nd ed. New York: St. Martin's, 1995.

**Holman, C. H., and W. Harmon. *Handbook to Literature.* 7th ed. New York: Macmillan, 1995.
An excellent dictionary of the words and phrases used in the study of English and American literature.

Jackson, G. M. *Encyclopedia of Traditional Epics.* Santa Barbara: CA: ABC-Clio, 1994.

**Literary Criticism Index.* 2nd ed. Ed. A. R. Weiner and S. Means. Metuchen, NJ: Scarecrow, 1993.
Indexes about 85 standard bibliographies of literary criticism. For each writer, there are listings of criticisms and places to find his or her specific works.

**Magill's Bibliography of Literary Criticism.* Ed. F. Magill. 4 vols. Englewood Cliffs, NJ: Salem, 1979.
An index to selected critical articles, books, or chapters in books that deal with specific works of western literature. Includes listings for 2,500 works of literature by 600 different authors.

Research Guide for Undergraduate Students: English and American Literature. 4th ed. New York: MLA, 1996.

African-American Literature

See also Ethnic Studies, page 341.

Bibliographic Guide to Black Studies. New York: Hall, 1980–present (annually).

A Bibliographical Guide to African-American Women Writers. Ed. C. L. Jordan. Westport, CT: Greenwood, 1993.

Black American Fiction: A Bibliography. Ed. C. Fairbanks and E. A. Engeldinger. Metuchen, NJ: Scarecrow, 1978.

Black American Writers Past and Present: A Biographical and Bibliographical Dictionary, Ed. T. G. Rush et al. 2 vols. Metuchen, NJ: Scarecrow, 1975.

Black Americans in Autobiography: An Annotated Bibliography of Autobiographies and Autobiographical Books Written Since the Civil War. Durham, NC: Duke UP, 1984.

Conjuring: Black Women, Fiction, and Literary Tradition. Bloomington: Indiana UP, 1985.

Gilkin, R. *Black American Women in Literature.* Jefferson, NC: McFarland, 1989.

Oxford Companion to African American Literature. New York: Oxford, 1997.

Poetry of the Negro: 1746–1970. Ed. L. Hughes and A. Bontemps. New York: Doubleday, 1970.

Schomburg Center Guide to Black Literature from the Eighteenth Century to the Present. Detroit: Gale, 1996.

Werner, C. *Black American Women Novelists.* Englewood Cliffs, NJ: Salem, 1989.

American Literature

American Bibliography. Ed. C. Evans. 14 vols. Magnolia, MA: Smith, 1967.

American Literary Scholarship. Durham, NC: Duke UP, 1963–present. Annually.

American Writers. 4 vols. New York: Scribner's, 1961–1981. Supplements.

Articles on American Literature. (Separate titles covering 1900–1950, 1950–1967, and 1968–75). Durham, NC: Duke UP, 1954, 1970, and 1979.

Bibliographical Guide to the Study of Literature of the USA. Ed. C. Gohdes. 5th ed. Durham, NC: Duke UP, 1984.

A Bibliographical Guide to the Study of Western American Literature. Ed. R. W. Etulain. Lincoln: U of Nebraska P, 1982.

Bibliography of American Literature. New Haven; Yale UP, 1955–present.

Bibliography of Bibliographies in American Literature. Ed. C. H. Nilon. New York: Bowker, 1970.

Cambridge Handbook of American Literature. Ed. J. Salzman. New York: Cambridge UP, 1986.

Literary History of the United States. Ed. R. E. Spiller et al. 4th ed. 2 vols. New York: Macmillan, 1974.

Mathiessen, F. O. *American Renaissance: Art and Expression in the Age of Emerson and Whitman.* London: Oxford UP, 1968.

Modern American Literature. Ed. D. Nyren. 4th ed. New York: Unger, 1969–1976. Supplements.

Oxford Companion to American Literature. Ed. J. D. Hart. 6th ed. New York: Oxford UP, 1995.

The Transcendentalists: A Review of Research and Criticism. Ed. J. Myerson. New York: MLA, 1984.

British Literature

Baker, E. A. *History of the English Novel.* 11 vols. New York: Barnes and Noble, 1975 (reprint of 1924–1967 ed.).

Bibliographical Resources for the Study of Nineteenth Century English Fiction. Ed. G. N. Ray. Folcroft, PA: Folcroft, 1964.

British Writers. Ed. I. Scott-Kilvert. 8 vols. New York: Scribner's, 1979–1983. Supplements, 1987 and 1992.

British Writers and Their Works. 10 vols. Lincoln: U of Nebraska P, 1964–1970.

Cambridge Bibliography of English Literature. Ed. G. Wilson. 5 vols. New York: Cambridge UP, 1965.

Cambridge Guide to English Literature. Ed. I Overby. 2nd ed. New York: Cambridge UP, 1994.

Cambridge History of the English Literature. 15 vols. Cambridge: Cambridge UP, 1961 and 1992.

Encyclopedia of Victorian Britain. Ed. S. Mitchell. New York: Garland, 1987.

The English Romantic Poets: A Review of Research and Criticism. 4th ed. New York: MLA, 1985.

Evans, G. L., and B. Evans. *The Shakespeare Companion.* New York: Scribner's, 1978.

Modern British Literature. 4 vols. Literary Criticism Series. New York: Ungar, 1966–1975. Supplements, 1985–present.

New Cambridge Bibliography of English Literature. 5 vols. New York: Cambridge UP, 1969–1977.

Oxford Companion to English Literature. Ed. M. Drabble. 5th ed. Oxford: Clarendon, 1995.

Oxford History of English Literature. Oxford: Clarendon, 1945–present.

Romantic Movement: A Selective and Critical Bibliography. West Cornwall, CT: Locust Hill, 1980–present.

Drama and Theater

American Drama Criticism: Interpretations, 1890–1977. Ed. F. E. Eddleman. New Haven, CT: Shoe String, 1979. Supplements 1984, 1989, 1992, and 1996.

Bailey. J. *A Guide to Reference and Bibliography for Theatre Research.* 2nd ed. Columbus: Ohio State U, 1983.

British Theatre, A Bibliography from the Beginning to 1985. Romsey, UK: Motley, 1989.

Cambridge Guide to American Theatre. Ed. D. B. Wilmeth and T. L. Miller. New York: Cambridge UP, 1993.

Cambridge Guide to Theatre. Ed. E. Banham. 2nd ed. New York: Cambridge UP, 1995.

Catalog of the Theatre and Drama Collections. Boston: Hall, 1967. Supplements.

Contemporary Dramatists. Ed. J. Vinson. 5th ed. New York: St. James, 1993.

Critical Survey of Drama. Ed. F. N. Magill. 8 vols. Englewood Cliffs, NJ: Salem, 1994.

Drama Criticism. 5 vols. Detroit, MI: Gale, 1991–1995.

Index to Full Length Plays: 1895–1964. 3 vols. Westwood: Faxon, 1956–1965.

Index to Plays in Periodicals. Metuchen, NJ: Scarecrow, 1979 and 1977–1987. Supplement, 1990.

McGraw-Hill Encyclopedia of World Drama. 2nd ed. 5 vols. New York: McGraw, 1983.

Oxford Companion to the Theatre. 4th ed. Fair Lawn, NJ: Oxford UP, 1984.

Play Index. New York: Wilson, 1953–present.

Silvester, R. *United States Theatre, A Bibliography from the Beginning to 1990.* Boston: Hall, 1993.

A Survey and Bibliography of Renaissance Drama. 4 vols. Lincoln: U of Nebraska P, 1975–1978.

Language Studies

American Literature and Language: A Guide to Information Sources. Detroit, MI: Gale, 1982.

Cambridge Encyclopedia of the English Language. New York: Cambridge, 1995.

Cambridge Encyclopedia of Language. Ed. D. Crystal. New York: Cambridge UP: 1988.

Campbell, G. L. *Compendium of the World's Languages.* 2 vols. New York: Routledge, 1991.

Crystal, D. *An Encyclopedic Dictionary of Language and Languages.* Oxford: Blackwell, 1993.

A Dictionary of American English on Historical Principals. Ed. W. Craigie and J. R. Hulbert. 4 vols. Chicago: U of Chicago P, 1938–1944.

Dictionary of American Regional English. Ed. F. Cassidy. Cambridge: Harvard UP, 1985–present (in progress).

International Encyclopedia of Linguistics. 4 vols. New York: Oxford UP, 1991.

Linguistics: A Guide to Reference Literature. Englewood, CO: Libraries Unlimited, 1991.

The Oxford Companion to the English Language. Ed. T. McArthur. New York: Oxford UP, 1992.

Oxford English Dictionary. 2nd ed. Ed. J. A. Simpson et al. 20 vols. New York: Oxford UP, 1989.

Random House Historical Dictionary of American Slang. New York: Random House, 1994–present (in progress).

The World's Writing Systems. New York: Oxford, 1996.

Mythology and Folklore

American Folklore: A Bibliography. Metuchen, NJ: Scarecrow, 1977.

American Folklore, An Encyclopedia. Ed. J. H. Brunvand. New York: Garland, 1996.

The Arthurian Encyclopedia. Ed. N. J. Lacy. New York: Bedrick, 1987.

Arthurian Legend and Literature: An Annotated Bibliography. 2 vols. New York: Garland, 1983.

Ashlimar, D. L. *Guide to Folktales in the English Language.* Westport, CT: Greenwood, 1987.

Bullfinch's Mythology. New York: Avenel, 1978.

Campbell, J. *Historical Atlas of World Mythology.* San Francisco: Harper, 1983–present (in progress).

Dictionary of Celtic Myth and Legend. Ed. M. J. Green. London: Thames & Hudson, 1992.

Dictionary of Classical Mythology. Ed. R. S. Bell. Santa Barbara, CA: ABC-Clio, 1982.

Dictionary of Native American Mythology. New York: Oxford, 1994.

Fable Scholarship: An Annotated Bibliography. Ed. P. Carnes. New York: Garland, 1982.

Facts on File Encyclopedia of World Mythology and Legend. Ed. A. S. Mercatante. New York: Facts on File, 1988.

Folklore and Literature in the United States: An Annotated Bibliography. Ed. S. S. Jones. New York: Garland, 1984.

Folklore of World Holidays. Detroit, MI: Gale, 1992.

Frazer, J. *The Golden Bough.* New York: St. Martin's, 1955.

Grimal, P. *Dictionary of Classical Mythology.* New York: Blackwell, 1986.

Index to Fairy Tales, 1949–1972. Ed. N. O. Ireland. Metuchen, NJ: Scarecrow, 1973. Supplements.

Larousse Dictionary of World Folklore. Ed. A. Jones. New York: Larousse, 1995.

Mythological and Fabulous Creatures: A Source Book and Research Guide. Westport, CT: Greenwood, 1987.

Oxford Guide to Classical Mythology in the Arts, 1300–1990s. Ed. J. D. Reid. New York: Oxford UP, 1993.

Steinfirst, S. *Folklore and Folklife: A Guide to English-Language Reference Sources.* New York: Garland, 1992.

Storyteller's Sourcebook. 2nd ed. Detroit, MI: Gale, 1996.

World Mythology: An Annotated Guide to Collections and Anthologies. Lanham, MD: Scarecrow, 1996.

Novel, The

American Fiction: A Contribution Toward a Bibliography. 3 vols. Ed. L. H. Wright. San Marino, CA: Huntington Library, 1969 and 1979.

The Contemporary English Novel: An Annotated Bibliography of Secondary Sources. Ed. H. W. Drescher and B. Kahrmann. New York: IPS, 1973.

The Contemporary Novel: A Checklist of Critical Literature on the English Novel Since 1945. Lanham, MD: Scarecrow, 1996.

The Continental Novel: A Checklist of Criticism in English, 1900–1960. Metuchen, NJ: Scarecrow, 1967–1980. Supplement, 1983.

Critical Survey of Long Fiction. Ed. F. N. Magill. 8 vols. Englewood Cliffs, NJ: Salem, 1991.

English Novel Explication: Criticism to 1972. Ed. H. Palmer and J. Dyson. New Haven, CT: Shoe String, 1973. Supplements, 1976–present.

Facts on File Bibliography of American Fiction, 1588–1865. New York: Facts on File, 1994.

Facts on File Bibliography of American Fiction, 1866–1918. 2 vols. New York: Facts on File, 1993.

Facts on File Bibliography of American Fiction, 1919–1988. 2 vols. New York: Facts on File, 1991.

Kellman, S. G. *The Modern American Novel: An Annotated Bibliography.* Englewood Cliffs, NJ: Salem, 1991.

Poetry

American and British Poetry: A Guide to the Criticism, 1925–1978. Athens, OH: Swallow, 1984; supp. 1995.

Columbia Granger's Index to Poetry. Ed. W. J. Smith. New York: Columbia UP, 1996.

Critical Survey of Poetry. Ed. F. N. Magill. 8 vols. Englewood Cliffs, NJ: Salem, 1982.

English Poetry: Select Bibliographical Guides. Ed. A. E. Dyson. New York: Oxford UP, 1971.

Guide to American Poetry Explication. 2 vols. Boston: Hall, 1989.

Martinez, N. C. *Guide to British Poetry Explication.* 4 vols. Boston: Hall, 1991–1995.

New Princeton Encyclopedia of Poetry and Poetics. 3rd ed. Princeton, NJ: Princeton UP, 1993.

Poetry Explication: A Checklist of Interpretations Since 1925 of British and American Poems Past and Present. Boston: Hall, 1980.

Subject Index to Poetry for Children and Young People. Ed. D. B. Frizzell-Smith and E. L. Andrews. Chicago: ALA, 1977.

Waggoner, H. H. *American Poetry: The Puritans through Walt Whitman.* New York: Scribner's, 1988.

Short Story

American Short-Fiction Criticism and Scholarship, 1959–1977: A Checklist. Ed. J. Weixlmann. Athens: Ohio UP, 1982.

Critical Survey of Short Fiction. Ed. F. N. Magill. 7 vols. Englewood Cliffs, NJ: Salem, 1993.

Short Story Index. Ed. D. E. Cook and I. S. Monro. New York: Wilson, 1953. Supplements.

Reference Guide to Short Fiction. Ed. by N. Watson. Detroit: St. James, 1994.

Twentieth-Century Short Story Explication. Ed. W. S. Walker. 3rd ed. Hamden, CT: Shoe String, 1977. Supplements. Also, new series began in 1993.

World Literature

See also Foreign Language Studies, pages 343–45.

Benet's Reader's Encyclopedia. 4th ed. New York: Harper & Row, 1996.

Columbia Dictionary of Modern European Literature. 2nd ed. Ed. J.-A. Bede and W. Edgerton. Columbia UP, 1980.

Encyclopedia of World Literature in the 20th Century. New York: Ungar, 1967 and 1981.

Jackson, G. M. *Encyclopedia of Traditional Epics.* New York: Oxford, 1997.

Electronic Sources to Literature and Language Studies

ARTS AND HUMANITIES SEARCH
BOOK REVIEW INDEX
EXPANDED ACADEMIC INDEX
LLBA (Linguistics and Language Behavior Abstracts)
MLA BIBLIOGRAPHY
WILSONDISC: HUMANITIES INDEX

Indexes to Articles in Literature and Language Studies Journals

**Abstracts of English Studies.* Urbana, IL: NCTE, 1958–date.
Provides abstracts to monographs and journal articles. Tenth issue each year features a subject index.

**Abstracts of Folklore Studies.* Austin: U of Texas P, 1962–1975. (Ceased publication.)
Indexes folklore journals, such as *Dovetail, Kentucky Folklore Record, Relics,* and others.

Book Review Digest. New York: Wilson, 1905–present.

Book Review Index. Detroit, MI: Gale, 1965–present.

**Humanities Index.* New York: Wilson, 1974–present.
Provides general indexing to literary and language topics in several key journals.

Index to Book Reviews in the Humanities. Detroit, MI: Thompson, 1960–present.

**MLA International Bibliography of Books and Articles on the Modern Language and Literatures.* New York: MLA, 1921–present. Annually.
The best overall index to major literary figures and language topics.

Mathematics

Basic Sources and Guides to Mathematics Literature

Biographical Dictionary of Mathematicians. 4 vols. New York: Scribner's, 1991.

CRC Handbook of Mathematical Sciences. Ed. W. Beyer. 6th ed. West Palm Beach, FL: CRC, 1987.

Encyclopaedia of Mathematics. 10 vols. Norwell, MA: Reidel/Kluwer, 1988–present (in progress).

***Encyclopedic Dictionary of Mathematics*. Ed. K. Ito. 2nd ed. 4 vols. Cambridge: MIT P, 1987.
Provides thorough but concise coverage of 450 different concepts and phenomena of mathematics (e.g., algebraic groups). Also includes bibliographies listing important sources of research.

Hoggar, S. G. *Mathematics for Computer Graphics*. New York: Cambridge UP, 1993.
This work draws on many areas of pure math, applying them to computer graphics.

Information Sources in Science and Technology. 2nd ed. Englewood, CO: Libraries Unlimited, 1994.

Mathematical Journals: An Annotated Guide. Comp. D. F. Liang. Metuchen, NJ: Scarecrow, 1992.

The Mathematics Dictionary. 5th ed. New York: Reinhold, 1992.

Motz, L., and J. H. Weaver. *The Story of Mathematics*. New York: Plenum, 1993.
This work provides an excellent history of mathematics.

Rosenfeld, L. B. et al. *Internet Compendium: Subject Guides to Health and Science Resources*. New York: Neal-Schuman, 1995.

Using the Mathematical Literature: A Practical Guide. Ed. B. K. Schaefer. New York: Dekker, 1979.

The VNR Concise Encyclopedia of Mathematics. 2nd ed. Ed. W. Gellert et al. New York: Reinhold, 1989.

Wolfram, S. *Guide for Mathematics, Version 2*. New York: Addison-Wesley, 1992.

The Words of Mathematics, An Etymological Dictionary of Mathematical Terms Used in English. Washington, DC: Mathematical Assn. of America, 1994.

Bibliographies to Mathematics Books and Other Sources

Annotated Bibliography of Expository Writing in the Mathematical Sciences. Ed. M. P. Gaffney and L. A. Steen. Washington, DC: Mathematics Assn., 1976.

Omega Bibliography of Mathematical Logic. Ed. G. H. Muller and W. Lenski. 6 vols. New York: Springer-Verlag, 1987.

Schaaf, W. I. *The High School Math Library*. 8th ed. Reston, VA: NCTM, 1987.

Vestpocket Bibliographies. Ed. W. I. Schaaf. See miscellaneous issues of the Journal of Recreational Mathematics, 1983–present.

Electronic Sources to Mathematics Literature
MATHSCI
WILSONDISC: GENERAL SCIENCE INDEX

Indexes to Articles in Mathematics Journals

***General Science Index*. New York: Wilson, 1978–present.
Covers about 100 science periodicals, including *American Mathematical Monthly, Journal of Recreational Mathematics,* and *Mathematics Magazine*.

Mathematical Reviews. Providence, RI: AMS, 1940–present.

Medical Studies

Basic Sources and Guides to Medical Studies Literature

Alternative Medicine, The Definitive Guide. Puyallup, WA: Future Medical Pubs., 1993.

American Medical Association Encyclopedia of Medicine. New York: Random, 1989.

Author's Guide to BioMedical Journals. Ed. M. A. Leibert. Larchmont, New York: Leibert, 1994.

Author's Guide to Journals in the Health Field. Ed. D. Ardell and J. James. New York: Haworth, 1980.

Black's Medical Dictionary. 37th ed. Lanham, MD: Barnes and Noble, 1992.

Cambridge World History of Human Disease. Ed. K. F. Kipple. New York: Cambridge UP, 1993.

Core Collections in Nursing and Allied Health Sciences. Phoenix, AZ: Oryx, 1990.

Encyclopedia of Cancer. 3 vols. San Diego: Academic Press, 1996.

Information Sources in the Medical Sciences. Ed. L. T. Morton and S. Godbolt. 4th ed. London: Butterworth, 1992.

International Dictionary of Medicine and Biology. 3 vols. New York: Wiley, 1986.

***Introduction to Reference Sources in Health Sciences*. 3rd ed. Ed. F. Roper and J. Boorkman. Chicago: MLA, 1994.
Discusses and lists health science reference materials, bibliographic sources,

and other specialized sources (e.g., statistical). Explains how to use many of the sources described.

Polit, D., and B. Hungler. *Nursing Research: Principles and Methods.* 5th ed. Philadelphia: Lippincott, 1994.

Rosenfeld, L. B. et al. *Internet Compendium: Subject Guides to Health and Science Resources.* New York: Neal-Schuman, 1995.

**Stauch, K., et al. *Nursing: Illustrated Search Strategy and Sources.* 2nd ed. Ann Arbor, MI: Pierian P, 1993. Provides guidance in formulating a research plan as well as information on finding and using specific research tools. Also has a listing of recent sources in major areas of nursing (e.g., community health issues).

Bibliographies to Medical Studies Books and Other Sources

AIDS Information Sourcebook. 3rd ed. Phoenix, AZ: Oryx, 1991.

An Annotated Bibliography of Health Economics. Ed. A. J. Culyer at al. New York: St. Martin's, 1977.

Medical Reference Works, 1679–1966. Ed. J. Blake and C. Roos. Chicago: Medical Library Association, 1967. Supplements.

Nursing Studies Index. Ed. V. Henderson. 4 vols. Philadelphia: Lippincott, 1957–1972.

Electronic Sources to Medical Studies Literature

AIDSLINE
BIOSIS PREVIEWS
EMBASE
EXPANDED ACADEMIC INDEX
MEDLINE
NURSING AND ALLIED HEALTH
SCISEARCH
WILSONDISC: GENERAL SCIENCE
  INDEX

Indexes to Articles in Medical Studies Journals

***Cumulated Index Medicus.* Bethesda, MD: U.S. Department of Health and Human Services, 1959–present. Provides indexing to most medical journals published worldwide.

***Cumulative Index to Nursing and Allied Health Literature.* Glendale, CA: CINAHL, 1956–present.

***Indexes nursing literature in journals such as *Cancer Nurse, Current Reviews*

for Recovery Room Nurses, Journal of Practical Nursing, Journal of Nursing Education, and many more.

International Nursing Index. New York: AJN, 1970–present.

Music

Basic Sources and Guides to Music Literaure

Baker's Biographical Dictionary of Musicians. 8th ed. New York: Schirmer, 1992.

Dictionary of Music. Ed. A. Isaacs and E. Martin. New York: Facts on File, 1983.

Dictionary of Music Technology. Ed. C. Tristam. Westport, CT: Greenwood, 1992.

***Druesdow, J. *Library Research Guide to Music.* Ann Arbor: Pierian P, 1982. An easy-to-follow guide to starting, planning, and carrying out library research in music. Explains how to use the sources, as well as provides a listing of periodical indexes, bibliographies, and other reference tools.

Encyclopedia of Pop, Rock, and Soul. Ed. I. Stambler. New York: St. Martin's, 1989.

Garland Encyclopedia of World Music. Hamden, CT: Garland, 1997–present (in progress).

Information on Music: A Handbook of Reference Sources in European Languages. 3 vols. Englewood, CO: Libraries Unlimited, 1975–1984.

Information Sources in Music. Ed. L. Foreman. New Providence, NJ: Bowker-Saur, 1997.

International Cyclopedia of Music and Musicians. Ed. B. Bahle. 11th ed. New York: Dodd, 1985.

International Encyclopedia of Women Composers. Ed. A. Cohen. 2nd ed. New York: Books and Music USA, 1988.

Music Analyses, An Annotated Guide to the Literature. H. J. Diamond. New York: Schirmer, 1991.

***Music Reference and Research Materials.* Ed. V. Duckles and M. Keller. 5th ed. New York: Schirmer, 1997. A comprehensive and thorough bibliography of sources for research in music, including recordings and music history. Provides brief comments on many of the 3,200 sources listed.

New Grove Dictionary of American Music. Ed. H. Hitchcock and S. Sadie. 4 vols. New York: Grove, 1986.

New Grove Dictionary of Music and Musicians. Ed. S. Sadie. 20 vols. New York: Macmillan, 1980.
A very scholarly, comprehensive, and international encyclopedia for music and music history. Includes bibliographies of important resources for each major topic.

New Oxford Companion to Music. New York: Oxford UP, 1983.

New Oxford History of Music. 10 vols. London: Oxford, 1957–1974.

Rosenfeld, L. B. et al. *Internet Compendium: Subject Guides to Humanities Resources.* New York: Neal-Schuman, 1995.

Slonimsky, N. *Music Since 1900.* 5th ed. New York: Schirmer, 1992.

The Virtual Musician: A Complete Guide to Online Resources and Services. New York: Schirmer/Prentice Hall, 1996.

Women Composers Through the Ages. 12 vols. Ed. M. F. Schleifer and S. Glickman. Boston: G.K. Hall, 1996–present (in progress).

Bibliographies to Music Books and Other Sources

Bibliographic Guide to Music. Boston: Hall, 1976–present. Annually.

General Bibliography for Music Research. Ed. K. E. Mixter. 3rd ed. Detroit, MI: Information Coordinators, 1996.

General Index to Modern Musical Literature in the English Language Including Periodicals for the Years 1915–1926. 1927; rpt. New York: DaCapo, 1970.

Popular Music: An Annotated Index of American Popular Songs. Detroit, MI: Gale, 1963–present (continuing).

Electronic Sources to Music Literature

ARTS & HUMANITIES SEARCH
EXPANDED ACADEMIC INDEX
RILM ABSTRACTS (Repertoire Internationale de Littérature Musicale)
WILSONDISC: HUMANITIES INDEX

Indexes to Articles in Music Journals

Humanities Index. New York: Wilson, 1974–present.
Indexes topics in music in such journals as *American Music, Early Music, Journal of Musicology,* and *Musical Quarterly.*

Music Article Guide. Philadelphia: Information Services, 1966–present.
Indexes music education and instrumentation in such journals as *Brass and Wind News, Keyboard, Flute Journal, Piano Quarterly,* and many more.

Music Index. Warren, MI: Information Coordinations, 1949–present.
Indexes music journals such as *American Music Teacher, Choral Journal, Journal of Band Research, Journal of Music Therapy, Music Journal, Musical Quarterly,* and many others.

RILM (Repertoire Internationale de Littérature Musicale). New York: City U of New York, 1967–present.

Philosophy

Basic Sources and Guides to Philosophy Literature

A Companion to Aesthetics. Ed. D. E. Cooper. Cambridge, MA: Blackwell, 1993.

Biographical Dictionary of Twentieth-Century Philosophers. Ed. S. Brown et al. New York: Routledge, 1996.

Cambridge Dictionary of Philosophy. Ed. R. Audi. New York: Cambridge, 1995

Dictionary of Philosophy. Ed. A. R. Lacey. New York: Paul/Methuen, 1987.

Dictionary of the History of Ideas. Ed. P. Winer, 5 vols. New York: Scribner's, 1974.

Encyclopedia of Classical Philosophy. Ed. D. J. Zeyl. Westport, CT: Greenwood, 1997.

Encyclopedia of Ethics. 2 vols. Ed. L. C. Becker and C. B. Becker. New York: Garland, 1992.

Encyclopedia of Philosophy. Ed. P. Edwards. 8 vols. New York: Macmillan, 1967–1968. Supp. 1996.
An excellent source for background information on concepts (e.g., analytic and synthetic statements), movements (e.g., Darwinism), issues (e.g., certainty), and philosophers.

Ethics. 3 vols. Ed. J. K. Roth. Pasadena, CA: Salem Press, 1994.

Fifty Major Philosophers: A Reference Guide. Ed. D. Collinson. New York: Routledge, 1987.

Great Thinkers of the Western World. Ed. I. P. McGreal. New York: HarperCollins, 1992.

Handbook of Western Philosophy. Ed. G. H. R. Parkinson et al. New York: Macmillan, 1988.

Oxford Companion to Philosophy. New York: Oxford, 1995.

Philosophy: A Guide to the Reference Literature. Ed. H. E. Bynago. Littleton, CO: Libraries Unlimited, 1986.

Philosophy in Cyberspace: A Guide to Philosophy-Related Resources on the Internet. Ed. D. Alexander. Bowling Green, OH: Philosophy Documentation Center, 1995.

**Research Guide to Philosophy.* Ed. T. N. Tice and T. P. Slavens. Chicago: ALA, 1983.

　Consists of 30 bibliographical essays on sources in the history of philosophy (e.g., seventeenth century) and various areas of philosophy (e.g., logic). Concludes with a bibliography of reference works.

Rosenfeld, L. B. et al. *Internet Compendium: Subject Guides to Humanities Resources.* New York: Neal-Schuman, 1995.

World Philosophy: Essay Reviews of 225 Major Works. Ed. F. Magill. 5 vols. Englewood Cliffs, NJ· Salem, 1982.

Bibliographies to Philosophy Books and Other Sources

J. R. *World Philosophy: A Contemporary Bibliography.* Westport, CT: Greenwood, 1993.

The Classical World Bibliography of Philosophy, Religion, and Rhetoric. New York: Garland, 1978.

Philosophers Index: A Retrospective Index [1940–1966]. Bowling Green, OH: Bowling Green U, 1978.

Roth, J. K. *Ethics: An Annotated Bibliography.* Englewood Cliffs, NJ: Salem, 1991.

Electronic Sources to Philosophy Literature

ARTS & HUMANITIES SEARCH
EXPANDED ACADEMIC INDEX
PHILOSOPHER'S INDEX
WILSONDISC: HUMANITIES INDEX

Indexes to Articles in Philosophy Journals

**Humanities Index.* New York: Wilson, 1974–present.

　Provides a general index to philosophical topics in journals such as *British Journal of Philosophy, Environmental Ethics, International Philosophy Quarter, Journal of the History of Ideas, Journal of Philosophy,* and many others.

**Philosopher's Index. Bowling Green, OH: Bowling Green U, 1967–present.

　Indexes philosophy articles in journals such as *American Philosophical Quarterly, Humanist, Journal of the History of Ideas, Journal of Philosophy, Philosophical Review, Philosophy Today,* and many more.

Physics

Basic Sources and Guides to Physics Literature

Annual Review of Nuclear and Particle Science. Annual Reviews, Inc.: Palo Alto, CA: 1952–date.

The Astronomy and Astrophysics Encyclopedia. Ed. S. P. Maran. New York: Reinhold, 1992.

Cambridge Atlas of Astronomy. 3rd ed. New York: Cambridge, 1994.

Encyclopedia of Physics. 2nd ed. New York: VCH, 1991.

Encyclopedia of Physics. 3rd ed. New York: Van Nostrand Reinhold, 1990.

Facts on File Dictionary of Astronomy. 3rd ed. Ed. V. Illingworth. New York: Facts on File, 1994.

A Guide to the Literature of Astronomy. Ed. R. A. Seal. Englewood, CO: Libraries Unlimited, 1977.

Information Sources in Physics. 3rd ed. Ed. D. Shaw. New Providence, NJ: Bowker-Saur, 1994.

Information Sources in Science and Technology. 2nd ed. Englewood, CO: Libraries Unlimited, 1994.

An Introductory Guide to Information Sources in Physics. Ed. L. R. A. Melton. Bristol, England: Inst. of Physics, 1978.

Macmillan Encyclopedia of Physics. 4 vols. Ed. J. S. Rigden. New York: Macmillan, 1996.

Magill's Survey of Science: Physical Science Series. 6 vols. Ed. F. N. Magill. Englewood Cliffs, NJ: Salem, 1992.

NASA Atlas of the Solar System. New York: Cambridge, 1997.

Rosenfeld, L. B. et al. *Internet Compendium: Subject Guides to Health and Science Resources.* New York: Neal-Schuman, 1995.

Space Almanac. 2nd ed. New York: Arcsoft, 1992.

Bibliographies to Physics Books and Other Sources

**Physics Abstracts.* London: IEE, 1898–present. Bimonthly.

A guide to the most recent work in physics worldwide. It provides an abstract that you can use in your research even though the journal itself might be unavailable.

Solid State Physics Literature Guides. New York: Plenum, 1972–1981.

Electronic Sources to Physics Literature

INSPEC
SCISEARCH
SPIN (Searchable Physics Information Notices)
WILSONDISC: GENERAL SCIENCE INDEX

Indexes to Articles in Physics Journals

***Applied Science and Technology Index.* New York: Wilson, 1958–present. Indexes general physics topics in *Laser Focus, Monthly Weather Review, Physics Today,* and others. *Current Papers in Physics.* London: IEE, 1966–date. Bimonthly.

***Current Physics Index.* New York: American Institute of Physics, 1975–date. Consult this work for indexing to most articles in physics journals such as *Applied Physics, Journal of Chemical Physics, Nuclear Physics, Physical Review, Physics Letters,* and many more.

Political Science

Basic Sources and Guides to Political Science Literature

Blackwell Encyclopedia of Political Institutions. Ed. V. Boddanor. Oxford: Blackwell, 1987.

Congress A to Z. 2nd ed. Washington, DC: Congressional Quarterly, 1993.

Congress and Lawmaking: Researching the Legislative Process. 2nd ed. Santa Barbara, CA: ABC-Clio, 1989.

Diller, D. C. *Russia and the Independent States.* Washington, DC: Congressional Quarterly, 1993.

Dorsey Dictionary of American Government and Politics. Belmont, CA: Dorsey, 1988.

Encyclopedia of Arms Control and Disarmament. 3 vols. Ed. R. D. Burns. New York: Scribner's, 1993.

Encyclopedia of Democracy. 4 vols. Ed. S.M. Lipset. Washington, DC: CQ, 1995.

Encyclopedia of Government and Politics. 2 vols. Ed. M. Hawkesworth and M. Kogan. New York: Routledge, 1992.

Encyclopedia of Public Affairs Information Sources. Ed. P. Wasserman et al. Detroit, MI: Gale, 1988.

Encyclopedia of the Democratic Party and Encyclopedia of the Republican Party. 4 vols. Ed. G. T. Kurian. Armonk, New York: Sharpe, 1997.

Encyclopedia of the United Nations and International Relations. 2nd ed. New York: Taylor and Francis, 1990.

Encyclopedia of the American Presidency. 4 vols. Ed. L. W. Levy and L. Fisher. New York: Simon & Schuster, 1994.

The Executive Office of the President, A Historical, Biographical and Bibliographical Guide. Westport, CT: Greenwood, 1997.

Guide to Official Publications of Foreign Countries. Chicago: ALA, 1990.

Information Sources of Political Science. Ed. F. L. Holler. 4th ed. Santa Barbara, CA: ABC-Clio, 1986.

Lowery, R. C. *Political Science: Illustrated Search Strategy and Sources.* Ann Arbor, MI: Pierian P, 1993.

Martin, F. S. and R. Goehlert. *How to Research Congress.* Washington, DC: CQ, 1996.

Maxwell, Bruce. *How to Access the Federal Government on the Internet.* Washington, DC: CQ, 1996.

***Morehead, J. *Introduction to United States Information Sources.* 5th ed. Littleton, CO: Libraries Unlimited, 1996. Covers all forms of information sources (books, periodicals, databases) for research on American politics and government, international relations, and the study of foreign governments.

Political Handbook of the World. Ed. A. S. Banks. New York: McGraw. Annually.

Political Science: A Guide to Reference and Information Sources. Ed. H. York. Englewood, CO: Libraries Unlimited, 1990.

Rosenfeld, L. B. et al. *Internet Compendium: Subject Guides to Social Sciences, Business, and Law Resources.* New York: Neal-Schuman, 1995.

Safire, W. *Definitive Guide to the New Language of Politics.* 4th ed. New York: Random, 1993.

State Yellow Book: A Directory. New York: Monitor, 1989–present. Semiannually.

The Statesman's Yearbook. New York: St. Martin's, 1964–date. Annually.

Survey of Social Science: Government and Politics Series. 5 vols. Ed. F. N. Magill and J. M. Bessette. Englewood Cliffs, NJ: Salem, 1995.

Urwin, D.W. *A Dictionary of European History and Politics,* 1945–1995. New York: Longman, 1996.

Wars and Peace Treaties 1816–1991. New York: Routledge, 1992.

Yearbook of the United Nations. Lake Success, NY: United Nations, 1947–present. Annually.

Bibliographies to Political Science Books and Other Sources

Edelheit, A. J. *The Rise and Fall of the Soviet Union: A Selected Bibliography of Sources in English.* Westport, CT: Greenwood, 1992.

Free-thought in the United States: A Descriptive Bibliography. Westport, CT: Greenwood, 1978.

International Bibliography of Political Science. New York: IPS, 1979. Supplements.

Monthly Catalog of U.S. Government Publications. Washington, DC: GPO, 1895–present.

Political Science: A Bibliographical Guide to the Literature. Metuchen, NJ: Scarecrow, 1965. Supplements, 1966–present.

Skidmore, C., and T. J. Spahn. *From Radical Left to Extreme Right: A Bibliography.* 3rd ed. Metuchen, NJ: Scarecrow, 1987.

Electronic Sources to Political Science Literature

ASI
CIS
CONGRESSIONAL RECORD ABSTRACTS
EXPANDED ACADEMIC INDEX
FEDERAL REGISTER ABSTRACTS
GPO MONTHLY CATALOG
NATIONAL NEWSPAPER INDEX
PAIS
UNITED STATES POLITICAL SCIENCE DOCUMENTS
WASHINGTON PRESSTEXT
WILSONDISC: SOCIAL SCIENCES INDEX
WORLD AFFAIRS REPORT

Indexes to Articles in Political Science Journals

***ABC: Pol Sci.* Santa Barbara, CA: ABC-Clio, 1969–present.

Indexes the tables of contents of about 300 international journals in the original language.

***International Political Science Abstracts.* Olso: International Political Science Assn., 1951–present.
Comprehensive, worldwide coverage of more than 600 periodicals; also provides abstracts in English.

***PAIS International in Print* (formerly *PAIS Bulletin*). New York: PAIS, 1915–present.
Indexes government publications and books, as well as such journals as Annals of the *American Academy of Political and Social Science* and *International Studies Quarterly.*

***Social Sciences Index.* New York: Wilson, 197–present.
Indexes articles in such journals as *American Journal of Political Science, American Political Science Review, Political Science Quarterly,* and many others.

Psychology

Basic Sources and Guides to Psychology Literature

American Handbook of Psychiatry. Ed. S. Arieti. 2nd ed. 8 vols. New York: Basic, 1974–1981.

Baxter, P. *Psychology: A Guide to Reference and Information Sources.* Englewood, CO: Libraries Unlimited, 1993.

Borchardt, D. H. *How to Find Out in Psychology.* Elmsford, NY: Pergamon, 1986.

Diagnostic and Statistical Manual of Mental Disorders. 4th ed. Washington, DC: American Psychiatric Assn., 1994.

Encyclopedia of Human Behavior. 4 vols. Ed. V. S. Ramachandran. San Diego: Academic Press, 1994.

***Encyclopedia of Psychology.* Ed. R. J. Corsini. 2nd ed. 4 vols. New York: Wiley, 1984.
A scholarly, thorough introduction to all aspects of psychology including its major theorists. Most of the articles include references to other sources, all of which are listed in the extensive bibliography in the index volume.

Encyclopedia of Sleep and Dreaming. Ed. M. A. Carskadon. New York: Macmillan, 1993.

International Encyclopedia of Psychiatry, Psychology, Psychoanalysis, and Neurology. 12 vols. New York: VNR, 1997.

Library Research Guide to Psychology. Ann
Arbor, MI: Pierian P, 1984.
**Library Use: A Handbook for Psychology.*
Ed. J. C. Reed and R. M. Baxter. 2nd
ed. Washington, DC: APA, 1992.
A thorough overview of the research
process in psychology. Provides guidance in choosing and narrowing topics
as well as suggesting research sources
to consult in psychology and such re-
lated fields as education and manage-
ment. Also explains how to use sources
such as *Psychological Abstracts.*
Oxford Companion to the Mind. Ed. R.
Gregory. New York: Oxford UP, 1987.
Rosenfeld, L. B. et al. *Internet Compendium: Subject Guides to Social Sciences,
Business, and Law Resources.* New
York: Neal-Schuman, 1995.
Survey of Social Science: Psychology Series.
6 vols. Ed. F. Magill. Englewood Cliffs,
NJ: Salem, 1993.

Bibliographies to Psychology Books and Other Sources

Annual Reviews of Psychology. Palo Alto,
CA: Annual Reviews, 1950–date.
Bibliographical Guide to Psychology.
Boston: Hall, 1982–present. Annually.
*Psychoanalysis, Psychology, and Litera-
ture: A Bibliography.* Ed. N. Kiell. 2nd
ed. 2 vols. Metuchen, NJ: Scarecrow,
1982. Supplement, 1990.
Psychological Abstracts. Washington, DC:
APA, 1927–present.
Psychological Index. 42 vols. Princeton, NJ:
Psychological Review, 1895–1936. Su-
perseded by *Psychological Abstracts.*

Electronic Sources to Psychology Literature

CHILD ABUSE AND NEGLECT
ERIC
EXPANDED ACADEMIC INDEX
MENTAL HEALTH ABSTRACTS
PSYCINFO
PSYCLIT
SOCIAL SCISEARCH
SOCIOLOGICAL ABSTRACTS
WILSONDISC: SOCIAL SCIENCES
INDEX

Indexes to Articles in Psychology Journals

*Child Development Abstracts and Bibliog-
raphy.* Chicago: U of Chicago P,
1927–present.
**Psychological Abstracts.* Washington, DC:
APA, 1927–present.

Indexes and provides brief abstracts to
psychology journals such as *American
Journal of Psychology, Behavioral Science, Psychological Review,* and many
more.
**Sociological Index.* New York: Interna-
tional Sociological Assn., 1952–present.
Indexes such journals as *American
Journal of Community Psychology,
Journal of Drug Issues, Sex Roles,* and
many others.

Religion

Basic Sources and Guides to Religion Literature

The Anchor Bible Dictionary. 6 vols. Ed. D.
N. Freedman et al. New York: Double-
day, 1992.
*Churches and Church Membership in the
U.S. 1990.* Ed. M. B. Bradley et al. At-
lanta, GA: Glenmary Research Center,
1992.
Concise Encyclopedia of Islam. Ed. C.
Glasse. San Francisco: Harper, 1989.
Dictionary of Feminist Theologies.
Louisville, KY: Westminster/John Knox,
1996.
Eliade, M., et al. *Eliade Guide to World Re-
ligions.* San Francisco: Harper, 1991.
Encyclopedia Judaica. 16 vols. Ed. C. Roth.
New York: Macmillan, 1972. (Annual
yearbooks serve to supplement.)
*Encyclopedia of African American Reli-
gions.* Ed. L. G. Murphy, J. G. Melton,
and G. L. Ward. New York: Garland,
1993.
Encyclopedia of American Religions. Ed. J.
G. Melton. 5th ed. Detroit: Gale, 1996.
*Encyclopedia of the American Religious Ex-
perience.* 3 vols. Ed. C. Lippy and P.
Williams. New York: Scribner's, 1987.
Encyclopedia of Native American Religions.
New York: Facts on File, 1992.
**Encyclopedia of Religion.* 16 vols. Ed. M.
Eliade. New York: Macmillan, 1987.
A scholarly, thorough treatment of
worldwide religions, religious thinkers,
and religious issues (e.g., the afterlife).
Useful bibliographies follow nearly all
articles.
Harper Atlas of the Bible. Ed. J. Pritchard.
New York: Harper, 1987.
*The International Standard Bible Encyclo-
pedia.* Ed. G. W. Bromley. 4 vols.
Grand Rapids, MI: Eerdmans,
1979–1988.
Introduction to Theological Research. Ed.
C. J. Barber. Moody, 1982.

***Library Research Guide to Religion and Theology.* Ed. J. Kennedy. 2nd ed. Ann Arbor, MI: Pierian P, 1984.
A good, step-by-step introduction to the basic sources in religious studies. Also includes a bibliography of sources in specific areas (e.g., the Bible, comparative religion).

Melton, J. G., and M. A. Koszegi. *Religious Information Sources: A Worldwide Guide.* New York: Garland, 1992.

The Muslim Almanac: A Reference Work on the History, Faith, Culture, and People of Islam. Detroit: Gale, 1996.

New Catholic Encyclopedia. 17 vols. New York: McGraw, 1977–1979. Supplement, 1989.

The New Standard Jewish Encyclopedia. Ed. G. Wigoder. New York: Facts on File, 1992.

Religion: A Cross-Cultural Encyclopedia. Santa Barbara, CA: ABC-Clio, 1996.

Research Guide to Religious Studies. Ed. J. F. Wilson and T. Slavens. Chicago: ALA, 1982.

Rosenfeld, L. B. et al. *Internet Compendium: Subject Guides to Humanities Resources.* New York: Neal-Schuman, 1995.

Who's Who in Religion. Chicago: Marquis, 1975/1976–present.

Yearbook of American and Canadian Churches. New York: Abingdon. Annually.

Bibliographies to Religion Books and Other Sources

A Critical Bibliography of Writings on Judaism. Lewiston, NY: Mellen, 1989.

Reference Works for Theological Research: An Annotated Selective Bibliographical Guide. Ed. R. Kepple. 3nd ed. UP of America, 1992.

Religion and Society in North America; An Annotated Bibliography. Ed. R. Brunkow. Santa Barbara, CA: ABC-Clio, 1983.

Religious Books and Serials in Print. New York: Bowker, 1987.

Wiersbe, W. W. *A Basic Library for Bible Students.* Grand Rapids, MI: Baker, 1981.

Electronic Sources for Religion Literature

EXPANDED ACADEMIC INDEX
RELIGION INDEX
WILSONDISC: HUMANITIES INDEX

Indexes to Articles in Religion Journals

The Catholic Periodical and Literature Index. New York: Catholic Library Assn., 1934–present.
Indexes 170 Catholic periodicals.

***Humanities Index.* New York: Wilson, 1974–present.
Indexes religious journals such as *Church History, Harvard Theological Review,* and *Muslim World.*

***Index of Articles on Jewish Studies.* Jerusalem: Jewish National & Univ. Library P, 1969–present.
Indexes 10,000 periodicals for all phases of Jewish religion and studies.

***Religion: Index One: Periodicals, Religion and Theological Abstracts.* (Formerly *Index to Religious Periodicals Literature*). Chicago: ATLA, 1949–present.
Indexes religious articles in journals such as *Biblical Research, Christian Scholar, Commonweal, Harvard Theological Review, Journal of Biblical Literature,* and many others.

Sociology and Social Work

Basic Sources and Guides to Sociology and Social Work Literature

American Families: A Research Guide and Historical Handbook. Ed. J. M. Hawes and E. I. Nybakken. Westport, CT: Greenwood, 1991.

Child Abuse and Neglect: An Information and Research Guide. New York: Garland, 1992.

Encyclopedia of Adolescence. 2 vols. New York: Garland, 1991.

Encyclopedia of Child Abuse. New York: Facts on File, 1989.

Encyclopedia of Homelessness. New York: Facts on File, 1994.

Encyclopedia of Homosexuality. 2 vols. Ed. W. R. Dynes. New York: Garland, 1990.

Encyclopedia of Marriage and the Family. 2 vols. Ed. D. Levinson. New York: Macmillan, 1995.

Encyclopedia of Marriage, Divorce, and the Family. New York: Facts on File, 1989.

Encyclopedia of Social Work. 19th ed. Ed. R. L. Edwards. 3 vols. New York: NASW, 1995.

***Encyclopedia of Sociology.* 4 vols. Ed. E. F. Borgatta and M. L. Borgatta. New York: Macmillan, 1992.

The first authoritative, scholarly encyclopedia devoted to sociology. Articles
cover concepts, theories, and research
and provide good lists of references for
further research.

Handbook of Sociology. Ed. N. Smelser.
Newbury Park, CA: Sage, 1988.

Knox, G. W. *National Gangs Resource
Handbook: An Encyclopedic Reference.*
Bristol, IN: Wyndham Hall, 1994.

Library Research Guide to Sociology. Ed. P.
McMillan and J. R. Kennedy. Ann Arbor, MI: Pierian P, 1981.

Rosenfeld, L. B. et al. *Internet Compendi-
um: Subject Guides to Social Sciences,
Business, and Law Resources.* New
York: Neal-Schuman, 1995.

The Social Science Encyclopedia. 2nd ed.
New York: Routledge, 1996.

Social Work Almanac. 2nd ed. Silver
Spring, MD: NASW, 1995.

The Social Work Dictionary. 3rd ed. Silver
Springs, MD: NASW, 1995.

***Sociology, A Guide to Reference and Information Sources.* Ed. S. Aby. Littleton,
CO: Libraries Unlimited, 1987.
Good starting place when trying to find
which indexes, bibliographies, and other reference books might be relevant.
Covers 600 major resources in sociology and related fields, giving descriptive
and evaluative information for each.

*Statistical Handbook on Adolescents in
America.* Phoenix, AZ: Oryx, 1996.

*Statistical Handbook on Violence in Ameri-
ca.* Phoenix, AZ: Oryx, 1995.

*Statistical Handbook on the American
Family.* Phoenix, AZ: Oryx, 1992.

Statistical Record of Children. 2nd ed. Detroit: Gale, 1997.

Statistical Record of Older Americans. 2nd
ed. Detroit, MI: Gale, 1996.

***Student Sociologist's Handbook.* Ed. P. B.
Bart and L. Frankel. 4th ed. New York:
McGraw, 1986.
Along with listing recommended
sources for researching sociological
topics, also includes sections on trends
in the field and on writing different
types of sociology papers.

Bibliographies to Sociology and Social Work Books and Other Sources

Families in Transition. Ed. J. Sadler. New
Haven, CT: Anchor, 1988.

Henslin, J. M. *Homelessness: An Annotated
Bibliography.* New York: Garland, 1993.

*Homelessness in America, 1893–1992: An
Annotated Bibliography.* Ed. B. Lubin
et al. Westport, CT: Greenwood, 1994.

*Reference Sources in Social Work: An An-
notated Bibliography.* Ed. J. H. Conrad.
Metuchen, NJ: Scarecrow, 1982.

*Sociological Aspects of Poverty: A Bibliogra-
phy.* Ed. H. P. Chalfant. Monticello, IL:
Vance Biblios., 1980.

Electronic Sources to Sociology and Social Work Literature

CHILD ABUSE AND NEGLECT
EXPANDED ACADEMIC INDEX
FAMILY RESOURCES
NCJRS (National Criminal Justice
Reference Service)
SOCIAL SCISEARCH
SOCIOLOGICAL ABSTRACTS
WILSONDISC: SOCIAL SCIENCES
INDEX

Indexes to Articles in Sociology and Social Work Journals

Popular Periodical Index. Roslyn, PA: PPI,
1973–present.
Indexes contemporary and regional is-
sues in magazines such as *GEO, Life,
Ohio Magazine, Playboy, Rolling Stone,
Texas Monthly,* and others.

***Social Sciences Index.* New York: Wilson,
1974–present.
Indexes articles in such journals as
Child Welfare, Families in Society, and
Social Problems.

***Sociological Abstracts.* New York: Sociological Abstracts, 1952–present.
Indexes and provides brief descriptions
of articles in journals such as *American
Journal of Sociology, Environment and
Behavior, Journal of Applied Social Psychology, Journal of Marriage and the
Family, Social Education, Social Research, Sociological Inquiry, Sociology,*
and many others.

Social Work Research and Abstracts. New
York: NASW, 1964–present.

Speech

See also Drama and Theater, page 353, and
Journalism and Mass Communications,
pages 349.

Basic Sources and Guides to Speech Literature

*African American Orators: A Bio-critical
Sourcebook.* Westport, Ct: Greenwood.
1996.

*American Orators of the 20th Century:
Critical Studies and Sources.* Westport,
CT: Greenwood, 1987.
Lanham, R. A. *Handlist of Rhetorical
Terms.* Berkeley: U of California P,
1991.
*Lend Me Your Ears: Great Speeches in His-
tory.* 2nd ed. New York: Norton, 1997.
**Research Guide in Speech.* Ed. G. Tand-
berg. Morristown, NJ: General Learning
P, 1974.
> Dated, but nevertheless a very useful
source for guidance on all stages of
preparing oral presentations. Also includes a brief history of oratory and a
selective listing of recommended
sources for research in various subject
areas as well as the field of speech.
Sprague, J., and D. Stuart. *The Speaker's
Handbook.* 4th ed. New York: Harcourt, 1996.

*Bibliographies to Speech Books
and Other Sources*

*American Orators Before 1900: Critical
Studies and Sources.* Westport, CT:
Greenwood, 1987.
*Radio and Television: A Selected Annotat-
ed Bibliography.* Metuchen, NJ: Scare-
crow, 1978. Supplements, 1982 and
1989.
*Rhetoric and Public Address: A Bibliogra-
phy: 1947–1961.* Madison: U of Wis-
consin P, 1964. (Continued annually in
Speech Monographs.)
*Table of Contents of the Quarterly Journal
of Speech, Speech Monographs, and
Speech Teacher.* Ed. J. McPhee. New
York: Farrar (in association with the
Speech Association of America), 1985.

*Electronic Sources to Speech
Literature*

COMMUNICATIONS INDEX
ERIC
EXPANDED ACADEMIC INDEX
LLBA (Language and Language
Behavior Abstracts)
MLA BIBLIOGRAPHIES
SOCIAL SCISEARCH
WILSONDISC: HUMANITIES INDEX

*Indexes to Articles in Speech
Journals*

**Humanities Index.* New York: Wilson,
1974–present.
> Indexes such speech journals as *Com-
munication, Journal of Communication, Quarterly Journal of Speech,*

Speech Monographs, and *Studies in
Public Communication.*
MLA International Bibliography. New
York: MLA, 1921–present.
> Indexes rhetorical subjects.

Women's Studies
*Basic Sources and Guides
to Women's Studies Literature*

Bloomsbury Guide to Women's Literature.
Ed. C. Buck. New York. Prentice-Hall,
1992.
*Encyclopedia of Child Bearing: Critical
Perspectives.* Ed. B. K. Rothman.
Phoenix, AZ: Oryx, 1993.
Fishburn, K. *Women in Popular Culture: A
Reference Guide.* Westport, CT: Green-
wood, 1982.
Handbook of American Women's History.
Ed. A. H. Zophy. New York: Garland,
1990.
*Index to Women of the World from Ancient
to Modern Times: Biographies and Por-
traits.* Westwood, CA: Faxon, 1970.
Supplement, 1988.
Larousse Dictionary of Women. Ed. M. Par-
ry. New York: Larousse, 1996
Olsen, K. *Chronology of Women's History.*
Westport, CT: Greenwood, 1994.
Primer on Sexual Harassment. Lanham,
MD: BNA, 1992.
Rosenfeld, L. B. et al. *Internet Compendi-
um: Subject Guides to Social Sciences,
Business, and Law Resources.* New
York: Neal-Schuman, 1995.
**Searing, S. *Introduction to Library Re-
search in Women's Studies.* Boulder,
CO: Westview, 1985.
> A multidisciplinary listing of sources for
researching women's issues and prob-
lems in the social sciences.
*Second to None: A Documentary History of
American Women.* 2 vols. Lincoln: Uni-
versity of Nebraska, 1994.
Sherrow, Victoria. *Women and the Mili-
tary, An Encyclopedia.* Santa Barbara,
CA: ABC-Clio, 1996.
Snyder, P. *European Women's Almanac.*
New York: Columbia UP, 1992.
*Statistical Handbook on Women in Ameri-
ca.* 2nd ed. Phoenix, AZ: Oryx, 1996.
Statistical Record of Women Worldwide.
2nd ed. Ed. L. Schmittroth. Detroit, MI:
Gale, 1995.
Who's Who of American Women. Chicago:
Marquis, 1958–present.
*Women in the United States Military,
1901–1995, A Research Guide and An-*

notated Bibliography. Westport, CT: Greenwood, 1996.

Women's Issues. 3 vols. Ed. M. McFadden. Englewood Cliffs, NJ: Salem/Magills, 1997.

Women's Legal Guide. Golden, CO: Fulcrum, 1996.

**Women's Studies Encyclopedia.* 3 vols. Westport, CT: Greenwood, 1989–1991. A multidisciplinary reference source on all issues relating to women. Vol. 1 covers views from the sciences (1989); vol. 2 deals with literature, arts, and learning (1990); vol. 3 covers history, philosophy, and religion (1991).

Bibliographies to Women's Studies Books and Other Sources

American Women and Politics: A Selected Bibliography and Research Guide. New York: Garland, 1984.

American Women Writers: A Critical Reference Guide. 4 vols. Ed. L. Mainiero and L. L. Faust. New York: Continuum, 1982. Supplement, 1993.

Annotated Bibliography of Feminist Criticism. Ed. M. Humm. Boston: Hall, 1987.

Annotated Bibliography of Twentieth Century Critical Studies of Women and Literature; 1660–1800. New York: Garland, 1977.

Bibliographic Guide to Studies on the Status of Women: Development and Population Trends. Paris: UNESCO, 1983.

Biographies of American Women. Santa Barbara, CA: ABC-Clio, 1990.

Feminist Companion to Literature in English. Ed. V. Blain et al. New Haven: Yale UP, 1990.

Feminist Resources for Schools and Colleges: A Guide. Ed. A. Chapman. Feminist P, 1986.

Fischer, G. V. *Journal of Women's History Guide to Periodical Literature (1980–1990).* Bloomington: U of Indiana P, 1992.

Older Women in 20th-Century America: A Selected Annotated Bibliography. New York: Garland, 1982.

Women and Work: Paid and Unpaid: A Selected Annotated Bibliography. Ed. M. A. Ferber. New York: Garland, 1987.

Women in America: A Guide to Information Sources. Ed. V. R. Terris. Detroit, MI: Gale, 1980.

Women's Studies: A Recommended Core Bibliography. Ed. E. Stineman and C. Loeb. Littleton, OH: Libraries Unlimited, 1979.

Electronic Sources to Women's Studies Literature

ERIC
EXPANDED ACADEMIC INDEX
SOCIAL SCISEARCH
SOCIOLOGICAL ABSTRACTS
WILSONDISC: SOCIAL SCIENCES INDEX and HUMANITIES INDEX

Indexes to Articles on Women's Studies Journals

**Social Sciences Index.* New York: Wilson, 1974–present.
  Indexes such journals as *Feminist Studies, Ms., Signs, Womanpower, Woman Activist, Woman's Journal, Women and Literature, Women's Studies,* and *Women's World.*

Women's Studies Abstracts. Rush, NY: Rush, 1972–present.

**Women's Studies Index (1989–present).* Boston: Hall, 1992–present. Annually. Currently, the best source for immediate information on women's issues.

APPENDIX B
Finding Internet Sources for A Selected Discipline

The following list of Web sites, in addition to the ones found by your keyword and subject searches, will launch your investigation of Internet resources. We have listed those disciplines most used by freshman for their research. Keep in mind that a keyword search will find one of these sites even if the Universal Resource Locator (URL) has changed.

Art

The Parthnet
http://home.mtholyoke.edu/~klconner/parthenet.html
> This resource gives you information on ancient and classical art, the treasures of the Renaissance, 19th Century American works, impressionism, and many other periods. It will also link you with major museums and their collections.

World Wide Arts Resources
http://wwar.world-arts-resources.com
> This site provides an artist index as well as an index to exhibits, festivals, meetings, and performances. Its search engine will take you to fine arts departments, online courses, syllabi, and art institutions.

WebLouvre
http://sunsite.unc.edu/wm/
> This internet version of the Musée du Louvre enables you to visit the painting exhibits, the sculptures, the Louvre's Auditorium, and miscellaneous exhibits, such as the medieval art collection. It even includes a short tour of Paris.

Astronomy

American Astronomical Society
http://www.aas.org
> This site gives you the *Astrophysical Journal,* providing articles, reviews, and educational information. It gives links to other astronomical sites on the Web.

Mount Wilson Observatory
http://www.mtwilson.edu
> This site takes you into the Mount Wilson Observatory for outstanding photography of the universe and for online journals, documents, agencies, and activities in astronomical science.

The Northern Lights Planetarium, Norway

http://www.uit.no/npt/homepage-npt.
en.html
This site takes you into the planetarium, displays the northern lights in vivid colors, and enables you to research such topics as *Aurora Borealis.*

The Universe at Our Doorstep

http://neptune.cgy.oanet.comp
This site links you to NASA programs, such as the space station, the shuttle program, or Project Galileo. It provides maps of the planets, views of Earth from many different angles, and plenty of planetary information.

Athletics

Outside Online

http://outside.starwave.com:80
This site is devoted to outdoor sports such as biking, skiing, backpacking, and camping with reviews of current sports and equipment.

Sportsline USA

http://www.sportsline.com/index.html
This site focuses on professional sports, such as auto racing, baseball, golf, and many others. Its Newsroom page provides news, photographs, and links to other sites.

ESPNET Sports Zone

http://espnet.sportzone.com
This site, provided by the ESPN sports network, gives up-to-date sports information as well as behind-the-scene articles.

Business

All Business Network

http://www.all-biz.com
This site provides a search engine to businesses with relevant information for the following—newsletters, organizations, news groups, and magazines.

Finance: The World Wide Web Virtual Library

http://www.cob.ohio-state.edu/dept/
fin/overview.html
The Finance Department of Ohio State University has established a site that will link you to hundreds of articles and resource materials on banks, insurers, market news, jobs, and miscellaneous data for students.

Nijenrode Business Webserver

http://www.nigenrode.nl/nbr/index.
html
This site serves primarily students and faculty at business schools with a search engine that finds news, business journals, career opportunities in accounting, banking, finance, marketing, and other related fields.

Communications

Communication Resources on the Web

http://alnilam.ucs.indiana.edu:1027/
sources/comm.html
This large database takes you to resources and Web sites on associations, book reviews, bibliographies, libraries, media, information science programs, and departments of communication in various universities.

Computer and Internet Technology

Byte Magazine

http://www.byte.comp
This site provides the major print articles from *Byte* magazine with product information on computer products, such as Netscape or Wordperfect.

Internet Society

http://www.isoc.org/indextxt.html
This site is supported by the companies, agencies, and foundations that launched the Internet and that keep it functioning. It gives you vital information with articles from the ISOC Forum newsletter.

OCP's Guide to Online High Tech Resources

http://ocprometheus.org
With a search engine that performs keyword searches, this site brings you a wealth of full-text articles, online magazines, technical documents, and Web links to high-tech issues.

Virtual Computer Library

http://www.utexas.edu/computer/ucl
This site gives you access to academic computing centers at the major universities along with books, articles, and bibliographies.

Current Events

New York Times on the Web

http://www.nytimes.com
This site presents current news of the day from the print edition with compilations of articles on arts and leisure, travel, and other special features.

Trib.com.—The Internet Newspaper

http://www.trib.com
This site is an online newspaper with complete articles on news, weather, and sports from around the world with links to Reuter's, the Associated Press, and other wire services.

USA Today

http://www.usatoday.com
USA Today online contains sections on news, life, money, sports, and special features. An index gives access to previous articles and a search engine takes you to specific articles on your chosen subject.

Wall Street Journal

http://www.wsj.com
This online edition features headlines and some articles from the print edition with a classroom edition for secondary school students and teachers.

Education

Chronicle of Education

http://chronicle.merit.edu
This site gives you "Academe This Week" from *The Chronicle of Education,* a weekly printed magazine about education on the undergraduate and graduate levels. You will need to be a subscriber to gain full access.

Educom

http://educom.edu
This site has full-text online articles with a focus on educational technology in its *Educom Review,* a focus on information technology in *Edupage,* and general news from *Educom Update.*

Edweb

http://edweb.cnidr.org:90
This site focuses on educational issues and resource materials for grades K–12 with articles on Web education, Web history, and Web resources.

Online Educational Resources

http://quest.arc.nasa.gov/OER
This site by NASA provides an extensive list of educational articles and documents on everything from the space shuttle to planetary exploration.

ERIC (Educational Resource and Information Center)

http://ericir.syr.edu/ithome
ERIC contains about 1 million documents, available by a keyword search, on all aspects of teaching and learning, lesson plans, administration, bibliographies, and almost any topic related to the classroom.

Environment

Envirolink

http://envirolink.org
This site has a search engine that allows access to environmental articles, photographs, action alerts, organizations, and additional Web sources.

Medicine and Global Survival

http://www.healthnet.org/MGS/MGS.html
This online journal features articles on environmental destruction, overpopulation, infectious diseases, the consequences of war, and, in general, the health of the globe. It provides links to other journals, newsletters, and government documents that explore environmental issues.

Government

Bureau of the Census

http://www.census.gov
This site from the U. S. Department of Commerce provides census data on geography, housing, and the population. It allows you to examine specific information about your targeted county.

Fedworld

http:///www.fedworld.gov
>   This site gives you links to Web sites of the government departments as well as lists of free catalogs. It links you to the Internal Revenue Service and other government agencies.

Library of Congress

http://www.lcweb.loc.gov
>   This site provides the Library of Congress catalog online for books by author, subject, and title. It also links you to historical collections and research tools.

Thomas

http://thomas.loc.gov
>   This site gives you access to congressional legislation and documents indexed by topic, by bill number if you have it, and by title. It also allows you to search the Congressional Record, The Constitution, and other government documents. It links you to the House, the Senate, the Government Printing Office, and the General Accounting Office.

White House Web

http://www.whitehouse.gov
>   This site provides a graphical tour, messages from the president and the vice-president, and accounts of life at the White House. Visitors to this site can even leave a message for the president in the guest book.

Health and Medicine

Global Health Network

http://www.pitt.edu/HOME/
GHNet.html
>   This site provides you with access to documents in public health as provided by scholars at The World Health Organization, NASA, The Pan American Health Organization, and others. It links you to agencies, organizations, and health networks.

Martindale's Health Science Guide

http://www-sci.lib.uci.edu/HSG/
HSGuide.html
>   This giant database gives you access to several medical centers for online journals and documents in medicine, nursing, nutrition, public health, medical law, and veterinary work.

Medweb: Medical Libraries

http://www.emory.edu/WHSC/
medweb.medlibs.html
>   Emory University provides a site that connects you with medical libraries and their storehouses of information. It also gives links to other health related Web sites.

National Institutes of Health

http://www.nih.gov
>   NIH leads the nation in medical research, so this site provides substantive information on numerous topics, from cancer and diabetes to malpractice and medical ethics.

History

Archiving Early America

http://earlyamerica.com
>   This site displays 18th Century documents in their original form for reading and downloading, such as the Bill of Rights and the speeches of Washington, Paine, Jefferson, and others.

Humanities Hub

http://www.gu.edu.au/gwis/hub.hom.
html
>   This site provides resources in the humanities and social sciences with links to anthropology, architecture, cultural studies, film, gender studies, government, history, philosophy, sociology, and women.

The Humbul Gateway

http://info.ox.ac.uk/departments/
humanities/international.html
>   This site provides historical esources, references, libraries, and bulletin boards with links to downloadable texts.

Literature

The English Server

http://english-server.hss.cmu.edu
>   Carnegie Mellon University provides academic resources in the humanities, including drama, fiction, film, television, and history with the added bonus of calls for papers and a link for downloading freeware and shareware.

Literature Directory

http://web.syr.edu/~~fjzwick/sites/
lit.html
As the name describes it, this site provides a directory, with links, to specific pieces of literature.

Project Gutenberg

http://promo.net/pg
This site provides literary texts in the public domain that can be downloaded via FTP and that are divided into three divisions: light literature such as fables, heavy literature such as *The Scarlet Letter,* and reference works.

Voice of the Shuttle

http://humanitas.ucsb.edu
For the literary scholar, this site gives a massive collection of bibliographies, textual criticism, newsgroups, and links to classical studies, history, philosophy, and other related disciplines.

Philosophy

The American Philosophical Association

http://www.oxy.edu/apa.html
This site provides articles, bibliographies, software, a bulletin board, gopher server, and links to other philosophical sites containing college courses, journals, texts, and newsletters.

Psychology

Clinical Psychology Resources

http://www.psychologie.uni-bonn.de/
kap/links-20.htm
This site features articles on assessment, behavior, disorders, psychotherapy, and other related issues. It has links to online journals and psychology organizations. It provides a keyword index to both articles and books.

Psych Web

http://www.gasou.edu/psychweb/
psychweb.htm#top
This site features a collection of articles from *Psychiatric Times,* reports from the National Institute of Health, information from universities, and links to psychology journals and other sites on the Internet. It includes, online, Freud's *The Interpretation of Dreams.*

Religion

Comparative Religion

http://weber.u.washington.edu/
~~madin
This comprehensive site gives references and resources to all religions and religious studies and religious organizations.

Vanderbilt Divinity School

http://www.library.vanderbilt.edu/
divinity/homelib.html
This source gives you references and interpretations to the Bible, links to other religious Web sites, and on-line journals, such as *Biblical Archaeologist.*

Science

The Academy of Natural Sciences Related Links

http://www.acnatsci.org/links.html
This site will link you to hundreds of articles and resource materials on various issues and topics in the natural sciences.

Discovery Channel Online

http://www.discovery.com
This site is an online version of television's Discovery Channel, and it features a keyword search engine.

Discover Magazine

http://www.dc.enews.com/magazines/
discover
This site is a online version of *Discover Magazine* including the texts of many articles. Its Archive Library enables you to examine articles from past issues.

National Academy of Sciences

http://www.nas.edu
This comprehensive site combines the resources of the National Academy of Engineering, the Institute of Medicine, and the National Research Council. It focuses on math and science education, and it has links to scientific societies.

Network Science

http://www.awod.com/netsci
The NetSci engine searches out biotechnological literature with links to other scientific Web sites. It focuses mainly on chemistry and pharmaceuticals.

Social Science

Political Science Resources on the Web

http://www.lib.umich.edu/libhome/
Documents.center/polisci.html
This site at the University of Michigan
is a vast data file on government information—local, state, federal, foreign,
and international. It is a good site for
political theory and international relations.

Praxis

http://caster.ssu.upenn.edu/~~restes/
praxis.html
This site provides a massive collection
of articles on socioeconomic topics
with links to other social science resources.

Social Science Information Gateway (SOSIG)

http://sosig.esrc.bris.ac.uk/Welcome.
html#socialsciences
The SOSIG site provides a keyword
search that makes available to you
many Web sites in an alphabetical list.

Sociology

http://hakatai.mcli.dist.maricopa.edu/
smc/ml/sociology.html
This site gives you access to hundreds
of sites that provide articles and resource materials on almost all aspects
of sociology issues.

Writing

Research Links for Writers

http://www.siu.edu/departments/cola/
english/seraph9k/research.html
This site gives you a method for finding and accessing various articles and
discussions about writing, especially research writing.

WWW Resources for Rhetoric and Composition

http://www.ind.net/Internet/comp.html
This site provides a number of links to
issues on writing and the teaching of
writing.

Internet Resources for English Teachers and Students

http://www.umass.edu/english/
resource.html
This site at the University of Massachusetts provides links to articles and in-
structional materials for the English
class.

Women's Studies

The Women's Resource Project

http://sunsite.unc.edu/cheryb/women
This site links you to libraries on the
Web that have collections on Women's
Studies. It also has links to women's
programs and women's resources on
the Web.

Women's Studies Resources

http:www.inform.umd.edu:8080/EdRes/
Topic/WomensStudies
This site features a search engine for a
key word search to women's issues and
provides directories to bibliographies,
classic texts, references, course syllabi
from various universities, and links to
other Web sites.

Women's Studies Librarian

http://www.library.wisc.edu/libraries/
WomensStudies
This site at the University of Wisconsin
provides information on important contributions by women in Science,
Health, and Technology with links to
their activities in literature, government,
and business.

Index

Note: **Bold** page numbers indicate main discussion.

Credits

Page 9, Figure 1 Text and artwork copyright © 1998 by YAHOO! Inc. All rights reserved. YAHOO! And the YAHOO! Logo are trademarks of YAHOO! Inc. Reprinted by permission. Page 10, Figure 2 Reproduced with the permission of Digital Equipment Corporation. AltaVista, the AltaVista logo and the Digital logo are trademarks of the Digital Equipment Corporation. Page 31, Figure 4 Reproduced with the permission of Digital Equipment Corporation. AltaVista, the AltaVista logo and the Digital logo are trademarks of Digital Equipment Corporation. Page 39, Figure 5 From *Bibliographic Index*, April 1997, p. 181. Reprinted by permission of The H.W. Wilson Company. Page 39, Figure 6 From "Mainstreaming in Education." Reprinted with permission of R. R. Bowker, a Reed Reference Publishing Company, from *Books in Print Subject Guide 1996-1997*, Vol. 3. Copyright © 1996 by Reed Elsevier Inc. Page 42, Figure 7 Reprinted from *Magill's Bibliography of Literary Criticism*, Vol. 2, p. 709. By permission of the publisher, Salem Press, Inc. Copyright © 1979,by Frank N. Magill. Page 43, Figure 8 Entry "Frost, Robert (1874-1963)." Reprinted by permission of the Modern Language Association of America from 1983 *MLA International Bibliography of Books and Articles on the Modern Languages and Literatures*. Copyright © 1983 by the Modern Language Association of America. Page 44, Figure 9 From *Encyclopedia of Psychology*, 2nd Edition, Vol. 1, p. 287 edited by Raymond J. Corsini. Copyright © 1994 John Wiley & Sons, Inc. Reprinted by permission of John Wiley & Sons, Inc. Page 44, Figure10 From *Out of the Storm: The End of the Civil War* by Noah Andre Trudeau. Copyright © 1994 by Noah Andre Trudeau. Reprinted by permission of Little, Brown and Company. Page 46, Figure 11 From *The Reader's Guide to Periodical Literature (Unabridged)* Vol. 94, No. 5, July 1994, p. 242. Reprinted by permission of The H.W. Wilson Company. Page 48, Figure 12 Reprinted with the permission of the American Psychological Association, publisher of *Psychological Abstracts®* and the PsycINFO® database (Copyright 1997 by the American Psychological Association). All rights reserved. Pages 48 and 49, Figures 13 and 14 From *Dissertation Abstracts International*, Vol. 58, 1997. Copyright © 1997 by University Microfilms, Inc. Reprinted by permission. Page 51, Figure 15 From *Biography Index*, 1997. Reprinted by permission of The H.W. Wilson Company. Page 52, Figure 16 From "Ann Sexton" by Susan Resnick Parr. Excerpted with permission of Charles Scribner's Sons Reference Books, an imprint of Simon & Schuster Macmillan, from *American Writers: A Collection of Literary Biographies*, Supplement II, Part 2, A. Walton Litz, Editor in Chief. Copyright © 1981 Charles Scribner's Sons. Page 53, Figure 17 From *The New York Times Index*, 1996, Vol. 84, p. 483. Copyright ©1996 by The New York Times Co. Reprinted by permission. Page 54, Figure 18 From *The CQ Researcher*, Vol. 7.27, July 18, 1997. Reprinted by permission of Congressional Quarterly, Inc. Page 60, Figure 22 Reproduced from Edition 20 of the *Dewey Decimal Classification*, published in 1989, by permission of Forest Press, a division of OCLC Online Computer Library Center, owner of copyright. Page 65, Figure 24 Source: George E. Hall and Courtenay M. Slater, eds., *1993 County and City Extra*. Reproduced with permission of Slater–Hall Information Products, from Bernan Press. Lanham, MD, 1993 (copyright). Page 87, Figure 25 From *Child Development*, 1997. Copyright © 1997 by The Society for Research in Child Development, Inc. Reprinted by permission. Page 88, Figure 26 From *Book Review Digest*, August 1997, Vol. 93, No. 5, p. 324. Reprinted by permission of The H.W. Wilson Company. Pages 90–91, Figure 27 "Second Thoughts About Integration" by Jerelyn Eddings in *U.S. News & World Report*, July 28, 1997. Copyright, July 28, 1997, U.S. News & World Report. Reprinted by permission. Page 110 From "The Love Song of J. Alfred Prufrock" in *Collected Poems 1909-1962* by T.S. Eliot. Reprinted by permission of Faber and Faber Limited. Page 161 "The Skaters" by John Gould Fletcher. Page 197, Figure 32 From "Cognitive Aspects of Psychomotor Performance" by Edwin A. Locke and Judith F. Bryan from *Journal of Applied Psychology*, Vol. 50, 1966. Copyright © 1966 by the American Psychological Association. Reprinted by permission of the author. Page 198, Figure 33 From "Pattern in Language" by Anna H. Live from *The Journal of General Education*, Vol. 18, July 1996 by Penn State Press. Reprinted by permission. Page 296, Table 1 Figure, "Psychiatrists' Attitudes Toward Etiological Theories of Infantile Autism" from "A National Survey of Mental Health Professionals Concerning the Causes of Early Infantile Autism" by B.J. Gallagher, B.J. Jones, and Meoghan Byrne from *Journal of Clinical Psychology*, 46, 1990, p. 936. Reprinted by permission of Clinical Psychology Publishing Company, Inc. and the author. Page 302 Figure from "Early Recognition of Autism" by Julie Osterling and Geraldine Dawson in *Journal of Autism and Developmental Disorders*, Vol. 24, No. 3, June 1994. Reprinted by permission of Plenum Publishing Corporation and the author.